D0991958

The Ruined Cottage
and
The Pedlar

The Cornell Wordsworth

General Editor: Stephen Parrish
Associate Editor: Mark L. Reed

Advisory Editors: M. H. Abrams, Geoffrey Hartman, Jonathan Wordsworth

---

The Salisbury Plain Poems, edited by Stephen Gill
The Ruined Cottage and *The Pedlar*, edited by James Butler
The Prelude, 1798–1799; edited by Stephen Parrish
Home at Grasmere, edited by Beth Darlington

The Ruined Cottage and *The Pedlar*

by William Wordsworth

Edited by
JAMES BUTLER

CORNELL UNIVERSITY PRESS

ITHACA, NEW YORK

THIS BOOK HAS BEEN PUBLISHED WITH THE AID OF A GRANT FROM THE HULL MEMORIAL PUBLICATION FUND OF CORNELL UNIVERSITY.

First published 1979 by Cornell University Press.

Printed in the United States of America by Vail-Ballou Press, Inc.

Library of Congress Cataloging in Publication Data

Wordsworth, William, 1770–1850.
The ruined cottage and The pedlar.

(The Cornell Wordsworth)
Includes bibliographical references.
I. Wordsworth, William, 1770–1850. The pedlar, 1978.
II. Butler, James, 1945– III. Title: The ruined cottage.
PR5869.R8 1978 821'.7 78-58066
ISBN 0-8014-1153-X

The Cornell Wordsworth

The individual volumes of the Cornell Wordsworth series, some devoted to long poems, some to collections of shorter poems, have two common aims. The first is to bring the early Wordsworth into view. Wordsworth's practice of leaving his poems unpublished for years after their completion, and his lifelong habit of revision—Ernest de Selincourt called it "obsessive"—have obscured the original, often the best, versions of his work. These original versions are here presented in the form of clean, continuous "reading texts" from which all layers of later revision have been stripped away. The second aim of the series is to provide, for the first time, a complete and accurate record of variant readings, from Wordsworth's earliest drafts down to the final lifetime (or first posthumous) publication. The most important manuscripts are shown in full transcription; on pages facing the transcriptions of the most complex and interesting of these manuscripts, photographs of the manuscript pages are also provided. Besides the transcriptions and the photographs, on which draft revisions may be seen, and an *apparatus criticus* in which printed variants are collected, a third device for the study of revisions is adopted: when two versions of a poem match sufficiently well, they are arrayed on facing pages so that the steps by which one was converted into the other become visible.

Volumes in the series are unnumbered, but upon publication their titles are inserted into the list of volumes in print in the order in which the poems were written. A more detailed introduction to the series may be found in the first volume published, *The Salisbury Plain Poems*, edited by Stephen Gill.

S. M. Parrish

Ithaca, New York

Contents

Preface

In 1832, two years before his death, Coleridge remarked, "I have often wished that the first two books of the Excursion had been published separately, under the name of 'The Deserted Cottage.' They would have formed, what indeed they are, one of the most beautiful poems in the language."[1] Coleridge's memory may have failed him slightly—the first book of *The Excursion* encompassed *The Ruined Cottage*, composed as a separate work in 1797—but his high opinion of the poem has been supported by later critics. F. R. Leavis in 1936 declared it "the finest thing Wordsworth wrote"; thirty-five years later, he repeated his praise of this "utterly convincing creative achievement." According to Herbert Read, Wordsworth's poem "contains the germ of all his subsequent development"; for Jonathan Wordsworth, it is among the most moving works of tragic literature. "As Wordsworth's first mature work," writes Mark Reed, *The Ruined Cottage* "is hardly less significant [than *Lyrical Ballads*] as a point of commencement for the modern English poetic tradition."[2]

After Wordsworth's death, his publishers reversed the poet's decision, arrived at fifty years earlier, not to present *The Ruined Cottage* as a separate work, and since 1850 it has appeared in print more often than *The Excursion* itself. But for a century the text reprinted was simply the first book of the last approved version (1850) of *The Excursion*, which incorporated revisions made in 1820, 1827, 1832, 1837, and particularly 1845. In this last revision, Wordsworth—perhaps stung by John Wilson's attack in his *Recreations of Christopher North* (1842) on the lack of religious sensibility in the poem—inserted into *The Excursion*, Book I, lines such as those about the enlightened spirit "whose meditative sympathies repose / Upon the breast of Faith" and about Margaret's soul, fixed "on the Cross."[3] As a consequence, the

[1] *Specimens of the Table Talk of the Late Samuel Taylor Coleridge* (London, 1835), II, 69.

[2] F. R. Leavis, *Revaluations: Tradition and Revolution in English Poetry* (London, 1936), p. 179, and "Wordsworth: The Creative Conditions," in *Twentieth-Century Literature in Retrospect*, ed. Reuben A. Brower (Cambridge, Mass., 1971), p. 330; Herbert Read, *Wordsworth: The Clark Lectures, 1929–1930* (London, 1930), p. 133; Jonathan Wordsworth, *The Music of Humanity* (London, 1969), pp. 152–153; Mark L. Reed, review of *The Music of Humanity*, *Journal of English and Germanic Philology*, 69 (1970), 528.

[3] *The Poetical Works of William Wordsworth*, VI (London, 1850), p. 37.

text that appeared in several editions for Victorian readers differs from what was published in *The Excursion* in 1814, and the revisions seriously distort the text of the independent poem that survives in complete manuscripts of 1798, 1799, and 1803–1804.

Five distinct stages of composition, from 1797 to 1804, mark the complex history of the independent poem:

First Stage: Spring 1797

RUINED COTTAGE MS. A (Dove Cottage MS. 13), written between sometime in March and 4–7 June, contains most of what became lines 152–243 of the MS. B text. MS. A begins abruptly with the Pedlar's contrast between the ruined cottage he now sees and the way he remembers it from the time when Margaret was alive. He describes the former happiness of Margaret and her husband, and tells of the illness and failed harvests that reduced them to poverty. The manuscript ends with the Pedlar's account of the restlessness and mental disturbance of Margaret's husband, now unable to support his family.

The RACEDOWN NOTEBOOK (DC MS. 11) contains *Ruined Cottage* work written between sometime in March and 4–7 June. Stubs show that some form of the poem's original conclusion was in the notebook (lines corresponding to MS. B, ll. 499–513), and remaining leaves have a passage in which Margaret finds the money that her husband received for enlisting in the army (MS. B, ll. 321–325).

A LETTER FROM COLERIDGE TO JOHN ESTLIN, 10 JUNE 1797—the manuscript is at Avon County Library (Bristol Reference Library)—bears a transcript by Dorothy Wordsworth of the original conclusion of *The Ruined Cottage* (lines corresponding to MS. B, ll. 491–528).

At least one manuscript from this first stage of composition is missing: by 4–7 June—or perhaps as late as the second week in July—Wordsworth had probably completed a unified version of the poem (including some lines about the Pedlar's visits to the cottage) that was some 200 to 370 lines long.

Second Stage: 25 January–ca. 10 March 1798

In the CHRISTABEL NOTEBOOK (DC MS. 15), Wordsworth made a fair copy of lines from *The Ruined Cottage* which contribute to MS. B, lines 122–165, and—after skipping two pages—lines containing the end of the Pedlar's third visit to the cottage, the whole of his fourth, and (now torn out of the notebook) the original conclusion to the poem (MS. B, ll. 470–528).

The ALFOXDEN NOTEBOOK (DC MS. 14) was used for *Ruined Cottage* drafts; stubs and remaining leaves show Wordsworth working on an introduction that includes a brief history of the Pedlar (contributing to MS. B, ll. 1–147), on the moral transition between Parts One and Two (MS. B, ll. 261–296), and on the Pedlar's second and third visits to the cottage (contributing to MS. B, ll. 416–462).

Ruined Cottage MS. B (DC MS. 17) incorporated previous materials into a 528-line poem, soon expanded to about double its original length by the following additions: (1) a passage about the Pedlar's reaction to Margaret's suffering (corresponding to MS. D, ll. 362–375); (2) a long history of the growth of the Pedlar's mind (contributing to MS. E, ll. 24–374); (3) a reconciling conclusion (155 lines, 45 of which contribute to MS. D, ll. 493–538).

Ruined Cottage MS. B² is a transcript in a letter (the manuscript is at Dove Cottage) from Dorothy Wordsworth to Mary Hutchinson, 5[–6] March, of 381 lines of the poem "immediately and solely connected with the Cottage." Dorothy described the entire poem as "grown to the length of 900 Lines."

In a letter from Coleridge to George Coleridge, ca. 10 March (the manuscript is at Coleridge Cottage, Nether Stowey), Coleridge copied out the opening 18 lines of MS. B's reconciling conclusion.

Third Stage: February–November, 1799

Ruined Cottage MS. D is a copy of the poem, 538 lines long, made by Dorothy Wordsworth in a pocket notebook (DC MS. 16). The text includes part of the reconciling conclusion but omits the long history of the Pedlar's mental development. The excluded lines about the Pedlar were transcribed in the notebook as an addendum.

Peter Bell MS. 2 (DC MS. 33) includes a draft for Margaret's character not incorporated into the poem until *Pedlar* MS. E (ll. 445–451).

Fourth Stage: 21 December 1801–8 July 1802

Wordsworth returned to *Ruined Cottage* MS. D to create an independent poem, solely about the Pedlar, from the 1799 addendum. New composition was linked with the 1799 copying in MS. D to form *The Pedlar*, 1802, by about 10 February 1802. MS. D preserves 233 lines of a poem about 280 lines long.

The Alfoxden Notebook, leaf 31, contains 43 lines of *The Pedlar*, 1802—all that survives of a transcript perhaps written either about 10 February or on 8 July.

Fifth Stage: 21 November 1803–18 March 1804

In Pedlar MS. E (DC MS. 37), the story of Margaret and the history of the Pedlar are recombined in an 883-line poem. The title *The Pedlar* is now used by the Wordsworths to refer to the combined poem.

Pedlar MS. E² (DC MS. 37), a fragment sewn into MS. E, was written about 6 March. It was the original first gathering of DC MS. 44—the copy of Wordsworth's unpublished poems prepared for Coleridge to take to Malta—and contains about 363 lines.

PEDLAR MS. M, written between about 6 and 18 March, is a part of the notebook (DC MS. 44) of unpublished poems copied for Coleridge. Dorothy wrote out *The Pedlar* in about 929 lines.

The account may be briefly told: Begun in 1797 as a stark story of Margaret's decline and death, *The Ruined Cottage* in 1798 acquired a history of the Pedlar who narrates her tale, as well as a tranquil conclusion. Wordsworth separated the Pedlar's history from the main poem in 1799, and his sister copied the surplus Pedlar passages as an addendum to *The Ruined Cottage*. In 1802 these overflow passages became a separate poem about the Pedlar's mental development; in 1803–1804 this account of the Pedlar and the story of Margaret were recombined. The Wordsworths used the title *The Pedlar* in 1802 to signify just the history of the Pedlar but in 1803–1804 to mean the combined work. For clarity, the shorter poem solely about the Pedlar is referred to below with its date appended: *The Pedlar*, 1802.

Not until 1949 did an edition presenting one of the four full-length manuscripts appear. Helen Darbishire included a 742-line text of *Ruined Cottage* MS. B (1798) in an appendix to *The Excursion* in Volume V of *The Poetical Works of William Wordsworth* (Oxford, 1949). Unfortunately, she did not distinguish between the original 528-line fair copy and draft insertions and additions. One result is that the lines are not always in their proper sequence. Twenty years later, Jonathan Wordsworth presented in *The Music of Humanity* his edition of *Ruined Cottage* MS. D (1799); he also provided, under the title *The Pedlar*, the surplus Pedlar material copied as an addendum to this manuscript (these passages, not a true "poem" in 1799, contribute to *The Pedlar*, 1802). What is printed in *The Music of Humanity* is the only reliable text of any of the four complete manuscripts. *Ruined Cottage* MS. D, Jonathan Wordsworth forcefully argues, is "the best balanced and most coherent surviving version" of the poem (p. 31). Lively discussion has followed this assertion. Many agree; of those who do not, some (such as F. W. Bateson) make claims for a text nearer the poem's beginnings, and others (such as F. R. Leavis) suggest that the complex interplay between the Poet and the Pedlar in the combined work makes that version the form in which the poem should be read.[4]

This edition presents a full textual history of *The Ruined Cottage*, *The Pedlar*, 1802, and *The Pedlar*, from the origin of *The Ruined Cottage* in 1797 until the last manuscript in which *The Pedlar* remains a separate work (MS. M, 1804)—

[4] F. W. Bateson, "Cottage Restored," *New Statesman* (22 August 1969), pp. 246–247; Leavis, "Wordsworth: The Creative Conditions," p. 332. The excellence of the combined text is also argued by Neil H. Hertz, "Wordsworth and the Tears of Adam," *Studies in Romanticism*, 7 (1967), 15–33; by Reeve Parker, "'Finer Distance': The Narrative Art of Wordsworth's 'The Wanderer,'" *English Literary History*, 39 (1972), 87–111; and by Peter J. Manning, "Wordsworth, Margaret, and the Pedlar," *Studies in Romanticism*, 15 (1976), 195–220.

twelve extant manuscripts in all. Manuscript and published variants for the poem after it became part of *The Excursion* will be included in the Cornell Wordsworth edition of that work. Of the three reading texts provided, two are of manuscript poems that have never before appeared in print: the first is *The Ruined Cottage* in the complete version closest to the tragic poem that Wordsworth read to Coleridge in June 1797 (it faces a reading text of the 1799 MS. D); the second is *The Pedlar*, which Wordsworth prepared in 1803–1804 after reconsidering his decision to divide Margaret's story and the Pedlar's history (it faces a transcription of the text copied into MS. M in March 1804, for Coleridge to take to Malta). Furthermore, the successive additions by which Wordsworth expanded *The Ruined Cottage* with an account of the Pedlar and a reconciling conclusion can be traced in the transcription of MS. B, and the later division of the poem is shown in the transcription of MS. D. A new poem—which Wordsworth created from his surplus lines about the Pedlar and gave thought to publishing (*The Pedlar*, 1802)—is here identified and appears in print for the first time. With these texts, one need no longer lament the deficiency Coleridge noted in 1832.

Preparation of this volume, as of all volumes in this series, was made possible by the Trustees of Dove Cottage, who generously gave access to manuscripts at the Wordsworth Library at Grasmere and authorized their publication. Timely photographic assistance was provided by John West, curator of the Wordsworth Museum at Grasmere; additional photographs are reproduced by permission of the Avon County Library (Bristol Reference Library) and the British Library Board. Hilton Kelliher and Jared Curtis shared with me their valuable work on the watermarks and collation of MS. M. An earlier form of part of my introduction appeared as "The Chronology of Wordsworth's *The Ruined Cottage* after 1800," in *Studies in Philology*, 74 (1977), 89–112, and I am grateful to the editor and The University of North Carolina Press for permission to draw on it here. I am indebted, as anyone who writes on *The Ruined Cottage* must be, to *The Music of Humanity* by Jonathan Wordsworth. He and my other editorial partners (especially Stephen Parrish, Mark Reed, Paul Betz, and Stephen Gill) assisted me in more ways than I can now remember or adequately acknowledge. My research at Grasmere has been supported by the National Endowment for the Humanities, the American Council of Learned Societies, the Johnson Fund of the American Philosophical Society, and La Salle College. My wife, Joanne, actively participated in work on this volume and cheerfully endured some of the pains of Margaret.

James Butler

Philadelphia, Pennsylvania

Abbreviations

Alfoxden	Alfoxden Notebook (Dove Cottage MS. 14).
ASP	*Adventures on Salisbury Plain.*
Butler	James Butler, "The Chronology of Wordsworth's *The Ruined Cottage* after 1800," *Studies in Philology*, 74 (1977), 89–112.
Chronology: EY	Mark L. Reed, *Wordsworth: The Chronology of the Early Years, 1770–1799* (Cambridge, Mass., 1967).
Chronology: MY	Mark L. Reed, *Wordsworth: The Chronology of the Middle Years, 1800–1815* (Cambridge, Mass., 1975).
DC MS.	Dove Cottage manuscript (1785–1814, revised numbering).
DCP	Dove Cottage miscellaneous manuscript, unnumbered.
DW	Dorothy Wordsworth.
EY	*Letters of William and Dorothy Wordsworth: The Early Years, 1787–1805*, ed. Ernest de Selincourt (2d ed.; rev. Chester L. Shaver; Oxford, 1967).
Finch	John Alban Finch, "*The Ruined Cottage* Restored: Three Stages of Composition," in *Bicentenary Wordsworth Studies in Memory of John Alban Finch*, ed. Jonathan Wordsworth (Ithaca, 1970), pp. 29–49.
Jacobus	Mary Jacobus, *Tradition and Experiment in Wordsworth's "Lyrical Ballads" (1798)* (Oxford, 1976).
JEGP	*Journal of English and Germanic Philology.*
Journals	*The Journals of Dorothy Wordsworth*, ed. Mary Moorman (Oxford, 1971).
LY	*Letters of William and Dorothy Wordsworth: The Later Years, 1821–1850*, ed. Ernest de Selincourt (3 vols.; Oxford, 1939).
Lyon	Judson Stanley Lyon, *The Excursion: A Study* (New Haven, 1950).
Meyer	George Wilbur Meyer, *Wordsworth's Formative Years* (Ann Arbor, Mich., 1943).
M of H	Jonathan Wordsworth, *The Music of Humanity: A Critical Study of Wordsworth's "Ruined Cottage"* (London, 1969).
Moorman	Mary Moorman, *William Wordsworth: A Biography* (2 vols.; Oxford, 1957, 1965).
Prelude	*The Prelude* (1805 text).
Prelude 1799	"*The Prelude*," *1798–1799*, ed. Stephen Parrish (Ithaca, 1977). Line references to the two-part *Prelude* are to the reading text on pp. 43–67.
PW	*The Poetical Works of William Wordsworth*, ed. Ernest de Selincourt and Helen Darbishire (5 vols.; Oxford, 1940–1949; rev. 1952–1959).

Raysor	Thomas M. Raysor, "Wordsworth's Early Drafts of *The Ruined Cottage* in 1797–1798," *Journal of English and Germanic Philology*, 55 (1956), 1–7.
RC	*The Ruined Cottage.*
SPP	*The Salisbury Plain Poems of William Wordsworth*, ed. Stephen Gill (Ithaca, 1975).
STC	Samuel Taylor Coleridge.
STCL	*Collected Letters of Samuel Taylor Coleridge*, ed. Earl Leslie Griggs (6 vols.; Oxford, 1956–1971).
Thompson	T. W. Thompson, *Wordsworth's Hawkshead*, ed. Robert Woof (Oxford, 1970).
Wordsworth and Gill	Jonathan Wordsworth and Stephen Gill, "The Two-Part *Prelude* of 1798–9," *Journal of English and Germanic Philology*, 72 (1973), 503–525.
WW	William Wordsworth.

The Ruined Cottage
and
The Pedlar

Introduction

I

When in early June 1797 Coleridge "leaped over a gate and bounded down a pathless field" (*LY*, III, 1263) to the Wordsworths' cottage at Racedown, the *annus mirabilis* of English Romanticism began. Soon after Coleridge's arrival, acquaintance developed into admiration and intimacy: Dorothy wrote to Mary Hutchinson that Coleridge "is a wonderful man," whose "conversation teems with soul, mind, and spirit" (*EY*, p. 188); Coleridge wrote to Southey that Wordsworth "is a very great man—the only man, to whom *at all times* & in *all modes of excellence* I feel myself inferior" (*STCL*, I, 334). In the year to come was the writing of *The Rime of the Ancient Mariner*, *Christabel*, *Kubla Khan*, and Wordsworth's contributions to *Lyrical Ballads* (1798), as well as the fruitful exchange of ideas that developed when the Wordsworths moved to Alfoxden to be close to Coleridge at Nether Stowey. As Hazlitt remembered after visiting Alfoxden in 1798, it was a time when one felt "the sense of a new style and a new spirit in poetry."[1]

At the very beginning of this *annus mirabilis*—just after Coleridge "bounded down a pathless field"—Dorothy reported, "The first thing that was read after he came was William's new poem *The Ruined Cottage* with which he was much delighted" (*EY*, p. 189). Forty-six years later, Wordsworth remembered an earlier date than 1797 for the composition of *The Ruined Cottage*. Speaking of *The Excursion* (whose first book incorporated the poem), he told Isabella Fenwick:

> Towards the close of the first book, stand the lines that were first written beginning "Nine Tedious years" & ending ["]Last human tenant of these ruined walls." These were composed in 95. at Race Down & for several passages describing the employment & demeanour of Margaret during her affliction I was indebted to observations made in Dorsetshire & afterwards at Alfoxden in Somersetshire where I resided in 97. & 98. [DCP]

But the poet's memory is about eighteen months in error. Along with the other dates in notes Wordsworth dictated in 1843, this one is approximate; there seems no reason to doubt Dorothy's statement in June 1797 that *The Ruined Cottage* was then a "new poem," for most of those lines referred to in

[1] "My First Acquaintance with Poets," in *The Complete Works of William Hazlitt*, ed. P. P. Howe, XVII (London, 1933), 117.

the Fenwick note were copied out by Dorothy for Coleridge to send to John Estlin about 10 June 1797. As Jonathan Wordsworth suggests, it seems likely that Coleridge would have sent a recent example of his friend's work (*M of H*, p. 12). In style and content, *The Ruined Cottage* is certainly not work of 1795: this "common tale, / By moving accidents uncharactered" (MS. B, ll. 290–291)[2] looks forward to *Lyrical Ballads* and *Michael*, rather than back to *Adventures on Salisbury Plain*. Wordsworth probably remembered the place of composition more accurately than the date, since he did begin the poem at Racedown, where he and Dorothy found their first adult home together in late September 1795.

Even though Wordsworth's comments in the Fenwick note place the date of *The Ruined Cottage* a year and a half too early, his remarks do indicate some of the poem's sources in his own "observations" at Racedown and Alfoxden. Although *The Ruined Cottage* is not a work of social protest, the story of failed harvests and high prices that caused Margaret's husband to enlist as a paid recruit does accurately reflect social conditions. The harvest of 1794 was bad, and the winter of 1794–1795 among the worst on record, destroying much of the grain in the ground. Wheat that normally cost about fifty shillings per British imperial quarter (eight bushels) climbed to ninety-two in 1795,[3] an increase that led to bread riots in Nottingham, Coventry, and Sussex. Throughout the poetry of his Racedown period, Wordsworth depicts this problem: in *The Borderers*, for example, the Female Beggar laments, "My poor Babe / Was crying, as I thought, crying for bread / When I had none to give him" (*PW*, I, 143; ll. 398–400). In the *Baker's Cart* fragment that anticipates *The Ruined Cottage*, the narrator describes the plight of a nameless woman:

> I have seen the Baker's horse
> As he had been accustomed at your door
> Stop with the loaded wain, when oer his head
> Smack went the whip and you were left, as if
> You were not born to live, or there had been
> No bread in all the land. [DC MS. 13, 4ʳ]

A diary kept by Joseph Gill, the steward at Racedown, shows that a baker's cart did pass by, and Wordsworth may well have seen events such as those he recounted in verse (Moorman, I, 314n). The first surviving letter Wordsworth sent from Racedown indicates that "the country people here are wretchedly poor" (*EY*, p. 154), as does Dorothy's earliest known Racedown letter: "The peasants are miserably poor; their cottages are shapeless struc-

---

[2] In this introduction, a reference to line numbers from *RC* MS. B, D, or E indicates the relevant reading text in this volume. Citation of a leaf number means that the quotation is drawn from the manuscript itself.

[3] T. S. Ashton, *An Economic History of England: The Eighteenth Century* (London, 1955), p. 239.

tures (I may almost say) of wood and clay—indeed they are not at all beyond what might be expected in savage life" (*EY*, p. 162). Those shapeless clay walls appear in Wordsworth's work on *The Ruined Cottage* (Alfoxden, 16ᵛ; MS. B, l. 30), along with the general dearth and the war with France. Wordsworth chose, however, to distance his story—thus giving it more than contemporary relevance—by placing these events a decade earlier:

> —You may remember, now some ten years gone,
> Two blighting seasons when the fields were left
> With half a tillage. It pleased heaven to add
> A worse affliction in the plague of war:
> A happy land was stricken to the heart;
> 'Twas a sad time of sorrow and distress. [MS. B, ll. 185–190]

There is no record of an actual individual as source for the story of Margaret, but many women must have been left in her situation when their husbands found it necessary to take the ten-guinea bounty for militiamen enlisting for service against the French.[4] The social background of *The Ruined Cottage* also produced, in the year it was first composed (1797), Frederick Morton Eden's bleak *State of the Poor* and, in the year it was expanded (1798), Malthus' even more dire *Essay on the Principle of Population as It Affects the Future Improvement of Society*.

Jonathan Wordsworth identifies one literary source of *The Ruined Cottage* as Goethe's *Der Wandrer*, probably in the translation of William Taylor of Norwich.[5] There Wordsworth could have found a dialogue between a wanderer and a woman living in the midst of a ruin still showing "Traces of man's arranging hand" (*M of H*, p. 264, l. 15). Several details may have been appropriated for *The Ruined Cottage*, but there is no source in Goethe for Margaret's central story. For this the poet probably drew on Southey's *Joan of Arc*; Wordsworth saw parts of the poem in manuscript in 1795 and read the published work in 1796.[6] Perhaps he also saw the excerpt Coleridge included in the first issue of *The Watchman* (1 March 1796):

> The death of a common Soldier from *Book the Seventh*, l. 320.
>
> Of unrecorded name
> Died the mean man, yet did he leave behind,
> One who did never say her daily prayers
> Of him forgetful; who to every tale

---

[4] J. Steven Watson, *The Reign of George III, 1760–1815* (Oxford, 1960), p. 376.

[5] *M of H*, pp. 3–4. Jonathan Wordsworth acknowledges his indebtedness to Mary Jacobus (p. 261), and I draw on both here (*M of H*, 50–67, 261–263; Jacobus, pp. 143–148). An English translation of *Der Wandrer* may be found in *M of H*, pp. 264–268.

[6] *EY*, pp. 153–154, 163, 169. The influence of Southey's poem was pointed out by E. P. Thompson, "Disenchantment or Default?: A Lay Sermon," in *Power and Consciousness*, ed. Conor Cruise O'Brien and William Dean Vanech (New York, 1969), p. 151.

> Of the distant war lending an eager ear,
> Grew pale and trembled. At her cottage door
> The wretched one shall sit, and with dim eye
> Gaze o'er the plain, where, on his parting steps,
> Her last look hung. Nor ever shall she know
> Her husband dead, but tortured with vain hope
> Gaze on—then heartsick turn to her poor babe,
> And weep it fatherless![7]

The poor, trembling, wretched woman; her tortured vigil at her cottage door as she awaits news of her soldier husband; her uncertainty whether she is a wife or widow; her mind deranged with vain hope; her poor babe—all are paralleled in *The Ruined Cottage*. Behind both the Wordsworth and Southey poems are Goldsmith's *Deserted Village* (1770), Fawcett's *Art of War* (1795), and perhaps Langhorne's *Country Justice* (1774–1777).[8] Southey in 1799 borrowed from *The Ruined Cottage* for his *Henry the Hermit* and for one of his *English Eclogues*, also named *The Ruined Cottage*. Similarly, Lamb, who heard Wordsworth read some version of *The Ruined Cottage* in July 1797 and perhaps later saw more of it, seems to echo the poem in his *Rosamund Gray* (1798). In short, some of the plot and several details of Wordsworth's *Ruined Cottage* were common knowledge in the intellectual circle in which he moved.

On the other hand, *The Ruined Cottage* can be seen as the culmination of elements present in Wordsworth's own poetry from the beginning. In *An Evening Walk*, for example, a female beggar—her husband killed in the American war—wanders along the road with her two babes. The poet comments, "For hope's deserted well why wistful look? / Chok'd is the pathway, and the pitcher broke" (*PW*, I, 26; ll. 255–256). The deserted well, choked pathway, and broken pitcher, here metaphoric, become literal as well in Wordsworth's later use of them in *The Ruined Cottage*. The woman in *Salisbury Plain* was once living happily with her husband and children, as was Margaret in *The Ruined Cottage*. But the Female Vagrant's husband was forced to go to war to feed his family. After accompanying him to America, all die, except the Female Vagrant, who must now shelter herself in ruins. Some fragments related to *Adventures on Salisbury Plain* in DC MS. 2 also anticipate events of *The Ruined Cottage*: a traveler finds a ragged woman alone in "a dwelling wild," suckling her three-year-old child because of the shortage of bread. She then tells the traveler how she came to this state from the happiness

[7] *The Watchman*, ed. Lewis Patton (Princeton, N.J., 1970), p. 45. The original *RC* may in turn have influenced Southey's revision of *Joan of Arc* for its second edition in 1798 (Jacobus, p. 143, n. 4).

[8] Arthur Beatty, *Joseph Fawcett: The Art of War; Its Relation to the Early Development of William Wordsworth*, University of Wisconsin Studies by the Department of English, no. 2 (Madison, 1918), pp. 224–269; Roger Sharrock, "Wordsworth and John Langhorne's 'The Country Justice,'" *Notes and Queries*, n.s. 1 (1954), 302–304. See also the chapter "Sources and Analogues" in Lyon, pp. 29–60.

she and her husband once enjoyed.[9] Margaret's abandonment in *The Ruined Cottage* is a stock situation in Wordsworth's poetry: one thinks of Martha Ray in *The Thorn*, Emily in *The White Doe of Rylstone*, and Ellen in *The Excursion*, Book VI. With the combination of personal observations, some drawing on literary sources, and some use of his own characteristic plots, Wordsworth at Racedown had the materials to begin *The Ruined Cottage*.

II

The two earliest manuscripts of *The Ruined Cottage*—MS. A (DC MS. 13) and the Racedown Notebook (DC MS. 11)—were written about the same time, and it is difficult to say which is earlier. MS. A is part of a folio notebook, reconstructed from several leaves at the Wordsworth Library and a photocopy of one leaf at the Pierpont Morgan Library as a gathering of twelve leaves, of which 2–5 and 7–12 are intact.[10] Wordsworth used 5^v and 7–12 for Ariosto and Chaucer translations in 1801–1802, but the passages on 2–5^r—all in Wordsworth's hand—represent work of the Racedown period:

2^r	*Argument for Suicide*
2^v	*Old Man Travelling, Animal Tranquillity and Decay*
3^r	*Description of a Beggar*
3^v	*Yet Once Again* fragment (*PW*, V, 340)
4^r	*The Baker's Cart* fragment
4^v	*Incipient Madness*
5^r	*Ruined Cottage* MS. A

Placement in the manuscript is not a good criterion for determining the order of entry in Wordsworth's notebooks, but here the entries on the rectos may be in chronological sequence. *Argument for Suicide* seems related to *The Borderers* (especially, as de Selincourt notes in *PW*, I, 375, to some of the speeches of Rivers-Oswald). Since Wordsworth was "ardent" in work on his play on 24 October 1796 (*EY*, p. 172) and "nearly finished" with it by 25 February 1797 (*EY*, p. 177), he probably composed *Argument for Suicide* during this period. *Description of a Beggar* certainly was written between the latter half of 1796 and early 1797; April–May 1797 is the most probable time of its composition. Though clearly related to *Ruined Cottage* MS. A, the *Baker's Cart* fragment must precede it, since here Wordsworth leaves a blank for the woman's name and has not yet developed either her story or his subtle psychological analysis of what in the fragment is called her "sick and extravagant mind." For *Ruined Cottage* MS. A itself, the suggestion in *Chronology*: *EY*, p. 338, of a date between March and Coleridge's arrival between June 4 and 7, 1797, seems accurate: Wordsworth would not have had time to do

---

[9] These fragments appear in *SPP*, pp. 287–303.

[10] This manuscript is described in *Chronology: EY*, p. 346. Leaf 3 is at the Pierpont Morgan Library, New York.

much with the poem while engaged with the tremendous labor of *The Borderers*, and it is hard to believe he could have read his "new poem," *The Ruined Cottage*, to Coleridge in June before he had worked out the details that appear in this manuscript.

MS. A includes most of what eventually became lines 152–243 of the MS. B text. In the opening passage of MS. A, Margaret is dead but well remembered by the speaker; he contrasts the present decay of her cottage to the way it once was. Even in the early stages of composition of *The Ruined Cottage*, Wordsworth had a pedlar in mind for narrator, since that character is in MS. A "a wanderer among the cottages," with his "pack of winter raiment." This narrator describes the past happiness of Margaret and her husband (Wordsworth leaves a blank in place of his name). But a dearth had fallen on the land, and the husband became ill. When he recovered—his savings exhausted and his mind unsettled—he wandered the fields. Here the manuscript ends, although the reconstructed notebook has a missing leaf following *Ruined Cottage* MS. A that could have contained additional lines.

The *Ruined Cottage* passages in this manuscript are written with relatively few corrections, but one set of lines gave Wordsworth a good deal of difficulty. After describing the "wild colt," the "unstalled heifer," and "the potter's ass" that now inhabit the ruined cottage, he drafted lines about "a poor man's horse":

> A wretched covert 'tis for man or beast
> And when the poor mans horse that shelters there
> Turns from the beating wind and open sky
> The iron links with which his feet are clogg'd
> Mix their dull clanking with the heavy sound
> Of falling rain a melancholy. [DC MS. 13, 5^{r}]

Wordsworth pursued this image, eventually adding a broken pane of glass which, to the narrator passing it "but two nights gone," "seemed akin to life" as it "glitter'd to the moon." But the clanking chains, beating wind, and glittering pane hark back to Wordsworth's earlier images in *Adventures on Salisbury Plain* and, particularly, in *The Borderers*:

> But two nights gone,
> The darkness overtook me—wind and rain
> Beat hard upon my head—and yet I saw
> A glow-worm, through the covert of the furze,
> Shine calmly as if nothing ailed the sky:
> At which I half accused the God in Heaven.—
> You must forgive me, Sirs.[11]

[11] *PW*, I, 144, ll. 422–428 and *apparatus criticus*. This similarity is noted by Finch, pp. 35–36, and he also suggests several other verbal parallels between *RC* MS. A and poems of spring 1797 (pp. 35–38).

Wordsworth eventually decided that the MS. A drafts about a night trip to a gloomy ruin, echoing with eerie noise within, had no place in his calm, straightforward tale of Margaret; the poet transferred the lines to the opposite verso and composed a poem he entitled *Incipient Madness*.[12] Although certainly inferior to *The Ruined Cottage*, the poem is interesting for the contrast it offers to Wordsworth's old style. "Life's every-day appearances" (*Prelude*, XII, 369)—the dignity and nobility of the commonplace—now replace the gothic sensationalism of the earlier Racedown poetry. If the subjects are still suffering and the disordered mind (as they are in *The Ruined Cottage*), they are seen with a new calmness as evincing the fundamental worth of the sufferer and the value of his emotions. Wordsworth's claim in his Preface to the *Lyrical Ballads* (1800) that "the human mind is capable of excitement without the application of gross and violent stimulants" provides a theory implicit in the exclusion of such stimulants from MS. A.[13]

The Racedown Notebook contains evidence of two additional passages of *The Ruined Cottage*. The earlier of the two passages was begun by Dorothy Wordsworth on 7^v, and continues backward onto 6^r.[14] From the stubs that remain, one can surmise that some or all of the concluding lines of the MS. B text were here: initial or terminal letters of lines corresponding to 499–513 are clearly discernible, and traces of ink suggest that more of the section might have been included as well. The second passage must have been written later because Dorothy continued her lines from 5^v to 8^r; the natural assumption is that leaves 6 and 7 were already filled or torn out. This second passage picks up the story of Margaret from about where MS. A left off. She finds a purse of gold in the casement and knows her husband has placed it there (MS. B, ll. 321–325).

Since Wordsworth told Isabella Fenwick in 1843 that the concluding lines of Margaret's tale were the first to be written, the passage torn out of the Racedown Notebook might be earlier than anything in MS. A. On the other hand, Wordsworth may have remembered (as Jonathan Wordsworth suggests in *M of H*, p. 11) that he wrote the conclusion before he finished the central part of the poem and may have confused his account nearly half a century later. Like MS. A, however, the Racedown Notebook sections work out fundamental elements of the story that must precede the reading of the

[12] Although composition of *Incipient Madness* is sometimes discussed as preceding *RC* MS. A (Finch, p. 33; Meyer, p. 222, n. 8), I agree with those scholars who find that a careful comparison of the manuscripts shows it to be later (Raysor, p. 4; *Chronology: EY*, p. 338; *M of H*, pp. 7–8).

[13] *The Prose Works of William Wordsworth*, ed. W. J. B. Owen and Jane Worthington Smyser (Oxford, 1974), I, 128.

[14] Finch, pp. 34–35, said that this draft is in the hand of Mary Hutchinson and must therefore date from her Racedown visit between 28 November 1796 and 4 June 1797. But the hand can now be identified as DW's.

"new poem" to Coleridge. The period between March and 4–7 June 1797 also seems the probable time for these entries.

Coleridge was so enthusiastic about *The Ruined Cottage* that he "procured Miss Wordsworth to transcribe" some of the poem to enclose in his letter of 10 June 1797 to John Estlin (*STCL*, I, 327). Dorothy copied onto the inside recto of the folded sheet a passage nearly identical with the conclusion of MS. B (ll. 491–528),[15] and these lines provide tantalizing clues about the state of the poem at that time. In the first place, the lines differ at some points from those suggested by the opening letters of the same passage on the Racedown stubs; they match what appears in the later manuscripts of 1798 and 1799. Dorothy must have copied the lines for Estlin from some other manuscript, later than the Racedown one and now lost. In addition, the Pedlar's direct address ("See'st thou that path"; "Stranger, here / In sickness she remained") demonstrates that the poem in 1797 had a character functioning as an auditor, and that he and the Pedlar were not yet the old acquaintances they became in later versions. Since these final lines tell first of Margaret's questioning of each passing soldier about her husband's fate, then of the gradual decay of her cottage, and finally of her death, Wordsworth also must have had the major events of the poem either planned or actually written by 10 June 1797.

What, then, was the state of the poem Coleridge heard in early June, 1797? Manuscripts of 1798 show that the poem's introduction and the account of the Pedlar's history (to at least MS. B, l. 122) belong to a later stage of composition, as does the moral transition between Parts One and Two (MS. B, ll. 243–296). On the other hand, much of Part One (MS. A), Margaret's discovery of the money (Racedown Notebook), and the conclusion (letter to Estlin) were almost certainly written before Coleridge's arrival at Racedown. But the bulk of Part Two—the tale of Margaret's decline chronicled through the Pedlar's successive visits to her cottage—cannot be assigned with certainty to either 1797 or 1798. Since Dorothy's transcript for Estlin of the poem's concluding lines comes from a manuscript no longer surviving, such a manuscript could have contained a complete text of the poem, including the Pedlar's visits to the cottage. Another possibility is that Coleridge heard only fragments of a work in process—MS. A, Margaret's finding of the gold, and the conclusion—with Wordsworth's explanation of what he still planned to write. Since Charles Lamb, writing to Wordsworth

[15] Mary Hutchinson probably took another copy of the poem's conclusion with her when she left Racedown about 4 June 1797. DW wrote her on 5[–6] March 1798, after transcribing much of the poem to MS. B, l. 484, "You have the rest to the end of Margaret's story" (*EY*, p. 209). Meyer (p. 222) and Raysor (p. 3) argue that DW's statement shows that the conclusion of *RC* was the only part written by early June 1797. But DW says nothing about how much of the poem Mary knew, referring instead to that part she had.

in 1814 about *The Excursion*, remembered that he had "known the story of Margaret . . . even as long back as I saw you first at Stowey,"[16] he must have heard some version of the poem about the second week in July. It may be, as Jonathan Wordsworth suggests (*M of H*, pp. 14–15), that a work without the Pedlar's visits would not be described as "the story of Margaret" by someone who had read *The Excursion*, but Lamb's memory is of an old occurrence, and the matter is further complicated by the possibility that Lamb saw a text of the later MS. B.[17] It is not impossible that Wordsworth wrote about the Pedlar's trips to the cottage between his reading of the work to Coleridge in June and the visit of Lamb in July. But if this section of the poem was not written by July 1797, then its composition probably did not take place until 1798. The Wordsworths moved into Alfoxden House in mid-July, and William's main literary labor for the next several months was revising *The Borderers* for a possible stage performance. There is no record that Wordsworth again worked on *The Ruined Cottage* before late January 1798.

The first two manuscripts of 1798 provide more evidence about the state of the poem in 1797, but it is evidence that is difficult to evaluate. What seems to be the earlier of the two manuscripts is DC MS. 15, usually called the *Christabel* Notebook because it contains the first known version of that poem. The notebook opens, after a stub, with *A Night-Piece*, which—since its composition draws on an event described in Dorothy's journal for 25 January 1798 (*Journals*, p. 2)—must have been written on or after that date. Then on the following leaf (3^r), William in his neatest hand began (after leaving the top quarter of the page blank) a fair copy of some lines from the beginning of *The Ruined Cottage* that are closely related to the MS. A text. He continued onto 3^v, copying in all lines corresponding to MS. B, 122–125, 142–145, 126–129, 146–160, 163–165, and 157–162. He then left the bottom three-quarters of 3^v blank, skipped 4^r, and began to copy again about the middle of 4^v:

> yet I saw the idle loom
> Still in its place. His sunday garments hung
> Upon the self-same nail, his very staff
> Stood undisturb'd behind the door. And when
> I pass'd this way, beaten by autumn winds
> She told me that her little babe was dead

---

[16] 9 August 1814; *The Letters of Charles and Mary Anne Lamb*, ed. Edwin W. Marrs, Jr., III (Ithaca, 1978), 95. For the date of Lamb's visit, see *Chronology: EY*, p. 201.

[17] Lamb's novel *A Tale of Rosamund Gray and Old Blind Margaret* (London, 1798) has verbal parallels with the history of the Pedlar added in *RC* MS. B, completed in March 1798. Lamb finished his novel by 7 March 1798 (*New Letters of Robert Southey*, ed. Kenneth Curry [New York, 1965], I, 161–162). In *Rosamund Gray*, for example, "Margaret retained a spirit unbroken by calamity. There was a principle *within*, which it seemed as if no outward circumstances could reach. It was a *religious* principle" (p. 8). She shares other traits with WW's Pedlar as well. Although there is no record that Lamb saw or heard this MS. B version of *RC*, the number of echoes raises the possibility.

And she was left alone. That very time
I yet remember, through the miry lane
She went with me a mile when the bare trees
Trickled with foggy damps, and in such sort
That any heart had ached to hear her beggd
That wheresoe'er I went I still would ask
For him whom she had lost. Five tedious years

The "Five tedious years" leads into the conclusion of the poem, and the following stub has the initial letters of MS. B, lines 483–514; its verso probably contained lines 515–528, although little can be seen here.

No other material in the *Christabel* Notebook can be dated before 1798, and the position of *The Ruined Cottage* work immediately after *A Night-Piece* suggests a date after 25 January but before a clearly later version of the poem contained in a letter from Dorothy to Mary Hutchinson, 5[–6] March 1798. A slight possibility remains that the *Christabel* Notebook entries were written in the summer of 1797. In the more likely case, though, that they were written early in 1798, the earliest transcript of the second phase of work on *The Ruined Cottage* would be this fair copy with its interesting blank spaces. Here Wordsworth copied the lines dealing with the end of the Pedlar's third visit to the cottage and all of the fourth, and in the absence of 1798 drafts it is an attractive hypothesis that these lines were first composed the previous summer. If they were, then at least part of the sequence detailing the Pedlar's visits was in the original poem.

But the blank spaces in the *Christabel* Notebook should make one cautious about maintaining that all four visits were composed (in the form in which we now have them) as early as 1797. The only ready explanation for Wordsworth's skipping almost two full pages between a point near the beginning and the conclusion of his poem is that he meant to link both ends with a middle. Perhaps 74 lines would fit in the space left; Wordsworth already had about 53 lines available for use from MS. A, and the full sequence of the Pedlar's visits would take another 174. The lines already in the *Christabel* Notebook imply several events not treated in MS. A: Robert's enlistment, Margaret's decline, the parting with the elder child, and at least something about the Pedlar's successive visits to the cottage. These matters would have to be treated with the utmost brevity to fit between the parts of the poem now in the notebook, and it may be that Wordsworth's spacing there has some other significance.[18]

[18] John Finch argued that this spacing in the *Christabel* Notebook indicates the original *RC* was about 174 lines long (Finch, pp. 40–43). Jonathan Wordsworth, the editor of *Bicentenary Wordsworth Studies in Memory of John Alban Finch* (Ithaca, 1970), says, however, that before his death Finch had come to think that the gap left in *RC* copying in this notebook would not have been sufficient for the events implied by the passages about the Pedlar's third and fourth visits (p. 43n).

A second manuscript of early 1798—DC MS. 14, known as the Alfoxden Notebook—also bears on the problem of when Wordsworth composed the passages on the Pedlar's visits. The Alfoxden Notebook, like the *Christabel* one, opened with some version of *A Night-Piece*, so *The Ruined Cottage* entries were probably written on or after 25 January and before Dorothy's letter of 5[–6] March 1798. Wordsworth used this notebook for drafts, so more certainty is possible in judging just what part of the poem he was working on in early 1798. Unfortunately, much of the *Ruined Cottage* section has been torn out, but it is usually possible to guess from the remaining initial letters on the rectos which lines later used in the MS. B text stood in the notebook. Stubs and surviving leaves show that passages about the Pedlar's second and third visits to the cottage were in the Alfoxden Notebook (MS. B, ll. 416?–432?, 447?–462), along with the moral transition between Parts One and Two (MS. B, ll. 261–296) and work on an introduction—including a brief history of the Pedlar—to replace the abrupt beginning of MS. A (the introduction contributes to MS. B, ll. 1–147).[19] There are also several passages of philosophic blank verse related to the Pedlar's history but not used for it.

The puzzle here, though, is again the Pedlar's visits to the cottage. There is no extant draft work on the first or fourth visit in the Alfoxden Notebook (some of the events of the first—Robert's disappearance and Margaret's discovery of the money—are touched on in the Racedown Notebook, and a fair copy of all of the fourth appears in the *Christabel* Notebook). Of course, more could have appeared on leaves now too mutilated to permit one to see initial letters. Since some work on the second and third visit is visible in the Alfoxden Notebook, Wordsworth was at least revising these segments and—along with the other parts of the poem—probably expanding them. Other evidence points to the same conclusion. About the time the Alfoxden Notebook was in use for these drafts, Dorothy entered this observation in her journal: "The moss rubbed from the pailings by the sheep, that leave locks of wool, and the red marks with which they are spotted, upon the wood" (*Journals*, p. 5; 4 February 1798). The same details find their way into her brother's poem, as part of the second visit to the cottage:

I saw the corner stones,
Till then unmarked, on either side the door
With dull red stains discoloured and stuck o'er
With tufts and hairs of wool, as if the sheep
That feed upon the commons thither came
As to a couching-place and rubbed their sides
Even at her threshold. [MS. B, ll. 388–394]

[19] These stubs are discussed further in the Alfoxden Notebook headnote, below. I am indebted to Mark Reed (*Chronology: EY*, p. 321) and John Finch (pp. 44–45) for their work in identifying what once stood on these stubs. Their line numbers differ from mine, since I cite this volume's reading text of MS. B, and they refer to the version of MS. B in *PW*, V.

We can say, therefore, that in early 1798, Woodsworth worked on the Pedlar's trips to the cottage, even if the evidence is not sufficient to permit us to say with certainty whether the passages about those visits were first composed then or in the previous summer.

What conclusions can now be drawn about *The Ruined Cottage* of 1797? That Coleridge and Lamb were so impressed with what they heard suggests that Wordsworth may have actually composed a "new poem," as Dorothy called it, instead of a series of disconnected fragments. The fair copy of the poem's conclusion in the 10 June letter to John Estlin shows that some manuscript is now missing; that manuscript is a likely candidate for what might have been the one containing the whole work. On the other hand, Wordsworth could have worked on the poem between the visit of Coleridge and that of Lamb a month later. In any case, the 1797 *Ruined Cottage* was much shorter than the 528-line version completed in early 1798 and given here as the first reading text. The 1797 poem must have begun abruptly, omitted much scene-setting and description of the Pedlar, and skipped the moral transition between Parts One and Two. But the probability is that at least some of the Pedlar's visits go back to 1797. As early as MS. A, the narrator is "A wanderer among the cottages" (l. 191); he is with Margaret when she tells of her husband's illness, and the Racedown fragment shows that he knows Margaret's reaction on finding the purse of money. The fair copy in the *Christabel* Notebook also indicates that some of the Pedlar's visits were early. Without doubt, though, Wordsworth expanded this section of the poem in 1798, so the number of visits (and the detail with which they were treated) in 1797 remain uncertain. If one accepts the possibility that Wordsworth left space in the *Christabel* Notebook for a complete text of the poem, then the first *Ruined Cottage* would have contained fewer than 200 lines, with a truncated account of the cottage visits. Jonathan Wordsworth accepts most of the visits-to-the-cottage sequence as early, and by eliminating the opening, the history of the Pedlar, and the moral transition between parts, he proposes a work of 370 to 400 lines written in 1797 (*M of H*, pp. 9–16). The question is a difficult one; most probably the poem was longer than 200 lines, but the drafting in the Alfoxden Notebook suggests that it was not long enough to include most or all of the visits to the cottage and reach 370 to 400 lines. Whatever its length, the surviving parts of the original work of 1797 are a powerful representation of a domestic tragedy, stark in its bare essentials. Margaret declines and dies—"Last human tenant of these ruined walls" (MS. B, l. 528)—with little editorial commentary.

III

By early March 1798 Wordsworth's philosophic discussions with Coleridge, and his own developing ideas, produced a quite different poem. Blank-verse fragments in the Alfoxden Notebook provide early indication of what Wordsworth was now to make of the story of Margaret. A long creative lull followed the growing intimacy with Coleridge that began in mid-1797, but these drafts of January–February 1798 show the philosophic fruits of their relationship:

> Why is it we feel
> So little for each other but for this
> That we with nature have no sympathy
> Or with such idle objects as have no power to hold
> Articulate language. [Alfoxden, 20^{v}][20]

Another try at the same idea expands this vision of the union and harmony of all things:

> And never for each other shall we feel
> As we may feel till we have sympathy
> With nature in her forms inanimate
> With objects such as have no power to hold
> Articulate language. In all forms of things
> There is a mind. [Alfoxden, 20^{v}–21^{r}]

Wordsworth eventually used these jottings to compose a new conclusion to *The Ruined Cottage*, and they clearly indicate the direction his thoughts were turning. His focus shifts from the unadorned account of Margaret's tragedy to the Pedlar's philosophic ideas—and how they developed—which cause the Pedlar to react in a particular way to that account. Margaret's decline and death can now enable the Pedlar to provide a lesson, as another Alfoxden draft that became part of the poem illustrates:

> We know that there is often found
> ~~And always~~
> In mournful thoughts and always might be found
> A power to virtue friendly. [Alfoxden, 16^{v}; MS. B, ll. 286–288]

Thus the character who relates a bare narrative gives way to the philosopher who can point a moral. Wordsworth, in his recasting of *The Ruined Cottage*, is himself becoming what in 1802 he described to John Wilson as a "great Poet": "He ought to a certain degree to rectify men's feelings, to give them new compositions of feeling, to render their feelings more sane pure and permanent, in short, more consonant to nature, that is, to eternal nature, and the great moving spirit of things" (*EY*, p. 355).

Wordsworth is, of course, indebted in these Alfoxden drafts to Coleridge's concept of the One Life, expressed in *The Aeolian Harp*, as well as in *Religious Musings*:

> 'Tis the sublime of man,
> Our noontide Majesty, to know ourselves

[20] In this passage and the following ones in this paragraph, I quote the unrevised base text.

> Parts and proportions of one wond'rous whole:
> This fraternizes man, this constitutes
> Our charities and bearings. But 'tis God
> Diffus'd thro' all, that doth make all one whole.[21]

Over these months of late 1797—part of a period Coleridge recalled when he "was with Wordsworth almost daily—& frequently for weeks together" (*STCL*, I, 525)—Wordsworth seems to have absorbed a philosophic system, if not necessarily its theological underpinnings, into which he could fit his own feelings about natural harmony.[22] Now in early 1798, the Pedlar, like Wordsworth, could view Margaret's tragedy from a different background and in a wider context, since "in all things / He saw one life, & felt that it was joy" (MS. B, 15^r). Wordsworth's turn to philosophic writing was now so pronounced that, on the very day Dorothy finished transcribing part of *The Ruined Cottage* for Mary Hutchinson, he wrote James Tobin of his plans for a grand philosophic poem of which *The Ruined Cottage* was now the largest part: "I have written 1300 lines of a poem in which I contrive to convey most of the knowledge of which I am possessed. My object is to give pictures of Nature, Man, and Society. Indeed I know not any thing which will not come within the scope of my plan."[23] Five days later he announced the title to James Losh: *The Recluse or Views of Nature, Man, and Society* (*EY*, p. 214). In the next decade and a half, *The Recluse* encompassed *The Prelude* (first perhaps as tailpiece, then as introduction), *Home at Grasmere*, *The Tuft of Primroses*, and *The Excursion*. But Wordsworth also faced a lifelong frustration because of his inability to complete the work Coleridge wanted, even though his friend kept goading him on. As late as 1817, in *Biographia Literaria*, Coleridge claimed that Wordsworth was "capable of producing" (even though their correspondence shows Coleridge disappointed with what had been produced in *The Excursion*) "the FIRST GENUINE PHILOSOPHIC POEM."[24] The merger—so clear in the 1798 revision of *The Ruined Cottage*—of philos-

[21] *Religious Musings*, ll. 141–146, in *Poems on Various Subjects* (London, 1796), pp. 148–149.

[22] Coleridge, Wordsworth, and the One Life are discussed in *M of H*, pp. 184–201, and in Jacobus, pp. 59–68. For the stresses of the poets' relationships and the differences in their thinking on this and other points, see Stephen Parrish, *The Art of the "Lyrical Ballads"* (Cambridge, Mass., 1973), pp. 34–79. Jonathan Wordsworth traces WW's development beyond his brief acceptance of the One Life in "Wordsworth's 'Borderers,'" *Proceedings of the British Academy*, 55 (1969), 211–228 (revised in *English Romantic Poets: Modern Essays in Criticism*, ed. M. H. Abrams, 2d ed. [London and New York, 1975], pp. 170–187).

[23] *EY*, p. 212 (6 March 1798). Exactly what WW included in his "1300 lines" is uncertain; see *Chronology: EY*, p. 223, n. 12.

[24] (London, 1817) II, 178. STC expressed his opinion of *The Excursion* to Lady Beaumont (*STCL*, IV, 564; 3 April 1815) and to WW (IV, 570–576; 22 May 1815). An account of WW's difficulty in writing *The Recluse*—and of his problem in reconciling the philosophic and narrative voices *RC* now included—is in James Butler, "Wordsworth's *Tuft of Primroses*: 'An Unrelenting Doom,'" *Studies in Romanticism*, 14 (1975), 237–248.

ophy with detailed observation of natural phenomena is, for good and ill, the source of Wordsworth's characteristic idiom. It was this period to which the poet looked back in 1843 when he declared that "no change has taken place in my manner for the last forty-five years" (*LY*, III, 1159).

Fortunately, extensive manuscript evidence survives from this vital stage in the development of *The Ruined Cottage*. Besides the *Christabel* and Alfoxden notebooks, discussed earlier, there is the first complete manuscript (DC MS. 17, MS. B), as well as a letter from Dorothy to Mary Hutchinson, 5[–6] March 1798 (known as MS. B^2), which contains a partial copy of MS. B. In its original form, MS. B consisted of thirty-four leaves of a homemade notebook. Dorothy copied a full text of *The Ruined Cottage* into MS. B, with the line number 255 at the end of Part One and 273 at the conclusion of Part Two, which also has the words "The End." In this 528-line state, the poem has the long introduction, a short account of the Pedlar's history, the moral transition between Parts One and Two, and the ending "she died, / Last human tenant of these ruined walls." This complete poem is the text closest to what Coleridge and Lamb heard, even though the Alfoxden drafts show that some parts were written later than 1797.

This version of the poem seems to have pleased Wordsworth for only a short time, however, because he drafted approximately thirty lines—Dorothy copied nine more—about the Pedlar's early education on 4^v and 5^v; a mark in the original text on 5^r shows where they were to be added. But Wordsworth wanted the Pedlar sequence to be longer still, too lengthy to fit on the blank versos, so ten additional leaves were inserted into the notebook between the original fifth and sixth leaves. Dorothy copied her brother's first addition; William's drafts and her transcripts then continue with a greatly expanded account of the Pedlar, showing the development of his philosophy. At the back of the notebook, after some canceled drafts by Wordsworth, twelve more leaves were added, on nine of which Dorothy copied a 146-line passage reconciling Margaret's tragedy with the idea of the One Life.

In the augmented history of the Pedlar, Wordsworth went back to trace the childhood of his character, beginning with a passage about the Pedlar's schooling and adding about 210 lines (6^r–15^r). Wordsworth's growing fascination with his own past experience and the way in which it affected his apprehension of reality produced a Pedlar sequence which is, in fact, the poet's first autobiographical work. It is not surprising that feelings here attributed to the Pedlar were later transferred to *The Prelude* (II, 416–434; III, 82, 122–127, 141–147, 156–167). The notes dictated to Isabella Fenwick in 1843 also record this similarity between the poet and his creation: "I am here called upon freely to acknowledge that the character I have represented in his person is chiefly an idea of what I fancied my own character might have become in his circumstances" (DCP). As in *The Prelude*, Wordsworth in these additions to *The Ruined Cottage* traces how "the foundations of his [the Pedlar's] mind were laid" (MS. B, 4^{v}), and how the ministry of nature prepared him "to recognize / The moral properties & scope of things" (MS. B, 11^{r}). The Pedlar finds contentment

> when, with bliss ineffable
> He felt the sentiment of being, spread
> O'er all that moves, & all that seemeth still. [MS. B, 14^{r}]

By the end of this passage, the Pedlar, Wordsworth idealized, has developed a mind that can look philosophically on the ruin and decay dramatized in the story of Margaret.

The bleak conclusion of the original poem—"and here she died, / Last human tenant of these ruined walls"—seems hardly appropriate for this new philosophic position, and Wordsworth drafted three attempts to change it (43^{v}–45^{r}). In the first two, the narrator has become "a better and a wiser man" for having heard the story; the third finds some consolation in the enduring beauty of nature. The poet crossed out all three drafts, and building on the lines about the One Life in the Alfoxden Notebook, he composed a long addendum (copied into MS. B by Dorothy). At the end of it, Wordsworth returned to a passage on 21^{v} presumably written for insertion after the Pedlar's description of the decay of the cottage but before his tale explaining how it came to such a state. Transferred to the end of the addendum, the image of the spear-grass, seen by the Pedlar with "mist & silent rain-drops silver'd o'er" (53^{r}), becomes a reconciling one as it transcends its "rank" appearance earlier in the poem (MS. B, l. 162). The Pedlar imparts his wisdom to the narrator:

> Be wise & chearful, & no longer read
> The forms of things with an unworthy eye
> She sleeps in the calm earth & peace is here. [MS. B, 53^{r}]

In this revision, the poem ends in tranquil acceptance, as the Pedlar and narrator "chearfully pursued" their "evening way."[25]

MS. B^{2} helps to date these additions. That manuscript, a letter from Dorothy to Mary Hutchinson, is written on a single sheet of the same kind of paper used to make MS. B. Although the letter is dated "Alfoxden March 5th [1798]," at the end of it Dorothy mentions having had tea with Thomas Poole "yesterday"; since Poole visited Alfoxden on 5 March, this long letter probably took two days to write (*Chronology: EY*, p. 223n). Dorothy copied 381 lines from *Ruined Cottage* MS. B for Mary and provided a brief summary of the rest. She introduced her copy as follows:

[25] Besides discussions of this conclusion in general works about WW and those about *RC* referred to in this introduction, see James H. Averill, "Suffering and Calm in Wordsworth's Early Poetry," *PMLA*, 91 (1976), 223–234.

You desire me, my dear Mary to send you a copy of the Ruined Cottage. This is impossible for it has grown to the length of 900 [9 written over an 8] lines. I will however send you a copy of that part which is immediately and solely connected with the Cottage. The Pedlar's character now makes a very, perhaps [deleted, changed to "certainly"] the *most*, considerable part of the poem. . . . [William's] faculties seem to expand every day, he composes with much more facility than he did, as to the *mechanism* of poetry, & his ideas flow faster than he can express them. After having described a hot summers noon the Poet supposes himself to come in sight of some tall trees upon a flat common.

After transcribing a passage about the meeting of the narrator and the Pedlar, Dorothy told Mary, "The poem then goes on describing his character & habits, & way of life, for above 200 lines." Dorothy omitted the passages about the Pedlar's character and then copied most of the story of Margaret; her work makes it clear that a few transitions and revisions were not yet made in MS. B by 5[-6] March.[26] At the conclusion of her transcript, Dorothy wrote:

Five tedious years
She lingered in unquiet widowhood a wife
And widow &c &c

you have the rest to the end of Margaret's story. There is much more about the Pedlar. I must now request that you will not let this poem go out of your own hands even into your brother Jacks.

Mary probably took a copy of the original concluding lines with her when she left the Wordsworths at Racedown in early June 1797; they are the lines Dorothy copied in Coleridge's letter to Estlin. Now in early March 1798, Mary had the parts "immediately and solely connected with the Cottage" of a poem expanded to 900 lines.

Although much about the Pedlar plainly predates MS. B², one long section in MS. B seems not to have been written by 5[-6] March. Dorothy excluded most of the material about the Pedlar's history—"above 200 lines," she said; in fact, she skipped about 270 lines of the numbered passage. The total is still within her estimate, and she may have had in mind that the inserted leaves add about 210 lines to what was already said about the Pedlar in the original version. But it seems unlikely that the unnumbered 80-line section about the Pedlar's adult life, written on the versos of leaves 15-18, would be included in Dorothy's "above 200 lines"; it would push the number to about 350. In this 80-line passage about the mature Pedlar, he is led by Nature to "sympathy with man" (16^{v}), and Jonathan Wordsworth points out similar passages from early 1798 (*M of H*, p. 162). But there is no way of knowing

[26] The differences between MSS. B and B² are included in an *apparatus criticus* to this volume's MS. B transcription. Raysor, misled by the fact that some parts of MS. B are later than MS. B²—and relying on printed texts only—errs in placing the entire MS. B² before MS. B (pp. 4-6).

whether this still further expansion of the Pedlar's story dates from soon after Dorothy's letter of 5[–6] March or closer to the date of the next manuscript that incorporates it (MS. D, 1799).

The reconciling addendum remains to be dated. Scholars have disagreed whether this was completed before or after Dorothy's letter to Mary, but it was certainly in process by about 10 March, when Coleridge copied out the first eighteen lines in a letter to his brother (*STCL*, I, 397–398). The question turns on whether one credits Dorothy's estimate of a total length of 900 lines and how one interprets her comment to Mary: "You have the rest to the end of Margaret's story. There is much more about the Pedlar." Although it has been argued that if the addendum had been written, Dorothy could not have told Mary she had the rest of Margaret's story (Finch, p. 47), the evidence suggests otherwise. After all, Margaret's story ends when she dies; the addendum records the Pedlar's philosophic reflections, and Dorothy does state, "There is much more about the Pedlar." Dorothy's estimate of lines in the entire poem puts the matter beyond doubt. Her "900 lines" has not often been taken literally, but the correction of 800 to 900 shows that she aimed at accuracy. The original *Ruined Cottage* in MS. B had 528 lines, quickly expanded to the number given at the end, 540. The inserted section about the Pedlar's youth is numbered and adds about 210; the addendum is 146 lines, with an early addition of 9 more counted in the totaling of lines on 43^{r}:

Original text of MS. B	528
Early addition in Part Two (36^{v}) (Pedlar's reaction to Margaret's suffering)	12
Insertion about Pedlar's youth	ca. 210
Reconciling addendum	146
Early addition in addendum (51^{v}) (transition between Pedlar's speech and narrator's reaction)	9
Total lines	ca. 905

She also tried to be exact about how much of the 900-line poem concerned the Pedlar's "character," changing "perhaps the most" to "certainly the most." Just what she counted is uncertain, but the following seems plausible:

Original Pedlar account in MS. B (ll. 40–104)	65
Insertion about Pedlar's youth	ca. 210
Pedlar's moral transition between parts (ll. 243–296)	54
Reconciling addendum	146
Early addition in addendum (51^{v}) (transition between Pedlar's speech and narrator's reaction)	9
Total lines	ca. 484

The addition of the addendum thus brings the poem to "900 lines," one-half of which are concerned with the Pedlar.[27] It is even tempting to conclude that Dorothy corrected her "800" to "900" and her "perhaps" to "certainly" because on the very two days she spent copying the poem for Mary, William finished composing the addendum with that facility and rapidity his sister's letter mentions.

Dating the addendum prior to 5[–6] March causes difficulty, however, in determining the order of Wordsworth's two major additions to the original text in MS. B. There now seems no certainty that the expansion of the Pedlar's history led the poet to write an addendum to agree with the Pedlar's new philosophy. The reverse could be true—perhaps composition of the reconciling addendum led to expansion of the Pedlar's history so that the sentiments he expresses can be seen to flow from his character, developed by past experiences. Three items bear on this problem of chronology: (1) Coleridge's letter to his brother (ca. 10 March 1798) contains the variant "These shadowy Sympathies" in place of the MS. B reading, "These quiet sympathies," in lines quoted from the beginning of the addendum. Perhaps Coleridge copied from Wordsworth's original draft, in which case Dorothy had not yet written her brother's lines into MS. B. Although the variant could be Coleridge's own change, this evidence suggests that the addendum may be later than the Pedlar expansion. (2) The number of lines in the addendum is added, in a penciled sum, to the line total at the end of Part Two in MS. B, but the Pedlar's history is not added in at the end of Part One. This evidence is weak, but it suggests that the Pedlar expansion may have been written later than the addendum. (3) The drafts in the Alfoxden Notebook related to the development of the Pedlar's philosophy were not used in expanding the Pedlar's history; drafts there (20^{v}–21^{r}) do, however, contribute to the addendum. This evidence seems inconclusive.

The order of composition of the Pedlar expansion and the reconciling addendum thus remains doubtful. What seems certain is that the passages included in MS. B—with the exception of the section about the mature Pedlar, and some revisions, transitions, and minor additions—were in existence by 5[–6] March 1798.

By 6 March *The Ruined Cottage* was in close to publishable form, and it was offered to Joseph Cottle about a week later. Coleridge acted as intermediary, proposing first a volume to contain Wordsworth's *The Borderers* and his own *Osorio*, and then one to include "Wordsworth's Salisbury Plain & Tale of a Woman [i.e., *The Ruined Cottage*] . . . with a few others which

---

[27] DW may also have thought of some or all of the meeting between the Pedlar and narrator as part of the description of the Pedlar's character.

he will add."[28] But *The Ruined Cottage* missed the chance of being considered by literary historians as the public beginning of the English Romantic Movement; Cottle printed *Lyrical Ballads* instead.

IV

The Wordsworths left for an eight-month stay in Germany in September, 1798, and in February of the following year William reworked some of his longer poems. "Wishing not to be in debt when I return to England," the poet wrote to Coleridge, "I have lately been employ'd in hewing down Peter Bell"; Wordsworth also "took courage to devote two days (O Wonder) to the Salisbury Plain," and it was "finished all but . . . [the woman's new] tale" (27 February 1799; *EY*, p. 256). *The Ruined Cottage* was, of course, another of those long works whose publication might keep Wordsworth out of debt, and the next manuscript of the poem probably dates from about this time.

Ruined Cottage MS. D (DC MS. 16) is one of Dorothy's pocket notebooks, and it contains copies of a number of her brother's poems. A complete listing of the contents of this notebook is in *Chronology: EY*, pp. 325–328; those passages that relate to questions about *The Ruined Cottage* are on leaves 28^{r}–69^{r}.[29] Dorothy copied *Adventures on Salisbury Plain* in two parts, the first on leaves 28^{r}–33^{r}. Then follows *Prelude* work from early 1799. The second part of *Adventures on Salisbury Plain* occupies 40^{r}–45^{v}, and Dorothy copied *The Ruined Cottage*—without the long history of the Pedlar and with an abbreviated version of his final discourse—on leaves 46^{r}–56^{r}. A passage developed from the Alfoxden Notebook ("In storm and tempest") is labeled "Fragment" on 56^{v} and continues for four lines on the following recto. Although now filled with a passage about the Pedlar written in 1802, the rest of 57^{r} and five more pages were originally left blank. The excluded sections about the Pedlar's history were then written, with some blank spaces, on 60^{r}–67^{r}. Finally, Dorothy transcribed that part of the Pedlar's concluding speech not used in her MS. D fair copy of *The Ruined Cottage* (67^{v}–69^{r}).

Dorothy's *Ruined Cottage* work was entered after the copying of *Adventures on Salisbury Plain*, since she had to squeeze some lines of *The Ruined Cottage* inadvertently skipped into the space left after the copying of the other poem (45^{v}).[30] This transcript of *Adventures on Salisbury Plain*—with a row of asterisks in place of the woman's story—is no doubt the outcome of Wordsworth's

[28] *STCL*, I, 400 (ca. 13 March). For the identification of "Tale of a Woman" with *RC*, see Moorman, I, 371, and *Chronology: EY*, p. 334.

[29] Before the renumbering of the Dove Cottage papers, this manuscript was known as 18A. Photographs and transcriptions of 28^{r}–33^{r} and 40^{r}–45^{v} are in *SPP*, pp. 158–205. Photographs and transcriptions of *Prelude* work on 39^{r} and 39^{v} are in *Prelude 1799*, pp. 144–145.

[30] A photograph of 45^{v} is in *SPP*, p. 204; see also the note to l. 792 of *ASP* on p. 201. Of course, placement of *RC* immediately after *ASP* in the notebook also suggests that *RC* is later.

work on the poem in February, 1799, so *Ruined Cottage* MS. D cannot be dated earlier than February.[31] The terminal date for this text of *The Ruined Cottage* is determined by its relationship with the two-part *Prelude*. On the page immediately after the conclusion of *The Ruined Cottage*, Dorothy copied a "Fragment" ("In storm and tempest") into her notebook, and in the overflow passages about the Pedlar she included a nineteen-line segment beginning "From Nature, & her overflowing soul" on 63^v. Both sections became part of *Prelude* MSS. RV, U, and V, and it is inconceivable that "In storm and tempest" could have been copied as a "Fragment" or that "From Nature" could have been entered as Pedlar surplus once each had found a home in the two-part *Prelude*. Without repeating detailed arguments advanced elsewhere, we can date MS. RV from about September to early December 1799; MSS. U and V were most likely copied between 26 November and 17 December of the same year.[32] Hence Dorothy transcribed *Ruined Cottage* MS. D between February and December 1799. The earlier part of this period—close to the time when William was reworking his other long poems and before he was occupied with preparation of *Prelude* MSS. RV, U, and V—seems the most probable time for the preparation of MS. D.[33]

Despite its 1799 date, *Ruined Cottage* MS D is more closely related to the original 528-line poem of early 1798, and to what Coleridge and Lamb heard in 1797, than to the combined version of the revised MS. B text. Wordsworth, perhaps uneasy about what his poem had become, in MS. D separated the history of the Pedlar from what he now considered, and entitled, *The Ruined Cottage*. The 350 lines about the Pedlar eventually included in the revision of MS. B are here reduced to these:

> With instantaneous joy I recognized
> That pride of nature and of lowly life,
> The venerable Armytage, a friend
> As dear to me as is the setting sun.
> Two days before
> We had been fellow-travellers. I knew
> That he was in this neighbourhood and now
> Delighted found him here in the cool shade. [MS. D, ll. 36–43]

[31] It is suggested in *SPP* (pp. 9–11) that *ASP* may have been copied after April 1799, because some of the *Prelude* work between *ASP*'s first and second parts may refer to WW's meeting with STC in Göttingen in April: since *ASP* is written around the *Prelude* drafts, it is later than they are. Jonathan Wordsworth, in his review of *SPP* in the *Times Literary Supplement* ("Startling the Earthworms," 3 December 1976, p. 1524), argues, however, that this manuscript of *ASP* was copied in February 1799.

[32] Wordsworth and Gill, pp. 516–519; *Chronology: MY*, pp. 629–630; *Prelude 1799*, pp. 22–34.

[33] Drafts for *RC* (toward MS. E, ll. 445–451) and the two-part *Prelude* (prior to MS. RV) also appear in *Peter Bell* MS. 2 (DC MS. 33). The *RC* lines were probably written about the same time as RC MS. D, but the draft may be slightly later since it is not used in MS. D. This passage is given in an *apparatus criticus* to the MS. E reading text, ll. 445–451.

Unlike the original version, however, MS. D does not end abruptly with Margaret's death. The reconciling image of the spear-grass and the mood of tranquillity remain, but the Pedlar's long introductory lesson about the One Life disappears—to resurface (somewhat changed) in the fourth book of *The Excursion* (*PW*, V, 148–150; ll. 1207–1275). Once again, as in 1798, *The Ruined Cottage* is what Dorothy earlier described to Mary Hutchinson as "Margaret's story" (*EY*, p. 209). The excluded passages about the Pedlar could be mined for inclusion in *The Prelude* as the poet's own experiences; what was left could be molded into a separate poem about the Pedlar.

V

We find no further mention of the overflow lines about the Pedlar until Dorothy's journal entry of 6 October 1800. During a visit of Coleridge to Dove Cottage, Dorothy noted: "After tea read The Pedlar. Determined not to print Christabel with the LB" (*Journals*, p. 43). Coleridge wrote to Humphry Davy three days later the reasons his poem would not appear in the second edition of *Lyrical Ballads*, consoling himself with a plan—never put into effect—"to publish the Christabel therefore with a long Blank Verse Poem of Wordsworth's entitled The Pedlar" (*STCL*, I, 631). Wordsworth, though, does not seem to have begun revising his Pedlar lines into a poem suitable for publication until December, 1801. Beginning then, and continuing for the next several months, Dorothy's journal contains important references to work on *The Pedlar*, 1802, as well as one to revision of *The Ruined Cottage*.[34]

[21 December 1801] Wm sate beside me and read the Pedlar, he was in good spirits, and full of hope of what he should do with it. [*Journals*, p. 70]
[22 December] Wm composed a few lines of the Pedlar. [p. 71]
[23 December] William worked at The Ruined Cottage and made himself very ill. [p. 73]
[25 January 1802] William tired with composition. [p. 79]
[26 January] We sate nicely together and talked by the fire till we were both tired, for Wm wrote out part of his poem and endeavoured to alter it, and so made himself ill. I copied out the rest for him. [p. 80]

---

[34] Some of the confusion over what the Wordsworths meant in 1801–1802 by "the Pedlar" has cleared. Evidence that "the Pedlar" may have referred to an independent poem—separate from the story of Margaret and solely about the Pedlar—is presented in *M of H* (pp. 164–166), but Jonathan Wordsworth saw the matter as undecided. Later scholarly work, however, confirms that the Wordsworth circle used the title "The Pedlar" in 1801–1802 to mean an independent poem, about as long as the 280 lines mentioned by DW in her journal on 8 July 1802 (Butler, pp. 99–111). MSS. E and E², in which the account of the Pedlar and Margaret's story are rejoined, date not from 1801–1802, as is assumed in *PW* (V, 409–410), but from two years later (Butler, pp. 92–98). In 1804 the title "Pedlar" encompassed the two-part poem and not just the work solely about the Pedlar it signified in 1801–1802. The appropriate evidence is set out below.

[30 January] William worked at the Pedlar all the morning. He kept the dinner waiting till 4 o'clock—he was much tired. [p. 82]
[1 February] William worked hard at the Pedlar and tired himself. [p. 83]
[7 February] William had had a bad night and was working at his poem. We sate by the fire and did not walk, but read the pedlar thinking it done but lo, though Wm could find fault with no one part of it—it was uninteresting and must be altered. Poor William. [p. 85]
[10 February] While I was writing out the Poem as we hope for a final writing, a letter was brought me. . . . After Molly went we read the first part of the poem and were delighted with it, but Wm afterwards got to some ugly places and went to bed tired out. [pp. 87–88]
[11 February] William sadly tired and working still at the Pedlar. [p. 88]
[12 February] William working again. I recopied the Pedlar, but poor William all the time at work. . . . I almost finished writing The Pedlar, but poor William wore himself and me out with labour. [pp. 89–90]
[13 February] . . . still at work at the Pedlar, altering and refitting. [p. 90]
[14 February] William left me at work altering some passages of the Pedlar, and went into the orchard. . . . I worked hard, got the backs pasted the writing finished, and all quite trim. [p. 90]
[16 February] He was better—had altered the pedlar. [p. 92]
[28 February] Wm very ill, employed with the pedlar. [In margin, "Disaster pedlar" added; p. 96]
[3 March] I was so unlucky as to propose to rewrite The Pedlar. Wm got to work and was worn to death. [pp. 96–97]
[6 March] I wrote the Pedlar, and finished it before I went to Mr. Simpson's to drink tea. [p. 98]
[7 March] I stitched up the Pedlar. [p. 98]
[9 March] We sate by the fire in the evening and read the Pedlar over. William worked a little and altered it in a few places. [p. 99]
[10 March] William has since Tea been talking about publishing the Yorkshire Wolds poem [i.e., *Peter Bell*] with the Pedlar. [p. 99]
[8 July] William was looking at the Pedlar when I got up. He arranged it, and after tea I wrote it out—280 lines. [p. 146]

Five manuscripts of *The Pedlar*, 1802, seem to be described here: (1) a manuscript from which William read on 21 December 1801 and which was possibly used for revisions by the poet and for copying by William and Dorothy before they thought the poem "done" on 7 February; (2) a manuscript dating from 10 February in which Dorothy wrote out the poem "as we hope for a final writing"; (3) a manuscript copied by Dorothy that was "almost finished" on 12 February and probably completed on 14 February; (4) a rewriting of *The Pedlar*, 1802, by Dorothy—after some "disaster" on 28 February—which was "finished" on 6 March and "stitched up" on 7 March; (5) a manuscript of 280 lines copied by Dorothy on 8 July after Wordsworth "arranged" a previous manuscript. Numbers 2 and 3 might in fact be the same manuscript, but Dorothy's saying she "recopied" on 12 February makes it seem possible that she was copying the poem again after William's revisions on 10 and 11 February.

Only two of these *Pedlar*, 1802, manuscripts survive. From the first one, *Ruined Cottage* MS D, Wordsworth read his extra passages with high hopes on 21 December, and he returned to it to create his new poem. In 1799, Dorothy had left a gap of nearly six pages between the "Fragment" ("In storm and tempest") and the Pedlar passages excluded from *The Ruined Cottage*. Another gap in copying, slightly less than a full page on 64^v, occurs at a break in the account, presumably left to explain how the Pedlar took up his calling. In 1801–1802, the Wordsworths filled these gaps with additional material about the Pedlar, giving him a new name—Patrick Drummond—and a Scottish rather than a Cumbrian background. The source of these lines is certainly James Patrick, "the intellectual Pedlar," as Wordsworth himself later indicated in the Fenwick note to *The Excursion*: "An Individual named Patrick, by birth and education a Scotchman, followed this humble occupation for many years & afterwards settled in the Town of Kendal.— He married a kinswoman of my wife's, & her sister Sarah was brought up from early Childhood under the good man's eye" (DCP). On 27 January 1802, Dorothy mentioned receiving from Sara Hutchinson "a sweet long letter, with a most interesting account of Mr Patrick" (*Journals*, p. 80). Sara's letter does not survive, but Wordsworth almost certainly used information it provided to write these lines about Patrick Drummond, whose songs and tales bewitched the "fair-hair'd, fair fac'd" "little Girl ten years of age" (MS. D, 57^r).

What is probably the first work written into MS. D in 1801 is a scrawled pencil draft in Wordsworth's hand on 59^v. In this draft, Wordsworth described the meeting of the speaker with the Pedlar in order to let him then tell his long history. The lines are, of course, a logical place to begin shaping the surplus passages into a poem, and it seems probable that these are the lines Dorothy refers to when she first mentions work on *The Pedlar*, 1802: "Wm composed a few lines of the Pedlar" (22 December 1801). Dorothy records no further composition until late January, and since the Wordsworths spent nearly a month with the Clarksons at Eusemere (leaving Grasmere 28 December and returning 23 January),[35] it is likely that little if anything was then accomplished. But from 25 January to 10 March, her journal details extensive *Pedlar*, 1802, work. In MS. D, some of the work referred to in these journal entries takes the form of alteration of what was written in 1799, as well as complete crossing out of a number of passages, and some pencil drafts—later erased and overwritten in ink by William and Dorothy—at the first gap left two years before (57^r–59^r). In short, the manuscript shows numerous revisions, quite sufficient in detail to make Wordsworth, as Dorothy says, "tired" and "very ill."

---

[35] *Journals*, pp. 74, 78.

At last, however, the passages were worked over enough to permit them to be formed into a poem. A fair copy begins on the first page of the first gap left in 1799 (57^{r}); Dorothy copied out thirty-one lines, beginning "Him had I seen the day before—alone," working from the earlier passages but incorporating Wordsworth's revisions and pencil-draft additions.[36] Wordsworth next wrote about fifty lines before Dorothy resumed work on the fair copy. The passage is numbered in pencil every twenty lines, and those numbers continue throughout the MS. D addendum, jumping from page to page to include uncanceled 1799 lines in the 1802 poem. Dorothy copied a new twenty-five-line passage into a second gap (64^{v}), but this 1802 writing is linked and numbered in sequence with the original 1799 sections coming before and after it.

On 8 July—having worked through three or four manuscripts after MS. D—Dorothy indicated in her journal that *The Pedlar* was 280 lines long. The MS. D version suggests a poem of roughly the same length, although it is difficult to identify precisely the lines with which Wordsworth intended to conclude it. The last pencil number is 220 on 65^{v}, followed eleven and one-half lines later by a penciled "IX" and a few illegible words. There is also a a large "P," which Wordsworth used on 64^{v} to indicate the placement of the additional fair copy. Unfortunately, the concluding insert was not made in MS. D—there was apparently no room for it. Although fourteen and one-half undeleted lines remain in the manuscript, the absence of the number 240 where it should be suggests that whether or not the undeleted lines once concluded *The Pedlar*, 1802, when the numbering was done the poem continued on to an insert on a now missing manuscript. Thus MS. D provides definite evidence for only about 230 lines of the new poem. One possibility for what may have followed on the insert is suggested by the later MS. E text of 1803–1804: at this point in the poem, there are thirty-five and one-half more lines about the Pedlar before the story of Margaret resumes. In fact, a draft toward a few lines of this missing passage (MS. E, ll. 350–355) appears inside the front cover of MS. D. Although no certainty is possible, the large "P" on 66^{r} in MS. D may indicate an insert of lines which subsequently form the conclusion of the Pedlar's story in MS. E.

The MS. D version of *The Pedlar*, 1802, was probably near completion about 7 February 1802; Wordsworth's reading of the poem and "thinking it done" on that date seem to imply something like the continuous text

[36] The poem's precipitate beginning is analogous to the dangling question—"Was it for this"—with which the two-part *Prelude* opens; in each case, WW seems to have let an abrupt beginning stand while he arranged various sections of a poem. Line 12 in the MS. D numbering of *The Pedlar*, 1802, is the first line (there numbered as l. 23) on the sole surviving leaf in the later Alfoxden Notebook version (see below). The more finished Alfoxden Notebook copy of *The Pedlar*, 1802, thus expanded the beginning by eleven lines.

provided by MS. D. Furthermore, Dorothy's "writing out the Poem" on 10 February might mean a fresh manuscript, and her recopying of *The Pedlar* on 12 February certainly suggests a new one, very likely the manuscript on which she "worked hard, got the backs pasted the writing finished, and all quite trim" on 14 February. Thus between late December 1801 and mid-February 1802, a new poem—*The Pedlar*, 1802—took shape in MS. D.

The only other surviving manuscript from 1802 is a single leaf (no. 31)—preceded by one stub and followed by several more—at the back of the Alfoxden Notebook. This passage is certainly later than the text prepared in early February, since it incorporates corrections made in MS. D. This surviving leaf has twenty-one lines on its recto and twenty-two on its verso; the number 40 is penciled before its eighteenth line, and the number 60 follows twenty lines later. The opening line is thus line 23 of the poem, and the preceding twenty-two lines must have stood on the opposite verso, now a closely cut stub. Following leaf 31 are nine stubs, and the versos of the first three are torn so as to show traces of ink (a tiny ink mark is also visible at the top of stub 38^r). A recent restoration of the notebook has added four more stubs after stub 39. Since forty-three lines are on the surviving leaf (which ends at line 65), nine more leaves would have space for a poem 452 lines long. If the four restored stubs are accepted, a total of 624 lines would be possible. Clearly, what could *not* have stood in the Alfoxden Notebook is the double-barreled *Ruined Cottage*; the story of Margaret was in itself 538 lines (in MS. D) and the description of the Pedlar would add about 280 lines. Instead this numbered fair-copy passage about the Pedlar, continuing on through at least three more leaves now removed from the notebook, is probably a transcript of the new poem concerning the Pedlar constructed in MS. D. The number of stubs also suggests that the Alfoxden Notebook may have contained other work besides this *Pedlar*, 1802, fair copy.

Dorothy Wordsworth's journal provides two possibilities for the date of this Alfoxden manuscript of *The Pedlar*, 1802. As mentioned above, the journal entries imply three or four fair copies of the poem postdating the completion of revision in MS. D about 7 February. The Alfoxden manuscript could not be the one of 14 February 1802 since Dorothy's description of pasting up the backs of it cannot apply to this leather-bound notebook. In addition, the entry in the margin for 28 February ("Disaster pedlar"), followed on 3 March by a decision to rewrite *The Pedlar*, implies that this fair-copy manuscript was accidentally destroyed or misplaced. Dorothy "stitched up" another fair copy on 7 March, but again this description suggests a homemade notebook rather than the commercially prepared Alfoxden. This manuscript of 7 March apparently does not survive; perhaps it was dismembered in the process of arranging *The Pedlar*, 1802, for recopying on 8 July. Be that as it may, the Alfoxden Notebook fair copy is thus most likely either a manuscript possibly transcribed on 10 February or the one written after tea on 8 July. The 8 July alternative has the advantage of accounting for a manuscript otherwise missing, and some verbal differences do suggest the possibility of manuscripts intermediary between MS. D and the Alfoxden text. But a case could also be made for the 10 February date. On the surviving Alfoxden leaf, all but nine of the forty-three original lines have been crossed out or—a number of sewing holes show—were once covered over by another piece of paper. That leaf might come from a relatively early stage in the arranging of *The Pedlar* in 1802, rather than from the conclusion of that work. The 10 February date would also explain why Dorothy used blank pages from an old notebook to copy the work: the Wordsworths were evidently in need of paper and on the tenth sent for some through Fletcher, the Keswick carrier (*Journals*, p. 87). The evidence, however, is not sufficient to prove that either 10 February or 8 July was the date when this Alfoxden fair copy of *The Pedlar*, 1802, was written, and one cannot rule out the possibility that revisions on this leaf were made in late 1803 or early 1804, when MS. E was being prepared.

Any explanation for the presence of only a single leaf of *The Pedlar*, 1802, in the Alfoxden Notebook must be speculative. Presumably the other pages were removed to prepare a new manuscript. Since the surviving Alfoxden leaf contained only nine lines not deleted or sewn over by another piece of paper, perhaps whoever cut out the pages did not think it worthwhile to remove this leaf for its nine lines, or perhaps the sewn-on sheet contained all that was necessary. One can only be grateful that the leaf is still in the notebook, since it provides additional evidence for the existence of Wordsworth's 1802 poem describing his philosophic pedlar.

The lack of a complete text of *The Pedlar*, 1802, makes critical judgment difficult, but some differences between this and earlier Pedlar accounts are clear. The 1799 Pedlar sequence had certainly been diminished by the transfer of two of its most impressive sections to *The Prelude*,[37] and the 1802 poem reflects this loss. Wordsworth's main addition, drawing on Sara Hutchinson's memories of James Patrick, emphasizes the gentle humanity of the Pedlar. Drummond seems both more melancholy ("And thus did Patrick gather when a Boy / Some gloomy notions" [MS. D, 58^v]) and more conventionally religious than in earlier incarnations:

> Pure livers were they all—austere & grave
> And fearing God the very children taught
> Stern self respect, a reverence for God's word
> And piety, scarce known on English land. [MS. D, 58^v]

[37] The nineteen-line passage "From Nature and her overflowing soul" (MS. D, 63^v–64^r) was included in the two-part *Prelude* in late 1799 (*Prelude 1799*, II, 446–464). The second passage—thirty-three lines beginning "though he was untaught" in MS. D, 66^v—may have been moved to form *Prelude*, III, 82, 122–127, 141–147, and 156–167, in late 1801 (*M of H*, p. 167, n. 1; Wordsworth and Gill, pp. 523–524); it is in any case not part of *The Pedlar*, 1802.

The combined effect of excisions and additions is to change *The Pedlar* from a philosophic exposition to a character sketch which resembles some of the *Lyrical Ballads* and the poems of 1802 in which Wordsworth returned to portrayals of character.[38]

Dorothy's journal shows that Wordsworth gave some thought in March 1802 to publishing this new poem (*Journals*, p. 99), but it is uncertain how long her brother thought of *The Pedlar*, 1802, as separate from *The Ruined Cottage*. Unless Wordsworth changed his mind more than once in 1802, the reference on 8 July (*Journals*, p. 146) to the length of *The Pedlar* as 280 lines means that it was still then an independent poem. But included in *Ruined Cottage* MS. D is a revision from "The old man ceased" to "Here Drummon" (55^{r}). The name Drummond does not appear in the later MS. E (late 1803–early 1804), so this MS. D correction may represent a decision to join the two parts sometime prior to the preparation of MS. E. *The Pedlar*, 1802, would then have been considered part of *The Ruined Cottage*, even though a new manuscript reflecting that combination may not have been immediately copied out. Such may be the import of a penciled sum opposite line 35 of *Ruined Cottage* MS. D: 35 + 276 = 311. If a 276-line *Pedlar* had been put with MS. D (or if leaves containing the poem—perhaps even leaves torn out of the Alfoxden Notebook—had been laid in), the Wordsworths would have had a readable text.

VI

Begun in 1797 as the story of Margaret, expanded in 1798 with a Pedlar's history, divided in 1799 into separate parts (one of which contributed to an independent work solely about the Pedlar in 1802), the poem achieved its final shape in MSS. E, E^{2}, and M: Wordsworth rejoined Margaret's story and the account of the Pedlar. The combined poem now also took over the title *The Pedlar*, since Dorothy calls it that when preparing MS. M (*EY*, p. 448), and Wordsworth wrote to Sir George Beaumont on Christmas Day, 1804, about Coleridge's reading from MS. M the preceding spring, "Of this Poem [*The Recluse*], that of 'the Pedlar' which Coleridge read you is part" (*EY*, p. 518).

MS. E (DC MS. 37) is a homemade notebook with nineteen surviving leaves—its original thirteenth leaf is now only a stub. The first ten leaves are five bifolia of torn and folded paper watermarked J APPLETON over the date 1794. The remaining nine, and the stub, are five bifolia of torn and folded paper watermarked with a crowned horn-in-shield above GR. The leaves of both kinds of paper are about 12 centimeters wide and 19 centimeters

[38] For the context in which *The Pedlar*, 1802, was written, see Jared R. Curtis, *Wordsworth's Experiments with Tradition: The Lyric Poems of 1802* (Ithaca, 1971), particularly pp. 27–30, 97–113.

Watermarks of the paper used in *Pedlar* manuscripts. Left: image of Britannia in a crowned oval and the date 1802; from a letter of Dorothy Wordsworth to Catherine Clarkson, 13 November 1803 (*EY*, pp. 416–421). Right: crowned horn-in-shield above GR; from a letter of Dorothy Wordsworth to Catherine Clarkson, [25] March 1804 (*EY*, pp. 458–462). Reproduced by permission of the British Library Board from Add. MS. 36997, ff. 5, 11. The left photograph is 72 percent of actual size; the right photograph is 85 percent of actual size.

high. Sewn into MS. E after its tenth leaf is MS. E^2, copied from MS. E but incomplete, containing only the opening one-third of the poem and ending in mid-sentence. MS. E^2 is one gathering of seven leaves and a stub; the leaves are about 10.7 centimeters wide and 16.9 centimeters high, formed from torn and folded paper watermarked with an image of Britannia in a crowned oval—with the date 1802 at the bottom inside the oval—and countermarked C HALE. Both MSS. E and E^2 are fair copies in Dorothy's hand, although Wordsworth has made corrections.

The paper used in the construction of these homemade notebooks helps establish their date, since the Wordsworths used the same supply of paper for writing letters as for constructing notebooks.[39] Every letter known to survive in manuscript that the Wordsworths wrote from Grasmere during the period from 13 November 1803 to 31 August 1804 has one of the notebook papers' watermarks. The Britannia/C HALE paper first appears on 13 November (*EY*, pp. 416–421); MS. E's two papers show up slightly later, the J APPLETON on 12 December (*EY*, pp. 426–428), and the crowned-horn-in-shield above GR on 15 January 1804 (*EY*, pp. 428–431).[40] Late 1803 thus seems the earliest possible date for these manuscripts of *The Pedlar*. A *terminus ad quem* is provided by the fact that comparative readings indicate that E^2 was copied from E and M was copied from E^2 until it stopped, then from E. MS. M (DC MS. 44) opens with *The Pedlar*, but it also contains most of Wordsworth's then unpublished poetry copied for Coleridge, who took this notebook to Malta (*Chronology*: *MY*, pp. 619–624, 636). On 8 February 1804 Coleridge requested transcriptions of the poems, and he renewed his appeal on 15 February (*STCL*, II, 1060, 1065). Dorothy wrote to him on 6 March, "We have transcribed all William's smaller Poems for you, and have begun the Poem on his Life and the Pedlar" (*EY*, p. 448). The last packet was sent to Coleridge by 18 March (*EY*, p. 459); work on MSS. E and E^2 must therefore have preceded that date.

About MS. E^2 it is possible to be more specific. The C HALE/1802 paper of MS. E^2 is identical with the paper used in the homemade MS. M, and M is gathered in eights, as is the single gathering that forms MS. E^2. In fact, the fragmentary MS. E^2 ends with the same line that concludes the first

[39] John Finch redated early *Home at Grasmere* manuscripts by matching the paper in them with that found in letters ("On the Dating of *Home at Grasmere*," in *Bicentenary Wordsworth Studies*, pp. 14–28).

[40] STC stayed with the Wordsworths from 20 December 1803 to 14 January 1804, and he no doubt used their supply of paper. The paper used for two letters to Mrs. Coleridge written in early January (*STCL*, II, 1024–1026) is watermarked with the image of Britannia in a crowned oval and the date 1802; the paper used for two letters to Southey (11 January and 13 January; *STCL*, II, 1026–1031) is watermarked with the crowned horn-in-shield above GR. I am indebted to the Victoria University Library, Toronto, and the Pierpont Morgan Library, New York, for permission to refer to these STC letters. A complete list of the Wordsworths' letters with the watermarks of MSS. E and E^2 appears in Butler, pp. 93–94.

gathering in MS. M: "Of ordinary life, unvex'd, unwarp'd" (MS. M, l. 363). The evidence suggests that MS. E² was once the first gathering of MS. M, and this conclusion is confirmed when one examines the last pages of the present first gathering in MS. M. Although much of this gathering is copied at the rate of twenty-eight to thirty lines per page, Dorothy spaced her lines out to twenty-two to twenty-five per page for the last four pages. Clearly, the second gathering was already written, and she spaced out the lines of the recopied first gathering to lead into it. There are a number of revisions in MS. E² and a bad ink spill on leaf 3^r, so Dorothy recopied this original first gathering of MS. M. The manuscript now known as E² is thus fragmentary not because any of it has been lost but because it was once part of another manuscript. In order to preserve the revisions in MS. E², this replaced gathering was then stitched into MS. E. Since Dorothy reported on 6 March 1804 that the copy of *The Pedlar* for Coleridge was now begun (*EY*, p. 448), MS. E² must have been written quite close to that date as the first part of the process of copying that produced MS. M.

It is difficult to be definite about the writing of MS. E, except for the range of dates suggested by the Wordsworths' first known use of its two papers (mid-December 1803 and mid-January 1804) and the copying from it of MS. E² (about 6 March 1804).[41] Two references by Coleridge to *The Recluse* provide additional information, however. On 14 October 1803 Coleridge wrote to Thomas Poole, "I rejoice therefore with a deep & true Joy, that he [Wordsworth] has at length yielded to my urgent & repeated—almost unremitting—requests & remonstrances—& will go on with the Recluse exclusively.—A Great Work, in which he will sail; on an open Ocean, & a steady wind" (*STCL*, II, 1013), repeating phrasing from a notebook entry written between 9 October and the date of the letter.[42] Despite Coleridge's optimism of mid-October, Dorothy wrote on 13 November, "William has not yet done any thing of importance at his great work,"[43]

---

[41] Several factors make it probable that the crowned horn-in-shield above GR and the J APPLETON are watermark and countermark of the same sheets, of which only half sheets now survive in the Wordsworth papers: (1) the papers are the same size, with chain lines 2.6 centimeters apart; (2) the letters JA within the bottom of the shield in the horn-in-shield watermark probably signify J. Appleton; (3) both types of paper seem to be torn along a central chain line; this is most obvious on the manuscript of the letter printed in *EY*, pp. 490–493. There is, of course, no way of knowing whether the full sheet was torn in half by the stationer or by the Wordsworths. In either case, it is quite possible that the J APPLETON and the horn-in-shield papers entered the Wordsworth household at the same time.

[42] *The Notebooks of Samuel Taylor Coleridge*, ed. Kathleen Coburn (3 vols.; London, 1957–1973), entry 1546.

[43] *EY*, p. 421. The "great work" is identified as *The Prelude* by Chester Shaver, the editor of *EY*, but in light of STC's letter of 14 October, DW almost certainly meant *The Recluse*. Besides, the Wordsworths consistently referred to *The Prelude* as "the poem on William's early life" (*EY*, pp. 436, 440, 447, 448, 454, 459, 470, 518) or "the poem to Coleridge" (*EY*, p. 463; *Journals*, p. 74).

and on 21 November, "William has written two little poems on subjects suggested by our Tour in Scotland—that is all he has actually done lately, but he is very well and I hope will soon be more seriously employed" (*EY*, p. 423). Since Wordsworth's letter to Beaumont, 25 December 1804, makes clear that *The Pedlar* is part of his magnum opus, *The Recluse*, the writing of MS. E was likely the outcome of Wordsworth's October plan—not put into effect by late November—to labor at his great work. Certainly from late January or early February 1804 Wordsworth worked intensively at *The Prelude*, so *Pedlar* MS. E probably may be dated between 21 November 1803 and early February 1804.

If one had to hypothesize a more exact time for MS. E, the last two weeks in January seem most likely. Coleridge had just left after a month's stay at Grasmere, and his encouragings may have spurred Wordsworth into action on both *The Pedlar* and *The Prelude* (Coleridge wrote to Richard Sharp on the morning after he left Grasmere telling him of his hopes for *The Recluse* [*STCL*, II, 1034]). Coleridge's month-long illness must have been difficult for the Grasmere household—Dorothy complained to Mrs. Clarkson that what with caring for the family and Coleridge, she had "*so much to do* that I seemed to have scarcely the quiet and leisure necessary to make me feel fit to write a letter that would give you any comfort" (15 January; *EY*, p. 430)—but now that he was gone, William had the leisure to write and Dorothy to copy. The evidence that suggests mid- to late January for the work that produced MS. E is, however, not conclusive.[44]

Whatever the exact date of MS. E, Wordsworth no longer thought of the philosophic description of the Pedlar as separate from the account of Margaret. Instead, philosophy and narrative are combined into one book of Wordsworth's intended epic, *The Recluse*, as Wordsworth himself wrote De Quincey on 6 March 1804:

> I am now writing a Poem on my own earlier life. . . . This Poem will not be published these many years, and never during my lifetime, till I have finished a larger and more important work to which it is tributary. Of this larger work I have written one Book and several scattered fragments: it is a moral and Philosophical Poem; the subject whatever I find most interesting, in Nature Man Society, most adapted to Poetic illustration. To this work I mean to devote the Prime of my life and the chief force of my mind. [*EY*, p. 454]

The reintroduction of passages about the Pedlar into *The Ruined Cottage* thus helps set the narrative-philosophic-dramatic mode of *The Excursion*; the Pedlar himself evolves in a later manuscript (DC MS. 71) into the Wanderer. At about the same time in 1804 that Wordsworth was beginning to decide

[44] Although WW's letter to John Thelwall, mid- or late January, about work on "a Poem of considerable labour" (*EY*, p. 432) probably refers to *The Prelude*, there is at least some chance that the poet might have meant *The Pedlar*.

the structure, content, and length of *The Prelude*, he—by rejoining the story of Margaret and the history of the Pedlar—mapped out what he intended to do in *The Recluse*. Indeed, the decision to use dramatic speakers to develop philosophic points in at least part of *The Recluse* freed the more autobiographical details for Wordsworth's *Prelude*, which now expanded rapidly.[45]

By the time Dorothy copied *Pedlar* MS. M (about 6–18 March 1804), Wordsworth had made numerous minor alterations in his poem, as well as three more lengthy changes affecting the Pedlar's role as commentator on Margaret's story by improving his philosophic standing. A passage in MS. M (ll. 100–122) praises the Pedlar as one of the silent poets: such men may lack "the accomplishment of verse," but are "endued with highest gifts, / The vision and the faculty divine." The Pedlar himself, "Though born in low estate, and earning bread / By a low calling," "Was as the prime and choice of sterling minds." MS. E omits an account—written in 1798—of the youthful "turbulence / Of his own heart"; restoration of the section in MS. M (ll. 299–318) again shows that the Pedlar's calm reaction to Margaret's death is a hard-won attitude developed through a combination of youthful and mature experiences. Finally, Wordsworth in MS. M cuts out one of the scenes added in 1802 about James Patrick and Sara Hutchinson (MS. E, ll. 83–98); the Pedlar's singing songs with the little girl and crying over her innocence are more suited to the character sketch of *The Pedlar*, 1802, than to the philosophic function the Pedlar's history once again served in 1804.[46]

With MSS. E, E², and M, the seven-year history of *The Ruined Cottage* and *The Pedlar* comes to a close. In the next complete copy (DC MS. 71), *The Pedlar* becomes the first book of *The Excursion*. But it is the separate poem Coleridge remembered in 1814—perhaps recalling his reading of *The Pedlar* to Beaumont ten years before or what he heard of *The Ruined Cottage* after bounding down a field to Racedown seven years before that—when he judged the work to be "the finest Poem in our Language, comparing it with any of the same or similar Length" (*STCL*, IV, 564).

---

[45] For an account of work on *The Prelude* in early 1804, see *Chronology: MY*, pp. 633–652, and Jonathan Wordsworth, "The Five-Book *Prelude* of Early Spring 1804," *JEGP*, 76 (1977), 1–25.

[46] The differences between MSS. E and M are discussed further in Reeve Parker, "'Finer Distance': The Narrative Art of Wordsworth's 'The Wanderer,'" *English Literary History*, 39 (1972), 105n, 110–111. The three changes were all made by the time of the copying of MS. E² (about 6 March), the original first gathering of MS. M.

Editorial Procedure

Like other volumes in this series, this edition provides two kinds of texts: (1) "reading texts," from which all complexities and variant readings are stripped away, and (2) transcriptions of manuscripts, usually with facing photographic reproductions of the manuscripts. Editorial procedures have been adapted to the different aims of these two styles of presentation.

The reading texts are designed to represent three full-length manuscripts (*Ruined Cottage* MSS. B and D, *Pedlar* MS. E) in their earliest complete states, so far as they can now be recovered. The editing of MS. B, the first full text, presents particular problems, since in making her fair copy Dorothy Wordsworth left a few gaps for transitions, which were later filled by her brother. The manuscript also has occasional minor corrections of meter, grammar, and internal inconsistencies. Since these later transitions and corrections would probably have been included had the original poem been prepared for publication (and do not distort the work's first impulse), they are here accepted as parts of the reading text, and each is identified in the notes. In *Ruined Cottage* MS. D, the first-level revision has been made by erasure. While it is sometimes possible to guess at the erased words on the basis of what is in the earlier MS. B, the guesses are offered in notes to the transcription, and the reading text presents the manuscript as it appeared after revision by erasure. *Pedlar* MS. E is also revised by erasure, but a lighter touch and the nature of the paper allow more certitude about what underlies the revisions. Therefore here the original readings, now erased, are, when legible, incorporated in the reading text. When a reading in the base text of MS. B, D, or E differs from the reading in both preceding and following manuscripts, these principles determine whether the reading text is emended: (1) if the variant is revised to read like both earlier and later manuscripts, the alteration is taken to be a correction of a copyist's error and is thus accepted in the reading text; (2) if the variant involves such common copyist's errors as the addition or omission of "s," "ed," or an article, the reading text is emended whether or not the base text is corrected; (3) if any other variant is not revised to read like both earlier and later manuscripts (and it is not obviously a copyist's error), it is preserved in the reading text since it may possibly represent Wordsworth's intent at one stage. In all three cases, notes to the reading texts provide complete details.

Reading-text punctuation is based on the pointing in Wordsworth's manuscripts and what he approved in the first printed text (*The Excursion*, 1814). The punctuation of the underlying manuscript guided that of each reading text; sometimes alterations and additions seemed necessary (particularly in the carelessly punctuated MSS. B and D), and other manuscripts and *The Excursion*, 1814, were then consulted, with more weight being given to the manuscripts' punctuation. The capitals and paragraphing of the manuscripts are preserved. Except for the ampersand, which is expanded, the Wordsworths' spelling is also preserved; a few obvious copyist's errors and Dorothy's idiosyncratic word separation, however, have been amended. Brackets enclosing blank spaces indicate blanks left in the manuscripts. As in earlier volumes in this series, letters no longer visible owing to defects in the manuscript have been supplied.

In the other main sort of text, transcription of a manuscript, the aim is to show with reasonable typographic accuracy everything in the manuscript that could be helpful to a study of the poem's growth and development. Even false starts and corrected letters can sometimes reveal the writer's intention, and they are here recorded, though reinforced letters and random marks are normally not. Passages in Wordsworth's hand are discriminated from those in Dorothy's by the use of roman type for his and italic for hers, although identification of hands must occasionally be conjectural, especially in the case of scattered words or parts of words. Revisions are shown in type of reduced size, and an effort has been made to show deletion marks, spacing, and other such physical features so that they resemble those of the manuscript itself, though some minor adjustments have been made in the interest of clarity; doubled-back lines are shown approximately as they appear in the manuscript. In the numbering of leaves, stubs are counted, but not pasted-down end papers. Editorial line numbers in the transcriptions of MSS. B and D correspond to those of the reading texts; these numbers are carried in the left-hand margins. Similarly, transcriptions of manuscripts contributing to MS. B (MS. A, the Racedown Notebook, the letter of Coleridge to Estlin, the *Christabel* Notebook, and the Alfoxden Notebook) carry either the precise MS. B line numbers in the left-hand margins or the pertinent range of roughly corresponding line numbers within brackets at the top of each page. Those passages about the Pedlar inserted into MS. B and later copied as an addendum to MS. D carry bracketed line references to MS. E at the top of the page if they were subsequently used in MS. E.

Readings of manuscripts that are relatively uncomplicated are presented in an *apparatus criticus* to transcriptions or reading texts. All variant readings—with the exception of single-letter miswritings corrected by the copyist—are shown; variants are in Dorothy's hand and in ink in the manuscripts, unless otherwise noted. Further details of presentation are given in the headnotes.

To avoid unnecessary elaboration in textual notes, all quotations from manuscripts are printed in roman type.

The following symbol is used in reading texts, transcriptions, and the *apparatus criticus*:

[? ?]	Illegible words; each question mark represents one word.

The following symbol is used in both reading texts and transcriptions:

[ ]	Gap or blank in the manuscript.

The following symbols are used in transcriptions; the first three also appear in the *apparatus criticus*:

[?peace]	Conjectural reading.
d} has}	An overwriting: original reading, "has," converted to "had" by writing the "d" upon the "s".
{s	A short addition, sometimes only a mark of punctuation.
[—?—?—]	Deleted and illegible word or words.
[?love/?live]	Alternate readings seem equally possible.
That more	Word or words written over an erasure; the original is now uncertain. Notes record the reading of the immediately preceding manuscript, and any visible letters are shown in boldface type.

The following abbreviations are used in the *apparatus criticus*; the first one also appears in the headnotes and notes.

161a, 161b	The first and second halves, respectively, of a line of verse.
alt	Alternate reading; the original is not deleted.
del to	Reading changed to another reading; the original is deleted.
del	Reading deleted.

The Ruined Cottage

Parallel Reading Texts of MSS. B (1798) and D (1799)

MS. B: Reading Text

The Ruined Cottage.
A Poem.——

Give me a spark of nature's fire,
Tis the best learning I desire.
. . . . .
My Muse though homely in attire
May touch the heart.
Burns.——

Part 1st.——

Twas Summer; and the sun was mounted high.
Along the south the uplands feebly glared
Through a pale steam, and all the northern downs
In clearer air ascending shewed their brown
5 And [ ] surfaces distinct with shades
Of deep embattled clouds that lay in spots
Determined and unmoved, with steady beams
Of clear and pleasant sunshine interposed;
Pleasant to him who on the soft cool grass
10 Extends his careless limbs beside the root
Of some huge oak whose aged branches make
A twilight of their own, a dewy shade
Where the wren warbles, while the dreaming man,
Half conscious of that soothing melody,
15 With sidelong eye looks out upon the scene,
By those impending branches made [ ]
More soft and distant. Other lot was mine.
Across a bare wide Common I had toiled
With languid feet which by the slippery ground

For that part of the Fenwick note relating to *RC*, see Appendix II, below.

Epigraph WW misquotes *Epistle to J. L.*****k* [Lapraik], *An Old Scotch Bard*, ll. 73–74, 77–78. In l. 1 of the epigraph, the "Gi" in "Give" is torn away.

1–7 (D, 1–8) The opening is an adaptation of a passage from *An Evening Walk* (1793), along with revisions made of it at Windy Brow in 1794 (*PW*, I, 8; ll. 53–56 and *apparatus criticus*).

7 The last two letters of "beams" have worn away.

10 The word "careless" was inserted and makes the line complete.

MS. D: Reading Text

The Ruined Cottage.
1st Part

'Twas summer and the sun was mounted high.
Along the south the uplands feebly glared
Through a pale steam, and all the northern downs
In clearer air ascending shewed far off
[5] Their surfaces with shadows dappled o'er 5
Of deep embattled clouds: far as the sight
Could reach those many shadows lay in spots
Determined and unmoved, with steady beams
Of clear and pleasant sunshine interposed;
Pleasant to him who on the soft cool moss 10
[10] Extends his careless limbs beside the root
Of some huge oak whose aged branches make
A twilight of their own, a dewy shade
Where the wren warbles while the dreaming man,
Half-conscious of that soothing melody, 15
[15] With side-long eye looks out upon the scene,
By those impending branches made more soft,
More soft and distant. Other lot was mine.
Across a bare wide Common I had toiled
With languid feet which by the slipp'ry ground 20

Bracketed line numbers in the left-hand margins refer to corresponding lines in the MS. B reading text. Notes that apply to both versions of *RC* are given below the MS. B reading text, with line references to the MS. D reading text in parentheses. For that part of the Fenwick note relating to *RC*, see Appendix II, below.

20 Were baffled still; and when I sought repose
On the brown earth my limbs from very heat
Could find no rest nor my weak arm disperse
The insect host which gathered round my face
And joined their murmurs to the tedious noise
25 Of seeds of bursting gorse which crackled round.
I rose and turned towards a group of trees
Which midway in the level stood alone,
And thither come at length, beneath a shade
Of clustering elms that sprang from the same root
30 I found a ruined Cottage, four clay walls
That stared upon each other.—'Twas a spot!
The wandering gypsey in a stormy night
Would pass it with his moveables to house
On the open plain beneath the imperfect arch
35 Of a cold lime-kiln. As I looked around
Beside the door I saw an aged Man
Stretched on a bench whose edge with short bright moss
Was green and studded o'er with fungus flowers;
An iron-pointed staff lay at his side.
40 Him had I seen the day before—alone
And in the middle of the public way
Standing to rest himself. His eyes were turned
Towards the setting sun, while with that staff
Behind him fixed he propped a long white pack
45 Which crossed his shoulders: wares for maids who live
In lonely villages or straggling huts.
I knew him—he was born of lowly race
On Cumbrian hills, and I have seen the tear
Stand in his luminous eye when he described
50 The house in which his early days were passed
And found I was no stranger to the spot.
I loved to hear him talk of former days
And tell how when a child ere yet of age
To be a shepherd he had learned to read
55 His bible in a school that stood alone,
Sole building on a mountain's dreary edge,
Far from the sight of city spire, or sound

20b–22 The original reading—"my limbs from very heat / Could find no rest nor my weak arm disperse"—was revised prior to DW's line numbering.

26 The original reading ("I turned my steps") was revised to "I rose & turned" in connection with WW's revisions in ll. 20b–22 (see the note above).

32–35 The "gypsey" and the "lime-kiln" also appear in *ASP*, ll. 176–177 (*SPP*, p. 128).

[20] Were baffled still, and when I stretched myself
On the brown earth my limbs from very heat
Could find no rest nor my weak arm disperse
The insect host which gathered round my face
And joined their murmurs to the tedious noise 25
[25] Of seeds of bursting gorse that crackled round.
I rose and turned towards a group of trees
Which midway in that level stood alone,
And thither come at length, beneath a shade
Of clustering elms that sprang from the same root 30
[30] I found a ruined house, four naked walls
That stared upon each other. I looked round
And near the door I saw an aged Man,
Alone, and stretched upon the cottage bench;
[39] An iron-pointed staff lay at his side. 35
With instantaneous joy I recognized
That pride of nature and of lowly life,
The venerable Armytage, a friend
As dear to me as is the setting sun.
Two days before 40
We had been fellow-travellers. I knew
That he was in this neighbourhood and now
Delighted found him here in the cool shade.
He lay, his pack of rustic merchandize

Of Minster clock. He from his native hills
Had wandered far: much had he seen of men,
60 Their manners, their enjoyments and pursuits,
Their passions and their feelings, chiefly those
Essential and eternal in the heart,
Which 'mid the simpler forms of rural life
Exist more simple in their elements
65 And speak a plainer language. He possessed
No vulgar mind though he had passed his life
In this poor occupation, first assumed
From impulses of curious thought, and now
Continued many a year, and now pursued
70 From habit and necessity. His eye
Flashing poetic fire, he would repeat
The songs of Burns, and as we trudged along
Together did we make the hollow grove
Ring with our transports. Though he was untaught,
75 In the dead lore of schools undisciplined,
Why should he grieve? He was a chosen son:
To him was given an ear which deeply felt
The voice of Nature in the obscure wind,
The sounding mountain and the running stream.
80 To every natural form, rock, fruit, and flower,
Even the loose stones that cover the highway,
He gave a moral life; he saw them feel
Or linked them to some feeling. In all shapes
He found a secret and mysterious soul,
85 A fragrance and a spirit of strange meaning.
Though poor in outward shew, he was most rich;
He had a world about him—'twas his own,
He made it—for it only lived to him
And to the God who looked into his mind.
90 Such sympathies would often bear him far
In outward gesture, and in visible look,
Beyond the common seeming of mankind.
Some called it madness—such it might have been,
But that he had an eye which evermore
95 Looked deep into the shades of difference
As they lie hid in all exterior forms,
Which from a stone, a tree, a withered leaf,

---

74 The word "though" was inserted and makes the line complete.

To the broad ocean and the azure heavens
Spangled with kindred multitudes of stars,
100 Could find no surface where its power might sleep,
Which spake perpetual logic to his soul,
And by an unrelenting agency
Did bind his feelings even as in a chain.
So was he framed, though humble and obscure
105 Had been his lot. Now on the Bench he lay
Stretched at his length, and with that weary load
Pillowed his head—I guess he had no thought
Of his way-wandering life. His eyes were shut;
The shadows of the breezy elms above
110 Dappled his face. With thirsty heat oppressed
At length I hailed him, glad to see his hat
Bedewed with water-drops, as if the brim
Had newly scooped a running stream. He rose
And, pointing to a sun-flower, bade me climb
115 The [ ] wall where that same gaudy flower
Looked out upon the road. It was a plot
Of garden-ground, now wild, its matted weeds
Marked with the steps of those whom as they pass['d],
The gooseberry trees that shot in long [ ],
120 Or currants shewing on a leafless stem
Their scanty strings, had tempted to o'erleap
The broken wall. Within that cheerless spot,
Where two tall hedgerows of thick willow boughs
Joined in a damp cold nook, I found a well
125 Half choaked [ ].
I slaked my thirst and to the shady bench
Returned, and while I stood unbonneted
To catch the current of the breezy air
The old man said, "I see around me [ ]
130 Things which you cannot see. We die, my Friend,
Nor we alone, but that which each man loved
And prized in his peculiar nook of earth
Dies with him or is changed, and very soon
Even of the good is no memorial left.

---

118 WW altered "[?them] who" to "those whom"; DW's fair copy has "pass," but the sense requires "pass'd" (the reading in MSS. D, E, and M).

131 The word "each" was inserted and makes the line complete.

[107] Pillowing his head—I guess he had no thought 45
Of his way-wandering life. His eyes were shut;
The shadows of the breezy elms above
[110] Dappled his face. With thirsty heat oppress'd
At length I hailed him, glad to see his hat
Bedewed with water-drops, as if the brim 50
Had newly scoop'd a running stream. He rose
And pointing to a sun-flower bade me climb
[115] The [ ] wall where that same gaudy flower
Looked out upon the road. It was a plot
Of garden-ground, now wild, its matted weeds 55
Marked with the steps of those whom as they pass'd,
The goose-berry trees that shot in long lank slips,
[120] Or currants hanging from their leafless stems
In scanty strings, had tempted to o'erleap
The broken wall. Within that cheerless spot, 60
Where two tall hedgerows of thick willow boughs
Joined in a damp cold nook, I found a well
[125] Half-choked [with willow flowers and weeds.]
I slaked my thirst and to the shady bench
Returned, and while I stood unbonneted 65
To catch the motion of the cooler air
The old Man said, "I see around me here
[130] Things which you cannot see: we die, my Friend,
Nor we alone, but that which each man loved
And prized in his peculiar nook of earth 70
Dies with him or is changed, and very soon
Even of the good is no memorial left.
The Poets in their elegies and songs
Lamenting the departed call the groves,
They call upon the hills and streams to mourn, 75
And senseless rocks, nor idly; for they speak
In these their invocations with a voice
Obedient to the strong creative power
Of human passion. Sympathies there are
More tranquil, yet perhaps of kindred birth, 80
That steal upon the meditative mind

---

63 DW left a gap after "Half-choked"; WW penciled in "with willow flowers & weeds," and later altered the line in ink to read, "Half-cover'd up with willow-flowers & grass."
67 WW's addition of "here" to DW's fair copy completes the line.

135 The waters of that spring if they could feel
Might mourn. They are not as they were; the bond
Of brotherhood is broken—time has been
When every day the touch of human hand
Disturbed their stillness, and they ministered
140 To human comfort. As I stooped to drink,
Few minutes gone, at that deserted well
What feelings came to me! A spider's web
Across its mouth hung to the water's edge,
And on the wet and slimy foot-stone lay
145 The useless fragment of a wooden bowl;
It moved my very heart. The time has been
When I could never pass this road but she
Who lived within these walls, when I appeared,
A daughter's welcome gave me, and I loved her
150 As my own child. Oh Sir! the good die first,
And they whose hearts are dry as summer dust
Burn to the socket. Many a passenger
Has blessed poor Margaret for her gentle looks
When she upheld the cool refreshment drawn
155 From that forsaken well, and no one came
But he was welcome, no one went away
But that it seemed she loved him. She is dead,
The worm is on her cheek, and this poor hut,
Stripped of its outward garb of houshold flowers,
160 Of rose and jasmine, offers to the wind
A cold bare wall whose earthy top is tricked
With weeds and the rank spear-grass. She is dead,
And nettles rot and adders sun themselves
Where we have sat together while she nursed
165 Her infant at her bosom. The wild colt,
The unstalled heifer and the Potter's ass,
Find shelter now within the chimney wall
Where I have seen her evening hearth-stone blaze
And through the window spread upon the road
170 Its chearful light.— You will forgive me, Sir,
I feel I play the truant with my tale.

140–145 (D, 88–91) Cf. *An Evening Walk* (1793), ll. 255–256: "For hope's deserted well why wistful look? / Chok'd is the pathway, and the pitcher broke" (*PW*, I, 26). Both poems echo Ecclesiastes, 12:6.

158 (D, 104) Cf. *ASP*, l. 743 (*SPP*, p. 152): "Say that the worm is on my cheek."

And grow with thought. Beside yon spring I stood
And eyed its waters till we seemed to feel
One sadness, they and I. For them a bond
[137] Of brotherhood is broken: time has been 85
When every day the touch of human hand
Disturbed their stillness, and they ministered
[140] To human comfort. When I stooped to drink,
A spider's web hung to the water's edge,
And on the wet and slimy foot-stone lay 90
[145] The useless fragment of a wooden bowl;
It moved my very heart. The day has been
When I could never pass this road but she
Who lived within these walls, when I appeared,
A daughter's welcome gave me, and I loved her 95
[150] As my own child. O Sir! the good die first,
And they whose hearts are dry as summer dust
Burn to the socket. Many a passenger
Has blessed poor Margaret for her gentle looks
When she upheld the cool refreshment drawn 100
[155] From that forsaken spring, and no one came
But he was welcome, no one went away
But that it seemed she loved him. She is dead,
The worm is on her cheek, and this poor hut,
Stripp'd of its outward garb of houshold flowers, 105
[160] Of rose and sweet-briar, offers to the wind
A cold bare wall whose earthy top is tricked
With weeds and the rank spear-grass. She is dead,
And nettles rot and adders sun themselves
Where we have sate together while she nurs'd 110
[165] Her infant at her breast. The unshod Colt,
The wandring heifer and the Potter's ass,
Find shelter now within the chimney-wall
Where I have seen her evening hearth-stone blaze
And through the window spread upon the road 115
[170] Its chearful light.— You will forgive me, Sir,
But often on this cottage do I muse
As on a picture, till my wiser mind
Sinks, yielding to the foolishness of grief.

---

89 A deletion and a revision over erasure altered the original text which probably read as does the revised MS. B: "At that deserted well a spider's web / Across its mouth hung to the water's edge."

117–119 DW's fair copy here has a two-line gap, filled by WW with three lines.

She had a husband, an industrious man,
Sober and steady; I have heard her say
That he was up and busy at his loom
175 In summer ere the mower's scythe had swept
The dewy grass, and in the early spring
Ere the last star had vanished. They who passed
At evening, from behind the garden fence
Might hear his busy spade, which he would ply
180 After his daily work till the day-light
Was gone and every leaf and every flower
Were lost in the dark hedges. So they lived
In peace and comfort, and two pretty babes
Were their best hope next to the God in Heaven.
185 —You may remember, now some ten years gone,
Two blighting seasons when the fields were left
With half a tillage. It pleased heaven to add
A worse affliction in the plague of war:
A happy land was stricken to the heart;
190 'Twas a sad time of sorrow and distress:
A wanderer among the cottages,
I with my pack of winter raiment saw
The hardships of that season: many rich
Sunk down as in [a] dream among the poor,
195 And of the poor did many cease to be,
And their place knew them not. Meanwhile, abridged
Of daily comforts, gladly reconciled
To numerous self denials, Margaret
Went struggling on through those calamitous years
200 With chearful hope: but ere the second spring
A fever seized her husband. In disease
He lingered long, and when his strength returned
He found the little he had stored to meet
The hour of accident or crippling age
205 Was all consumed. As I have said, 'twas now
A time of trouble; shoals of artisans

---

190 WW's revision of "It was" to "T'was" makes the line metrical and restores the reading of the earlier MS. A.

194 DW left out the indefinite article, which is in the earlier MS. A and in later manuscripts.

196 (D, 144) Cf. *Paradise Lost*, VII, 144: "Whom thir place knows here no more"; and Psalm 103: 16: "And the place thereof shall know it no more."

196b–201a DW left a gap here in her fair copy, and WW added these lines as the necessary transition.

She had a husband, an industrious man, 120
Sober and steady; I have heard her say
That he was up and busy at his loom
[175] In summer ere the mower's scythe had swept
The dewy grass, and in the early spring
Ere the last star had vanished. They who pass'd 125
At evening, from behind the garden-fence
Might hear his busy spade, which he would ply
[180] After his daily work till the day-light
Was gone and every leaf and flower were lost
In the dark hedges. So they pass'd their days 130
In peace and comfort, and two pretty babes
Were their best hope next to the God in Heaven.
[185] —You may remember, now some ten years gone,
Two blighting seasons when the fields were left
With half a harvest. It pleased heaven to add 135
A worse affliction in the plague of war:
A happy land was stricken to the heart;
[190] 'Twas a sad time of sorrow and distress:
A wanderer among the cottages,
I with my pack of winter raiment saw 140
The hardships of that season: many rich
Sunk down as in a dream among the poor,
[195] And of the poor did many cease to be,
And their place knew them not. Meanwhile, abridg'd
Of daily comforts, gladly reconciled 145
To numerous self-denials, Margaret
Went struggling on through those calamitous years
[200] With chearful hope: but ere the second autumn
A fever seized her husband. In disease
He lingered long, and when his strength returned 150
He found the little he had stored to meet
The hour of accident or crippling age
[205] Was all consumed. As I have said, 'twas now
A time of trouble; shoals of artisans

Were from their daily labour turned away
To hang for bread on parish charity,
They and their wives and children—happier far
210 Could they have lived as do the little birds
That peck along the hedges, or the kite
That makes her dwelling in the mountain rocks.
Ill fared it now with Robert, he who dwelt
In this poor cottage; at his door he stood
215 And whistled many a snatch of merry tunes
That had no mirth in them, or with his knife
Carved uncouth figures on the heads of sticks,
Then idly sought about through every nook
Of house or garden any casual task
220 Of use or ornament, and with a strange,
Amusing but uneasy novelty
He blended where he might the various tasks
Of summer, autumn, winter, and of spring.
The passenger might see him at the door
225 With his small hammer on the threshold stone
Pointing lame buckle-tongues and rusty nails,
The treasured store of an old houshold box,
Or braiding cords or weaving bells and caps
Of rushes, play-things for his babes.
230 But this endured not; his good-humour soon
Became a weight in which no pleasure was,
And poverty brought on a petted mood
And a sore temper: day by day he drooped,
And he would leave his home, and to the town
235 Without an errand would he turn his steps
Or wander here and there among the fields.
One while he would speak lightly of his babes
And with a cruel tongue: at other times
He played with them wild freaks of merriment:
240 And 'twas a piteous thing to see the looks
Of the poor innocent children. 'Every smile,'
Said Margaret to me here beneath these trees,

210–211 (D, 158–159) Finch (p. 36) first pointed out the parallel with *Animal Tranquillity and Decay* (1797): "The little hedgerow birds, / That peck along the road" (*PW*, IV, 247; ll. 1–2).

211 DW corrected "[?road]" to "hedges," the reading in the earlier MS. A and in later manuscripts.

229/230 DW here left a two-line gap in her fair copy.

Were from their daily labour turned away 155
To hang for bread on parish charity,
They and their wives and children—happier far
[210] Could they have lived as do the little birds
That peck along the hedges or the kite
That makes her dwelling in the mountain rocks. 160
Ill fared it now with Robert, he who dwelt
In this poor cottage; at his door he stood
[215] And whistled many a snatch of merry tunes
That had no mirth in them, or with his knife
Carved uncouth figures on the heads of sticks, 165
Then idly sought about through every nook
Of house or garden any casual task
[220] Of use or ornament, and with a strange,
Amusing but uneasy novelty
He blended where he might the various tasks 170
Of summer, autumn, winter, and of spring.
[230] But this endured not; his good-humour soon
Became a weight in which no pleasure was,
And poverty brought on a petted mood
And a sore temper: day by day he drooped, 175
And he would leave his home, and to the town
[235] Without an errand would he turn his steps
Or wander here and there among the fields.
One while he would speak lightly of his babes
And with a cruel tongue: at other times 180
He played with them wild freaks of merriment:
[240] And 'twas a piteous thing to see the looks
Of the poor innocent children. 'Every smile,'
Said Margaret to me here beneath these trees,

'Made my heart bleed.'" At this the old Man paused
And looking up to those enormous elms
245 He said, "'Tis now the hour of deepest noon.
At this still season of repose and peace,
This hour when all things which are not at rest
Are chearful, while this multitude of flies
Fills all the air with happy melody,
250 Why should a tear be in an old Man's eye?
Why should we thus with an untoward mind
And in the weakness of humanity
From natural wisdom turn our hearts away,
To natural comfort shut our eyes and ears,
255 And feeding on disquiet thus disturb
[ ] of Nature with our restless thoughts?"

2nd Part

He spake with somewhat of a solemn tone:
But when he ended there was in his face
Such easy chearfulness, a look so mild
260 That for a little time it stole away
All recollection, and that simple tale
Passed from my mind like a forgotten sound.
A while on trivial things we held discourse,
To me soon tasteless. In my own despite
265 I thought of that poor woman as of one
Whom I had known and loved. He had rehearsed
Her homely tale with such familiar power,
With such a countenance of love, an eye
So busy, that the things of which he spake
270 Seemed present, and, attention now relaxed,
There was a heartfelt chillness in my veins.
I rose, and turning from that breezy shade
Went out into the open air, and stood
To drink the comfort of the warmer sun.
275 Long time I had not stayed ere, looking round
Upon that tranquil ruin, and impelled
By a mild force of curious pensiveness,

---

256 For the gap in DW's fair copy, MS. B[2] reads "The tone."
262 The "d" on "sound" has worn away.
269 The "e" on "spake" has worn away.
273–274 DW broke the line in the wrong place: "Went out into the open air, and stood to drink / The comfort of the warmer sun."

'Made my heart bleed.'" At this the old Man paus'd 185
And looking up to those enormous elms
[245] He said, "'Tis now the hour of deepest noon.
At this still season of repose and peace,
This hour when all things which are not at rest
Are chearful, while this multitude of flies 190
Fills all the air with happy melody,
[250] Why should a tear be in an old man's eye?
Why should we thus with an untoward mind
And in the weakness of humanity
From natural wisdom turn our hearts away, 195
To natural comfort shut our eyes and ears,
[255] And feeding on disquiet thus disturb
The calm of Nature with our restless thoughts?"

End of the first Part

Second Part

He spake with somewhat of a solemn tone:
But when he ended there was in his face 200
Such easy chearfulness, a look so mild
[260] That for a little time it stole away
All recollection, and that simple tale
Passed from my mind like a forgotten sound.
A while on trivial things we held discourse, 205
To me soon tasteless. In my own despite
[265] I thought of that poor woman as of one
Whom I had known and loved. He had rehearsed
Her homely tale with such familiar power,
With such a[n active] countenance, an eye 210
So busy, that the things of which he spake
[270] Seemed present, and, attention now relaxed,
There was a heartfelt chillness in my veins.
I rose, and turning from that breezy shade
Went out into the open air and stood 215
To drink the comfort of the warmer sun.
[275] Long time I had not stayed ere, looking round
Upon that tranquil ruin, I returned

---

210 WW penciled "active" into a gap left by DW; the expansion of "a" to "an" is editorial.

I begg'd of the old man that for my sake
He would resume his story. He replied,
280 "It were a wantonness, and would demand
Severe reproof, if we were men whose hearts
Could hold vain dalliance with the misery
Even of the dead, contented thence to draw
A momentary pleasure never marked
285 By reason, barren of all future good.
But we have known that there is often found
In mournful thoughts, and always might be found,
A power to virtue friendly; were't not so,
I am a dreamer among men—indeed
290 An idle dreamer. 'Tis a common tale,
By moving accidents uncharactered,
A tale of silent suffering, hardly clothed
In bodily form, and to the grosser sense
But ill adapted, scarcely palpable
295 To him who does not think. But at your bidding
I will proceed.
While thus it fared with those
To whom this Cottage till that hapless year
Had been a blessed home, it was my chance
To travel in a country far remote.
300 And glad I was when, halting by yon gate
Which leads from the green lane, again I saw
These lofty elm-trees. Long I did not rest:
With many pleasant thoughts I cheered my way
O'er the flat common. At the door arrived,
305 I knocked, and when I entered with the hope
Of usual greeting, Margaret looked at me
A little while, then turned her head away
Speechless, and sitting down upon a chair
Wept bitterly. I wist not what to do
310 Or how to speak to her. Poor wretch! at last
She rose from off her seat—and then—Oh Sir!
I cannot *tell* how she pronounced my name:
With fervent love and with a face of grief
Unutterably helpless and a look

---

291 (D, 232) Cf. *Hart-Leap Well* (*PW*, II, 252; l. 97): "The moving accident is not my trade"; and WW's reference to a "moving accident" in *EY*, p. 256. The phrase echoes *Othello*, I, iii, 97: "Of moving accidents by flood or field."

And begged of the old man that for my sake
He would resume his story. He replied, 220
[280] "It were a wantonness and would demand
Severe reproof, if we were men whose hearts
Could hold vain dalliance with the misery
Even of the dead, contented thence to draw
A momentary pleasure never marked 225
[285] By reason, barren of all future good.
But we have known that there is often found
In mournful thoughts, and always might be found,
A power to virtue friendly; were't not so,
I am a dreamer among men, indeed 230
[290] An idle dreamer. 'Tis a common tale,
By moving accidents uncharactered,
A tale of silent suffering, hardly clothed
In bodily form, and to the grosser sense
But ill adapted, scarcely palpable 235
[295] To him who does not think. But at your bidding
I will proceed.
While thus it fared with them
To whom this cottage till that hapless year
Had been a blessed home, it was my chance
To travel in a country far remote. 240
[300] And glad I was when, halting by yon gate
That leads from the green lane, again I saw
These lofty elm-trees. Long I did not rest:
With many pleasant thoughts I cheer'd my way
O'er the flat common. At the door arrived, 245
[305] I knocked, and when I entered with the hope
Of usual greeting, Margaret looked at me
A little while, then turned her head away
Speechless, and sitting down upon a chair
Wept bitterly. I wist not what to do 250
[310] Or how to speak to her. Poor wretch! at last
She rose from off her seat—and then, oh Sir!
I cannot tell how she pronounced my name:
With fervent love, and with a face of grief
Unutterably helpless, and a look 255

315 That seemed to cling upon me, she inquired
If I had seen her husband. As she spake
A strange surprize and fear came o'er my heart
And I could make no answer—then she told
That he had disappeared, just two months gone.
320 He left his house; two wretched days had passed,
And on the third by the first break of light,
Within her casement full in view she saw
A purse of gold. 'I trembled at the sight,'
Said Margaret, 'for I knew it was his hand
325 That placed it there, and on that very day
By one, a stranger, from my husband sent,
The tidings came that he had joined a troop
Of soldiers going to a distant land.
He left me thus—Poor Man! he had not heart
330 To take a farewell of me, and he feared
That I should follow with my babes and sink
Beneath the misery of a soldier's life.'
This tale did Margaret tell with many tears:
And when she ended I had little power
335 To give her comfort and was glad to take
Such words of hope from her own mouth as served
To chear us both—but long we had not talked
Ere we built up a pile of better thoughts,
And with a brighter eye she looked around
340 As if she had been shedding tears of joy.
We parted. It was then the early spring;
I left her busy with her garden tools;
And well remember, o'er the fence she looked,
And while I paced along the foot-way path
345 Called out, and sent a blessing after me
With tender chearfulness and with a voice
That seemed the very sound of happy thoughts.

I roved o'er many a hill and many a dale
With this my weary load, in heat and cold,
350 Through many a wood, and many an open plain,
In sunshine or in shade, in wet or fair,

---

323 (D, 264) A purse of gold] The manpower shortage during the war with France caused the British government to offer a bounty for those who enlisted; militiamen who signed up for service in Europe received ten guineas.

330 The word "he" was inserted and makes the line complete.

341 WW altered " 'Twas the" to "It was then the," probably for the sake of the meter.

[315] That seem'd to cling upon me, she enquir'd
If I had seen her husband. As she spake
A strange surprize and fear came to my heart,
Nor had I power to answer ere she told
That he had disappeared—just two months gone. 260
[320] He left his house; two wretched days had passed,
And on the third by the first break of light,
Within her casement full in view she saw
A purse of gold. 'I trembled at the sight,'
Said Margaret, 'for I knew it was his hand 265
[325] That placed it there, and on that very day
By one, a stranger, from my husband sent,
The tidings came that he had joined a troop
Of soldiers going to a distant land.
He left me thus—Poor Man! he had not heart 270
[330] To take a farewell of me, and he feared
That I should follow with my babes, and sink
Beneath the misery of a soldier's life.'
This tale did Margaret tell with many tears:
And when she ended I had little power 275
[335] To give her comfort, and was glad to take
Such words of hope from her own mouth as serv'd
To cheer us both: but long we had not talked
Ere we built up a pile of better thoughts,
And with a brighter eye she looked around 280
[340] As if she had been shedding tears of joy.
We parted. It was then the early spring;
I left her busy with her garden tools;
And well remember, o'er that fence she looked,
And while I paced along the foot-way path 285
[345] Called out, and sent a blessing after me
With tender chearfulness and with a voice
That seemed the very sound of happy thoughts.
I roved o'er many a hill and many a dale
With this my weary load, in heat and cold, 290
[350] Through many a wood, and many an open ground,
In sunshine or in shade, in wet or fair,

259 DW's fair copy here has a one-line gap, filled by WW.

Now blithe, now drooping—as it might befal—
My best companions now the driving winds
And now the music of my own sad steps,
355 With many short-lived thoughts that passed between
And disappeared. I measured back this road
Towards the wane of summer, when the wheat
Was yellow and the soft and bladed grass
Sprung up afresh and o'er the hay-field spread
360 Its tender green. When I had reached the door
I found that she was absent. In the shade
Where now we sit I waited her return.
Her cottage in its outward look appeared
As chearful as before; in any shew
365 Of neatness little changed, but that I thought
The honeysuckle crowded round the door
And from the wall hung down in heavier tufts,
And knots of worthless stone-crop started out
Along the window's edge and grew like weeds
370 Against the lower panes. I turned aside
And strolled into her garden. It was changed:
The unprofitable bindweed spread his bells
From side to side, and with unwieldy wreaths
Had dragged the rose from its sustaining wall
375 And bowed it down to earth; the border tufts—
Daisy, and thrift, and lowly camomile,
And thyme—had straggled out into the paths
Which they were used to deck. Ere this an hour
Was wasted. Back I turned my restless steps,
380 And as I walked before the door it chanced
A stranger passed, and guessing whom I sought
He said that she was used to ramble far.
The sun was sinking in the west, and now
I sate with sad impatience. From within
385 Her solitary infant cried aloud.
The spot though fair seemed very desolate,
The longer I remained more desolate.

---

356 For the deleted original ("came this way"), DW left alternate readings which make the line complete: "measured back this road"; "came this way again." The position of DW's manuscript line number opposite "measured back this road" suggests that it may be the preferred reading (see p. 231, below).

358 (D, 300) Cf. *A Midsummer Night's Dream*, I, i, 211: "Decking with liquid pearl the bladed grass."

Now blithe, now drooping, as it might befal,
My best companions now the driving winds
And now the 'trotting brooks' and whispering trees 295
And now the music of my own sad steps,
[355] With many a short-lived thought that pass'd between
And disappeared. I came this way again
Towards the wane of summer, when the wheat
Was yellow, and the soft and bladed grass 300
Sprang up afresh and o'er the hay-field spread
[360] Its tender green. When I had reached the door
I found that she was absent. In the shade
Where now we sit I waited her return.
Her cottage in its outward look appeared 305
As chearful as before; in any shew
[365] Of neatness little changed, but that I thought
The honeysuckle crowded round the door
And from the wall hung down in heavier wreathes,
And knots of worthless stone-crop started out 310
Along the window's edge, and grew like weeds
[370] Against the lower panes. I turned aside
And stroll'd into her garden.— It was chang'd:
The unprofitable bindweed spread his bells
From side to side and with unwieldy wreaths 315
Had dragg'd the rose from its sustaining wall
[375] And bent it down to earth; the border-tufts—
Daisy and thrift and lowly camomile
And thyme—had straggled out into the paths
Which they were used to deck. Ere this an hour 320
Was wasted. Back I turned my restless steps,
[380] And as I walked before the door it chanced
A stranger passed, and guessing whom I sought
He said that she was used to ramble far.
The sun was sinking in the west, and now 325
I sate with sad impatience. From within
[385] Her solitary infant cried aloud.
The spot though fair seemed very desolate,
The longer I remained more desolate.

---

295 The quotation is from Burns's *To W. S****n* [Simpson], *Ochiltree*, stanza xv, l. 3; WW also quoted it at the end of his first note on *The River Duddon*: "Adown some trotting burn's meander" (*PW*, III, 504).

And looking round I saw the corner stones,
Till then unmarked, on either side the door
390 With dull red stains discoloured and stuck o'er
With tufts and hairs of wool, as if the sheep
That feed upon the commons thither came
As to a couching-place and rubbed their sides
Even at her threshold. The church-clock struck eight;
395 I turn'd and saw her distant a few steps.
Her face was pale and thin, her figure too
Was changed. As she unlocked the door she said,
'It grieves me you have waited here so long,
But in good truth I've wandered much of late
400 And sometimes, to my shame I speak, have need
Of my best prayers to bring me back again.'
While on the board she spread our evening meal
She told me she had lost her eldest child,
That he for months had been a serving-boy
405 Apprenticed by the parish. 'I am changed,
And to myself,' said she, 'have done much wrong,
And to this helpless infant. I have slept
Weeping, and weeping I have waked; my tears
Have flowed as if my body were not such
410 As others are, and I could never die.
But I am now in mind and in my heart
More easy, and I hope,' said she, 'that heaven
Will give me patience to endure the things
Which I behold at home.' It would have grieved

388–394 (D, 330–336) WW probably drew this observation from his sister's Alfoxden journal, 4 February 1798: "The moss rubbed from the pailings by the sheep, that leave locks of wool, and the red marks with which they are spotted, upon the wood" (*Journals*, p. 5).

394b–395 DW's fair copy here has a gap, filled by WW.

403 Although "eldest" was acceptable in the sense of "first-born," the word was altered in DW's hand to "elder," probably for consistency with "two pretty babes" in l. 183.

406 The words "said she" were inserted and make the line complete.

411 WW deleted "& heart" to "in my heart" for the sake of the meter; although the ampersand is deleted, the sense requires the inclusion of "and."

And, looking round, I saw the corner-stones, 330
Till then unmark'd, on either side the door
[390] With dull red stains discoloured and stuck o'er
With tufts and hairs of wool, as if the sheep
That feed upon the commons thither came
Familiarly and found a couching-place 335
Even at her threshold.— The house-clock struck eight;
[395] I turned and saw her distant a few steps.
Her face was pale and thin, her figure too
Was chang'd. As she unlocked the door she said,
'It grieves me you have waited here so long, 340
But in good truth I've wandered much of late
[400] And sometimes, to my shame I speak, have need
Of my best prayers to bring me back again.'
While on the board she spread our evening meal
She told me she had lost her elder child, 345
That he for months had been a serving-boy
[405] Apprenticed by the parish. 'I perceive
You look at me, and you have cause. Today
I have been travelling far, and many days
About the fields I wander, knowing this 350
Only, that what I seek I cannot find.
And so I waste my time: for I am changed;
And to myself,' said she, 'have done much wrong,
And to this helpless infant. I have slept
Weeping, and weeping I have waked; my tears 355
Have flow'd as if my body were not such
[410] As others are, and I could never die.
But I am now in mind and in my heart
More easy, and I hope,' said she, 'that heaven
Will give me patience to endure the things 360
[414] Which I behold at home.' It would have grieved
Your very heart to see her. Sir, I feel
The story linger in my heart. I fear
'Tis long and tedious, but my spirit clings
To that poor woman: so familiarly 365
Do I perceive her manner, and her look
And presence, and so deeply do I feel
Her goodness, that not seldom in my walks
A momentary trance comes over me;

---

362 WW penciled "soul" as an alternate for "heart"; later manuscripts read "soul."

415 Your very soul to see her: evermore
Her eye-lids drooped, her eyes were downward cast;
And when she at her table gave me food
She did not look at me. Her voice was low,
Her body was subdued. In every act
420 Pertaining to her house affairs appeared
The careless stillness which a thinking mind
Gives to an idle matter—still she sighed,
But yet no motion of the breast was seen,
No heaving of the heart. While by the fire
425 We sate together, sighs came on my ear;
I knew not how and hardly whence they came.
I took my staff, and when I kissed her babe
The tears were in her eyes. I left her then
With the best hope and comfort I could give;
430 She thanked me for my will, but for my hope
It seemed she did not thank me. I returned
And took my rounds along this road again
Ere on its sunny bank the primrose flower
Had chronicled the earliest day of spring.
435 I found her sad and drooping; she had learned
No tidings of her husband: if he lived
She knew not that he lived; if he were dead
She knew not he was dead. She seemed not changed
In person or appearance, but her house
440 Bespoke a sleepy hand of negligence;
The floor was neither dry nor neat, the hearth
Was comfortless [ ],
The windows they were dim, and her few books,
Which one upon the other heretofore
445 Had been piled up against the corner panes
In seemly order, now with straggling leaves

---

417 DW left a gap after "And"; WW filled in the rest of the line.
418b–419a Later insertion by DW into her fair copy, possibly to correct a copying error; the insertion precedes her line numbering.
441–442 DW's fair copy here has a two-line gap, filled by WW.

And to myself I seem to muse on one 370
By sorrow laid asleep or borne away,
A human being destined to awake
To human life, or something very near
To human life, when he shall come again
For whom she suffered. Sir, it would have griev'd 375
[415] Your very soul to see her: evermore
Her eye-lids droop'd, her eyes were downward cast;
And when she at her table gave me food
She did not look at me. Her voice was low,
Her body was subdued. In every act 380
[420] Pertaining to her house-affairs appeared
The careless stillness which a thinking mind
Gives to an idle matter—still she sighed,
But yet no motion of the breast was seen,
No heaving of the heart. While by the fire 385
[425] We sate together, sighs came on my ear;
I knew not how, and hardly whence they came.
I took my staff, and when I kissed her babe
The tears stood in her eyes. I left her then
With the best hope and comfort I could give; 390
[430] She thanked me for my will, but for my hope
It seemed she did not thank me.

I returned
And took my rounds along this road again
Ere on its sunny bank the primrose flower
Had chronicled the earliest day of spring. 395
[435] I found her sad and drooping; she had learn'd
No tidings of her husband: if he lived
She knew not that he lived; if he were dead
She knew not he was dead. She seemed the same
In person [ ] appearance, but her house 400
[440] Bespoke a sleepy hand of negligence;
The floor was neither dry nor neat, the hearth
Was comfortless [ ],
The windows too were dim, and her few books,
Which, one upon the other, heretofore 405
[445] Had been piled up against the corner-panes
In seemly order, now with straggling leaves

---

400 After "person," "or" was erased, but no insertion was made; later manuscripts read "and."

Lay scattered here and there, open or shut
As they had chanced to fall. Her infant babe
Had from its mother caught the trick of grief
450 And sighed among its playthings. Once again
I turned towards the garden gate and saw
More plainly still that poverty and grief
Were now come nearer to her: all was hard,
With weeds defaced and knots of withered grass;
455 No ridges there appeared of clear black mould,
No winter greenness; of her herbs and flowers
It seemed the better part were gnawed away
Or trampled on the earth; a chain of straw
Which had been twisted round the tender stem
460 Of a young apple-tree lay at its root;
The bark was nibbled round by truant sheep.
Margaret stood near, her infant in her arms,
And seeing that my eye was on the tree
She said, 'I fear it will be dead and gone
465 Ere Robert come again.' Towards the house
Together we returned, and she enquired
If I had any hope. But for her babe
And for her little friendless Boy, she said,
She had no wish to live, that she must die
470 Of sorrow.— Yet I saw the idle loom
Still in its place. His sunday garments hung
Upon the self-same nail—his very staff
Stood undisturbed behind the door. And when
I passed this way beaten by autumn wind[s],
475 She told me that her little babe was dead
And she was left alone. That very time,
I yet remember, through the miry lane
She went with me a mile, when the bare trees
Trickled with foggy damps, and in such sort
480 That any heart had ached to hear her begged
That wheresoe'er I went I still would ask
For him whom she had lost. Five tedious years
She lingered in unquiet widowhood,
A wife, and widow. Needs must it have been

---

449 (D, 410) trick] "A particular habit, way, or mode of acting" (*OED*).

457 The words "It seemed" were inserted and make the line complete.

474 DW wrote "wind" for "winds"—presumably a copying error since the *Christabel* Notebook and MSS. B², D, and E read "winds."

Lay scattered here and there, open or shut
As they had chanced to fall. Her infant babe
Had from its mother caught the trick of grief 410
[450] And sighed among its playthings. Once again
I turned towards the garden-gate and saw
More plainly still that poverty and grief
Were now come nearer to her: the earth was hard,
With weeds defaced and knots of withered grass; 415
[455] No ridges there appeared of clear black mould,
No winter greenness; of her herbs and flowers
It seemed the better part were gnawed away
Or trampled on the earth; a chain of straw
Which had been twisted round the tender stem 420
[460] Of a young apple-tree lay at its root;
The bark was nibbled round by truant sheep.
Margaret stood near, her infant in her arms,
And seeing that my eye was on the tree
She said, 'I fear it will be dead and gone 425
[465] Ere Robert come again.' Towards the house
Together we returned, and she inquired
If I had any hope. But for her Babe
And for her little friendless Boy, she said,
She had no wish to live, that she must die 430
[470] Of sorrow. Yet I saw the idle loom
Still in its place. His sunday garments hung
Upon the self-same nail, his very staff
Stood undisturbed behind the door. And when
I passed this way beaten by Autumn winds 435
[475] She told me that her little babe was dead
And she was left alone. That very time,
I yet remember, through the miry lane
She walked with me a mile, when the bare trees
Trickled with foggy damps, and in such sort 440
[480] That any heart had ached to hear her begg'd
That wheresoe'er I went I still would ask
For him whom she had lost. We parted then,
Our final parting, for from that time forth
Did many seasons pass ere I returned 445
Into this tract again.

Five tedious years
She lingered in unquiet widowhood,
A wife and widow. Needs must it have been

485 A sore heart-wasting. I have heard, my Friend,
That in that broken arbour she would sit
The idle length of half a sabbath day,
There—where you see the toadstool's lazy head—
And when a dog passed by she still would quit
490 The shade and look abroad. On this old Bench
For hours she sate, and evermore her eye
Was busy in the distance, shaping things
Which made her heart beat quick. Seest thou that path?
(The greensward now has broken its grey line)
495 There, to and fro she paced through many a day
Of the warm summer, from a belt of flax
That girt her waist spinning the long-drawn thread
With backward steps.— Yet ever as there passed
A man whose garments shewed the Soldier's red,
500 Or crippled Mendicant in Sailor's garb,
The little Child who sate to turn the wheel
Ceased from his toil, and she with faltering voice,
Expecting still to learn her husband's fate,
Made many a fond inquiry; and when they
505 Whose presence gave no comfort were gone by,

---

485 WW altered "Master! I have heard" to "I have heard my Friend." The concluding lines preserve a state of the poem before the Pedlar became well known to the poet in this MS. B version; WW revised here and in l. 526 for consistency with, for example, ll. 47–52 and l. 130.

490–491 (D, 454–455) Cf. *The Borderers*, ll. 570–573:

I met a peasant near the spot; he told me,
These ten years she had sate all day alone
Within those empty walls. [*PW*, I, 150]

495–502 (D, 459–466) Bridport in Dorset, near WW's home at Racedown, was the center in England for spinners producing twine for fishing lines and nets. WW's description of such spinning parallels the account given in Patricia Baines, *Spinning Wheels, Spinners, and Spinning* (London, 1977): "The long fibres [of flax or hemp] are more difficult to manage when held in the hand, so they were tied round the spinner's waist. . . . A child was employed to turn the wheel by means of a pole from one side while the spinners walked backwards from the rotating hooks on the other side, playing out fibres with each hand as they went and so making two yarns at a time which, on the return journey, were twisted together."

499 (D, 463) In MS. B, WW added an "s" to DW's "garment"; the earlier STC to Estlin manuscript reads "garments," as do MSS. D, E, and M. A verbal parallel to the description of the Soldier occurs in *ASP*, when a traveler meets an aged man, whose "ragged coat scarce showed the Soldier's faded red" (*SPP*, p. 123, l. 9).

501–509 (D, 465–473) An echo of *The Old Cumberland Beggar* is pointed out by Finch (p. 37):

She who tends
The toll-gate, when in summer at her door
She turns her wheel, if on the road she sees
The aged Beggar coming, quits her work,
And lifts the latch for him that he may pass.
[*PW*, IV, 235; ll. 32–36]

[485] A sore heart-wasting. I have heard, my friend,
That in that broken arbour she would sit 450
The idle length of half a sabbath day—
There, where you see the toadstool's lazy head—
And when a dog passed by she still would quit
[490] The shade and look abroad. On this old Bench
For hours she sate, and evermore her eye 455
Was busy in the distance, shaping things
Which made her heart beat quick. Seest thou that path?
(The green-sward now has broken its grey line)
[495] There to and fro she paced through many a day
Of the warm summer, from a belt of flax 460
That girt her waist spinning the long-drawn thread
With backward steps.— Yet ever as there passed
A man whose garments shewed the Soldier's red,
[500] Or crippled Mendicant in Sailor's garb,
The little child who sate to turn the wheel 465
Ceased from his toil, and she with faltering voice,
Expecting still to learn her husband's fate,
Made many a fond inquiry; and when they
[505] Whose presence gave no comfort were gone by,

Her heart was still more sad. And by yon gate
Which bars the traveller's road she often stood
And when a stranger horseman came, the latch
Would lift, and in his face look wistfully,
510 Most happy if from aught discovered there
Of tender feeling she might dare repeat
The same sad question. Meanwhile her poor hut
Sunk to decay, for he was gone whose hand,
At the first nippings of October frost,
515 Closed up each chink and with fresh bands of straw
Checquered the green-grown thatch. And so she sate
Through the long winter, reckless and alone,
Till this reft house by frost, and thaw, and rain
Was sapped; and when she slept the nightly damps
520 Did chill her breast, and in the stormy day
Her tattered clothes were ruffled by the wind
Even at the side of her own fire.— Yet still
She loved this wretched spot, nor would for worlds
Have parted hence; and still that length of road
525 And this rude bench one torturing hope endeared,
Fast rooted at her heart, and here, my friend,
In sickness she remained, and here she died,
Last human tenant of these ruined walls."

The End

---

517 (D, 481) WW uses "reckless" in a now obsolete sense: "Having no care or consideration for oneself" (*OED*).

518 DW revised "hut" to "house," the reading of the earlier STC to Estlin manuscript and of all subsequent manuscripts.

522–526 (D, 486–490) Finch noted (p. 37) echoes from *The Three Graves*, II, 5–6: "Fast rooted to the spot, you guess, / The wretched maiden stood" (*PW*, I, 309).

526 WW revised "& Stranger! here" to "& here my friend"; see the note to l. 485.

528 (D, 492) Cf. *Descriptive Sketches* (1793): "Sole human tenant of the piny waste" (*PW*, I, 54; l. 189).

Her heart was still more sad. And by yon gate 470
Which bars the traveller's road she often stood
And when a stranger horseman came, the latch
Would lift, and in his face look wistfully,
[510] Most happy if from aught discovered there
Of tender feeling she might dare repeat 475
The same sad question. Meanwhile her poor hut
Sunk to decay, for he was gone whose hand
At the first nippings of October frost
[515] Closed up each chink and with fresh bands of straw
Chequered the green-grown thatch. And so she lived 480
Through the long winter, reckless and alone,
Till this reft house by frost, and thaw, and rain
Was sapped; and when she slept the nightly damps
[520] Did chill her breast, and in the stormy day
Her tattered clothes were ruffled by the wind 485
Even at the side of her own fire. Yet still
She loved this wretched spot, nor would for worlds
Have parted hence; and still that length of road
[525] And this rude bench one torturing hope endeared,
Fast rooted at her heart, and here, my friend, 490
In sickness she remained, and here she died,
[528] Last human tenant of these ruined walls."
The old Man ceased: he saw that I was mov'd;
From that low Bench, rising instinctively,
I turned aside in weakness, nor had power 495
To thank him for the tale which he had told.
I stood, and leaning o'er the garden-gate
Reviewed that Woman's suff'rings, and it seemed
To comfort me while with a brother's love
I blessed her in the impotence of grief. 500
At length [ ] the [ ]
Fondly, and traced with milder interest
That secret spirit of humanity
Which, 'mid the calm oblivious tendencies
Of nature, 'mid her plants, her weeds, and flowers, 505
And silent overgrowings, still survived.
The old man, seeing this, resumed and said,
"My Friend, enough to sorrow have you given,

---

501 After "length," "upon" was erased; after "the," "hut I fix'd my eyes" was erased. No insertion was made in MS. D, but MS. E reads, "At length towards the Cottage I return'd."

The purposes of wisdom ask no more;
Be wise and chearful, and no longer read 510
The forms of things with an unworthy eye.
She sleeps in the calm earth, and peace is here.
I well remember that those very plumes,
Those weeds, and the high spear-grass on that wall,
By mist and silent rain-drops silver'd o'er, 515
As once I passed did to my heart convey
So still an image of tranquillity,
So calm and still, and looked so beautiful
Amid the uneasy thoughts which filled my mind,
That what we feel of sorrow and despair 520
From ruin and from change, and all the grief
The passing shews of being leave behind,
Appeared an idle dream that could not live
Where meditation was. I turned away
And walked along my road in happiness." 525
He ceased. By this the sun declining shot
A slant and mellow radiance which began
To fall upon us where beneath the trees
We sate on that low bench, and now we felt,
Admonished thus, the sweet hour coming on. 530
A linnet warbled from those lofty elms,
A thrush sang loud, and other melodies,
At distance heard, peopled the milder air.
The old man rose and hoisted up his load.
Together casting then a farewell look 535
Upon those silent walls, we left the shade
And ere the stars were visible attained
A rustic inn, our evening resting-place.

The End

526–538 The conclusion uses some of the conventions of the pastoral, as presented, for example, in the last lines of *Lycidas*:

And now the Sun had stretch'd out all the hills,
And now was dropt into the Western bay;
At last he rose, and twitch'd his Mantle blew:
To morrow to fresh Woods, and Pastures new.

The Ruined Cottage

Transcriptions and Photographic Reproductions

MS. A

Ruined Cottage MS. A is leaf 5^r of a gathering of twelve folio sheets (DC MS. 13), of which 2 to 5 and 7 to 12 survive. The leaves are 24.5 centimeters wide by 39 centimeters high; they are watermarked either with a crowned shield containing a fleur-de-lys or with W ELGAR over the date 1795. The chain lines are at intervals of 2.8 centimeters. Wordsworth wrote the *Ruined Cottage* material—mainly fair copy but degenerating into drafting—in the spring of 1797. The dating of other work in the notebook is discussed on page 7, above; the fragments on 4^r (*The Baker's Cart*) and 4^v (*Incipient Madness*) are transcribed in Appendix I.

MS. A is separated into two columns by a vertical pencil line. Following a photograph of the entire sheet, photographs of the top and bottom halves of each column are presented with facing transcriptions, labeled [Col. 1a] to [Col. 2b]. A faint red line runs horizontally across the manuscript page 2.7 centimeters from the top; Wordsworth observed this margin by beginning his *Ruined Cottage* passage below it in Column 1a, although a later draft begins above it. Similar red lines run vertically 2.0 centimeters from the left edge and 3.9 centimeters from the right edge; another runs horizontally 1.5 centimeters from the bottom of the page. Only the left-hand margin was observed and that for only a few verses in Column 1a, noted in the transcription.

The order of entry for passages in MS. A is often difficult to determine. The text may have started in Column 1a with lines 166/167 ("the poor man's horse") to 170. Elsewhere in this DC MS. 13, Wordsworth used the left-hand column for his main text and the right-hand one for revision. Successive revisions related to "the poor man's horse" sheltering within the ruin fill three-quarters of the right-hand column; these drafts were eventually used in *Incipient Madness* on the facing 4^v. The speaker's repeated visits to a ruin, coupled with the account of the poverty-stricken woman of "sick and extravagant" mind in the *Baker's Cart* fragment, eventually produced *The Ruined Cottage.* Wordsworth may have written parts of Margaret's story (lines contributing to MS. B, ll. 152–243) in blank spaces left in MS. A after work on "the poor man's horse"; at any rate, the text does not run continuously from the top of Column 1a to the end of Column 2b but has gaps, and jumps backward from the foot of Column 2b to the bottom of Column 1b.

Editorial line numbers in the left-hand margins of the transcriptions refer to corresponding lines in MS. B.

[illegible] husband was [illegible] to come [illegible] road
[illegible] Her husband was a man
[illegible]
[illegible]
[illegible]
many a passenger
Was blest poor Margaret for her gentle looks
When she upheld the cool refreshment drawn
From that forsaken well, and no one came
But he was welcome no one went away
But that it seemed she loved him — She is dead
And nettles rot and adders sun themselves
Upon the floor where I have seen her sit
And rock her baby in the cradle. She
Is gone to
Is dead and in her grave — [illegible] And this poor hut
Stripp'd of its outward garb of household flowers
Of rose and jasmine offers to the wind
~~[illegible] wall [illegible] weeds~~
~~[illegible] grass~~
A cold bare wall whose top you see is trick'd
With weeds and the rank spear grass — from this casement
You see the swallow's nest has dropp'd away
[illegible] her cold
[illegible] the poor man's horse
That feeds along the lanes from cold nights
Finds shelter now within the chimney wall
Where I have seen her evening hearth-stone blaze
And through the window spread upon the road
Its cheerful light. You see the
[illegible] to the sky yet stained with smoke
You see the swallow's nest has dropp'd away
A wretched covert 'tis for man or beast
And when the poor man's horse that shelters there
Turns from the beating wind and open sky
The iron links with which his feet are clogg'd
Mix their dull clanking with the heavy sound
Of falling rain / a melancholy
[illegible] poor man's horse that hither comes

[ ] husband was industrious; in his mood
[ ]er & Steady
Her husband was a man
[ ]ffectonate & kind and in his mood
Sober & steady but I forget my tale
Her was kind hearted in his mood

152 many a passenger
153 Has blest poor Margaret for her gentle looks
154 When she upheld the cool refreshment drawn
155 From that forsaken well, and no one came
156 But he was welcome no one went away
157 But that it seemed she loved him—She is dead
163 And nettles rot and adders sun themselves
164 Upon the floor where I have seen sit
165; 157 And rock her baby in its cradle. She
gone to —
158 Is dead and in her grave. } ~~This~~ And this poor hut
159 Stripp'd of its outward garb of household flower
160 Of rose and jasmine offer to the wind
~~A cold bare wall whose~~ top ~~is trick with weeds~~
~~And the rank spear grass~~
earthy
161 A cold bare wall whose^top ~~you see~~ is trick
162 With weeds and the rank spear grass—from this ~~casement~~
casement
You see the swallows nest has dropp'd away
165 Tis a sad change ~~the~~ wild colt
166 The unstall heifer & the potters ass
the poor man's horse
That feeds along the lanes, from cold night sho
wers
167 Finds shelter now within the chimney wall
168 Where I have seen her evenings hearth-stone blaze
169 And through the window spread upon the road
170 Its chearful light. You see the
Though open to the sky yet stained with smoke
You see the swallows nest has dropp'd away
A wretched covert 'tis for man or beast
And when the poor mans horse that shelters there
Turns from the beating wind and open sky
n
The iron lik } ks with which his feet are clogg'd
Mix their dull clanking with the heavy sound
Of falling rain a melancholy

The paper at the top is worn away; the six lines in reduced type are a revision of ll. 172–173, below (see Col. 1b). The faint red line mentioned in the headnote runs between the last two lines of WW's six-line revision.

166/167 The line beginning "That feeds," and the two following ones, observe the red margin line (see the headnote).

Of falling rain, a melancholy
And when the poor man's horse that hither comes
For shelter turns about
That open then the passengers may hear
The iron links with which his feet were clogged
Mix their dull clanking with the heavy sound
Of falling rain, a melancholy thing
To any man who has a heart to feel. —

She had a husband poor the gentlest an industrious man
Sober and quiet often I have heard her say
That he was up and busy at his loom
In summer ere the mower's scythe had swept
The dewy grass and in the early spring
Ere the last star had vanished. They who passed
At evening from behind the garden fence
Might hear his busy spade which he would ply
After his daily work till the daylight
Was gone and every leaf and every flower
Were lost in the dark hedges. So they liv'd
In peace and comfort and two pretty babes
Were their best hope next to the God in Heav'n.
You may remember (now some ten years gone)
Two blighting seasons when the fields were left
With half a harvest. — It pleased Heaven to add
A worse affliction in the plague of war
A happy land was stricken to the heart.

And whistled many a snatch of merry tunes
Which had no mirth in them: for half a day
He then would leave his home and to the town
Without an errand would he turn his steps
Or wander up and down among the fields
One while he would speak lightly of his babes
And with a cruel tongue, at other times
He play'd with them wild freaks of merriment
And every smile of the poor innocent babes
Said Margaret to me here beneath these trees
Made my heart bleed —

And when the poor mans horse that hither comes
For shelter turns [?ab]
And open sky the passenger may hear
were
The iron links with which his feet ~~are~~ cloggd
Mix their dull clanking with the heavy sound
Of falling rain, a melancholy thing
To any man who has a heart to feel.—

Poor Margaret

an industrious man
172 She had a husband ~~once a sober man~~
and sober
173 ~~I knew him~~ often I have heard her say
174 That he was up and busy at his loom
175 In summer er the mower scythe had swept
176 The dewy grass and in the early spring
ad
177 Ere the last star h[?as] vanished. They who past
178 At evening from behind the garden fence
179 Might hear his busy spade which he would ply
180 After his daily work till the day-light
181 Was gone, and every leaf and every flower
182 Were lost in the dark hedges. ~~there is a [?moo]~~
So they liv'd
183 In peace and comfort and two pretty babes
184 Were their best hope next to the God in Heav'n.
( )
185 —You may remember, now some ten years gone
186 Two blighting seasons when the fields were left
187 With half a harvest.— It pleased Heaven to add
188 A worse affliction ~~the~~ in the plague of war
189 A happy land was stricken to the heart.

---

215 And whistled many a snatch of merry tunes
216 Which had no mirth in them: for half a day
234 He then would leave his home and to the town
235 Without an errand would he turn his steps
236 Or wander up and down among the fields
237 One while he would speak light of his babes
238 And with a cruel tongue, at other times
239 He play'd with them wild freaks of merriment
241 And every smile of the poor innocent babes
242 Said Margaret to me beneath these trees
243 Made my heart bleed —

---

182 For the deleted half-line, cf. *Incipient Madness*, l. 7 (Appendix I, below). If WW did originally intend the passage later used in *Incipient Madness*, it hardly seems to fit at this point in Margaret's story. Perhaps the preceding eleven lines postdate the deleted half-line; the account of Margaret and Robert would then have filled the space left between the line "To any man who has a heart to feel.—" and l. 182b.

215 The text continues from l. 214 at the bottom of Col. 2b.

242/243 The leaf number (6)—now superseded after recent refoliation—is modern.

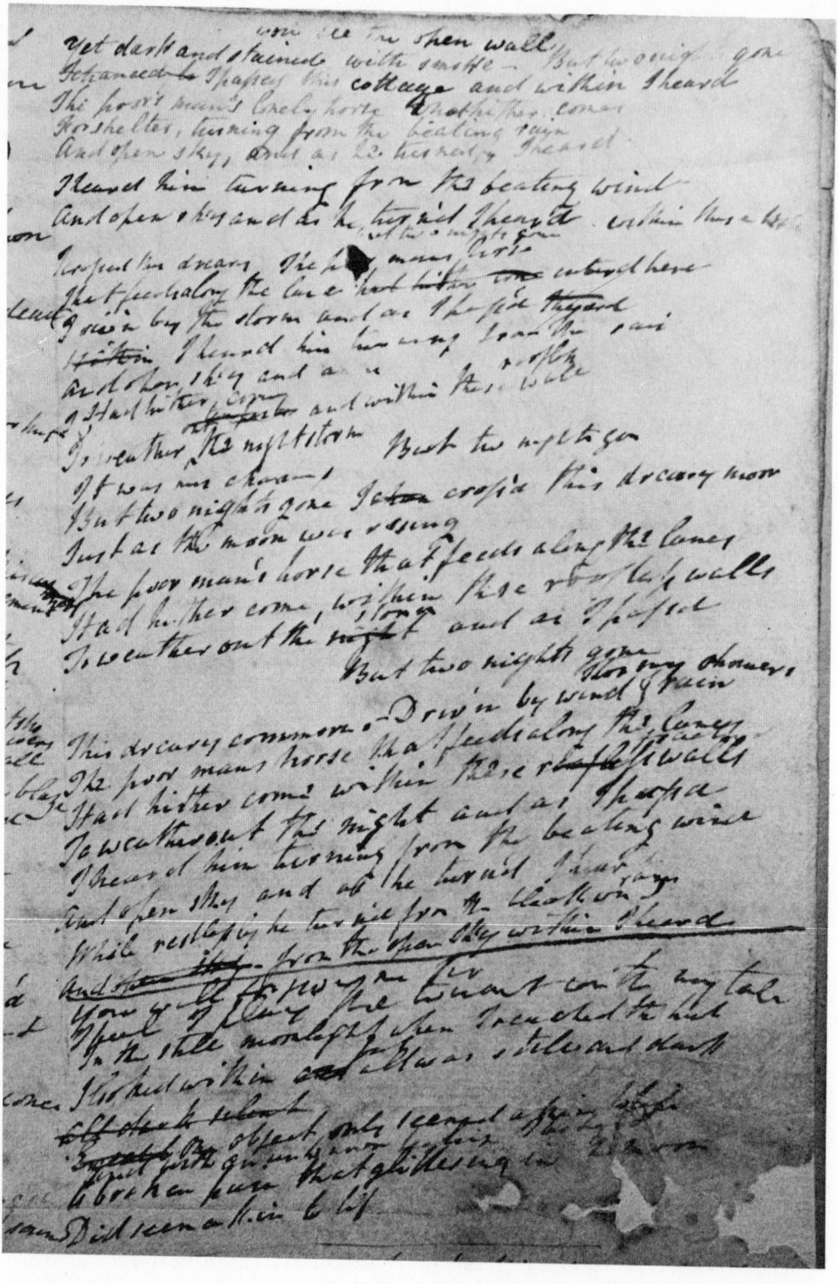

you see the open wall
Yet dark and stained with smoke— But two nights gone
~~I chanced to~~ I passed this cottage and within I heard
t} {at
The poor's man's lonely horse w{h }o hither comes
For shelter, turning from the beating rain
And open sky, and as he turned, I heard

I heard him turning from the beating wind—

{within these {W/wall
And open sky and as he turn'd I heard {
but two nights gone

I crossed this dreary
The poor mans horse
That feeds along the lane ~~had hither come~~ enterd here
Driv'n by the storm and as I pass'd ~~I heard~~
~~Within~~ I heard his turning from the beating rain
And open sky and as he
I Had hither come
roofless
~~out~~ ~~tempests~~ and within these wall
To weather^the night storm

n} But tw nights gon
It was my cha[?]{ce,
But two nights gone I ~~chan~~ cross'd this dreary moor
i}
Just as the moon was r[?]{sing
The poor man's horse that feeds along the lanes
Had hither come, within these roofless walls
storm
To weather out the ~~night~~ and as I passd

But two nights gone
stormy showers
This dreary common.— Driv'n by wind & rain
The poor mans horse that feeds along the lanes
fracturd
Had hither come within these ~~roofless~~ walls
To weather out the night and as I passd
I heard him turning from the beating wind
And open sky and as he turn'd I heard
rain
While restlessly he turn'd from the bleak wind
And ~~open sky~~ from the open sky within I heard

---

170 You will forgive me Sir
171 I feel I play the truant with my tale
In the still moonlight when I reached the hut
but
I looked within ~~and~~ all was still and dark
~~All dark silent~~
~~Except~~ One object only seemed akin to life
And with an unknown feeling I beheld
A broken pain that glittering in the moon
Did seem akin to lif

The faint red line referred to in the headnote runs below the sixth line of the transcription.
170–171 These lines were intended for insertion after l. 170a in Col. 1a.

But two nights gone I cross'd this dreary moor
In the still moonlight, when I reached the hut
I looked within but all was still & dark

Only within the ruin I beheld
At a small distance on the dusky ground
A broken pane which glitter'd to the moon
And seemed akin to life. — Another time
The winds of autumn drove me o'er the heath
Walk in a dark night by the [illegible] compelled
[illegible]
I was a [illegible] they were hard times
A wanderer among the cottages
I with my pack of winter raiment saw
What the poor suffer'd — Many rich
Sunk down as in a dream among the poor
And of the poor did many cease to be
And their place knew them not. 'Twas at this time
As Margaret told me on this very bench
A fever seiz'd her husband. In disease
He linger'd long and when his strength returned
He found the little he had stor'd to meet
The hour of accident or crippling age
Was all consumed. [illegible] in the land
[illegible] of trouble [illegible] Artisans [illegible] was now
Were from the merchants [illegible] turned away
To hang for bread on parish charity
They and their wives and children, happier far
Could they have lived as do the little birds
That peck along the hedges, or the kite
That makes her dwelling in the mountain rocks
Ill fared it now with

[illegible]

But two nights gone I cross'd this dreary moor
clear
In the ~~still~~ moonlight, when I reached the hut
I looked within but all was still & dark

Only within the ruin, I beheld
At a small distance on the dusky ground
A broken pain which glitter'd to the moon
And seemed akin to life.— Another time
The winds of autumn drove me oer the heath
evening
Heath in a dark night by the storm compelled
the hardships of that season

---

unhappy
~~A dearth was in the land~~ They were hard times
190 'Twas a sad time of [?sorrow ?& ?distress]
191 A wanderer among the cottages
192 I with my pack of winter raiment, saw
[?~~hard~~] ~~evils~~ [?] all then
193 What ~~the poor~~ suffer'd— Many ~~of the~~ rich
What evils [?then/?there] [?] were suffered
194 Sunk down as in a dream among the poor
195 And of the poor did many cease to be
196 And their place knew them not. Twas at this time
As Margaret told me on this very bench
201 A Fever seized her husband. In disease
202 He linger'd long and when his strength return'd
203 He found the little he had stor'd to meet
204 The hour of accident or crippling age
205 Was all consumed. ~~A dearth was in the land~~
as I have said twas now
[?~~season~~]
206 A time of trouble Shoals of Artisans
daily labour
207 Were from the merchants turn'd away
208 To hang for bread on parish charity
209 They and their wives and children, happier far
210 Could they have liv'd as do the little birds
211 That peck along the hedges, or the kite
212 That makes her dwelling in the mountain rocks
213 Ill fared it now with
214 at his door he st[ ]

---

193 WW revised the first four words to "the hardships of that season"—the words that appear above the preceding horizontal line.
213 WW leaves a blank for the husband's name.
214 The last three letters of "stood" are torn away. The text here jumps to l. 215 in the left-hand column (Col. 1b).

Lines from the Racedown Notebook

The Racedown Notebook (DC MS. 11) has leaves 17.8 centimeters wide by 11 centimeters high; 32 leaves are intact: 13 to 24, 27 to 37, and 42 to 50. *Ruined Cottage* work is on 5^{v} to 8^{r}: one-third of leaves 5 and 8 is torn away, and there are stubs only at 6 and 7. The paper is watermarked with a fleur-de-lys within a highly ornamented frame surmounted by a trefoil device and is countermarked TP; the chain lines are 2.6 centimeters apart.

The pages in the Racedown Notebook were not used in order. The *Ruined Cottage* material in the notebook dates from the spring of 1797. Preceding leaves contain a prose note for *Salisbury Plain* (late 1795; in *SPP*, pp. 305–306) and two pieces from 1793 (*Chronology: EY*, pp. 25, 304): (1) *In vain did Time & Nature toil to throw*; and (2) *How sweet the walk along the woody steep*—the conclusion of these lines is visible at the top of the photograph of 5^{v}. Following the *Ruined Cottage* passages are a few lines for *Descriptive Sketches* (1793 edition, ll. 626–631). Then follows work for *Imitation of Juvenal*, probably dating from the spring of 1796 (*Chronology: EY*, pp. 340–341).

Both main lines and revisions of the *Ruined Cottage* passages are in Dorothy Wordsworth's hand; she began on 7^{v} and worked backward to 7^{r} and—possibly—6^{r}. Leaves 6 and 7 were then torn out of the notebook, but letters surviving on the stubs correspond to initial or terminal letters in lines from the original conclusion of the poem. In the following presentation of stubs, a hyphen signifies a trace of illegible ink:

Stub 7^{v}	
Three lines of space or illegible writing in ink	
[A man whose garments shewed the Soldier's] red	B 499
-	[500?]
-	[501?]
[Ceased from his toil, & she with faltering vo]ice	502
[Expecting still to learn her husband's fa]te	503
One-line space	[504?]
[Whose presence gave no comfort were g]one by	505
[Her heart was still more sad. And by yo]n gate	506
Two-line space	
Stub 7^{r}	
Four lines of space or illegible writing in ink	
Of [tender feeling she might dare repeat]	511
The [same sad question. Meanwhile her poor hut]	512
Sun[k to decay, for he was gone whose hand,]	513
Was	
[?~~The~~]	

The
[?She]
Of the

Stub 6^{v}
No letters visible

Stub 6^{r}

-

[?A] [514?]
[?Cl] [515?]
[?C] [516?]
~~W~~
Three lines of illegible writing in ink

After the removal of leaves 6 and 7, Dorothy copied on 5^{v} and continued on 8^{r} a passage about Margaret's discovery of the money; her text (transcribed on the following page) works toward MS. B, ll. 321–325. At the top of 8^{r}, the significance of "Johannes [?Tanvers]," in an unknown hand, is unclear; the leaf number (3) visible in the photograph is modern and now superseded.

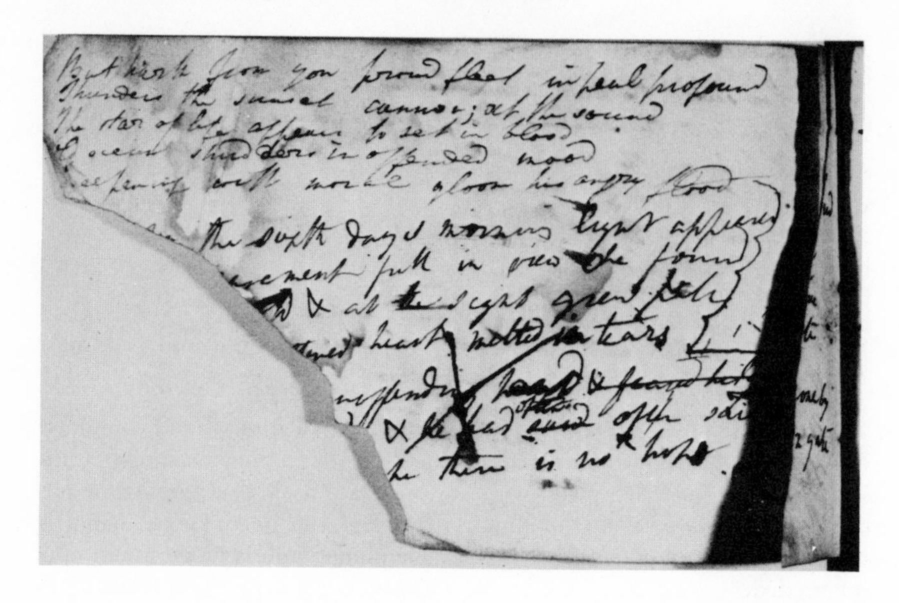

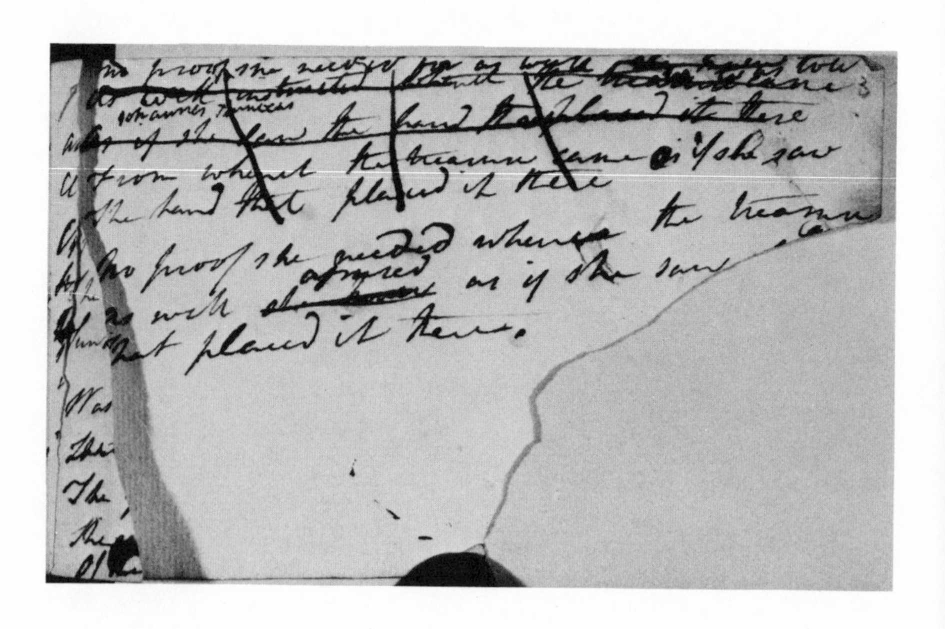

[5^v] [B, 321–323]

[ ] *the sixth days morning light appeared*
[ ]*asement full in view she found*
[ ]*ld & at the sight grew pale*
[ ]*ttered heart melted in tears*
eart [?G]
[ ]*noffending h* [?*and*] ~~*& feared his*~~ [?~~*god*~~]
~~*often*~~
[ ] *& he had* ~~*said*~~ *often said*
[ ]*pe there is no hope*

[8^r] [B, 323–325]

no proof she needed for as well ~~*she knew*~~
[?] *twas told*
~~*As well instructed whence the treasure came*~~
Johannes [?*Tanvers*]
~~*As if she saw the hand that placed it there*~~

a
From whence the treasure came [?*i*] *s if she saw*
The hand that placed it there

No proof she needed whence the treasure
ca[ ]
assured
As well ~~*she knew*~~ *as if she saw* [ ]
That placed it there.

Lines from the Letter of Coleridge to John Estlin, 10 June 1797

At Coleridge's request, Dorothy Wordsworth copied the original conclusion of *The Ruined Cottage* on the inside recto of his letter to John Estlin, 10 June 1797. The manuscript is now at the Avon County Library (Bristol Reference Library); it is a single sheet of white laid paper measuring 40.2 centimeters wide by 32 centimeters high (the inside recto thus measures 20.1 centimeters wide). Chain lines appear at intervals of 2.4 centimeters. The watermark is an image of Britannia in an oval, and the sheet is countermarked COLES over the date 1795. For the complete text of the letter, see *STCL*, I, 327–328.

Editorial line numbers in the left-hand margin of the transcription refer to corresponding lines in MS. B. In lines 509–510, the letter's seal has transferred the initial letters to the right edge of the paper; in line 499, the first comma has been smudged, perhaps in an attempt at deletion. The present condition of this manuscript, foxed and reinforced with archival silk, makes it especially difficult to determine which punctuation marks were added by either William or Dorothy after the lines had been copied; only the more certain cases are recorded in the following transcription.

her eye

Was busy in the distance, shaping things
That made her heart beat quick. Seest thou that path?
(The green-sward now has broken its grey line;)
There, to and fro she paced, through many a day
Of the warm summer: from a belt of flax
That girt her waist, spinning the long-drawn thread
With backward steps. Yet, ever as there passed
A man whose garments shewed the soldier's red,
Or crippled mendicant in sailor's garb,
The little child, who sat to turn the wheel,
Ceased from his toil; and she, with faultering voice,
Expecting still to learn her husband's fate,
Made many a fond inquiry; and when they,
Whose presence gave no comfort, were gone by,
Her heart was still more sad – And by yon gate
That bars the traveller's road, she often sat,
And if a stranger-horseman came, the latch
Would lift; & in his face look wistfully,
Most happy, if from aught discovered there
Of tender feeling, she might dare repeat
The same sad question — Meanwhile, her poor hut
Sunk to decay; for he was gone, whose hand,
At the first nippings of October frost,
Closed up each chink, and with fresh bands of straw
Chequered the green-grown thatch; and so she sat
Through the long winter, reckless and alone,
Till this reft house by frost, and thaw, and rain
Was sapped; and, when she slept, the nightly damps
Did chill her breast, and in the stormy day
Her tattered clothes were ruffled by the wind
Even by the side of her own fire. Yet still
She loved this wretched spot, nor would for worlds
Have parted hence: and still, that length of road,
And this rude bench one torturing hope endeared,
Fast rooted at her heart; and, Stranger, here
In sickness she remained, and here she died,
Last human tenant of these ruined walls –

491 *her eye*
492 *Was busy in the distance, shaping things*
493 *That made her heart beat quick. See'st thou that path?*
494 *{(The green-sward now has broken its grey line;)}*
495 *There, to and fro she paced, through many a day*
496 *Of the warm summer: from a belt of flax*
497 *That girt her waist {;} spinning the long-drawn thread*
498 *{With [?That]} backward steps. {Y yet}, ever as there passed*
499 *A man, whose garments shewed the Soldier's red,*
500 *Or crippled mendicant in Sailors garb,*
501 *{The [?]} little child, who sat to turn the wheel,*
502 *Ceased from his toil {;} and she, with faultering voice,*
503 *Expecting still to learn her husbands fate,*
504 *Made many a fond inquiry, {;} and when the {y [?]} ,*
505 *Whose presence gave no comfort, were gone by,*
506 *Her heart was still more sad — {A [?b]} nd by yon {ga [?]} te*
507 *That bars the traveller's road, she often sat,*
508 *And if a stranger-horseman came, the latch*
509 *Would lift; & in his face look wistfully,*
510 *Most happy, {if [?]} from aught discovered there*
511 *Of tender feeling, she might dare repeat*
512 *The same sad question — Meanwhile, her poor hut*
513 *Sunk to decay:—for he was gone, whose hand,*
514 *At the first nippings of October frost,*
515 *Closed up each chink, and with fresh bands of straw*
516 *Checquered the green-grown thatch; and so she sat*
517 *Through the long winter, reckless and alone,*
518 *'Till this reft house by frost, and thaw, and rain*
519 *Was sapped; and, when she slept, the nightly damps*
520 *Did chill her breast, and in the stormy day*
521 *Her tattered clothes were ruffled by the wind,*
522 *Even by the side of her own fire. Yet still*
523 *She loved t {his [?he]} wretch {e [?]} d spot, nor would for worlds*
524 *Have parted hence: and still, that lengh {t} h of road,*
525 *And this rude bench one torturing hope endeared,*
526 *Fast-rooted at her heard {t}; and, Stranger, here*
527 *In sickness she remained, and here she died,*
528 *{— Last human tenant of these ruined walls —*

Lines from the *Christabel* Notebook

The *Christabel* Notebook (DC MS. 15) is one of Dorothy Wordsworth's pocket notebooks, with a red leather cover and a flap for closure. The pages are 12.3 centimeters wide by 19.6 centimeters high; the white laid paper has chain lines 2.7 centimeters apart. The watermark seems to be a crowned horn-in-shield over GR; the countermark may be J L[?A]RKING. Eight leaves of a different size containing part of *Christabel* have been inserted; they are wove paper, cut to about 12.2 centimeters wide by 19.2 centimeters high, countermarked P&P over the date 1797. The notebook's contents are described in *Chronology: EY*, pp. 322–325, and in *Chronology: MY*, pp. 615–616; the probable date of the *Ruined Cottage* entries (late January or February 1798) is discussed on pp. 11–12, above.

Wordsworth's fair copy of *Ruined Cottage* lines begins on 3^{r} and continues onto 3^{v}; a draft for lines 147–157 of *The Old Cumberland Beggar* (*PW*, IV, 239) was later written at the top of 3^{r}, and a prose draft for that poem's note (*PW*, IV, 445) postdates the *Ruined Cottage* passage on 3^{v} (*Chronology: EY*, pp. 27, 322, 342–343). After writing onto 3^{r} and 3^{v} lines from near the beginning of *The Ruined Cottage*, the poet left 4^{r} blank and resumed his fair copy on 4^{v} with the end of the Pedlar's third and the whole of his fourth visit to the cottage. Leaf 5 is now only a stub, but the initial letters on its recto show that the text continued from 4^{v} onto 5^{r}. In the following presentation of the stub, an opening hyphen means that a portion of the initial letter can be seen but is indecipherable.

Stub 5^{r}

Sh[e lingered in unquiet widowhood]	B 483
A [wife, and widow. Needs must it have been]	484
A [sore heart-wasting. Master! I have heard]	485
Th[at in that broken arbour she would sit]	486
T[he idle length of half a sabbath day]	487
T[here—where you see the toadstool's lazy head]	488
An[d when a dog passed by she still would quit]	489
Th[e shade & look abroad. On this old Bench]	490
For [hours she sate, & evermore, her eye]	491
W[as busy in the distance, shaping things]	492
W[hich made her heart beat quick. Seest thou that path?]	493
(T[he greensward now has broken its grey line)]	494
T[here, to & fro she paced through many a day]	495
Of [the warm summer, from a belt of flax]	496
T[hat girt her waist spinning the long-drawn thread]	497
W[ith backward steps—Yet ever as there passed]	498

A [man whose garments shewed the Soldier's red] 499
Or [crippled Mendicant in Sailor's garb] 500
Th[e little Child who sate to turn the wheel] 501
Ce[ased from his toil, & she with faltering voice] 502
Ex[pecting still to learn her husband's fate] 503
M[ade many a fond inquiry & when they] 504
W[hose presence gave no comfort were gone by] 505
- [506?]
- [507?]
- [508?]
- [509?]
- [510?]
[?O] [511?]
[?T] [512?]
- [513?]
A[t the first nippings of October frost,] 514

The rest of the conclusion (corresponding to MS. B. ll. 515–528) probably stood on 5^{v}.

Editorial line numbers in the left-hand margins of the following transcriptions refer to corresponding lines in MS. B.

3

No man is dear to man, the poorest poor
Long for some moments in a weary life
When they can know & feel that they have been
Themselves the fathers & the dealers out
Of some small blessings, have been kind to such
As needed kindness, for this single cause
That we have all of us one human heart.—
This pleasure is to one kind being known
[illegible] in herself
By her own wants
within that cheerless spot
Where two tall hedgerows of thick willow boughs
Joined in a damp cold nook I found a well
Half-choak'd with weeds and grass—across its mouth
A spiders web hung to the water's edge
And on its wet and slimy footstone lay
The useless fragment of a wooden bowl
I slaked my thirst and to the shady bench
Returned, and while I stood unbonnetted
To catch the current of the breezy air
The old man said. O! Master time has been
When I could never pass this way, but she
Who lived within these walls, when I appeared
A daughter's welcome gave me, and I loved her
As my own child. Oh! Sir the good die first
And they whose hearts are dry as summer dust
Burn to the socket. Many a passenger
Has blest poor Margaret for her gentle looks
When she upheld the cool refreshment drawn
From that forsaken well and no one came
But he was welcome no one went away
But that it seemed she lov'd him. She is dead
The worm is on her cheek and this poor hut
Stripp'd of its outward garb of household flowers
Of rose and jasmine offers to the wind

122	within that chearless spot
123	Where two tall hedgerows of thick willow boughs
124	Joined in a damp cold nook I found a well
125; 143	Half-choak'd with weeds and grass—across its mouth
142–143	A spiders web hung to the water's edge
144	And on its wet and slimy foot stone lay
145	The useless fragment of a wooden bowl
126	—I slaked my thirst and to the shady bench
127	Returned, and while I stood unbonnetted
128	To catch the current of the breezy air
129; 146	The old man said, O! Master time has been
147	When I could never pass this way, but she
148	Who lived within these walls, when I appeared
149	A daughter's welcome gave me, and I loved her
150	As my own child. Oh! Sir the good die first
151	And they whose hearts are dry as summer dust
152	Burn to the socket.— Many a passenger
153	Has blest poor Margaret for her gentle looks
154	When she upheld the cool refreshment drawn
155	From that forsaken well and no one came
156	But he was welcome no one went away
157	But that it seemed she lov'd him. She is dead
158	The worm is on her cheek and this poor hut
159	Stripp'd of its outward garb of household flowers
160	Of rose and jasmine offers to the wind

And nettles rot and adders sun themselves
Where we have sat together while she rock'd
Her baby in its cradle. She is dead
The worm is on her cheek and this poor hut
Stripp'd of its outward garb of household flowers
Of rose and jasmine, offers to the wind
A cold bare wall whose earthy top is trick'd
With weeds and the rank speargrass. — From
this casement
You see the swallows nest has dropp'd away

The Old Cumberland Beggar

Description.

The class of Beggars to which the old man here described belongs is fast ... It consisted of poor & mostly old and infirm persons who confined themselves to a stated round in their neighbourhood and had certain fixed days on which at different houses they regularly received charity, sometimes in money, but mostly in provisions.

163 And nettles rot and adders sun themselves
164 Where we have sat together while she rock'd
165; 157 Her baby int its cradle. She is dead
158 The worm is on her cheek and this poor hut
159 Stripp'd of its outward garb of household flowers
160 Of rose and jasmine, offers to the wind
161 A cold bare wall whose earthy top is trick'd
162 With weeds and the rank speargrass.— From
this casement
You see the swallows nest has dropp'd away

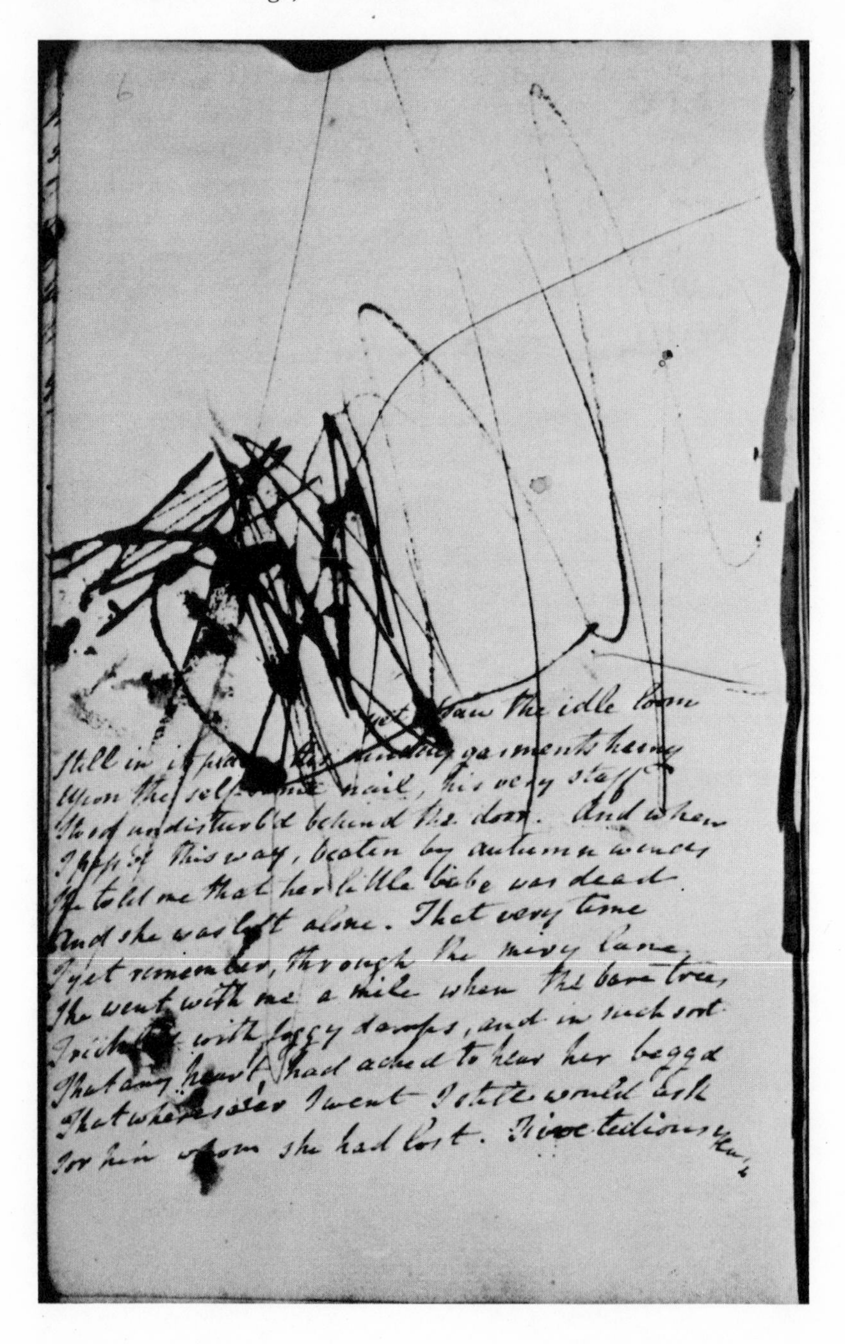
yet I saw the idle loom
Still in its place. His Sunday garments hung
Upon the selfsame nail, his very staff
Stood undisturbed behind the door. And when
I pass'd this way, beaten by autumn winds
She told me that her little babe was dead
And she was left alone. That very time
I yet remember, through the miry lane
She went with me a mile when the bare trees
Trickled with foggy damps, and in such sort
That any heart had ached to hear her begg'd
That wheresoe'er I went I still would ask
For him whom she had lost. Five tedious years

470 yet I saw the idle loom
·} {H
471 Still in its place,} {his sunday garments hung
472 Upon the self-same nail, his very staff
473 Stood undisturb'd behind the door. And when
474 I pass'd this way, beaten by autumn winds
475 She told me that her little babe was dead
476 And she was left alone. That very time
477 I yet remember, through the miry lane
478 She went with me a mile when the bare trees
479 Trickled with foggy damps, and in such sort
480 That any heart had ached to hear her beggd
e{
481 That whereso {'er I went I still would ask
482 For him whom she had lost. Five tedious years

Lines from the Alfoxden Notebook

The Alfoxden Notebook (DC MS. 14), bound in brown leather, has leaves measuring about 9.5 centimeters wide by 16 centimeters high. No watermark is visible; the chain lines are 2.6 centimeters apart. As recently restored, the notebook has fifty leaves (besides an opening and a closing paste-down), of which twenty-one leaves are intact:

Gathering	*Original leaf nos.*	*Intact leaf nos.*	*Stub nos.*
1, in 8 (first leaf a paste-down)	1–7	2, 6	1, 3–5, 7
2, in 8	8–15	15	8–14
3, in 8	16–23	16, 20–23	17–19
4, in 4?	24–27	24–27	–
5, in 8	28–35	28–29, 31	30, 32–35
6, in 4?	36–39	–	36–39
7, in 4?	40–43	–	40–43
8, in 8 (last leaf a paste-down)	44–50	45–50	44

Stubs 40–43 have no original paper and are the restorer's stubs only; it is possible that gathering 4 was in eight leaves and that four are now lost. The contents of this notebook are described in *Chronology: EY*, pp. 321–322.

Between late January and early March 1798, Wordsworth drafted onto 11ʳ–21ᵛ passages related to *The Ruined Cottage*. Much of this work is now torn out of the notebook, but letters surviving on the stubs suggest lines that were later used in the MS. B text. In the following presentation of stubs, a hyphen signifies a trace of illegible ink.

Stub 11ʳ
Seven lines of space or illegible letters
H [B 416?]
A [417?]
Sh [418?]
[?K]
[?In]
Gi[ves to an idle matter—still she sighed] 422
Bu[t yet no motion of the breast was seen] 423
[?Th]
We [sate together, sighs came on my ear] 425
I [knew not how and hardly whence they came.] 426
I [took my staff & when I kissed her babe] 427
Th[e tears were in her eyes. I left her then] 428

[?It]	[431?]
An	[432?]
[?D]	
A	

Stub 11v
At bottom of page

[?es]	[445?]
[?ng]	
[?ves]	[446?]

Stub 12r

L	[447?]
A	[448?]
Horizontal line, followed by a dozen lines of space or illegible letters	
W	[453? or 454?]
-	
N[o winter greenness; of her herbs & flowers]	456
T[he better part were gnawed away]	457
O[r trampled on the earth; a chain of straw]	458
W[hich had been twisted round the tender stem]	459
Of [a young apple-tree lay at its root]	460
{T	
{O[he bark was nibbled round by truant sheep]	461
M[argaret stood near, her infant in her arms]	462

Nothing can be identified from the scraps of writing on stub 12v or on the rectos and versos of stubs 13 and 14. Leaves 15 and 16 are intact and included in the following transcriptions; three stubs come after leaf 16:

Stub 17r
Two-line space

[?O]	[29?]
-	
-	
T	[32?]
W	[33?]
[?In]	
B	[36?]
[?S]	[37?]
W[as green and studded o'er with fungus flowers]	38
~~A~~	
A[n iron-pointed staff lay at his side]	39
H[im had I seen the day before—alone]	40
A[nd in the middle of the public way]	41
[?S]	[42?]
[?T]	[43?]
-	[44?]

[?W] [45?]
I[n lonely villages or straggling huts] 46
I [knew him—he was born of lowly race] 47
O[n Cumbrian hills, and I have seen the tear] 48
[?St] [49?]
Th[e house in which his early days were passed] 50
A[nd found I was no stranger to the spot] 51

Stub 17^{v}
Illegible terminal letters

Stub 18^{r}
-
Or
B
-
Two-line space
O
-
[?W]
-
-
A
Horizontal line
-
In
-
[?P]
[?S] [104? or 106?]
-
P[illowed his head—I guess he had no thought] 107
O[f his way-wandering life. His eyes were shut] 108
- [109?]
D[appled his face. With thirsty heat oppressed] 110
At [length I hailed him glad to see his hat] 111
B[edewed with water-drops, as if the brim] 112
H[ad newly scooped a running stream, he rose] 113

The fragmentary evidence is vexing, but clearly some version of the Pedlar's history was on leaves 17–18. If leaf 17^{v} continued on from the line corresponding to MS. B, line 51, perhaps twenty-six lines would fit on that verso, with perhaps a dozen more at the top of 18^{r} before the story of Margaret resumed (possibly at line 104 or 106). Wordsworth seems to have revised as he went along, and this is the most probable explanation for the difficulty in matching initial letters on 18^{r} with later fair copy. The verso of stub 18 probably contained lines corresponding to MS. B, 114–136—lines linked with 18^{r} and

19ʳ—and two visible word endings, one about four lines down from the top and the other at the bottom, support this conjecture:

Stub 18ᵛ

ssd [118?]

d [136?]

Stub 19ʳ

Of [brotherhood is broken—time has been] 137
W[hen every day the touch of human hand] 138
Di[sturbed their stillness, & they ministered] 139
To [human comfort. As I stooped to drink] 140
- [141?]
W[hat feelings came to me! A spider's web] 142
Ac[ross its mouth hung to the water's edge] 143
A[nd on the wet & slimy foot-stone lay] 144
T[he useless fragment of a wooden bowl] 145
I[t moved my very heart. The time has been] 146
W[hen I could never pass this road but she] 147
Horizontal line
-
[?To]
[?Th]
Al[ong the south the uplands feebly glared] 2
Th[rough a pale steam and all the northern downs] 3
In [clearer air ascending shewed their brown] 4
~~An~~[d surfaces distinct with shades] 5
Of [deep embattled clouds that lay in spots] 6
D[etermined and unmoved; with steady beams] 7
Of [clear and pleasant sunshine interposed] 8
-
[?~~P~~]
Of [some huge oak whose aged branches make] 11

Stub 19ᵛ
Illegible terminal letters. Perhaps lines corresponding to MS. B, 12–28, stood here, leading into lines on 17ʳ.

On leaves 17–19, Wordworth worked out lines up to about the point where he had begun MS. A (corresponding to MS. B, l. 152) several months before. The remaining 1798 *Ruined Cottage* work in the Alfoxden Notebook—passages of philosophic blank verse related to the Pedlar's character—is on leaves 20 and 21, which are fully transcribed on the following pages.

In 1802, Dorothy Wordsworth returned to the Alfoxden Notebook to write out a fair copy of *The Pedlar*, 1802, but only leaf 31 survives. Her copy probably began on leaf 30ᵛ and continued on some of the nine leaves that are now stubs (or thirteen, if the restorer's stubs are accepted) which follow leaf 31—see pp. 28–29, above. Stubs 32^v, 33^v, 34^v, and 38^r show slight traces of ink; only on 33^v can anything be guessed at:

Stub 33^v

[?s]	[E 264?]
ght	[265?]

Editorial line numbers in the left-hand margins of the following transcriptions of leaves 15, 16, 20, and 21 of the Alfoxden Notebook refer to corresponding lines in MS. B. The editorial line numbers on the transcription of leaf 31 refer to corresponding lines in MS. E.

261 All recollection and that simple
tale
262 Passd from my mind like a forgotten
sound
263 ~~A while we held discourse~~
263 A while on trivial things we held discourse
s
264 To me soon ta[?t]{ teless for I was depressd

271 A [?~~ch~~] chillness was among my veins
passing
272 I rose & & turning from that breezy shade
273 Went out into the open air & stood
274 To drink the comfort of the warmer sun—

265 And thought of that poor woman as of
one
266 Whom I had known & loved.
her aged

~~Who by my side was seated~~
263 A while on trivial things we held discourse
264 To me soon tasteless. In my own despight
265 I thought of that poor woman as of one
266 Whom I had known & loved. He had
rehearsed
267 Her homely tale with such familiar power
268 With such a countenance of love, an eye
269 So busy, that the things of which he spake
270 Semed present, and attention now relax'ed
There was a heartfelt
{~~I~~
271 {~~A felt a creeping~~ chillness in my veins
272 I rose and turning from that breezy shade
273 Went out into the open air & stood
274 To drink the comfort of the warmer sun
275 Long time I had not stayed
ere looking round

C

The line of revision below the third horizontal rule is a revision of l. 266.

The large "C" at the bottom of the page refers to a similar mark on 16v to which the text jumps. Hence the passages on 15v–16r probably precede these lines continuing from 15r onto 16v.

~~There would he~~ wander in the storm and there
Would feel
~~He felt~~ whateer there is of power in sounds
To breathe an elevated mood—by form
Or image unprofaned of sounds that
are
The ghostly language of the antient earth
Or make their dim abode in distant
winds

Not for whateer there is of power in sounds
That make their dim abode in distant
To breathe an elevated mood by form
Or [?imaged] unprofaned.
[?ese]
Oh listen listen how ~~sounds~~ that wind
away
While the last touch they le[?vae] upon the sense
Tells they [?have]
the firs
~~Hush they are coming—[?they] have passd~~
~~And [?run]~~ There would he stand
still
~~Beneath~~ In the ~~warm~~ covert of some [?lonesome]
rock
Or
Would gaze upon the moon untill its
light
Fell like a strain of music on his soul
And seem'd to sink into his very heart

[?] His eye was like the star of Jove
When in a storm its radiance comes & goes
As winds drive on the their invisible clouds
Some men there are who like inscects &c
dart and dart against the mighty
stream of tendency others with
no vulgar sense of their existence
To no vulgar end float calmly
down.

The draft on the upper two-thirds of the page is for "In storm and tempest" (see a more finished version on 20r–20v and the note on 20r). The lines deleted with vertical strokes were probably written first, with WW revising above them and then continuing his passage below.

Below the horizontal rule is a draft related to the Pedlar's character but not used for it.

There is a holy indolence
Compared to which our best activity
Is oftimes deadly bane
They rest upon their oars
Float down the mighty stream of tendency
In a ~~[illegible]~~ calm mood of holy indolence
A most wise passiveness in which the heart
Lies open and is well content to feel
As nature feels and to receive her shapes
As she has made them.

The mountain's outline and its steady form
Gave simple grandeur to his mind nor less
The changeful language of the countenance
Gave movement to his thoughts and multitude
With order and relation

He lov'd to contemplate
The mountains and the antient hills again
~~Within it in their solitude~~ to pause
And feel his spirit in their solitudes

there is a holy indolence
Com
[?To ?w] pared to which our best activity
Is oftimes deadly bane
They rest upon their oars
F
float down the mighty stream of tendency
a calm
In [?the] ~~deep~~ mood of holy indolence
A most wise passiveness in which the
heart
Lies open and is well content to feel
As nature feels and to receive her
shapes
As she has made them.

The mountain's outline and its steady
form[?s]
Gave simple grandeur to his mind nor less
The changeful language of its countenance
Gave movement to his thoughts and
multitude
With order and relation

He lov'd to contemplate
aged
The mountains and the ~~antient~~ hills
stand
to ~~feed~~
~~His spirit in their solitudes~~
And feed his spirit in their solitudes

The first of the two drafts above the rule is another unused sketch for the Pedlar's character (it probably contributes to *Excursion*, IX, 81–92; *PW*, V, 289). The second draft was used in the recopying of "In storm and tempest" on 20r–20v.

The passage below the line was not incorporated in *RC* or *The Pedlar*.

Him that tranquil ruin and impell'd
By a mild force of curious pensiveness
I begg'd of the old man that for my sake
He would resume his story. He replied
It were a wantonness and would demand
Severe reproof, if we were men whose hearts
Could hold vain dalliance with the misery
contented thence to draw
Even of the dead [illegible]
A momentary pleasure [illegible] never
marked
By reason, barren of all future
good
But we have known that there is often found
2
And always
In mournful thoughts and always
might be found
A power to virtue friendly; wer't not so
I am a dreamer among men indeed
An idle dreamer. 'Tis a common
tale
By moving accidents uncharacter'd
A tale of silent suffering hardly cloth'd
In bodily form and to the grosser sense
But ill adapted, scarcely palpable
bidding
To him who does not think. But at your [illegible]
I will proceed. While thus it fared
with those

a ruin cottage from [illegible] the path
level
[illegible]

[?peaceful]
276 (Upon that tranquil ruin and impell'd
277 By a mild force of curious pensiveness
278 I begg'd of the old man that for my
sake
i
279 He would resume his story. He repled
280 It were a wantonness and would demand
281 Severe reproof, if we were men whose
hearts
282 Could hold vain dalliance with the
misery
contented thence to draw
283 Even of the dead ~~and idly thence extract~~
momentary [?~~trivial~~] pleasure
284 ~~A passing pleasure felt but~~ never
marked
285 By reason, barren of all future
good
But we have known
286 ~~We know~~ that there is often found
2 1
~~And always~~
287 In mournful thoughts and always
might be found
288 A power to virtue friendly—wert not so
289 I am a dreamer among men—indeed
290 An idle dreamer. Tis a common
tale
291 By moving accidents uncharacter'd
292 A tale of silent suffering hardly cloath'd
293 In bodily form and to the grosser sense
294 But ill adapted scarcely palpable
But bidding
295 To him who does not think. At your ~~request~~
296 I will proceed. While thus it fared
with those

---

a ruin cottage four bare shapeless walls
{That level
{[?that] midway in that [?~~Common~~] stood alone

The large "C" at the top of the page indicates that the text here continues from a similar mark at the bottom of 15r.

286 WW's numbers are intended to reverse the order of "there" and "often."

The draft below the rule is related to *RC*, MS. B, ll. 27 and 30.

In storm and tempest and beneath the beam
Of quiet moons he wandered there — and there
Would feel whateer there is of power in sound
To breathe an elevated mood, by form
Or image unprofaned — there would he stand
Beneath some rock listening to sounds that are
The ghostly language of the antient earth
Or make their dim abode in distant winds
Thence did he drink the visionary power
I deem not profitless these fleeting moods
Of shadowy exaltation not for this

That they are kindred to our purer mind
And intellectual life but that the soul
Remembering how she felt but what she felt
Remembering not retains an obscure sense
Of possible sublimity at which
With growing faculties she doth aspire
With faculties still growing, feeling still
That whatsoever point they gain they still
Have something to pursue. But from these
There something of

he wanderd there
In storm and tempest and beneath
the beam
Of quiet moons ~~he wandered there~~—and there
Would feel whateer there is of power in sound,
To breathe an elevated mood, by form
Or image unprofaned—there would he
stand
~~Listening to sounds [?t]~~
are
Beneath some rock, listening to sounds that
The ghostly language of the antient
earth
Or make their dim abode in distant
winds
Thence did he drink the visionary power
I deem not profitless these fleeting moods
Of shadowy exaltation not for this

That they are kindred to our purer mind
And intellectual life but that the
soul
Remembring how she felt but what
she felt
Remembring not retains an obscure sense
Of possible sublimity at which her [~~?~~]
~~Een from the very dimness of the [?things]~~
s doth
With growing faculties t he [?] aspire
With facu l still growing, feeling still
That whatsoever point they Gain, There
still
Is something to pursue. But from these
haunts
Have something to they still

WW probably added the correction at the very top after the deletion in the second line.

"In storm and tempest," continuing onto 20v, is clearly related to WW's thinking about the Pedlar. The lines, however, do not appear in MS. B; they were copied after *RC* and before the Pedlar addendum in MS. D. In late 1799, the passage on Alfoxden, 20r, became part of *Prelude 1799* (II, 352–371).

In the fourth line from the bottom WW, writing rapidly, may have allowed the descender from a word above to serve as the "l" or the "t" of "faculties," then simply left off the end of the word.

lonesome
Of ~~untamed~~ nature he had skill to draw
A better & less transitory power
n
an i[?f] fluence now he drew a better power
habitual
less transient n
An influence more permanet t. To his
mind
The mountain's outline and its steady
[?impact] form
Gave simple grandeur and its presence
shaped
The measure and the prospect of
his soul
ese
To majesty, such virtue had th at
s
form
~~Perennial and~~
s aged hills
Of Mountain and the nor less
their coutence
The changeful language—of ~~its countenan~~
Gave movement to his thoughts
and multitude
With order & relation
G

Why is it we feel
So little for each other but for this
That we with nature have no sympathy
things
Or with such ~~idle objects~~ as have no
power to hold
Articulate language

And never for each other shall we feel
[?find]
As we may feel till we ~~have~~ sympathy
With nature in her forms inanimate
[?If ?such ?]
With objects such as have no power
to hold

The top draft continues from 20r; it contributes to *Prelude*, VII, 720–729.
The bottom draft continues onto the following page. It, and the middle one above, form the basis for the opening of the reconciling addendum in MS. B; see B, 46r.

Articulate language. In all forms of things
There is a mind

Transfigured by his feelings he
Even as a prophet—one whose appeared purposes
Were round him like a light—
One to whom solitary thought had nobleness he seem'd
The powers miraculous by which the
Walks through the world that lives soul
in solemn things
Of unknown modes of being which
Or in the heavens or in the heavens on earth
Exist by mighty combinations, bound & earth
Together by a link, & with a soul
Which makes all, one.

One evening when the sun was setting
And ere th unusual [illegible] glow he
The exceeding beauty of this earth perceived
The loveliness of nature and felt

Articulate language. In all forms of things
There is a mind

Transfigured by his feelings he
appeared
Even as a prophet—one whose purposes
Were round him like a light—
sublimed he seem'd
One to whom solitary thought had
given
The power miraculous by which the
soul
Walks through the world that lives
in future things

Of unknown modes of being which
on earth
Or in the heavens or in the heavens
& earth
Exist by mighty combinations, bound
Together by a link, & with a soul
Which makes all, one.

One evening when the sun was sinking
low
clearness
And with unusual [?~~clearness~~] he
perceived
The exceeding beauty of this earth
and felt
The loveliness of {N / nature}

The first two lines continue from 20v; the other three drafts are presumably about the Pedlar but were not incorporated in *RC* or *The Pedlar*.

To gaze
those
On that green hill and on [?the] scattered
trees

And feel a pleasant consciousness of life
In the [?impression] of that loveliness
Untill the sweet sensation called
the mind

~~Into itself and all external things~~
~~[?So ?]~~
Into itself by image from without
Unvisited: and all her reflex powers
u
Wrapp'd in a still dream forgetf[?f] llness

I lived without the knowledge that
I lived
Then by those beauteous forms brought
back again
To lose myself again as if my life
Did ebb & flow with a strange
mystery

These lines of philosophic blank verse, perhaps inspired by WW's thinking about the Pedlar, were not used in the delineation of his character.

The passage visible at the bottom of the photograph is probably related to "Away away it is the air" (*PW*, IV, 357–358), which appears on leaf 23v of the Alfoxden Notebook.

29 He by appointment waited for me here
Beneath these Elms, it being our joint way
To travel on together a few days.
— We were dear Friends I from my childhood up
Had known him, in a nook of Furness Fells
At Hawkshead where I went to School 9 years
One Room he had, the fifth part of a house
A place to which he drew from time to time
And found a kind of home or harbour there
— He was the best Old Man. And often I
Delight to recollect him, & his looks
And think of him and his affectionate ways
— In that same Town of Hawkshead where we dwelt
There was a little Girl ten years of age
But tiny for her years, a pretty dwarf
Fair-hair'd, fair-fac'd, & though of stature small
In heart as forward as a lusty child
This Girl when from his travels he re-turn'd
To his abiding-place would daily come
To play with the good Man, & he was wont
To tell her stories of his early life

[*The Pedlar*, 1802, Fragment]

E, 37 *He by appointment waited for me here*
E, 38 *Beneath these Elms, it being our joint wish*
E, 39 *To travel on together a few days.*
E, 40 *—We were dear Friends I from my childhood*
up
E, 41 *Had known him, in a nook of Furness Fells*
E, 42 *At Hawkshead where I went to School 9*
years
E, 43 *One* {*R* / *room*} *he had, the fifth part of a house*
E, 44 *A place to which he drew from time to time*
E, 45 *And found a kind of home or harbour there*

He lov'd me X
Paragraph {~~*O*~~ kindest / ~~*old*~~}
E, 95–96 *——He was the* ~~*best*~~ ~~*old*~~ *Man! And often I*
E, 97 *Delight to recollect him, & his looks*
E, 98 *And think of him and his affectionate ways*
To me & every one both old & youn{g / d}
E, 61 *——In that same Town of Hawkshead where*
we dwelt
E, 62 *There was a little Girl ten years of age*
E, 63 *But tiny for her years, a pretty dwarf*
E, 64 *Fair-hair'd, fair-fac'd, & though of stature*
small
E, 65 *In heart as forward as a lusty child*
E, 66 40 *This Girl when from his travels he ret{= / =turn'd}*
E, 67 *To his abiding-place would daily come*
E, 68 *To play with the good Man, & he was wont*
E, 69 *To tell her stories of his early life*
He loved me out of many rosy Boys

The passages here and on 31v were written four years later than the preceding 1798 work on *RC*; DW possibly copied these lines from *The Pedlar*, 1802, on 10 February or 8 July 1802 (see pp. 28–29, above).

95–96 The deletions, the revision ("kindest"), the copying instructions ("Paragraph" and "He lov'd me"), and the deletion mark for the next twelve lines are all in pencil. The × at the right of this line refers to a similar one on 31v, l. 46 ("He lov'd me"), to which the text jumped after lines at the bottom of this page and the top of the following one were deleted.

98/61 The interlining is in pencil.

66 The number 40 is in pencil.

The penciled line at the foot of the page is another copying instruction showing that ll. 46ff. on the following page should come after l. 45 on this page.

Or, what she better liked to sing to her
Scotch songs sometimes but oftener to repeat
Scotch poetry, old Ballads & old tales
Love Gregory, William Wallace and Rob Roy
All this while she was sitting on a stool
Between his knees, & oft would she stand up
Upon her Stool, & coax him with a kiss
To tell her more, and many a time would
Cry over her and she would wonder why
This standing at his threshold have I seen
Yea many times when he had little thought
That any one was near. And for myself
He lov'd me out of many rosy Boys
Singled out me, as he in sport hath said
For my grave looks too thoughtful for my years
His name was Drummond. The bare truth it was
That in his early childhood he had been
A Herd-callan for forty pence a year.
His history, I from himself have heard
Full often after I grew up, & he
Found in my heart as he would kindly say
A kindred heart to his. Among the Hills

E, 84 *Or, what she better liked to sing to her*
E, 85 *Scotch songs sometimes but oftener to repeat*
E, 86 *Scotch poetry, old Ballads & old Tales*
E, 87 *Love Gregory, William Wallace, and Rob Roy*

E, 88 *All this while she was sitting on a stool*
E, 89 *Between his knees, & oft would she stand up*
E, 90 *Upon her stool, & coax him with a kiss*
E, 91 *To tell her more, and many a time would h[ ]*
E, 92 *Cry over her and she would wonder why*
E, 93 *This standing at his threshold have I seen*
Glad was I when from his rounds
[?return]
E, 94 *Yea many times when he had little thought*
[?As]
E, 95 *That any one was near. And for myself* X
As I grew up &c
E, 46 X*He lov'd me out of many rosy Boys*
E, 47 *Singled out me, as he in sport hath said*
E, 48 *For my grave looks too thoughtful for my*
years
His name was Drummond. The bare truth it
was

E, 72 *60* *That in his early childhood he had been*
E, 73–74 *A Herd-Callan for forty pence a year.*
E, 99 *His history I from himself have heard*
E, 100 *Full often after I grew up, & he*
E, 101 *Found in my heart as he would kindly say*
E, 102 *A kindred heart to his. Among the Hills*

The deletion of the opening twelve lines is in pencil.
91 The last letter in this line is torn away; MS. E reads "he."
93/94 The interlining is in pencil and becomes l. 49 of the MS. E reading text.
94/95 The doubtful word is in pencil.
95–46 The penciled ×'s indicate that ll. 46ff. were to be inserted after l. 45 on 31r. "As I grew up &c" is in pencil; it is the beginning of l. 50 of the MS. E reading text.
72 The number 60 is in pencil.
A number of holes suggest that the last ten lines on this page were once covered with a sewn-on sheet.

MS. B, with Readings of MS. B^2 in an *Apparatus Criticus*

Ruined Cottage MS. B (DC MS. 17) is a homemade notebook originally consisting of thirty-four leaves, the last of which is now missing. Insertion of ten leaves after the original leaf 5 and the addition of twelve leaves at the end expanded the notebook; it now has fifty-five leaves, about 12.5 centimeters wide by 20.5 centimeters high, intact. MS. B was formed by the tearing and folding of sheets of paper watermarked with a fleur-de-lys and countermarked B over the date 1795 (illustrated in Alfred H. Shorter, *Paper Mills and Paper Makers in England, 1495–1800* [Hilversum, 1957], p. 272, fig. 7); the chain lines are 2.6 centimeters apart. *Peter Bell* MS. 1 (DC MS. 18) and several of the Wordsworths' letters (*EY*, pp. 199–212, 215–219) are written on the same kind of paper, as is a letter Coleridge wrote while staying at Alfoxden (*STCL*, I, 394–398). None of these other known uses of this paper precedes the terminal date of MS. B—5[–6] March 1798, when MS. B^2 was copied from it. MS. B^2 itself is written on a full sheet of the sort of paper used to construct MS. B.

At first a relatively straightforward fair copy of *The Ruined Cottage* in 528 lines, MS. B soon became a working manuscript in which the Pedlar's history was expanded and the reconciling conclusion appended. William's revisions and Dorothy's copies of them are scattered throughout the notebook's verso pages, with their points of insertion—themselves sometimes altered—indicated by various symbols. Furthermore, the addition of ten leaves between the original fifth and sixth leaves means that even the text on the rectos cannot be read continuously from page to page. Interpretation of the following transcription will thus be aided if the main stages of work in MS. B are spelled out here:

1. Fair copy of *The Ruined Cottage.*
   a. Original 528-line text on rectos of 2–5 and 16–26; 26^v; and the rectos of 27–43.
   b. Addition of 12 lines ("Sir I feel"—36^v) to make a 540-line text.
2. Pedlar expansion and reconciling addendum (the order of these two additions is uncertain—see p. 21, above).
   a. Pedlar expansion.
      i. Drafts on 4^v and 5^v intended for insertion at MS. B, l. 58b.
      ii. Fair copy and drafts on rectos of 6–15 and versos of 10, 12, 13, and 14. This second stage incorporates the first, and it was also intended for insertion at MS. B, l. 58b.
      iii. Drafts and fair copy on versos of 15–17 (revisions on 18^r and 18^v) intended for insertion at MS. B, l. 65b, after the inclusion of the second stage.

b. Reconciling addendum.
  i. Abortive drafts on 43ᵛ and 45ʳ.
  ii. Fair copy on the rectos of 46–54, bringing the addendum to 146 lines.
  iii. Addition on 51ᵛ, bringing the addendum to what was counted as 155 lines.

Notes to the transcriptions provide more detail of these revisions, particularly of minor ones omitted above.

Editorial numbers in the left-hand margins indicate lines in the MS. B reading text. For the large portions of this manuscript that do not contribute to the reading text—chiefly the Pedlar expansion and the addendum—but which are used in later texts, bracketed letters and numbers to the right at the top of the page refer to corresponding lines in MS. D and/or MS. E. Where lines in MS. B did not become part of the MS. D reading text but were copied as overflow in MS. D, a reference in brackets is made to the D leaf number, recto or verso, on which the passage begins. To make possible reference to lines on the leaves of fair-copy additions to MS. B, line numbers in the right-hand margins are serially assigned on each leaf.

That part of *The Ruined Cottage* sent by Dorothy to Mary Hutchinson on 5[–6] March 1798 (MS. B^2) is presented in an *apparatus criticus* to the base text of the numbered reading text lines in the MS. B transcription. Although the addendum and the first two stages of the Pedlar expansion were complete by early March, Dorothy transcribed only those lines "immediately and solely connected with the Cottage," beginning at MS. B, line 26, and continuing—with some gaps—to line 484. Dorothy's comments leading into her copy are quoted in the Introduction, p. 19, above. MS. B^2 enables one to see, in those lines copied by Dorothy, which revisions in MS. B were made prior to 5[–6] March and which were presumably made later. All changes made in MS. B^2 are in Dorothy's hand; she did not number the lines in her letter to Mary.

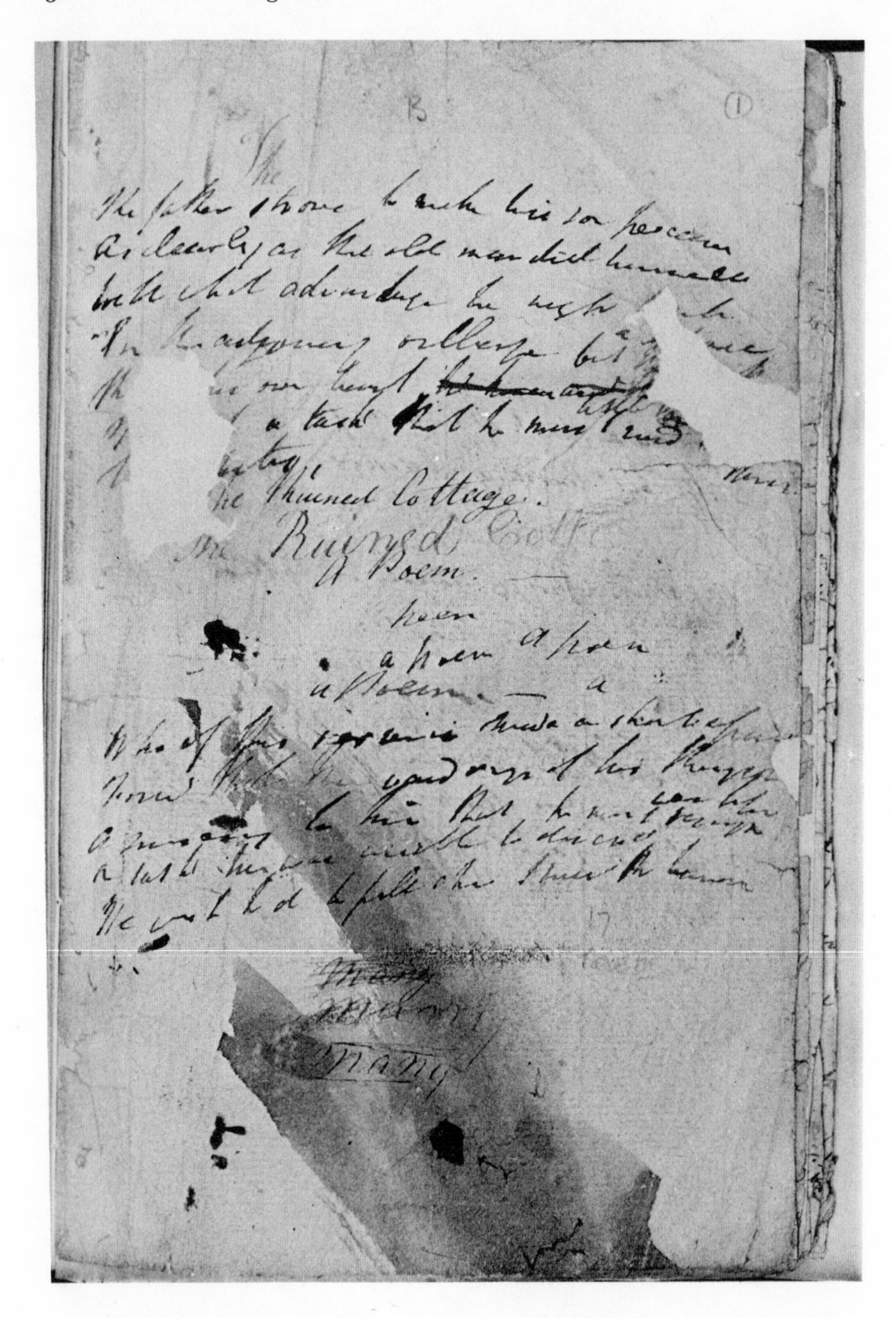
The Ruined Cottage.

A Poem.

[D, 64^r; E, 279–285]

The
The father strove to make his son perceive
As clearly as the old man did himself
t}
With what advan[?a]} age he might t[ ]ch
a [?school]
In the adjoining village but the [?Youth]
Th[ ] his own heart ~~he knew and [?]~~
[?]
[?] a task that he must [?]
[?]
[? ?]
The Ruined Cottage.
The Ruined Cottage
A Poem. ——
poem
a poem a poem
a Poem. — a
Who of this service made a short essay
Found that the wandrings of his thought
[?were ?then]
A misery to him that he must resign
A task he was unable to [?discharge]
[?Heaviest ?load ?he ?felt ?when ?shone ?the ?heavens]

~~Many~~
Many
Many

[?]

The drafts on this page are toward a passage on 14^v intended for insertion on 15^r. Two large holes in the upper half of 1^r affect the readings.

The circled numbers in pencil visible at the upper right-hand corner of this and following photographs are of recent origin, as is the penciled "B" at the top center of the photograph. In pencil below the last line, right of center, is "17 Case III," a now superseded Dove Cottage reference number; this page served as the front cover of the notebook until recent restoration.

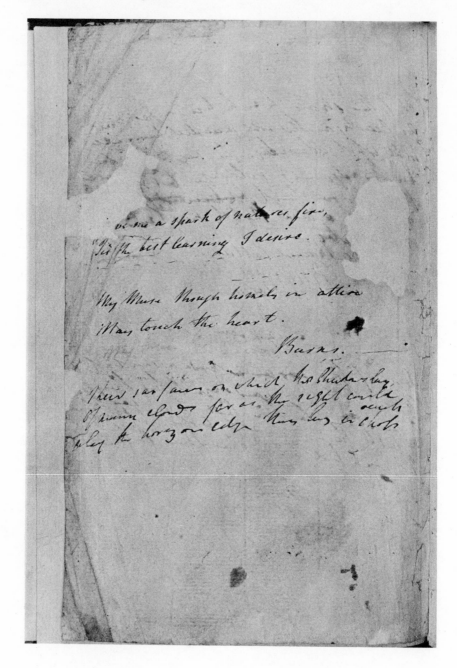

ve me a spark of natures fire,
Tis the best learning I desire.

My Muse though homely in attire
May touch the heart.

Burns.

[illegible]

[ ]ve me a spark of natures fire,
Tis the best learning I desire.

My Muse though homely in attire
May touch the heart.
May touch the [?heart]
Burns. ———

Their surfaces on which the Shadows lay,
Of many clouds far as the sight could
reach
Along the horizons edge [?those/?these] lay in spots

The opening two letters of "Give" in l. 1 are torn away. WW's repetition, "May touch the [?heart]," and the line under "Tis the best" are in pencil. The draft at the bottom is a revision of ll. 5–6 on 2^{r}.

(2)

Part 1st

Their surfaces with shadows all distinct
Of deep embattled clouds. Far as the sight
Could reach those many shadows lay in spots
Determined & unmoved

'Twas Summer; and the sun was mounted high
Along the south the uplands feebly glared
Through a pale steam and all the northern downs
In clearer air ascending shewed far off ~~their~~ ~~b~~
With shadows dappled o'er
And surfaces distinct with shades
Of clouds whose many shadows lay in spots
Of deep embattled clouds that lay in spots
Determined and unmoved; with steady beams
Of clear and pleasant sunshine interposed
Pleasant to him who on the soft cool moss ~~grass~~
Extends his careless limbs beside the root
Of some huge oak whose aged branches make
The noon
A twilight of their own, a dewy shade
Where the wren warbles, while the dreaming

13 man

Part 1st. ———
their surfaces with shadows all distinct
Of deep embattled clouds. Far as the sight
Could reach those many shadows lay in spots
Determined & unmoved

1 *Twas Summer; and the sun was mounted high.*
2 *Along the south the uplands feebly glared*
3 *Through a pale steam and all the northern*
downs
far off
4 *In clearer air ascending shewed ~~their brown~~*
X {with / [?all] shadows dappled oer
5 *And surfaces distinct with shades*
Of clouds whose many shadows lay in spots
6 *Of deep embattled clouds that lay in spots*
7 *Determined and unmoved; with steady bea[ ]*
8 *Of clear and pleasant sunshine interposed*
moss
9 *Pleasant to him who on the soft cool ~~grass~~*
careless
10 *Extends his ^ limbs beside the root*
boughs prolong
11 *Of some huge oak whose aged branches make*
The morning, making through a summers day
12 *A twilight of their own, a dewy shade*
13 *Where the wren warbles, while the dreaming*
man

13

1–25 After having described a hot summers noon the Poet supposes himself to come in sight of some tall trees upon a flat common *the text of B² begins at l. 26*

---

5 The X at the beginning of this line indicates where the revision at the top of the page should be added.
7 The last two letters of "beams" are worn away.

(3)

Half conscious of that soothing melody
~~[illegible]~~ upon the mossy earth
With sidelong eye looks out upon the scene
By those impending branches made
More soft and distant. Other lot was mine
Across a bare wide Common I had toiled
With languid feet which by the slippery ground
Were baffled still; and when I stretched myself ~~[illegible]~~
On the brown earth my limbs from very heat
Could find no rest nor my weak arm disperse
The insect host which gathered round my face
And joined their murmurs to the tedious noise
Of seeds of bursting gorse which crackled round
I rose & turned ~~my steps~~ towards a group of trees
Which midway in that level stood alone
And thither come at length beneath a shade
Of clustering elms that sprang from the same root
I found a ruined Cottage four clay walls
That stared upon each other_'Twas a spot
The wandering gypsey in a stormy night

14 *Half conscious of that soothing melody*
resting his head
~~His head reclined~~ upon the mossy earth
15 *With sidelong eye looks out upon the scene*
16 *By those impending branches made*
17 *More soft and distant. Other lot was mine*
18 *Across a bare wide Common I had toiled*
19 *With languid feet which by the slippery* [?~~grod~~]
I stretched mysel
ground
and when ~~I sought repose~~
20 [*20*] *Were baffled still; ~~my limbs from very heat~~*
21 On the brown earth my limbs from very heat
22 *Could find no rest nor my weak arm disperse*
23 *The insect host which gathered round my*
face
24 *And joined their murmurs to the tedious noise*
25 *Of seeds of bursting gorse which crackled round*
rose &
26 *I ^ turned ~~my steps~~ towards a group of trees*
{at
27 *Which midway in th {e level stood alone*
28 *And thither come at length beneath a*
shade
29 *Of clustering elms that sprang from the same*
root
30 *I found a ruined Cottage, four clay walls*
31 *That stared upon each other—'Twas a spot*
32 [*32*] *The wandering gypsey in a stormy night*

14–25 *not in MS. B²*
27 Which, that level, alone,
28 And, come, length,
{C
29 {clustering elms,
31b–35a *not in MS. B²*

14/15 The inserted line is in pencil, with the deleting stroke and correction in ink.
20 The line number is on the facing 2v.
20–21 The number 32 at the bottom of the facing page shows that l. 21 was added before the numbering. The initial correction in l. 20 matches l. 21 in ink color and is clearly related to the interlining.
26 Once l. 21 was added, the speaker was on the ground. The line under "my steps" was probably drawn to note the inconsistency of his walking; a correction was then made.
32 The line number is on the facing 2v.

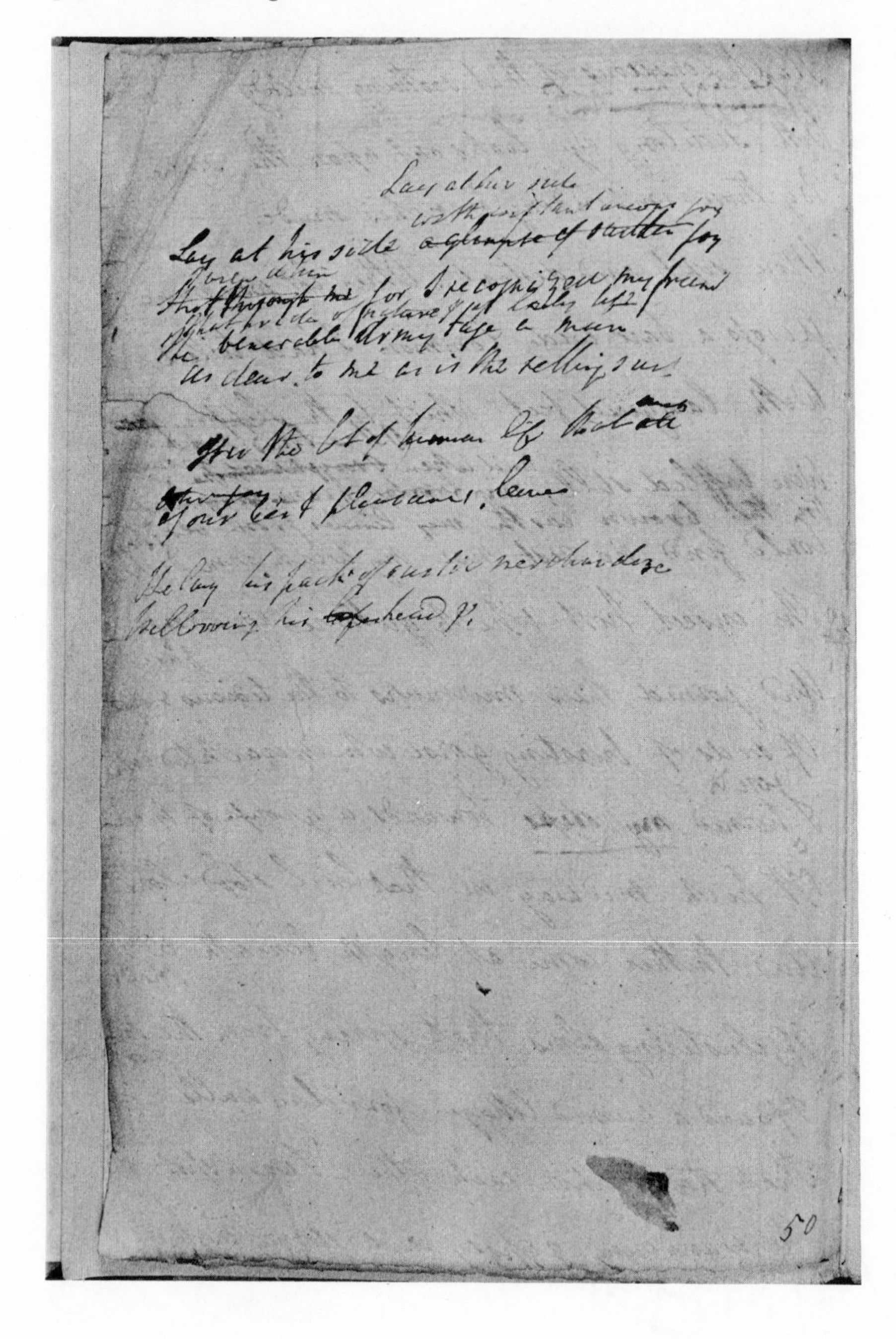

Lay at her side

Lay at his side a glimpse of ... joy

that brought me for I recognized my friend

the venerable Armytage a man

As dear to me as is the setting sun.

... the lot of human life ...

your best pleasures. Leave

He lay his pack of rustic merchandize

Pillowing his forehead ?

50

[3^{v}]

[D, 35–39, 44–45]

Lay at his side
with instantaneous joy
Lay at his side ~~a glimpse of sudden~~ joy
I view'd him
~~Shot through me~~ for I recognized my friend
That pride of nature & of lowly life
The venerable Armytage, a man
As dear to me as is the setting sun

[?much/ ?most]
It is the lot of human lif that ~~all~~
~~[?Other] joy,~~
Of our best pleasures, leave

He lay his pack of rustic merchandize
Pillowing his [?~~lifes~~] head &.

This draft, for insertion on 4^{r} after l. 37, is toward a shortened account of the Pedlar, who is now named Armytage; as such, it probably dates from 1799. A later draft is on 26^{v}.

The number 50, visible at the bottom right of the photograph, refers to the text on 4^{r}.

(4)

Would pass it with his moveables to house
On the open plain beneath the imperfect arch
Of a cold lime-kiln. ~~At~~ I looked around
~~Beside~~ And near the door I saw an aged Man
Stretched on a bench whose edge with short bright moss
an iron pointed staff
Was green and studded o'er with fungus flowers
~~Lay~~ at his side
~~An iron pointed staff lay at his side~~
Him had I seen the day before — alone
And in the middle of the public way
Standing to rest himself. His eyes were ~~turn~~
turned
Towards the setting sun while with that staff
Behind him fixed he propped a ~~long~~ long white pack
Which crossed his shoulders: wares for maids
who live
In lonely villages ~~or~~ straggling huts
I knew him — he was born of lowly race
On Cumbrian hills, and I have seen the tear
Stand in his luminous eye when he describ'd
The house in which his early ~~days were~~ youth was passed

33 *Would pass it with his moveables to house*
34 *On the open plain beneath the imperfect arch*
35 *Of a cold lime-kiln. ~~As~~ I looked around*
And near
36 *~~Beside~~ the door I saw an aged Man*
an iron-pointed staff
37 *Stretched on a bench whose edge with short bright*
moss
38 *Was green and studded o'er with fungus flowers*
Lay at his side
39 *~~An iron-pointed staff lay at his side~~*

40 *Him had I seen the day before —} alone*
41 *And in the middle of the public way*
42 *Standing to rest himself. His eyes were ~~turn'd~~*
turned
43 *Towards the setting sun while with that*
staff
44 *Behind him fixed he propped ^a ~~a~~long white*
pack
45 *Which crossed his shoulders: wares for maids*
who live
46 *In lonely villages* {*or* / [*?an*]} *straggling huts*
47 *I knew him —} he was born of lowly race*
48 *On Cumbrian hills, and I have seen the tear*
49 *Stand in his luminous eye when he described*
youth was
50 [*50*] *The house in which his early ~~days were~~ passed*

33–35a *not in MS. B²*
37–39 Stretched on a Bench
An iron-pointed staff lay at his side
40 before, —} alone,
41 in] on heath *del to* public way,
42 turned
43 sun,
44 fixed, a long
45 shoulders,
46 villages, or
47 —He
48 and] &
50 days *del to* youth w{as / ere} passed,

---

37 The draft on 3^v was intended to follow this line.
40–58a These lines were copied onto MS. D, 60^r, as Pedlar overflow.
47–49 What might look like deletions here are in fact random marks.
50 The line number is on the facing 3^v.

From that tenement

The many an evening to his distant home
Returned in solitude, and saw the hills
Grow larger in the darkness, alone
Beheld the stars come out above his head,
And travell'd through the wood, no comrade near,
To whom he might confess the things he saw.
So the foundations of his mind were laid.
In such communion, not from terror free,
While yet a child, and long before his time
He had perceived the presence and the power
Of greatness, and deep feelings had impress'd
Great objects on his mind with portraiture
And colour so distinct that on his mind
They lay like substances and almost seem'd
To haunt the bodily sense. He had received
A precious gift, for as he grew in years
With these impressions would he still compare
All shapes and forms that came into his mind
And being still unsatisfied with aught
Of dimmer character he thence attained
An active power to fasten images
Upon his thought, retouch'd till things
The liveliness of dreams. Nor did he fail

68

[D, 60r; E, 121–146]

[?same] bleak
From that [?~~low~~] tenement 1
He many an evening to his distant home 2
In solitude returning
~~Return'd in solitude, and~~ saw the hills 3
^ and beheld
Grow larger in the darkness, ~~all~~ alone 4
alone
Beheld the stars come out above his head, 5
forest no one
And travell'd through the ~~wood, no comrade~~ 6
near,
To whom he might confess the things he saw., 7
Thus
So the foundations of his mind were laid. 8
In such communion, not from terror free 9
,
While yet a child and long before his time 10
He had perceived the presence and the 11
power
Of Greatness, and deep feelings had impress'd 12
~~thought~~ a line &
Great objects ~~on his mind~~ with^portraiture 13
colour thought
And ~~outline~~ so distinct that on his ~~mind~~ 14
They lay like substances and almost 15
seem'd
To haunt the bodily sense.— He had 16
received
A precious gift, for as he grew in years 17
With these impressions would he still 18
compare
his [?ideal ?functions ? ?]
All shapes and forms that came into his 19
mind
[?]
And being still unsastified with aught 20
[?n]
In its int [?fluence] less intense
Of dimmer character he thence attained 21
An active power to fasten images 22
thought
Upon his ~~brain~~, retouch'd till [?they] 23
acquird
The liveliness of dreams. Nor did he fail 24

This draft, continuing onto 5v, is WW's first stage of Pedlar expansion. DW incorporated these lines into her copy of the second stage of the expansion—beginning on 6r—on the ten inserted leaves (see the headnote).

The mark in the upper left-hand corner matches a similar one in l. 58 on 5r indicating the place of insertion for these lines. The doubtful word and revisions in l. 1 are in pencil. Other uses of pencil on this page are as follows: l. 3, deleting line and revision; l. 6, deleting line and revision; l. 8, "Thus" revision; l. 10, the added comma; interlinings at ll. 18/19, 19/20, and 20/21.

The number 68, visible at the bottom right of the photograph, refers to the text on 5r.

And found I was no stranger to the spot (5)
I loved to hear him talk of former days
And tell how when a child ere yet of age
To be a Shepherd he had learned to read
His bible in a school that stood alone
Sole building on a mountains dreary edge
Far from the sight of city Spire, or sound
Of Minster clock. ‡ He from his native hills
Had wandered far. much ~~had he~~ seen of men
Their manners, their enjoyments & pursuits
Their passions & their feelings, chiefly those
Essential and eternal in the heart
Which 'mid the simpler forms of rural life
Exist more simple in their elements
And speak a plainer language. He possessed
No vulgar mind though he had passed his life
In this poor occupation, first assumed
From impulses of curious thought ~~& nor~~ from such

51 *And found I was no stranger to the spot*
52 *I loved to hear him talk of former days*
53 *And tell how when a child ere yet of age*
54 *To be a shepherd he had learned to read*
55 *His bible in a school that stood alone*
56 *Sole building on a mountains dreary edge*
57 *Far from the sight of city spire, or sound*
58 *Of Minster clock.* ⌶ *He from his native hills*
{H
{he did he see
59 ~~*Had*~~ *wandered far, much* ~~*had he seen*~~ *of men*
60 *Their manners, their enjoyments & pursuits*
61 *Their passions & their feelings, chiefly those*
62 *Essential and eternal in the heart*
63 *Which 'mid the simpler forms of rural*
life
64 *Exist more simple in their elements*
65 *And speak a plainer language.* X *He*
possessed
66 *No vulgar mind though he had passed his life*
67 *In this poor occupation, first assumed*
from such
68 [68] *From impulses of curious thought* ~~*& now*~~

---

52 I loved to hear him ~~tell how when a child~~
~~Ere yet of age to be a shepherd~~
talk of former days,
53 child,
55 alone,
58b–105a *omitted and DW writes:* The poem then goes on describing his [?ha]{ch}aracter & habits, & way of life, for above 200 lines

---

51–58a These lines were copied onto MS. D, 60r, as Pedlar overflow.
58 The mark here indicates the insertion point for the first stage of the Pedlar expansion (beginning on 4v) and thus also the second stage (beginning on 6r).
58b–65a These lines were copied onto MS. D, 65r, as Pedlar overflow.
59 The conclusion of the second-stage Pedlar expansion (on 15r) leads into l. 59, necessitating WW's deletions and revisions (in pencil) here.
65 The X is in pencil; it indicates where the third stage of the Pedlar expansion—the section about the mature man on the versos of 15–18—should be inserted.
68 The line number is on the facing 4v. In the original state of MS. B—before the leaves used for an augmented history of the Pedlar were added—the text continued from here onto the present 16r.

[illegible]

He sat and even in their fixed lineaments
He traced an ebbing and a flowing mind
Expression ever varying. In his heart
Love was not yet nor the pure joy of love
By sound diffused or by the breathing air
Or from the silent looks of happy things
Flowing, or from the universal face
Of earth & sky. . [illegible]
[illegible]

85

[D, 60^v, 61^v; E, 148–156, 175–180]

                [?ear] and [?eye]
                ⎧ear
Incessantly to turn his ⎩eye and eye 1
[?On] all things which the rolling seasons brought 2
  To feed such appetite nor this alone
                ⎧I
~~To feed such appetite~~^. ⎩*In caves forlorn* 3
  Sufficed but many an hour in^[?c]
And in the hollow depths of naked crags 4
He sat and even in their fix'd lineaments 5
He traced an ebbing and a flowing mind 6
Expression ever varying. In his heart 7
Love was not yet nor the pure joy of love 8
By sound diffused or by the breathing air 9
Or from the silent looks of happy things 10
Flowing, or from the universal face 11
Of earth & sky . . tuned by Nature 12
to sympathy with man 13

The correction in the first line—"[?ear] and [?eye]"—was made first in pencil, then overwritten in ink; faint traces of pencil underlie the l. 3 revision "nor this alone" and the l. 4 correction "Sufficed but many an hour."

12–13 WW's addition is in a lighter ink color; these lines (and a later draft on 16^v, ll. 8–10) contribute to E, 320–322 (D, 65^v).

The number 85, visible at the bottom of the photograph, refers to the text on 16^r, which faced 5^v before the insertion of ten leaves.

From that bleak tenement
He many an evening to his distant home
In solitude returning saw the hills
Grow larger in the darkness all alone
Beheld the stars come out above his head
And travelled through the wood, no comrade
To whom he might confess the things he
near he
saw.
So the foundations of his mind were laid.
In such communion not from terror free
While yet a child, and long before his time
He had perceived the presence & the power
Of greatness, and deep feelings had impressed
Great objects on his mind, with portraiture
And colour so distinct
They lay like substances, & almost seemed
To haunt the bodily sense. He had received
A precious gift for as he grew in years
With these impressions would he still compare

[D, 60r; E, 121–139]

From that bleak tenement	1
He many an evening to his distant home	2
In solitude returning saw the hills	3
Grow larger in the darkness all alone	4
Beheld the stars come out above his head	5
And travelled through the wood, no comrade	6
near	
To whom he might confess the things he	7
saw.	
So the foundations of his mind were laid.	8
In such communion not from terror free	9
While yet a child; and long before his	10
time	
He had perceived the presence & the power	11
~~*of jo*~~	
Of greatness, and deep feelings had impressed	12
Great objects on his mind, with portrai=	13
=ture	
And colour so distinct	14
They lay like substances, & almost seemed	15
To haunt the bodily sense. He had received	16
A precious gift for as he grew in years	17
With these impressions would he still compare	18

This page begins the second stage of the Pedlar expansion with DW's recopying of the first stage (4v and 5v) onto this first recto of the inserted leaves.

1 The final letter runs off the edge, but traces of it survive on 7r.

11/12 Deletion by partial erasure or smudging.

7

All ~~shapes~~ [his] ideal stores, his shapes, & forms
And being still unsatisfied with aught
Of dimmer character, he thence attained
An <u>active</u> power to fasten images
Upon his brain, & on their pictured lines
Intensely brooded, ~~&~~ even till they ~~attained~~ [acquired]
The liveliness of dreams. Nor did he fail
While yet a child, with a child's eagerness
Incessantly to turn his ear & eye
On all things which the rolling seasons [brought]
To feed such appetite; Nor this alone
Appeased his yearning. In the after day
Of boyhood, many an hour in caves forlorn
And in the hollow depths of naked crags
He sate, and even in their fixed lineaments
Or from the power of a peculiar eye
Or by creative feeling overborne
Or by predominance of thought oppressed
Even in their fixed and steady lineaments.

[D, 60v; E, 140–154]

his
All ~~shapes~~ ideal stores, his shapes, & forms 1
[20] *And being still unsatisfied with aught* 2
Of dimmer character, he thence attained 3
An active power to fasten images 4
Upon his brain, & on their pictured lines 5
acquired
Intensely brooded, ~~ti~~ even till they ~~attained~~ 6
The liveliness of dreams. Nor did he fail 7
While yet a child, with a child's eagerness 8
Incessantly to turn his ear & eye 9
On all things which the rolling seasons 10
brought
To feed such appetite; Nor this alone 11
Appeased his yearning. In the after day 12
Of boyhood, many an hour in caves forlorn 13
And in the hollow depths of naked crags 14
He sate, and even in their fixed lineaments 15
r }
O [*?f*] } *from the power of a peculiar eye* 16
Or by creative feeling overborne 17
f }
Or by predominance o [?] } *thought oppressed* 18
Even in their fixed and steady lineaments 19

---

2 The number 20, on the facing 6v, is in pencil. The second stage of the Pedlar expansion is numbered in twenties throughout.
3 The large comma after "character" may have started as an "s."

He traced an ebbing and a flowing mind
Expression ever-varying within his heart
here stop
Love was not yet, nor the pure joy of love
By sound diffused or by the breathing air
Or by the silent looks of happy things
Or flowing from the universal face
Of earth and sky. But he had felt the power
Of nature, & already was prepared
By his intense conceptions to receive
Deeply, the lesson deep of love, which he
Whom Nature, by whatever means, has taught
To feel intensely cannot but receive

year he had been
Ere his ninth ~~summer he was~~ sent abroad
To tend his father's sheep. Such was his task
Thenceforward ~~till~~ the later day of youth
Oh then what soul was his when on the tops
Of the high mountains he beheld the sun

[D, 61^r, 61^v; E, 155–156, 175–191]

He traced an ebbing and a flowing mind 1
Within
Expression ever-varying| ~~*In*~~ *his heart* 2
╳here stop
[*40*] *Love was not yet, nor the pure joy of love* 3
By sound diffused or by the breathing air 4
Or by the silent looks of happy things 5
Or flowing from the universal face 6
Of earth and sky. But he had felt the 7
power
Of nature, & already was prepared 8
By his intense conceptions to receive 9
Deeply, the lesson deep of love, which he 10
{,
Whom Nature {(*by whatever means, has* 11
taught
To feel intensely cannot but receive 12
year he had been
Ere his ninth ~~*summer he was*~~ *sent* 13
abroad
To tend his father's sheep. such was his 14
task
{ill
Thenceforward t{*o the later day of youth* 15
Oh! then what soul was his! when on 16
the tops
{*Of*
{[?~~*In*~~] *the high mountains he beheld the sun* 17

---

2 The vertical stroke is in ink, the X in pencil. WW's "here stop" is related to a rearrangement of passages shown by his copying instruction on the facing 7^v:

Thus informed
He had small need of books

The passage on 11^r in MS. B was thus moved to this place, and DW copied it here in MS. D, 61^r.

3 The penciled number is on the facing 7^v; the numbering precedes the rearrangement of passages.

11 The opening parenthesis is partially erased.

17 "[?In]" is partially erased.

Rise up and bathe the world in light. ⑨
He looked.
The Ocean and the earth beneath him lay
In gladness and deep joy. The clouds were touched
did he
And in their silent faces ~~he beheld~~ read
Unutterable love. Sound needed none
Nor any voice of joy: his spirit drank
The spectacle. Sensation, soul and form
All melted into him. They swallowed up
His animal being. In them did he live
And by them did he live. They were his life
mind
In such a deep of ~~soul~~. In such high hour
Of visitation from the living God
He did not feel the God; he felt his works;
Thought was not. In enjoyment it ex=
=pired
Such hour by prayer or praise was unprofaned
He neither prayed, nor offered thanks or praise
His mind was a thanksgiving to the power
That made him. It was blessedness & love.
A Shepherd on the lonely mountain tops

[D, 61v; E, 192–209]

Rise up and bathe the world in light. 1
He looked,
The Ocean and the earth beneath him lay 2
In gladness and deep joy. The clouds were 3
touched
did he
And in their silent faces ~~he beheld~~ read 4
Unutterable love. Sound needed none 5
[60] *Nor any voice of joy: his spirit drank* 6
e.} {S
The spectacl } {sensation, soul and form 7
All melted into him. They swallowed up 8
His animal being. In them did he live 9
And by them did he live. They were his 10
life
mind
{In such access of ~~soul,~~
{__________________ In such high hour 11
Of visitation from the living God 12
He did not feel the God: he felt his works 13
Thought was not. In enjoyment it ex= 14
=pired
Such hour by prayer or praise was unprofaned 15
He neither prayed, nor offered thanks or 16
praise
His mind was a thanksgiving to the power 17
That made him. It was blessedness & love. 18
A Shepherd on the lonely mountain tops 19

---

6 The penciled number is on the facing 8v.

11 The horizontal line may indicate a place where an addition was necessary. The position of the 80 on 9v opposite l. 8 on 10r suggests that the original half-line was not included in the numbering.

(10)

Such intercourse was his & in this sort
Was his existence oftentimes possessed
Oh then how beautiful, how bright appeared
The written promise; he had early learned
To reverence the volume which displays
The mystery, the life which cannot die
But in the mountains did he feel his faith
There did he see the writing—All things there
Looked immortality, revolving life
And greatness still revolving, infinite;
~~Then~~ there littleness was not, the least of things
Seemed infinite, and there his spirit shaped
Her prospects ~~[illegible]~~ nor did he believe—he saw
What wonder if his being ~~thus~~ became
Sublime and comprehensive, Low desires
Low thoughts had there no place, yet was his heart
Lowly; for he was meek in gratitude
Oft as he called to mind these ecstasies
And whence they flowed, & from them he acquired
~~Wisdom~~

[D, 62^{r}; E, 210–228]

Such intercourse was his & in this sort 1
Was his existence often times possessed 2
Ah! then how beautiful, how bright appeared 3
The written promise; he had early learned 4
To reverence the volume which displays 5
The mystery, the life which cannot die 6
But in the mountains did he feel his faith 7
[*80*] *There did he see the writing—All things there* 8
Looked immortality, revolving life 9
And greatness still revolving, infinite; 10
There
~~Then~~ ^ *littleness was not, the least of things* 11
Seemed infinite, and there his spirit shaped 12
nor
Her prospects {[?~~nor~~] / [?]} ^ {*d* / [?]}*id he believe—he saw* 13
What wonder if his being th{*us* / *en*} *became* 14
com
Sublime and apprehensive; Low desires 15
Low thoughts had there no place, yet was 16
his heart
Lowly; for he was meek in gratitude 17
Oft as he called to mind these ecstacies 18
And whence they flowed, & from them he 19
acquired
~~Wisdom~~ 20

---

8 The penciled 80 is on the facing 9^{v}. The number is 21 lines on from the number 60; possibly the original half-line on 9^{r} (l. 11) was not counted.
15 DW may have left alternate readings as a query for her brother.

Few books were his yet to the neighbouring town
He [illegible] what his earnings would afford
[illegible]
[illegible]
While at the stall he read. Among the
files
He gazed upon that mighty orb of song
The divine Milton. Other lore

Thus passed the time yet to the neigh-
bouring town
He often went with what small over-
plus
His earnings might supply & brought
away
The book which most had
tempted his desires
While at the stall he read. Among the
files
He gazed upon that mighty orb of song
The divine Milton

[D, 62^v; E, 234–240]

Few books were his yet to the neighbouring town 1
went with
He ~~carried~~ what his earnings would afford 2
From time to time and duly brought away
~~And bought such books~~ as tempted his desire 3
The volume which
While at the stall he read. Among the 4
hills
He gazed upon that mighty orb of song 5
The divine Milton. Other lore 6

Thus passed the time yet to the neigh- 7
-bouring town
He often went with what small over- 8
-plus
His earnings might supply & brought 9
away
book
The ~~volume~~, which [?~~firs~~] most had 10
tempted his desires
While at the stall he read. Among the 11
hills
He gazed upon that mighty orb of song 12
M
The divine {*milton* 13

WW's drafts and DW's copy are associated with the movement of the section beginning "Small need had he of books" on 11^r back to 8^r. After this rearrangement, the lines copied by DW form a transition between l. 5 on 11^r and l. 12 on 12^r. The line number 120 facing l. 13 on 12^r suggests that entry of this passage on 10^v follows the numbering; see the note to l. 13 on 12^r.

(11)

Wisdom which works ~~by~~ through patience; thence he learn'd
In many a calmer hour of sober thought
To look on nature with an humble heart
Self-question'd where it did not understand
And with a superstitious eye of love. X
~~He had~~ Small need, had he, of books; for many a tale
Traditionary round the mountains hung
And many a legend peopling the dark woods
Nourished Imagination in her growth,
And gave the mind that apprehensive power
By which she is made quick to recog-
:nize
The moral properties & scope of things —
Yet greedily he read & read again
Whate'er the rustic Vicar's shelf supplied
The life & death of Martyrs who sus-
=tained
Intolerable pangs, & here & there
A straggling volume torn & incomplete
Which left half-told the preternatural
tale

[D, 62^v, 61^r, E, 229–233, 157–169]

through
Wisdom which works ~~by~~^ patience; thence he learn'd 1
In many a calmer hour of sober thought 2
To look on nature with an humble heart 3
Self-question'd where it did not understand 4
And with a superstitious eye of love. X— 5
{S had he
~~He had~~ {*small need^ of books; for many a tale* 6
o}
Traditionary round the mu}untains hung 7
And many a legend peopling the dark woods 8
Nourished Imagination in her growth 9
And gave the mind that apprehensive power 10
By which she is made quick to recog-nize 11
The moral properties & scope of things 12
Yet greedily he read & read again 13
{V
Whate'er the rustic {vicar's shelf supplied 14
The life & death of Martyrs who sus-tained 15
Intolerable pangs, & here & there 16
A straggling volume torn & incomplete 17
Which left half told the preternatural tale 18

---

5 The X probably indicates the insertion point for the new lines on 10^v, needed after the passage from 11^r, l. 6, to 12^r, l. 11, had been transferred to 8^r, l. 2.

Romance of giants chronicle of fiends.
Profuse in garniture of wooden cuts
Strange & uncouth, dire faces, figures dire
Sharp-kneed, sharp elbowed & lean-ankled too
With long & ghostly shanks forms which once seen
Could never be forgotten. Things though low
Though low and humble not to be despised
By such as have observed the curious links
With which the perishable hours of life
Are bound together and the world of thought
Exists and is sustained. Within his store
The annual savings of a toilsome life
The Schoolmaster supplied; books that explain
The purer elements of truth involv'd
In lines and numbers, and by charm severe
Especially perceived where Nature droops
And feeling is suppress'd preserve the mind
Busy in solitude and poverty.
And thus employed he many a time o'erlooked
The listless hours when in the hollow vale
Hollow and green he lay on the green turf

[D, 61r, 62v; E, 170–175, 240–250]

Romance of giants chronicle of fiends 1
Profuse in garniture of wooden cuts 2
Strange & uncouth, dire faces, figures dire 3
ancled
Sharp kneed, sharp-elbowed & lean-ankled 4
too
With long & ghostly shanks forms which 5
once seen
Could never be forgotten. Things though 6
low ~~mean~~
low
Though ~~mean~~ and humble not to be despised 7
observed
By such as have ~~remarked~~ the curious links 8
Wi}
By {th which the perishable hours of life 9
Are bound together and the world of thought 10
Exists and is sustained. X ~~A different store~~ 11
The annual savings of a toilsome life 12
[*120*] The Schoolmaster supplied, books that explain 13
The purer elements of truth involv'd 14
In lines and numbers and by charm 15
severe
Especially perceived where Nature droops 16
And feeling is suppress'd preserve the 17
mind
Busy, in solitude and poverty. 18
{he o'erlook'd
And thus employed {[?] many a time forgot 19
listless {W
The creeping hours {when in the hollow 20
vale
Hollow and green he lay on the green 21
turf

4 A bad ink stain required the addition of "ancled."
11 The X indicates either the stopping place for the passage continuing from the previous page and transferred to 8r or the insertion point for new lines from 10v, or perhaps both.
13 The penciled number is on the facing 11v. There is no number 100 in this Pedlar expansion; the 120 comes 42 lines after the number 80, which is beside l. 8 on 10r. Miscounting is a possible but not entirely satisfactory explanation. If the transfer of the passage from 11r and 12r to 8r and the insertion of lines on 10v preceded the numbering, the number would be 8 off instead of 2.

[D, 63^r]

He trembled at her look, and reverenced then 12
her
When with ~~her~~ a moral beautity in her 13
face
She took him up and led him through 14
the stars.

Or of the day of vengeanc when the sea 1
Rose like a giant from his sleep and smote 2
{of
The hills, and when the firmament {h heav 3
Rained darkness which the race of men 4
beheld
~~And had no hope.~~ 5
Yea all the men that lived & had no hope

Yet not the less he found 6
In cold relation and the liflessness 7
Of truth by oversubtlety dislog'd 8
From grandeur & from love an idle toy 9
The dullest of all toys He saw in truth 10
A holy spirit & a breathing soul 11

What seems to be the earlier of these two drafts is the five-line passage beginning below the middle of the page; it does not appear in later texts. The second draft—"Yet not the less he found"—is in darker ink and runs over from the bottom of the page to the top. Certainly the second draft—and probably the first—were intended for insertion on 13^r.

A penciled 140 at the right edge near the middle of the page refers to the text on 13^r.

(13)

In lonesome idleness. What could he do?
Nature was at his heart, and he perceived
Though yet he knew not how, a wasting power
In all things which from her glad influence
Might tend to wean him. Therefore with her hues
Her forms, and with the spirit of her forms
He clothed the nakedness of austere truth.
While yet he linger'd in the elements
Of science, and among her simplest laws,
His triangles they were the stars of heaven,
The silent stars; his altitudes the crag
Which is the eagle's birth-place; or some peak
Familiar with forgotten years, which shews
Inscrib'd, as with the silence of the thought,
Upon its bleak and visionary sides,
The history of many a winter storm,
Or obscure records of the path of fire.
Yet with these lonesome sciences he still
Continued to amuse the heavier hours
Of solitude. And solitary thought
But now, before his twentieth year was pass'd,
Accumulated feelings press'd his heart
With an encreasing weight; he was o'erpower'd

[D, 63r, 63v; E, 251–271]

In lonesome idleness. What could he do? 1
Nature was at his heart, and he perceived 2
?}
Though yet he knew not how, a wasting } power 3
~~glad~~
{~~sweet~~
In all things which from her {[?] influence 4
tend to
Might^wean him, therefore, with her hues 5
~~And with her~~ 6
Her forms and with the spirit of her forms 7
He cloathed the nakedness of austere truth.
?}
~~He cloathed the nakedness of austere } truth~~ 8
While yet he linger'd in the elements 9
Of science, and among her simplest laws, 10
His triangles they were the stars of heaven, 11
The silent stars: his altitudes the crag 12
[*140*] Which is the eagle's birth-place; or some peak 13
Familiar with forgotten years, which shews, 14
Inscrib'd as with the silence of the thought, 15
Upon its bleak and visionary sides, 16
The history of many a winter storm, 17
Or obscure records of the path of fire. 18
Yet with these lonesome sciences; he still 19
Contrived to amuse the heavier hour 20
Of solitude X and solitary thought. 21
But now, before his twentieth years was passd
Accumulated feelings press'd his heart 22
With an encreasing weight; he was 23
oerpowerd

WW's question marks after words in ll. 3 and 8 possibly suggest his uncertainty about them.
11 There is an erasure of a letter or mark of punctuation after "triangles."
13 The number 140 is penciled on the facing 12v.
21 The X indicates the point of insertion for the draft "Yet not the less he found" (ll. 6–14) on 12v. The other draft on 12v was perhaps intended to follow (or replace) l. 18, although WW made no insertion mark.

Than in his earliest season did he love
The tempests uproar
By Nature and his spirit was on fire
With restless thoughts – his eye became disturb'd
And many a time he wish'd the winds might rage
When they were silent. far more fondly now
Than in his earliest season did he love
Tempestuous nights, the uproar and the sounds
That live in darkness: from his intellect
And from the stillness of abstracted thought
He sought repose, in vain – in vain

[D, 63v]

fondly
for more ~~deeply~~ now 1
Than in his earlier season did he love 2
The tempests uproar 3
B}
H} y Nature and his spirit was on fire 4
With restless thoughts—his eye became 5
disturb'd
n}
And may} y a time he wish'd the winds might 6
rage
When they were silent, far more fondly now 7
Than in his earlier season did he love 8
their voices & hear
Tempestuous nights the uproar and the 9
sounds
That live in darkness: from his intellect 10
And from the stillness of abstracted thought 11
He sought repose, in vain—in vain 12

This draft was to replace the deleted lines at the top of 14r.
4 The penciled number 160, visible in the photograph, probably refers to the text on 14r.

By nature, and his mind became disturbed
And many a time he wished the winds
When they were silent, ... his mystery
And from the stillness of abstracted thought
In vain he sought repose in vain he turned
To science for a cure. I have heard him say
That at this time he scanned the laws of light
Amid the roar of torrents where they send
From hollow clefts up to the clearer air
A cloud of mist which in the shining sun
Varies its rainbow hues. — but vainly thus
And vainly by all other means he strove
To mitigate the fever of his heart.

From nature & her overflowing soul
He had received so much, that all his thoughts
Were steeped in feeling. He was only then
Contented, when, with bliss ineffable
He felt the sentiment of being spread
O'er all that moves, & all that seemeth still,
O'er all, which lost beyond the reach of thought
And human knowledge, to the human eye
Invisible, yet liveth to the heart,
O'er all that leaps, & runs, & shouts, & sings
Or beats the gladsome air, o'er all that glides

[D, 63v]

By nature—and his mind became disturbd 1
And many a time he wish'd the winds might rage 2
When they were silent.} from his intellect 3
And from the stillness of abstracted thought
[*160*] In vain he sought repose in vain he turnd 4
To science for a cure, I have heard him say 5
That at this time he scann'd the laws of light 6
With a strange pleasure of disquietude
din
Amid the ~~sound~~ of torrents where they send 7
roar
From hollow clefts, up to the clearer air 8
A cloud of mist which in the shining sun 9
{but vainly thus
Varies its rainbow hues. — ~~In vain he strove~~ 10
180
And vainly by all other means he strove
his
To mitigate the fever of ~~the~~ heart 11
^
From nature & her overflowing soul 12
He had received so much, that all his thoughts 13
Were steeped in feeling. He was only then 14
Contented, when, with bliss ineffable 15
~~And wi~~
~~of gratitude~~
[~~? ? ? ?~~]
He felt the sentiment ^ of being, spread 16
O'er all that moves, & all that seemeth still, 17
O'er all, which lost beyond the reach of thought, 18
And human knowledge, to the human eye 19
Invisible, yet liveth to the heart; 20
Oer all that leaps, & runs, & shouts, & sings 21
{*or* {[*?all*] [?]
Or beats the gladsome air, { *that glides* 22

---

4 The 160 is in pencil on the facing 13v; the number 180—the last in this second stage of the Pedlar expansion—below l. 10 is also in pencil. Again, the numbering is a puzzle. Revision between the entry of 160 and that of 180 seems the most likely solution: the first draft written on 12v—"Or of the day" (ll. 1–5)—was counted in from the 140 facing 13r, making the 160 here accurate. Then WW added the second draft on 12v—"Yet not the less" (ll. 6–14)—and made the revision on 13v to replace the original lines at the top of 14r. The number 160 would then be superseded, but the 180 after l. 10 would be right.

9/10 The single word, "but," is in pencil.

12 The 19-line passage beginning in l. 12 and ending on 15r at l. 9 became part of *Prelude 1799* (II, 446–464).

15/16 The four illegible words and "of gratitude" are deleted in pencil.

16 The caret has been filled in with pencil and ink.

18 The comma after "thought" is smudged or partially erased.

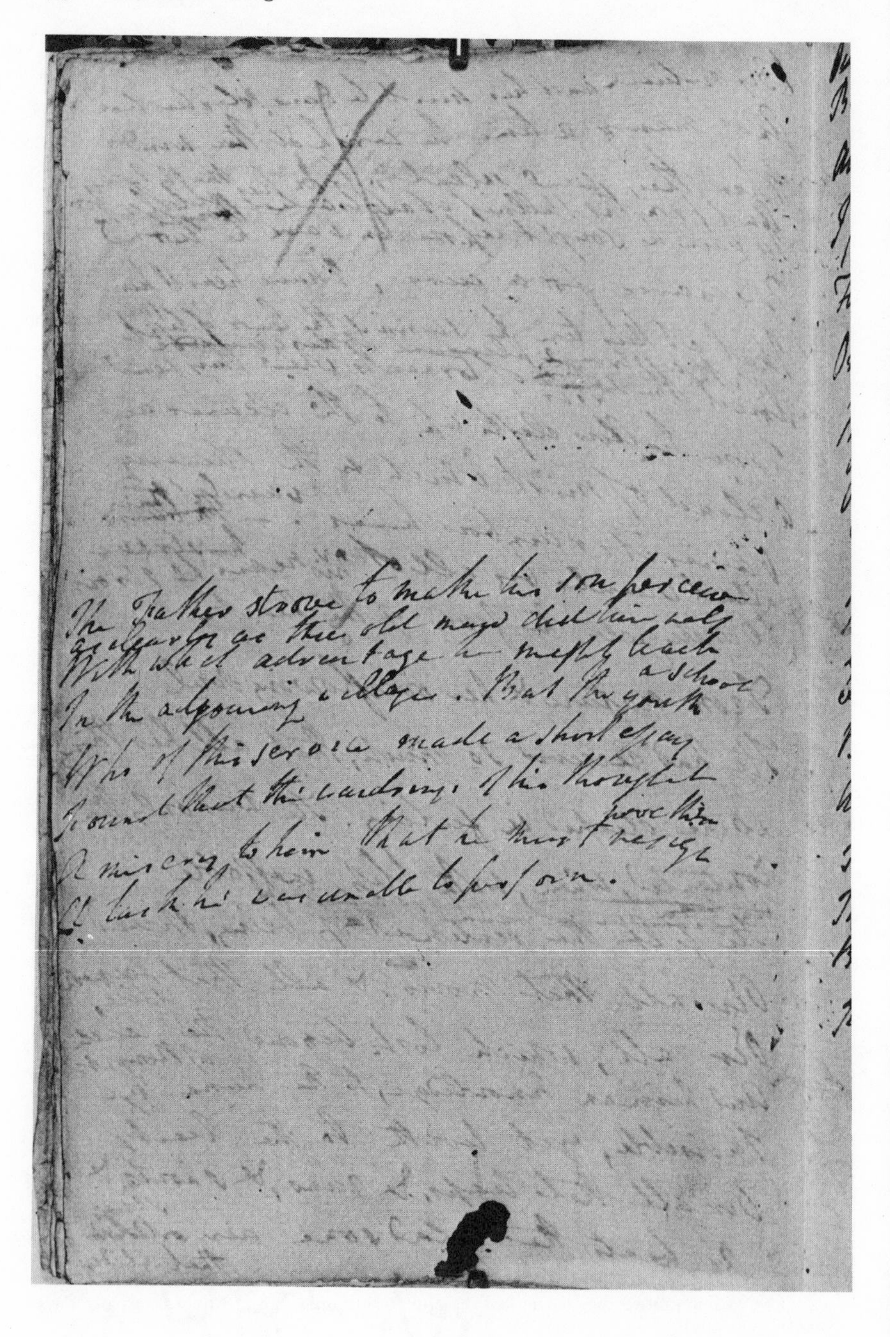
The Father strove to make his son perceive
As clearly as the old man did himself
With what advantage he might teach a school
In the adjoining village. that the youth
Who of this service made a short essay
Found that the wanderings of his thought were then
A misery to him, that he must resign
A task he was unable to perform.

[D, 64r; E, 279–285]

The Father strove to make his son perceive 1
As clearly as thee old man did himself
With what advantage he might teach 2
a school
In the adjoining village. But the youth 3
Who of this service made a short essay 4
Found that the wandrings of his thought 5
were then
A misery to him that he must resign 6
A task he was unable to perform. 7

This draft was intended for insertion on 15r below the horizontal line. Another version of these lines is on 1r.

~~In all that glides beneath the wave~~ (15)
Beneath the waves, yea in the wave itself
And mighty depth of waters. Wonder not
If such his transports were; for in all things
He saw one life & felt that it was joy.
One song they sang, & it was audible,
Most audible then, when the fleshly ear
~~[illegible]~~
O'ercome by grosser prelude of that strain
Forgot its functions, & slept undisturbed.
These things he had sustained in solitude
Even till his bodily strength began to yield
Beneath their weight. The mind within him burnt
And he resolved to quit his native hills.
He asked his fathers blessing, and assumed
This lowly occupation. The old man
Blessed him and prayed for him, yet with a heart
Forboding evil. From his native hills

[D, 64r, 65r; E, 294–299]

{~~O~~
{~~*o'er all that glides beneath the wave*~~ 1

{*ve,*
Beneath the wa{*y, yea in the wave itself* 2
And mighty depth of waters. Wonder not 3
If such his transports were; for in all 4
things
life
He saw one [?~~*soul*~~/?~~*mind*~~], *& felt that it was* 5
joy.
One song they sang, & it was audible, 6
Most audible, then, when, the fleshly ear 7
~~Amid the voice of breezes streams & [?wood]~~
Oer come by grosser prelude of that strain 8
Forgot its functions, & slept undisturb= 9
=ed.
These things he had sustained in 10
solitude
Even till his bodily strength began to 11
{~~yield~~
{sink yield
Beneath their weight. the mind within 12
him burnt
And he resolv'd to quit his native hills X∧/ 13

He asked his fathers blessing, and assumed 14
This lowly occupation, The old man 15
Bless'd him and prayed for him, yet 16
with a heart
Fr}
Forboding evil. H{om his native hills 17

---

13 The X is in ink traced over pencil. This mark and the horizontal line indicate where the draft on 14v should be placed.
17 Here ends the second-stage Pedlar expansion; the text then jumps back to 5r (l. 59) and continues from the bottom of 5r onto 16r.

In lonesome meditation Many a year
By curious thought he was content to toil
In this poor calling which he now pursued
From habit and necessity. He walked
Among the haunts of vulgar men
Unstained; the talisman of constant thought
And kind sensations in a gentle heart
Preserved him; every show of vice to him
Was a remembrancer of what he knew,
Or a fresh seed of wisdom, or produced
That tender interest which the virtuous feel
Among the wicked, which when truly felt
May bring the bad man nearer to the good,
But innocent of evil, cannot sink
The good man to the bad. Among the woods
A lone enthusiast & among the fields
In this way wandering, he had pass'd
The better portion of his time, & there
From day to day had his affections breathed
The wholesome air of nature; there he kept
In solitude, & solitary thought,
So pleasant were those comprehensive views
His mind in a just equipoize of love

[D, 65^{r}, E, 306–313]

these [? ?]
[?]
Many a year 1
Of did he toil
In lonesome meditation ~~and impelle'd~~ 2
live
By curious thought he was content to toil 3
In this poor ~~occupation~~ 4
calling which he now pursued
From habit and necessity. He walked 5
Among the haunts of vulgar men 6
Unstained; the talisman of constant thought 7
kind
And ~~pure~~ sensations in a gentle heart 8
vice
Preserv'd him; every shew of [?~~vice~~] to him 9
Was a remembrancer of what he knew, 10
Or a fresh seed of wisdom, or produced 11
the virtuous feel
That tender interest which ~~when truly~~ 12
~~felt~~
Among the wicked, which when truly felt 13
May bring the bad man nearer to the good, 14
But innocent of evil, cannot sink 15
The good man to the bad. *Among the woods,* 16
A lone enthusiast, & among the fields, 17
lived
itinerant ~~labour~~ in this labour
In this way-wandering business he had passed 18
obscure employment
The better portion of his time, & there 19
From day to day had his affections breathed 20
The wholesome air of nature; There 21
he kept
In solitude, & solitary thought, 22
So pleasant were those comprehen- 23
-sive views,
His mind in a just equipoize of love. 24

Here begins the third stage of the Pedlar expansion. The opening five-line draft is in darker ink; the text on this page originally began in l. 5 with "He walked," which was to be inserted at l. 70b on 16^{r}. After the addition of the opening five-line draft, this third-stage expansion was meant for insertion on 5^{r} at l. 65b.

(16)

Continued many a year & now pursued
From habit and necessity. His eye
Flashing poetic fire he would repeat
or ditty sweet and wild
The songs of Burns and as we trudged
Which he had [illegible] along
Together did we make the hollow grove
Ring with our transports though he was untaught
In the dead lore of schools undisciplined
Why should he grieve? He was a chosen son
He yet retained an ear which deeply felt
The voice of Nature in the obscure wind
The sounding mountain & the running stream
From deep analogies by him supplied
To every natural form, rock, fruit & flower
Even the loose stones that cover the high-way
He gave a moral life, he saw them feel
Or linked them to some feeling. In all shapes
He found a secret & mysterious soul
A fragrance & a spirit of strange meaning

69 *Continued many a year, & now pursued*
70 *From habit and necessity. His eye*
71 *Flashing poetic fire he would repeat*
or ditty sweet and wild
72 *The songs of Burns, and as we trudged*
along

Which h{e / [?is]} had fitted to the moor
land harp
[?the ?bare ?rock] and
73 *Together, did we make the hollow grove*
though
74 *Ring with our transports,^ he was untaught*
75 *In the dead lore of schools undisciplined*
76 *Why should he grieve? He was a chosen son*
~~In his old age~~
He yet retained
77 *~~To him was given~~ an ear which deeply ~~fe~~*
felt
78 *The voice of Nature in the obscure wind*
79 *The sounding mountain & the running*
stream
From deep analogies by thought supplied
~~Or by [? ? ? ? ?force]~~
or consciousness is not to be subdued
{*To*
80 {*In every natural form, rock, fruit, & flower*
81 *Even the loose stones that cover the high-*
-way
82 *He gave a moral life; he saw them feel*
83 *Or linked them to some feeling. In all*
shapes
84 *He found a secret & mysterious soul*
85 [*85*] *A fragrance & a spirit of strange meaning*

69–85 *not in MS. B*[2]

The text of the original 528-line *RC* continues onto 16^r from 5^r (l. 68), which preceded this page before the insertion of leaves on which the Pedlar expansion is written.

72–73 A revision of these lines is on 18^v.

73 What looks like a deleting line on the comma after "Together" is a mark showing through from 16^v.

74–103 This passage beginning "though he was untaught" was copied onto MS. D, 66^v–67^r, as Pedlar overflow; the lines eventually became part of *Prelude* (III, 82, 122–127, 141–147, 156–167).

77 The "fe" is partially erased.

85 The number is on 5^v, which once faced this page.

Serene it was unclouded by the cares
Of ordinary life, unvexed, unwarped
By partial bondage. In his steady course
No piteous revolutions had he felt,
No wild varieties of joy or grief.
Unoccupied by sorrow of its own
His heart lay open & by nature tuned
And constant disposition of his thoughts
To sympathy with man, he was alive
To all that was enjoyed where'er he went,
And all that was endured & in himself
Happy he had no pressure from within
Which made him turn aside from wretchedness
With coward fears. He could afford to suffer
With those whom he saw suffer. Hence it was
That in our best experience he was rich
And in the wisdom of our daily life
He had observed the progress and decay
Of many minds, of minds & bodies too
The history of many families
And how they prospered, how they were o'erthrown
By passion or mischance or such misrule
Among and the earth

[D, 65^v; E, 314–338]

and [?~~strong~~ ?pure] had been
[? ? ?]
Serene it was, unclouded by the cares 1
Of ordinary life, unvexed, unwarped 2
By partial bondage; In his steady course 3
No piteous revolutions had he felt, 4
No wild varieties of joy or grief. 5
~~Simple and uniform were all his days.~~
Unoccupied by sorrow of its own ~~his~~ 6
heart
~~*Lay open & by nature*~~ 7
His heart lay open; & by nature tuned 8
And constant disposition of his thoughts 9
To sympathy with man, he was alive 10
To all that was enjoyed where'er he went, 11
And all that was endured, & in himself 12
Happy and quiet in his chearfulness
Happy, he had no pressure from with 13
He had no painful
=in,
aside
Which made him turn ~~away~~ from wretched= 14
=ness
{H
With coward fears. {he could afford to 15
suffer
With those whom he saw suffer. Hence 16
it was
~~that [?als]~~
~~That in his various rounds he had~~
That not alone in stores which to its self,
The deep and solitary mind [?supplies]
That in our best experience he was rich, 17
As in the wisdom
The home-felt wisdom of our daily life 18
In his various roun
Hd had observd the progress and 19
decay
of minds & bodies too
Of many ~~fam~~ minds, ~~and many families~~ 20
The history of many families
And how they prosper'd, how they lived 21
in peace
And happiness and how they were 22
oerthrown
By passion or mischance or such misrule 23
~~Of government~~ 24
Among and masters of 25
the earth

The third-stage expansion of the Pedlar continues from 15^v.
1 The three illegible words above this line are in pencil.
5/6 Deleted in pencil (an illegible overwriting in pencil may have preceded the deletion). The numbers visible at the bottom right of the photograph refer to the text on 17^r.

(17) 8

Though poor in outward shew he was most rich
He had a world about him—'twas his own
He made it—for it only lived to him
And to the God who looked into his mind
Such sympathies would often bear him far
In outward gesture, & in visible look,
Beyond the common seeming of mankind
Some called it madness—such it might have been
But that he had an eye which evermore
Looked deep into the shades of difference
As they lie hid in all exterior forms
Near or remote, minute or vast, an eye
~~And by an unrelenting agency~~
~~Did bind his feelings even as in a chain~~
~~Which found no surface where its power might sleep~~
~~Which spake perpetual logic to his soul~~
Which from a stone, a tree, a withered leaf
To the broad ocean, & the azure heavens
Spangled with kindred multitudes of stars

99
~~104~~

86 *Though poor in outward shew he was most*
rich
87 *He had a world about him—'twas his own*
88 *He made it—for it only lived to him*
89 *And to the God who looked into his mind*
90 *Such sympathies would often bear him far*
91 *In outward gesture, & in visible look,*
92 *Beyond the common seeming of mankind*
93 *Some called it madness—such it might have*
been
94 *But that he had an eye which evermore*
95 *Looked deep into the shades of difference*
96 *As they lie h[?]/i d in all exterior forms*
Near or remote, minute or vast, an eye
~~*And by an unrelenting agency*~~
~~*Did bind his feelings even as in a chain*~~
Which found no surface where its power
might sleep
Which spake perpetual logic to his soul
97 *Which from a stone, a tree, a withered*
leaf
98 *To the broad ocean, & the azure heavens*
99 [99 / ~~101~~] *Spangled with kindred multitudes of*
stars

86–99 *not in MS.B*[2]

86–99 These lines were copied onto MS. D, 67^r, as Pedlar overflow.
99 The numbers are on the facing 16^v. DW made a copying error in the unnumbered lines on this page; they are correctly repeated on 18^r. She noticed her error in two stages, the first before the numbering and the second after it; this accounts for the deletion of 101 and insertion of 99. WW's inserted line after l. 96 is not included in DW's numbering.

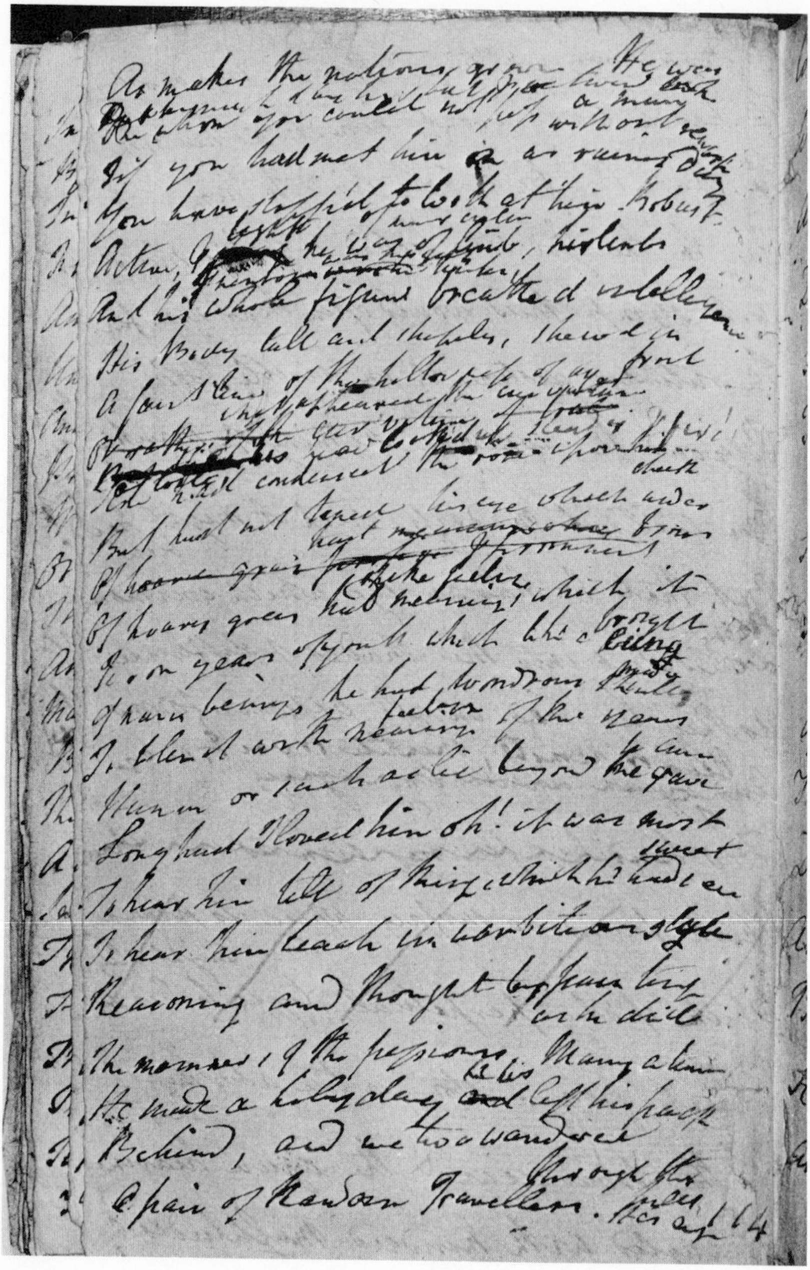

[D, 66r; E, 339, 363–374, 51–54]

As makes the nations groan He was 1
a man
Dis
[?] tinguishd by his [?] & active look
One whom you could not pass without remark 2
I on
if you had met him [?in] a rainy day 3
You have stopp'd to look at him. Robust 4
light of [?manner ?calm]
Active, & [?~~strong~~] he was of limb, his limbs 5
was his gait
& nervous ~~were his~~ limbs,
And his whole figure breathed intelligence 6
His Body tall and shapely, shewed in 7
front
A faint line of the hollowness of age 8
what appeared the curvature
~~Or rather, of the curvature of toil~~ 9
of his
~~But [?still]~~ [?his] head look'd up steady & fixe'd
Of toil,
Time had condensed the rose upon his 10
cheek
But had not tamed his eye which under 11
brows
~~had meanings which~~
~~Of hoary gray profuse & prominent~~ 12
spake feelings
Of hoary gray had meanings which it 13
brought
being
From years of youth which like a [?being] 14
made
Of many beings he had wondrous skill 15
feelings
To blend with meanings of the years 16
to come
Human or such as lie beyond the grave 17
Long had I loved him oh! it was most 18
sweet
To hear him tell of things which he had seen 19
style
To hear him teach in unambitious [?] 20
Reasoning and thought by painting 21
as he did
The manners & the passions. Many a time 22
[?he ?]
He made a holyday ~~and~~ left his pack 23
Behind, and we two wandered 24
through the
hills,
A pair of Random Travellers. His eye 25

The third-stage expansion of the Pedlar's history continues from 16v and ends—with the exception of some revisions to it on 18r and 18v—on this page. The final line here leads into l. 71 on 16r. The number 114, visible at the bottom right of the photograph, refers to the text on 18r.

(18)

Could find no surface where its power might
sleep
Which spake perpetual logic to his soul,
And by an unrelenting agency
Of terror and resources wh. this great, his
lights
Did bind his feelings even as in a chain.
So was he framed ~~though humble & obscure~~
~~Had been his lot.~~ ~~Stretched~~
Now on the Bench he
lay
else
Stretched at his ~~length~~, & with that weary
load
Pillowed his head - I guess he had no ~~thou~~
thought
Of his way-wandering life. His eyes were shut
The shadows of the breezy elms above
Dappled his face. With thirsty heat op=
pressed
At length I hailed him glad to see his hat
Bedewed with water-drops, as if the brim
Had newly scooped a running stream. He
rose
And, pointing to a sun-flower bade me
climb

100 *Could find no surface where its power might*
sleep
101 *Which spake perpetual logic to his soul,*
102 *And by an unrelenting agency*
Active and nervous was his gait, his
limbs
103 *Did bind his feelings even as in a chain.*
.
104 *So was he framed* } ~~*though humble & obscure*~~
105 ~~*Had been his lot*~~. ~~*Stretch*~~
Now on the Bench he
lay
ease
106 *Stretched at his length, & with that weary*
load
107 *Pillowed his head—I guess he had no* ~~*thou*~~
thought
108 *Of his way-wandering life. His eyes were shut*
109 *The shadows of the breezy elms above*
110 *Dappled his face. With thirsty heat op-*
pressed
111 *At length I hailed him glad to see his hat*
112 *Bedewed with water-drops, as if the brim*
. {He
113 *Had newly scooped a running stream* } {[?]
rose
114 [*114*] *And, pointing to a sun-flower bade me*
climb

100–105a *not in MS. B²*
105 *MS. B² resumes with half-line* Now on the Bench he lay,
106 ease,
107 thought
108 shut,
111 him,
113 stream. He rose,
114 And,] And sun-flower,

100–103 These lines were copied onto MS. D, 67ʳ, as Pedlar overflow.
102/103 The interlining is a revision of l. 5 on the facing 17ᵛ.
114 The number is on 17ᵛ.

His body tall and shapely shewed in front
A faint line of the hollowness of age
Or rather what appeared the curvature
Of toil, his head looked up steady and fair
Age had compressed the rose upon his cheek
Into a narrower circle of deep red

‡ and in that plot

Or many a ditty ~~wild~~ [sweet]

Which ~~had~~ he had fitted to the moorland [harp.]
His own sweet verses, and as we trudged
Together [did we make the] ~~the hollow rock and~~ hill [yell] [along] as given to

[18^{v}]

[66^{r}, 66^{v}; E, 367–368]

His body tall and shapely shewed in front 1
A faint line of the hollowness of age 2
Or rather what appeared the curvature 3
Of toil, his head look'd up steady and fixed 4
Age had compress'd the rose upon his cheek 5
Into a narrower circle of deep red. 6
    ⌿ and in that plot sweet 7
    and in that
    or many a ditty ~~wild~~ 8
    ^
    { ~~he~~
Which { [?had] he had fitted to the moorland harp 9
His own sweet verse and as we trudged along 10
    did we make the
Together ~~the [?bear] rock and~~ hollow grove 11

1–6 These lines are a revision of ll. 7–10 on 17^{v}.
7 The mark matches a similar one in l. 117 on 19^{r}, indicating insertion of these words.
8 The caret and the words "and in that" are in pencil.
8–11 These lines are a revision of ll. 72–73 on 16^{r}.

19

The wall where that same gaudy Flower
Looked out upon the road. It was a plot
Of garden-ground, now wild to matted weeds
Marked with the steps of those whose as when such as when they pass
The goose-berry trees that shot in long
Or currents hanging from them leafless stems
In scanty strings had tempted to o'er leap
The broken wall. Within that cheerless spot
Where two tall hedgerows of thick willow boughs
Joined in a damp cold nook I found a well
Half choaked
I slaked my thirst & to the shady bench
Returned & while I stood unbonneted
To catch the current of the breezy air
The old man said "I see around me
Things which you cannot see. We die my friend
Nor we alone but that which each man loved

131

115 *The wall where that same gaudy flower*
116 *Looked out upon the road. It was a plot*
117 *Of garden-ground, now wild,*[*its matted weeds*
such as when those
~~those~~ m
118 *Marked with the steps of* {[*?them*] *who* ^ *as they pass*
119 *The goose berry trees that shot in long*
hanging from their s
120 *Or currants* ~~*shewing on a*~~ *leafless stem*
In
121 ~~*Their*~~ *scanty strings had tempted to o'er leap*
122 *The broken wall. Within that cheerless spot*
123 *Where two tall hedgerows of thick willow boughs*
124 *Joined in a damp cold nook I found a well*
125 *Half choaked*
126 *I slaked my thirst & to the shady bench*
127 *Returned & while I stood unbonneted*
128 *To catch the current of the breezy air*
129 *The old man said "I see around me*
130 *Things which you cannot see. We die my Friend*
each
131 *Nor we alone but that which* ^ *man loved*

131

---

115 *no gap*
117 Of garden ground, now wild, & in that plot
118–122 *not in MS. B*[2]
125 Half choaked &c—
126 thirst,
127 Returned,
130 "Things die, my Friend,
131 Nor *over* Ev *erased* each *included*

---

117 The mark in the middle of this line refers to the insertion of "and in that plot" from l. 7 of 18v.

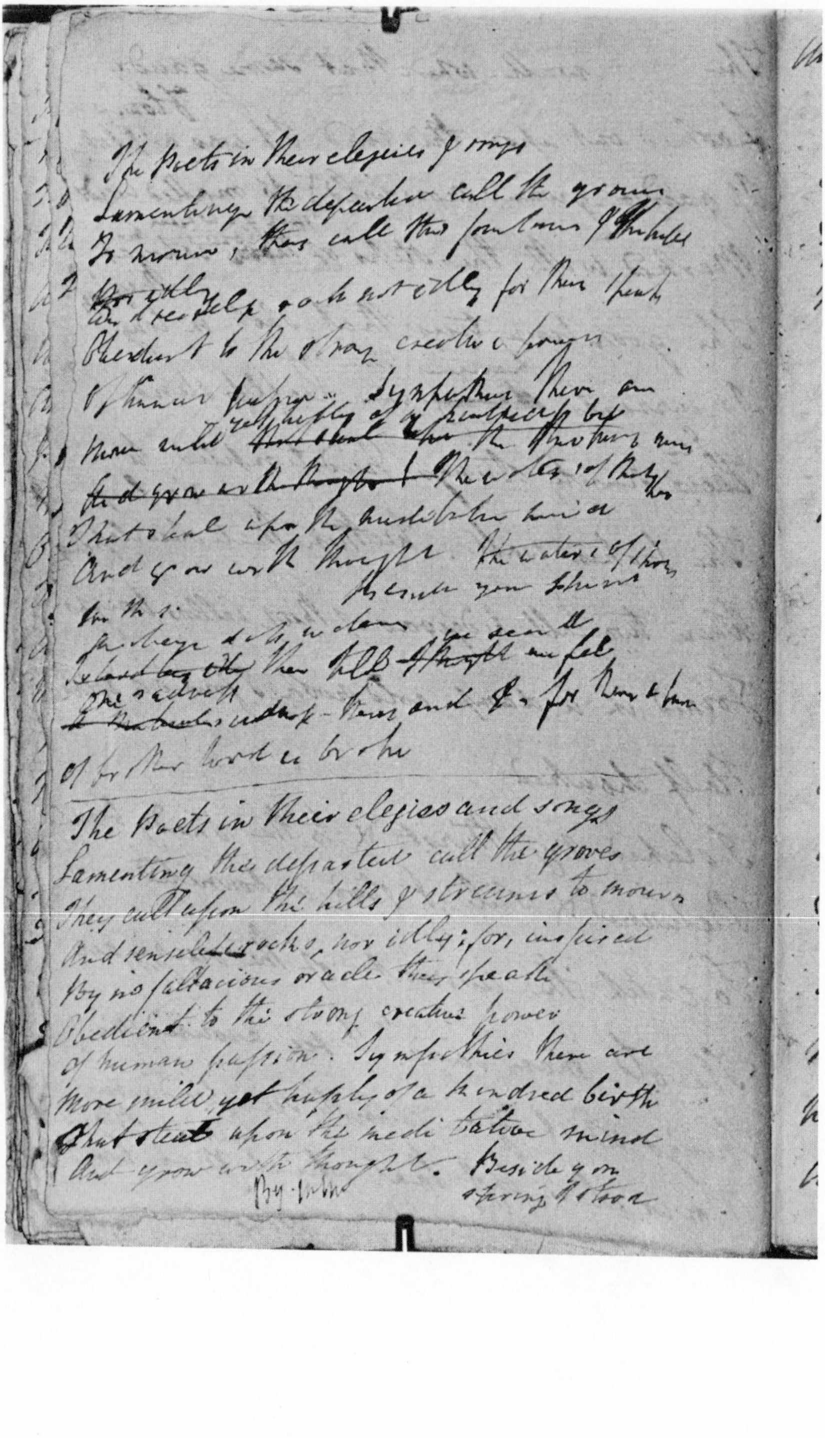

[D, 73–85; E, 411–423]

The Poets in their elegies & songs 1
Lamenting the departed call the groves 2
t }
To mourn, they call the fountains & [?]} he hills 3
~~Nor idly~~ 4
And senseless rock not idly for they speak 5
Obedient to the strong creative powers 6
Of human passion. . . Sympathies there are 7
yet haply of a kindred bir
More mild ~~that steal upon the thinking~~ [?mind] 8
~~And grow with thought~~ The waters of that [?spri] 9
That steal upon the meditative mind 10
And grow with thought ~~The waters~~ of spring 11
Beside yon Spring
[?In ?the ?s] 12
And eyed its waters we seem'd
~~I stood beside~~ them till ~~I thought~~ we fel 13
One sadness
~~A mutual~~ sadness—they and I—for them a bond 14
Of brotherhood is broke 15

The Poets in their elegies and songs 16
Lamenting the departed call the groves 17
They call upon the hills & streams to mourn 18
And senseless rocks, nor idly; for, inspired 19
By no fallacious oracle they speak 20
Obedient to the strong creative power 21
Of human passion. Sympathies there are 22
More mild, yet haply of a kindred birth 23
That steal upon the meditative mind 24
And grow with thought. Beside yon 25
spring I stood
By [?]

WW's addition—continuing onto 20v—was inserted in MS. D after the line that corresponds to l. 134 of MS. B. The first line of this draft on 19v is opposite l. 134 on 20r, but no mark for insertion is made there.

(20)

And prized in his peculiar nook of earth
Dies with him or is changed & very soon
Even of the good is no memorial left
The waters of that spring if they could feel
~~A feeling of~~
Might mourn. They are not as they were
the bond
Of brotherhood is broken. time has been
When every day the touch of human hand
Disturbed their stillness, & they ministered
When
To human comfort. ~~As~~ I stooped to drink
~~Few minutes gone~~ at that deserted well
At that deserted well a spiders web
~~What feelings came to me.~~ ~~A spider's web~~
or
Across its mouth ~~hung~~ to the water's edge
And on the wet & slimy foot stone lay
The useless fragment of a wooden bowl
day
It moved my very heart. The ~~time~~ has been
road
When I could never pass this ~~way~~ but she
Who lived within these walls, when I appeared
A daughter's welcome gave me & I loved her

140

132 *And prized in his peculiar nook of earth*
133 *Dies with him or is changed & very soon*
134 *Even of the good is no memorial left*
~~have aught~~
135 *The waters of that spring if they could feel*
~~Of feeling spirit in them~~
136 *Might mourn. They are not as they were*
the bond
h
137 *Of brotherhood is broken—time* [?*w*] *as been*
138 *When every day the touch of human hand*
139 *Disturbed their stillness, & they ministered*
When
140 *To human comfort.* ~~*As*~~ *I stooped to drink*
141 ~~*Few minutes gone*~~*, at that deserted well*
A that deserted well a spiders web
142 ~~*What feelings came to me! A spider's web*~~
~~as~~
143 *Across its mouth hung to the water's edge*
-
144 *And on the wet & slimy foots stone lay*
145 *The useless fragment of a wooden bowl*
day
146 *It moved my very heart. The* ~~*time*~~ *has been*
road
~~*road*~~
147 *When I could never pass this* [?] *but she*
~~*way*~~
148 *Who lived within these walls, when I appeared*
149 *A daughter's welcome gave me & I loved her*

149

---

133 him, changed,
134 left.
136 were,
137 broken; has
140 drink,
143 edge,
-st
144 footsto one,
145 bowl—
147 way
148 appeared,
149 me,

And eyed its waters till we seemed to feel
The sadness, they and I. For them a bond
Of brotherhood is broken time has been
When every day the touch of human hand
Disturbed their stillness and they ministered
To human comfort.

[D, 83–88; E, 421–426]

And eyed its waters till we seemed to feel 1
One sadness, they and I; For them a bond 2
Of brotherhood is broken time has been 3
When every day the touch of human hand 4
Disturbd their stillness and they minister'd 5
To human comfort. 6

The text of this addition continues from 19v.

(21)

As my own child—Oh Sir! the good die first
And they whose hearts are dry as summer dust
Burn to the socket. Many a passenger
Has blessed poor Margaret for her gentle looks
When she upheld the cool refreshment drawn
shrine
From that forsaken ~~well~~, & no one came
But he was welcome, no one went away
But that it seemed she loved him. She is dead
The worm is on her cheek and this poor hut
Stripped of its outward garb of houshold flowers
sweet-brier
Of rose & ~~jasmine~~ offers to the wind
A cold bare wall whose earthy top is tricked
With weeds & the rank spear-grass
She is dead
And nettles rot & adders sun themselves
Where we have sat together while she nursed
Her infant at her bosom—The wild colt
The unstalled heifer & the Potter's ass
Find shelter now within the chimney wall.

69

150 *As my own child. Oh Sir! the good die first*
151 *And they whose hearts are dry as summer*
dust
152 *Burn to the socket. Many a passenger*
153 *Has blessed poor Margaret for her gentle*
looks
154 *When she upheld the cool refreshment drawn*
spring
155 *From that forsaken ~~well~~, & no one came*
156 *But he was welcome, no one went away*
157 *But that it seemed she loved him. She is*
dead
158 *The worm is on her cheek and this poor hut*
159 *Stripped of its outward garb of houshold*
flowers
sweet-brier
160 *Of rose & ~~jasmine~~ offers to the wind*
a
161 *A cold bea{ re wall whose earthy top is*
tricked
162 *With weeds & the rank spear-grass*
She is dead
163 *And nettles rot & adders sun themselves*
164 *Where we have sat together while she*
nursed
165 *Her infant at her bosom. The wild colt*
166 *The unstalled heifer & the Potter's ass*
167 *Find shelter now within the chimney wall*
67

---

150 child— first,
157 dead,
158 cheek, &
159 flowers,
160 jasmine] sweet *del to* woodbine,
161 cold, bare
162 weeds, spear-grass—
163 rot,
164 sate together,
165 baby *del to* infant
166 heifer,

---

167 The number is an error for 167.

While I stood sitting in thought
He came to me and raised my friend
But I have spoken thus
With an ungrateful temper and have read
The forms of things with an unworthy eye
She sleeps in the calm earth and peace is here
I well remember that those very plumes
Those weeds & the high spear grass on that wall
By mist and silent rain drops silver'd o'er
As once I pass'd did to my ~~mind~~ heart convey
So still an image of tranquillity
So calm & still & look'd so beautiful

Amid the uneasy thoughts which fill'd my mind
That what we feel of sorrow or despair
From ruin and from change, and all the grief
The passing shews of being leave behind
Appeared an idle dream that could not live
Where meditation was. I turn'd away
And walk'd along the ~~road~~ [illegible] in happiness
You will forgive me Sir I feel I play
The truant with my tale. Poor Margaret

[illegible]

[D, 507–525; E, 852–870]

While I stood fixd in thought 1
He came to me and said my friend 2
But I have spoken thus 3
With an ungrateful temper and have read 4
The forms of things with an unworthy eye 5
She sleeps in the calm {[?earth] / [?]} and peace {is / [?] [?here]}
I well remember that those very plumes 6
Those weeds & the high spear grass on that wall 7
By mist and silent rain drops silver'd oer 8
As once I pass'd did to my ~~mind~~ heart convey 9
So still an image of tranquillity 10
So calm & still & looked so beautiful 11

Amid the uneasy thoughts which fill'd my mind 12
That what we feel of sorrow or despair 13
From ruin and from change, and all the grief 14
The passing shews of beings leave behind 15
Appeared an idle dream that could not live 16
Where meditation was. I turn'd away 17
And walk'd along the ~~road~~ my path in happiness 18
You will forgive me Sir I feel I play 19
The truant with my tale. Poor Margaret 20

and pleasantly did we pursue our way

This draft—presumably once intended for insertion after l. 170a on the facing 22r—became the climax of the addendum through its use of the spear-grass as an image of tranquillity; see 53r and 54r. The last line on 21v was added to the draft after WW decided to use this passage in the addendum.

(22)

Where I have seen her evening hearth-stone blaze
~~And spread its chearful light~~
And through the window spread upon the road
Its chearful light — You will forgive me Sir
I feel I play the truant with my tale
She had a husband an industrious man
Sober & steady I have heard her say
That he was up & busy at his loom
In summer ere the mowers scythe had swept
The dewy grass, & in the early spring
Ere the last star had vanished. was gone & They who passed
At evening, from behind the garden fence
Might hear his busy spade which he would ply
After his daily work till the day-light
Was gone & every leaf ~~and every flower~~ and flower were lost
~~were lost~~ In the dark hedges. So they passed their days lived
In peace & comfort & two pretty babes
Were their best hope next to the God in ~~Heaven~~

84

168 *Where I have seen her evening hearth-stone*
blaze
[?]
~~*And spread its chearful light*~~
169 *And through the window spread upon the road*
170 *Its chearful light— You will forgive me Sir*
171 *I feel I play the truant with my tale*
172 *She had a husband an industrious man*
173 *Sober & steady I have heard her say*
174 *That he was up & busy at his loom*
175 *In summer ere the mowers scythe had*
swept
176 *The dewy grass, & in the early spring*
was gone &
177 *Ere the last star had vanished. They who*
passed
178 *At evening, from behind the garden fence*
e }
179 *Might hear his busy spad*[?]} *which he*
would ply
h}
180 *After d*} *is daily work till the day-light*
and flower were lost
181 *Was gone & every leaf* ~~*and every flower*~~
I {I pass'd their days
182 ~~*Were lost*~~ {*in the dark hedges. So they*^ ~~*lived*~~
183 *In peace & comfort & two pretty babes*
184 *Were their best hope next to the God in Heaven*
84

---

168 blaze,
169 And, window,
170 me,
171 tale—
172 husband,
173 steady,
174 up,
175 mower's
176 &] and
177 They] He
179 Might hear *inserted above line* His spade,
180 his work,
181 gone, leaf, &
183 and comfort, &

---

182 WW first tried to change to a capital "I" by overwriting; he then placed an "I" slightly to the left. DW seems to have dotted the second "e" in "hedges."
184 The number below this line is an error, possibly with a short correcting stroke changing it to 184.

Meanwhile, abridgement
Of daily comforts gladly reconciled
To numerous self-denials, Margaret
Went struggling on through those calamitous years
With cheerful hope: but ere the second spring
A fever seized her husband. In disease

[D, 144–149, E, 477–482]

196 Meanwhile, abridged

197 Of m{d/f}aily comforts gladly reconciled
198 To numerous self denials, Margaret
199 Went struggling on through those calamitous years
200 With chearful hope: but ere the second spring
201 A fever seized her husband. In disease

196b–201a *not in MS. B*[2]

WW's draft fills a gap left on 23r for this transition.

(23)

— You may remember now some ten years gone
Two blighting seasons when the fields were left
With half a harvest; it pleased heaven to add
A worse affliction in the plague of war;
A happy land was stricken to the heart
'Twas a sad time of sorrow and distress
A wanderer among the cottages ~~I with~~
~~Of winter raiment saw the hardships~~
I with my pack of winter raiment saw
The hardships of that season many rich
Sunk down as in dream among the poor
And of the poor did many cease to be
And their place knew them not. ~~Many~~

Went struggling on through those calamitous years
With cheerful hope but ere the second spring
A fever seized her
He lingered long & when his strength returned
He found the little he had stored to meet

201

185 *—You may remember now some ten years gone*
186 *Two blighting seasons when the fields were left*
harvest ; it
187 *With half a ~~tillage~~. ~~It~~ pleased heaven to add*
188 *A worse affliction in the plague of war*
t
189 *A happy land was stricken to the heard*
T'
190 *~~It~~ was a sad time of sorrow and distress*
191 *A wanderer among the cottages, ~~I with my pack~~*
~~Of winter raiment saw the hardships of the~~
192 *I with my pack of winter raiment, saw*
193 *The hardships of that season many rich*
194 *Sunk down as in dream among the poor*
195 *And of the poor did many cease to be*
. ~~Margr~~
196 *And their place knew them not*
Went struggling on through those calamitous years
With chearful hope but ere the second spring
A fever seized
In disease
201 *~~In disease~~*
202 *He lingered long & when his strength return -ed*
203 *He found the little he had stored to meet*
2
101

---

185 remember, gone,
187 harvest.
189 heart—
190 & distress;
191–192 A wanderer among the cottages,
I with my pack of winter raiment saw
193 season. Many
194 down, in a dream,
195 be,
196a not— *on the next line DW writes:* It is now to be expressed that a fever seized Margarets husband
196b–201a *not in MS. B²*

196/201 DW left a two-and-one-half-line gap for WW to write in missing lines; her 201 at the bottom of the page shows that she counted this gap in her numbering. WW tried to use the space available, but he eventually wrote a five-line passage on 22v. Hence DW's MS. B line totals are now two numbers less than those of the reading text.

(24)

The hour of accident or crippling age
Was all consumed. As I have said 'twas now
A time of trouble shoals of artisans
Were from their daily labour turned away
To hang for bread on parish charity
They and their wives & children happier far
Would they have lived as do the little birds
That peck along the hedges, or the kite
That makes her dwelling in the mountain rocks
Ill fared it now with Robert, he who dwelt
In this poor cottage. at his door he stood
And whistled many a snatch of merry tunes
That had no mirth in them, or with his knife
Carved uncouth figures on the heads of sticks
Then idly sought about through every nook
Of house or garden any casual task
Of use or ornament & with a strange

218

204 *The hour of accident or crippling age*
205 *Was all consumed. As I have said 'twas*
now
206 *A time of trouble shoals of artisans*
207 *Were from their daily labour turned away*
208 *To hang for bread on parish charity*
209 *They and their wives & children happier*
far
C
210 [?*W*] *ould they have lived as do the little birds*
he *ges,*
211 *That peck along the* [?*roa*] *d* *,* *or the kite*
212 *That makes her dwelling in the mountain*
rocks
213 *Ill fared it now with Robert, he who*
dwelt
214 *In this poor cottage, at his door he stood*
215 *And whistled many a snatch of merry*
tunes
216 *That had no mirth in them, or with his*
knife
217 *Carved uncouth figures on the heads of*
sticks
218 *Then idly sought about through every nook*
219 *Of house or garden any casual task*
220 *Of use or ornament & with a strange*

218

---

206 trouble. Shoals
207 away,
208 charity,
209 They, & children,
210 Could
211 hedges,
212 rocks—
216 knif *next to margin, del to* knife
217 sticks,
218 about,
219 garden,
220 ornament,

(25)

amusing but uneasy novelty
He blended where he might the various tasks
Of summer, autumn, winter & of spring
The passenger might see him at the door
~~Beat~~
With his small hammer on the threshold stone
Pointing came buckle-tongues & rusty nails
The treasured store of an old houshold box
Or braiding cords or weaving bells & caps
Of rushes play-things for his babes

But this endured not his good-humour soon
Became a weight in which no pleasure was
And poverty brought on a petted mood
And a sore temper; day by day he drooped

233

221 *Amusing but uneasy novelty*
222 *He blended where he might the various*
tasks
223 *Of summer, autumn, winter & of spring*
224 *The passenger might see him at the door*
~~Pointi~~
225 *With his small hammer on the threshold*
stone
226 *Pointing lame buckle-tongues & rusty*
nails
227 *The treasured store of an old houshold*
box
228 *Or braiding cords or weaving bells & caps*
229 *Of rushes play-things for his babes*

230 *But this endured not his good-humour*
soon
231 *Became a weight in which no pleasure*
was
232 *And poverty brought on a petted mood*
233 *And a sore temper, day by day he drooped*
233

---

222 might,
223 winter, {& / or of spring.
225 ~~Poin~~ With his small hammer, on the threshold-stone
226 or rusty nails,
228–229 *Full transcription of these lines is useful*:
cords or weaving ~~caps~~ bells & caps
Or braiding ^ ~~caps and~~ ~~bells of rushes~~
~~bells~~ ~~of rushes~~
Of Rushes
^ Play-things for his babes
230 not;
231 was,
232 mood,

229/230 DW left a two-line gap, included in her numbering, for her brother to write in missing lines. The gap, however, was not filled. Since the reading text numbers were two higher than those of the manuscript at this point (see the note to 23r, 196/201), DW's count now matches the reading-text numbers.

(26)

And he would leave his home & to the town
Without an errand would he turn his steps
Or wander here & there among the fields
One while he would speak lightly of his babes
And with a cruel tongue, at other times
He played with them wild freaks of mer-
riment
And 'twas a piteous thing to see the looks
Of the poor innocent children. Every smile
Said Margaret to me here beneath these trees
Made my heart bleed. At this the old man
paused
And looking up to those enormous elms
He said 'tis now the hour of deepest noon
At this still season of repose & peace
This hour when all things which are not at
rest
Are chearful while this multitude of flies
Fills all the air with happy melody
Why should a tear be in an old Man's eye
Why should we thus with an untoward
mind

251

234 *And he would leave his home & to the town*
235 *Without an errand would he turn his steps*
236 *Or wander here & there among the fields*
237 *One while he would speak lightly of his babes*
238 *And with a cruel tongue, at other times*
239 *He played with them wild freaks of mer=*
=riment
240 *And 'twas a piteous thing to see the looks*
241 *Of the poor innocent children. Every smile*
242 *Said Margaret to me here beneath these trees*
243 *Made my heart bleed. At this the old Man*
paused
to
244 *And looking up {[?on] those enormous elms*
245 *He said 'tis now the hour of deepest noon*
246 *At this still season of repose & peace*
247 *This hour when all things which are not at*
rest
A
248 *C}re chearful while this multitude of flies*
249 *Fills all the air with happy melody*
e
250 *Why should a tear by} in an old Man's eye*
251 *Why should we thus with an untoward*
mind

251

---

236 fields;
237 babes,
238 tongue—at
241 Children.
242 Marg! me, trees,
243 bleed."
244 And, to elms,
245 "tis noon.
246 peace,
248 Are chearful,
250 be mans eye?
251 thus, mind,

And in the weakness of humanity
From natural wisdom turn our hearts
away
To natural comfort shut our eyes & ears
And feeding on disquiet thus disturb
of Nature with our
restless thoughts

255

I found a ruined house four naked walls
That stared upon each other. I look round
And near the door I saw an aged man
Alone & stretched upon the cottage bench
An iron pointed staff lay at his side
With instantaneous joy I recognized
That pride of nature & of lowly life
The venerable Armytage a friend
As dear to me as is the setting sun.

252 *And in the weakness of humanity*
253 *From natural wisdom turn our hearts*
away
254 *To natural comfort shut our eyes & ears*
255 *And feeding on disquiet thus disturb*
256 *of Nature with our*
restless thoughts

255

I found a ruined house four naked walls
That stared upon each other. I look round
And near the door I saw an aged man
Alone & stretched upon the cottage bench
An iron pointed staff lay at his side
With instantaneous joy I recognized
That pride of nature & of lowly life
The venerable Armytage, a friend
As dear to me as is the setting sun.

---

252 humanity,
253 From natural comfort {wisdom / turn} turn our hearts away,
254 ears,
255 the *erased at end of line*
256 *in the gap* [?Tone] *del to* The tone nature thoughts?

---

256 Penciled into the gap is the MS. B[2] reading "[The tone]" in the hand of a twentieth-century editor, Ernest de Selincourt. The number 255 below this line may be a counting error, since the five lines added here after the number 251 at the foot of 26^{r} make 256.

WW's draft below l. 256 works toward the abbreviated version of the Pedlar's history copied into MS. D (ll. 31–39). An earlier attempt at this passage is in MS. B, 3^{v}.

27

2nd Part

He spake with somewhat of a solemn tone
But when he ended there was in his face
Such easy chearfulness, a look so mild
That for a little time it stole away
All recollection and that simple tale
Passed from my mind like a forgotten sou[nd]
A while on trivial things we held dis[course]
To me soon tasteless. In my own despite
I thought of that poor woman as of one
Whom I had known & loved. He had re[hearsed]
Her homely tale with such familiar power
With such a [illegible] countenance [illegible], an eye
So busy, that the things of which he spa[ke]
Seemed present & attention now relax[ed]

14

2nd Part

257 *He spake with somewhat of a solemn tone*
258 *But when he ended there was in his face*
259 *Such easy chearfulness, a look so mild*
260 *That for a little time it stole away*
261 *All recollection and that simple tale*
262 *Passed from my mind like a forgotten soun[ ]*
263 *A while on trivial things we held dis*
=course
264 *To me soon tasteless. In my own despite*
265 *I thought of that poor woman as of one*
266 *Whom I had known & loved. He had re*
=hearsed
267 *Her homely tale with such familiar power*
tender kindly &c
268 *With such a ^ countenance ~~of love~~, an eye*
269 *So busy, that the things of which he spak[ ]*
270 *Seemed present &, attention now relaxed*

14

2nd Part] *not underlined*
257 tone &c *beginning a new line DW writes:* After about 20 lines descriptive of the Poet's feelings he goes on—
258–277 *not in MS. B²*

---

262 The "d" on "sound" has worn away.
269 The "e" on "spake" has worn away.

(28)

There was a heartfelt chillness in my veins
I rose, and turning from that breezy shade
Went out into the open air, and stood to drink
The comfort of the warmer sun
Long time I had not staid ere looking [round]
Upon that tranquil ruin, ~~& impelled~~ [I return'd]
~~By a mild force of curious pensiveness~~
I begg'd of the old man that for my sake
He would resume his story. He replied
It were a wantonness, & would demand
Severe reproof, if we were men whose [hearts]
Could hold vain dalliance with the misery
Even of the dead contented thence to draw
A momentary pleasure never marked
By reason, barren of all future good
But we have known that there is [often found]
In mournful thoughts & always might be [found]
31

271 *There was a heartfelt chillness in my veins*
272 *I rose, and turning from that breezy shade*
273 *Went out into the open air, and stood to drink*
274 *The comfort of the warmer sun*
275 *Long time I had not stayed ere looking ~~r~~*
round
I returned
276 [*20*] *Upon that tranquil ruin, ~~& impelled~~*
277 ~~*By a mild force of curious pensiveness*~~
278 *I begg'd of the old man that for my sake*
279 *He would resume his story. He replied*
280 *It were a wantonness, & would demand*
281 *Severe reproof, if we were men whose*
hearts
282 *Could hold vain dalliance with the misery*
283 *Even of the dead contented thence to draw*
284 *A momentary pleasure never marked*
285 *By reason, barren of all future good*
286 *But we have known that there is*
often found
287 *In mournful thoughts & always might be*
found

31

271–277 *not in MS. B*[2]
278 begged
280 wantonness,] wantonness
281 reproof,] reproof
282 misery,
283 dead,
284 pleasure,
285 good,
286 is often found,
287 In mournful thoughts *inserted above line* And always might be found,

---

273 "To drink" should begin the following line to make ll. 273 and 274 metrical, and the lines were so copied in MS. D.
275 Deletion by erasure.
276 The number 20 is on the facing 27v.

A power to virtue friendly went not so (29)
I am a dreamer among men—indeed
An idle dreamer. 'Tis a common tale
By moving accidents uncharactered
A tale of silent suffering, hardly clothed
In bodily form & to the grosser sense
But ill adapted, scarcely palpable
To him who does not think. But at your bidding
I will proceed

40 While thus it fared with them
To whom this Cottage till that hapless year
Had been a blessed home it was my chance
To travel in a country far remote
And glad I was when halting by yon gate
Which leads from the green lane again I saw
These lofty elm-trees. Long I did not rest
With many pleasant thoughts I cheered my way
O'er the flat common. At the door arrived
I knocked, & when I entered with the hope
40

re't
288 *A power to virtue friendly we[?re]} not so*
289 *I am a dreamer among men—indeed*
290 *An idle dreamer. 'Tis a common tale*
291 *By moving accidents uncharactered*
o
292 *A tale of silent suffering, hardly cl[?oa]} thed*
293 *In bodily form & to the grosser sense*
294 *But ill adapted, scarcely palpable*
295 *To him who does not think. But at your*
bidding
296 *I will proceed*
em
[40] *While thus it fared with ~~those~~*
297 *To whom this Cottage till that hapless year*
298 *Had been a blessed home it was my chance*
299 *To travel in a country far remote*
300 *And glad I was when halting by yon gate*
301 *Which leads from the green lane again I*
saw
g
302 *These lofty elm-trees. Lon[?d]} I did not rest*
303 *With many pleasant thoughts I cheered my*
way
304 *O'er the flat common. At the door arrived*
305 *I knocked, & when I entered with the hope*
49

---

ie
288 frei} ndly, were't
289 men,
290 tale,
292 clothed
293 form,
296 proceed. *no paragraph* them
297 cottage
299 remote,
300 when, gate,
302 Long rest—
a
304 [?I]} rrived,
305 And when I entered with the hope *incomplete line*

---

296 The number 40 is on the facing 28ᵛ.

Of usual greeting Margaret looked at me (30)
A little while, then turned her head away
Speechless. & sitting down upon a chair
Wept bitterly. I wist not what to do
Or how to speak to her, Poor wretch! at last
She rose from off her seat—and then—Oh Sir
I cannot <u>tell</u> how she pronounced my name
With fervent love & with a face of grief
Unutterably helpless & a look
That seemed to cling upon me she enquired
I could make
If I had seen her husband. As she spake
No answer, from
A strange surprize and fear came to my heart
And ere I could reply
And I could make no answer. then she told
That he had disappeared; just two months gone
He left his house, two wretched days had passed
And on the third by the first break of light
Within her casement full in view she saw
66

306 *Of usual greeting Margaret looked at me*
307 *A little while, then turned her head away*
308 *Speechless, & sitting down upon a chair*
309 *Wept bitterly. I wist not what to do*
310 *Or how to speak to her. Poor wretch! at last*
311 *She rose from off her seat—and then—Oh Sir*
312 *I cannot tell how she pronounced my name*
313 *With fervent love & with a face of grief*
314 *Unutterably helpless & a look*
315 *That seemed to cling upon me she inquired*
I could make
316 [*60*] *If I had seen her husband. As she spake*
No answer, from {to
317 *A strange surprize and fear came* {*o'er my heart*
And ere I could reply
318 *And I could make no answer—then she told*
319 *That hi had disappeared; just two months gone*
320 *He left his house, two wretched days had passed*
321 *And on the third by the first break of* *li*[?]{g}*ht*
322 *Within her casement full in view she saw*
66

306 greeting, Marg[t]
307 her head *omitted*
309 bitterly—
311 seat, & then—Oh Sir!
312 name,
313 love,
314 helpless,
315 me,
317 & fear came to
318 answer;
319 he had disappeared just
321 third, light,
322 view,

316 The number 60 is on the facing 29v.
319 DW's "hi" is an obvious miswriting for "he." Although nothing is visible under the erasure in this line, the spacing suggests "but" or "not."

A purse of gold." I trembled at the sight
Said Margaret "for I knew it was his hand
That placed it there, [deleted] [deleted] [deleted]:
[deleted] . [deleted] [deleted] [deleted] [deleted] a [deleted]
and on that very day

[deleted] [deleted] [deleted]
By one, a stranger, from my husband sent
The tidings came that he had joined a troop
Of soldiers going to a distant land
He left me thus - Poor Man! he had not heart
To take a farewell of me & he feared
That I should follow with my babes & sink
Beneath the misery of a soldier's life
This tale did Margaret tell with many tears
And when she ended I had little power
To give her comfort & was glad to take
Such words of hope from her own mouth as served
To chear us both - but long we had not talked

323 *A purse of gold. "I trembled at the sight*
324 *Said Margaret "for I knew it was his hand*
325 *That placed it there, ~~then turned her head a-~~*
~~-way~~
~~Speechless, and sitting down upon a chair~~
and on that very day
~~The tidings came~~
326 *By one, a stranger, from my husband sent*
327 *The tidings came that he had joined a troop*
328 *Of soldiers going to a distant land*
329 *He left me thus—Poor Man! he had not*
heart
he
330 *To take a farewell of me &^ feared*
331 *That I should follow with my babes &*
sink
332 *Beneath the misery of a soldier's life*
333 *This tale did Margaret tell with many tears*
334 *And when she ended I had little power*
335 *To give her comfort & was glad to take*
336 [*80*] *Such words of hope from her own mouth as*
served
337 *To chear us both—but long we had not*
talked

---

323 gold "I sight"
324 Margaret,
325 there—& on that very day,
326 sent,
328 soldiers, land,
330 me, & he
332 Soldier's life"
333 Marg[t]
335 comfort,
337 talked,

---

323 DW may have begun another letter before the opening "A" in this line.
325/326 DW repeats ll. 307b–308 and then cancels them.
336 The number 80 is on the facing 30[v].

(32)

Ere we built up a pile of better thoughts
And with a brighter eye she looked around
As if she had been shedding tears of joy
We parted It was then the early spring
I left her busy with her garden tools
And well remember o'er that fence she looked
And while I paced along the foot-way path
Called out, and sent a blessing after me
With tender chearfulness & with a voice
That seemed the very sound of happy thoughts

I rov'd o'er many a hill and many a dale
With this my weary load, in heat and cold
Through many a wood, and many an open ~~plain~~ ground
In sunshine & in shade, in wet or fair
Now blithe, now drooping as it might befal
My best companions now the driving winds
And now the "trotting brooks" and whispering trees
And now the music of my own sad steps

338 *Ere we built up a pile of better thoughts*
339 *And with a brighter eye she looked around*
340 *As if she had been shedding tears of joy*
{It n}the
341 *We parted.* { '~~T~~*was the* } ^ *early spring*
342 *I left her busy with her garden tools*
{at
343 *And well remember o'er th*{*e fence she looked*
344 *And while I paced along the foot-way path*
345 *Called out, and sent a blessing after me*
346 *With tender chearfulness & with a voice*
347 *That seemed the very sound of happy thoughts*

348 *I roved o'er many a hill and many a dale*
349 *With this my weary load, in heat and cold*
350 *Through many a wood, and many an open*
~~*plain*~~
ground
351 *In sunshine or in shade, in wet or fair*
352 *Now blithe, now drooping—as it might befal*
353 *My best companions now the driving winds*
And now the "trotting" brooks and whispering trees
354 *And now the music of my own sad steps*

---

338 thoughts,
340 joy.
341 —'Twas the
343 that
344 footway
345 and] &
346 chearfulness,
348 and] &
349 & cold,
350 wood & plain *del to* ground
351 sunshine,
352 drooping,
353/354 *inserted line included* brooks, & trees,

---

351 For the "o" in the first "or," DW began to make an ampersand.
353/354 The interlining is certainly early—it is in MS. B²—but the placement of 100 opposite l. 356 on 33r shows that it was not included prior to the numbering.

With many a short-lived thoughts that passed between
And disappeared I came this way again
measured back this road
Towards the wane of summer when the wheat
Was yellow & the soft and bladed grass
Sprung up afresh & o'er the hay-field spread
Its tender green. When I had reached the door
I found that she was absent. In the shade
Where now we sit I waited her return.
Her cottage in its outward look appeared
As chearful as before; in any shew
Of neatness little changed, but that I thought
The honey suckle crowded round the door
And from the wall hung down in heavier tufts
And knots of worthless stone crop started out
Along the window's edge & grew like weeds
Against the lower panes. I turned aside
And strolled into her garden. It was changed

{And a
355 {*With many short-lived thoughts that passed*
between

came this way again
356 *And dis-appeared. I ~~came this way~~*
[*100*] *measured back this road*

wane
357 *Towards the ~~wain~~ of summer when the wheat*
358 *Was yellow & the [?~~fr~~] soft and bladed grass*
~~again~~
359 *Sprung up afresh & o'er the hay-field*
spread
360 *Its tender green. When I had reached the*
door
361 *I found that she was absent. In the shade*
362 *Where now we sit I waited her return*
363 *Her cottage in its outward look appeared*
364 *As chearful as before; in any shew*
365 *Of neatness little changed, but that I thought*
366 *The honey suckle crowded round the door*
367 *And from the wall hung down in hea=*
loads
=vier ^ ~~*tufts*~~
368 *And knots of worthless stone-crop started*
out
369 *Along the window's edge & grew like weeds*
370 *Against the lower panes. I turned aside*
371 *And strolled into her garden. It was changed*

---

355 many a thought that past
356 disappeared. way again
357 wheat *next to margin, del to* wheat
358 the soft &
363 appeareded *with final* ed *erased*
364 before,
366 honey-suckle
367 And, tufts;

---

356 The number 100 is on the facing 32^v; it seems to be opposite the correction below the original line, so that revision probably precedes the numbering.

(34) (35)

The unprofitable bindweed spread his bells,
From side to side, & with unwieldy wreaths
Had dragged the rose from its sustaining wall
And ~~bowed~~ bent it down to earth. The border tufts
Daisy, & thrift & lowly camomile
And thyme had straggled out into the paths
Which they were used to deck. Ere this an hour
Was wasted back I turned my restless steps
And as I walked before the door it chanced
A stranger passed, & guessing whom I sought
He said that she was used to ramble far
The sun was sinking in the west & now
I sate with sad impatience. From within
Her solitary infant cried aloud
The spot though fair seemed very desolate
The longer I remained more desolate

372 *The unprofitable bindweed spread his bells*
373 *From side to side, & with unwieldy wreaths*
374 *Had dragged the rose from its sustaining*
wall
bent
375 *And ~~bowed~~ it down to earth, the border*
tufts
376 [*120*] *Daisy, & thrift & lowly camomile*
377 *And thyme had straggled out into the*
paths
378 *Which they were used to deck. Ere this an*
hour
379 *Was wasted back I turned my restless steps*
380 *And as I walked before the door it*
chanced
381 *A stranger passed, & guessing whom*
I sought
382 *He said that she was used to ramble far*
383 *The sun was sinking in the west & now*
384 *I sate with sad impatience. From within*
385 *Her solitary infant cried aloud*
386 *The spot though fair seemed very desolate*
387 *The longer I remained more desolate*

---

375 bent earth. The
376 thrift, camomile,
377 thyme, *comma erased*
379 wasted; my steps *then* steps *del to* restless steps
380 And, door,
381 passed &, sought,
382 far.
383 west,
385 aloud.
386 spot, though fair, desolate,

---

376 The number 120 is on the facing 33v.

(35)

And looking round I saw the corner stones,
Till then unmarked, on either side the door
With dull red stains discoloured & stuck o'er
With locks of wool as if the sheep
That feed upon the commons thither came
As to a couching-place & rubbed their sides
Even at her threshold. The church-clock struck eight
I turned and saw her distant a few steps

Her face was pale & thin her figure too
Was changed. As she unlocked the door she said
It grieves me you have waited here so long
But in good truth I've wandered much of late
And sometimes, to my shame I speak have need
~~Have need of my best prayers to bring me~~
Of my best prayers to bring me back again
While on the board she spread our evening meal
She told me she had lost her ~~eldest~~ elder child

388 *And looking round I saw the corner stones,*
389 *Till then unmarked, on either side the*
door
390 *With dull red stains discoloured & stuck*
o'er
locks
391 *With tufts & hairs of wool as if the sheep*
392 *That feed upon the commons thither came*
393 *As to a couching-place & rubbed their sides*
{The church-clock
394 *Even at her threshold.* {*I*
struck eight
395 I turn'd and saw her distant a few steps
[*140*]
396 *Her face was pale & thin, her figure too*
397 *Was changed. As she unlocked the door she said*
398 *It grieves me you have waited here so long*
399 *But in good truth I've wandered much of late*
{*have*
400 *And sometimes, to my shame I speak* {
need
~~*Have need of my best prayers to bring*~~ *me*
~~*me*~~
401 *Of my best prayers to bring me back again*
402 *While on the board she spread our evening* ~~*meal*~~
meal
403 *She told me she had lost her* ~~*eldest*~~ *child*
elder

---

388 And, looking round, stones,] stones
390 stains] stones discoloured,
391 wool,
392 The
394 The church clock
395 turned, & saw her, steps,
396 figure, too,
398 long,
400 some times, speak, have need
401 again.
402 meal
403 elder child,

394–395 DW left a two-and-one-half-line gap, included in her numbering (see the note to 395/396 below), for her brother to fill. He made his insertion, however, in one and one-half lines. Hence there is one line less in Part Two than the 273 recorded on 43^r.

395/396 The number 140 is on 34^v, but it did not face 35^r when the numbering was entered. The numbers from 34^v to the end of the original version of *RC* run as follows: 140, 200, 160, 180, 220, 140, 160, 1[overwritten 2]73. The last three numbers are errors for 240, 260, and—as corrected—273. What happened to the others was that after the poem was written out but before it was numbered, the gathering of four, which contains leaves 35, 36, 37, and 38, was inadvertently folded backward making the sequence 37, 38, 35, 36. The line numbers all came out right, but the number 140 faced 37^r in the mistaken folding of sheets. The order of the text is, of course, not affected, but the placement of the mistaken numbering here and elsewhere enables one to see which lines were included in the count and which excluded. Henceforth, the transcriptions will record numbers as they now stand in the manuscript, but their original placement in the misfolded gathering will be indicated in notes.

401 In the original numbering, done when the fold in the gathering of four (35, 36, 37, 38) was reversed, the number 180 on 38^v would have stood opposite this line.

You look at me & you have cause
And well you may. To day
I have been travelling far and many days
About the fields I wander knowing this
Only that what I seek I cannot find
And so I waste my time for I am chan

Sir I feel &c
next page

200

[D, 347–352; E, 684–689]

I perceive 1
& you have cause
You look at me and well you may To day 2
I have been travelling far and many days 3
About the fields I wander, knowing th[?is] 4
Only, that what I seek I cannot find 5
And so I waste my time for I am chang 6

^Sir I feel &c
next page

The draft at the top of this page was included in MS. D following a line corresponding to MS. B, 405a, which is on the facing 36r. A blot obscures the text of l. 4 here on 35v.

WW's copying instruction—"Sir I feel &c / next page"—refers to a draft on 36v (originally intended for inclusion at l. 431 on 37r). This notation on 35v, exactly opposite a matching caret on 36r, shows that the draft on 36v was then moved to l. 415.

The number 200, visible at the bottom right of the photograph, refers to the text on 36r; see the note to l. 421 on 36r.

(36)

That he for months had been a serving boy
Apprenticed by the parish I am changed
And to myself [said she] have done much wrong
And to this helpless infant. I have slept
Weeping & weeping I have waked my tears
Have flowed as if my body were not such
As others are & I could never die ~~but I am~~ ~~more~~
~~In spirit~~ [mind] ~~& heart more~~ easy
But I am now in mind ~~& heart~~ [in my heart]
More easy, & I hope said she that heaven
Will give me patience to endure the [things]
Which I behold at home. It would have [grieved]
Your very soul to see her. evermore
Her eye-lids drooped, her eyes were downward cast
And when ~~that~~ [the] [her] table gave me food
She did not look at me her voice was low
~~She did not [illegible] me~~ & ~~so easy [illegible]~~
Her body was subdued. In every act
Pertaining to her house affairs appeared
The careless stillness which a thinking ~~mind~~ soul

404 *That he for months had been a serving boy*
405 *Apprenticed by the parish. I am changed*
said she
406 *And to myself^have done much wrong*
407 *And to this helpless infant. I have slept*
408 *Weeping & weeping I have waked my tears*
409 *Have flowed as if my body were not such*
410 *As others are, & I could never die* ~~*but I am*~~
~~*now*~~
~~*mind*~~
~~*In spirit & heart more easy*~~
in my heart
411 *But I am now in mind* ~~*& heart*~~
412 *More easy, & I hope said she that heaven*
413 *Will give me patience to endure the*
things
414 *Which I behold at home. It would have*
grieved
415 *Your very soul to see her.^evermore*
416 *Her eye-lids drooped, her eyes were down-*
=ward cast
she {at her {g
{when ~~sh~~ {e table {[?]ave me food
417 *And* {
418 She did not look at me *her voice was low*
~~*She did not look at me*~~^ ~~*In every act*~~
419 *Her body was subdued. In every act*
420 *Pertaining to her house affairs appeared*
421 [*200*] *The careless stillness which a thinking*
~~*mind*~~ *soul*

---

404 serving-boy,
406 myself, said she,
408 Weeping, & waked,
410 die. *end of line*
412 hope, said she,
415 her.] her
416 eyelids cast] bent
417 And when she at her table gave me food
418 me—
421 soul

---

415 The caret refers to the intended insertion here of "Sir I feel" (following WW's instructions on 35v), a passage that is copied on 36v, and was previously intended for inclusion at l. 431 on 37r.

417–419 DW left a gap for WW to fill at l. 417, and she also seems to have made a copying error; she corrected it in ll. 418–419. When WW filled the gap, he repeated "She did not look at me" in l. 418, possibly to make the line level with DW's correction "her voice was low." The numbering from 180 to 200 on the misfolded sheets (see the note to 395/396 on 35r) shows that at least DW's correction precedes the numbering.

421 The 200 is on the facing 35v. The same number would also be opposite this line in the numbering of the misfolded gathering, but it is now out of sequence since it follows 140 opposite a line on 35r.

A human being destined to awake
To human life or something very near
To human life when he shall come again
For whom she suffered. Tis it would have grieved
Your very heart to see her. + even now

+ Sir I feel

The story linger in my heart I fear
Tis long & tedious but my spirit clings
To that poor woman so familiarly
Do I perceive her manner & her look
And presence so deeply do I feel
Her goodness that a vision of the mind
A momentary trance comes over me
And to myself I seem to muse on one
By sorrow laid asleep or borne away

[D, 362–376; E, 699–713]

A human being destined to awake 10
To human life or something very near 11
To human life when he shall come 12
again
For whom she suffered^ Sir it would 13
have griev'd
Your very heart to see her. X evermore 14

X
Sir I feel 1
The story linger in my heart I fear 2
u
Tis long & tedious by{t my spirit clings 3
To that poor woman so familiarly 4
Do I perceive her manner & her look 5
And presence [?&] *so deeply do I feel* 6
a vision of the mind
Her goodness that ~~*a trance comes over me*~~ 7
A momentary trance comes over me
And to my self I seem to muse on one 8
By sorrow laid asleep, or borne away 9

This draft begins at the middle of the page and runs over from the bottom to the top. Originally intended for insertion at the X in l. 431, exactly opposite on the facing 37r, these lines were then moved to l. 415 on 36r. WW's addition in ll. 13–14 here on 36v dovetails with the text on 36r. Although this passage is not included in MS. B², its composition before 5[–6] March 1798 seems certain. The twelve lines here in DW's hand must be what increased the total length of Part Two of *RC* from 273 to 285 lines (and, with the 255 lines in Part One added in, increased the overall length of the poem before the Pedlar expansion and the inclusion of the addendum to 540). See the numbers—and the note regarding them—on 43r.

(37)

gives to an idle matter. Still she sighed
But yet no motion of the breast was seen
No heaving of the heart. While by the fire
We sate together, sighs came on my ear
I knew not how and hardly whence they came.
I took my staff & when I kissed her babe
The tears were in her eyes. I left her then
With the best hope and comfort I could give
She thanked me for my will but for my + hope
It seemed she did not thank me. I returned
And took my rounds along this road again
Ere on its sunny bank the primrose flower
Had chronicled the earliest day of spring
I found her sad and drooping. She had learned
No tidings of her husband. if he lived
She knew not that he lived if he were dead
She knew not he was dead she seemed not changed

422 *Gives to an idle matter—still she sighed*
423 *But yet no motion of the breast was seen*
424 *No heaving of the heart.* While by the fire
425 We sate together, sighs came on my ear
426 I knew not how and hardly whence they
came.

w}
427 *I took my staff & [?k]}hen I kissed her babe*
428 *The tears were in her eyes. I left her then*
429 *With the best hope and comfort I could give*
430 *She thanked me for my will for my*
hope

X

431 *It seemed she did not thank me. I returned*
432 *And took my rounds along this road again*
433 *Ere on its sunny bank the primrose*
flower
434 *Had chronicled the earliest day of spring*
435 *I found her sad and drooping she had learned*
436 *No tidings of her husband, if he lived*
437 *She knew not that he lived it he*
were dead

[?]
438 *She knew not he was dead she seemed*
not changed

---

422 matter. Still
423 seen,
425 together,] together
426 how, or came.] came
427 staff, & when
429 and] & give.
430 will,
431 me:
433 Ere, bank,
434 spring.
435 and] &
437 lived, if dead,
438 dead— She

---

430 In the numbering of the misfolded gathering, 140 would have stood opposite this line (see the note to 395/396 on 35r).

431 The X here is the original point of insertion for "Sir I feel" on 36v, before that passage was transferred to l. 415 on 36r.

437 DW's "it" is an obvious miswriting for "if."

In person or appearance, but her house
Bespoke a sleepy hand of negligence
The floor was neither dry nor neat the hearth
Was comfortless

The windows they were dim & her few books
Which one upon the other heretofore
Had been piled up against the corner panes
In seemly order, now with straggling leaves
Lay scattered here & there, open or shut
As they had chanced to fall. Her infant babe
Had from its mothers caught the trick of grief
And sighed among its playthings once again
I turned towards the garden gate & saw
More plainly still that poverty & grief
Were now come nearer to her the earth was hard
With weeds defaced & knots of withered grass
No ridges there appeared of clear black mould

439 *In person or appearance, but her house*
440 *Bespoke a sleepy hand of negligence*
441 The floor was neither dry nor neat the hearth
442 Was comfortless

too
443 *The windows they were dim & her few books*
444 *Which one upon the other heretofore*
445 *Had been piled up against the corner*
panes
446 *In seemly order, now with straggling leaves*
r
447 *Lay scatte[?rd] ed here & there, open or shut*
448 *As they had chanced to fall. Her infant*
babe
449 *Had from its mother caught the trick of*
grief
6
450 [*14* *0*] *And sighed among its playthings once*
again
451 *I turned towards the garden gate & saw*
452 *More plainly still that poverty & grief*
the earth
453 *Were now come nearer to her,^ ~~all~~ was*
hard
454 *With weeds defaced & knots of withered*
grass
455 *No ridges there appeared of clear black*
mould

---

440 negligence,
441–442 *not in MS. B²*
443 dim,
444 one *inserted above line* the other] another
447 scattered open, or shut,
449 grief,
450 playthings;
451 gate,
452 {still / [?]}
453 the earth was hard
454 defaced, grass;
455 mould,

441–442 WW filled a gap in his sister's copying. The numbering from 140 to 160 in the misfolded gathering (see the note to 395/396 on 35r) includes either these two lines or a two-line gap.
450 The number 160 is opposite on 37v; it would also have faced this line in the numbering of the misfolded gathering, but it is now out of sequence.

(39)

No winter greenness. Of her herbs & flowers
It seemed
The better part were gnawed away
Or trampled on the earth; a chain of straw
Which had been twisted round the tender stem
Of a young apple-tree lay at its root
The bark was nibbled round by truant sheep
Margaret stood near, her infant in her arms
And seeing that my eye was on the tree
She said I fear it will be dead & gone
Ere Robert come again. Towards the house
Together we returned & she enquired
If I had any hope. But for her babe
And for her little friendless Boy she said
She had no wish to live that she must die
Of sorrow—Yet I saw the idle loom
Still in its place. His sunday garments hung

and
456 *No winter greenness; of her herbs & flowers*
It seemed
457 ^*The better part were gnawed away*
458 *Or trampled on the earth; a chain of straw*
459 *Which had been twisted round the tender*
stem
460 *Of a young apple-tree lay at its root*
461 *The bark was nibbled round by truant*
sheep
462 *Margaret stood near, her infant in her*
arms
463 *And seeing that my eye was on the tree*
464 *She said I fear it will be dead & gone*
465 *Ere Robert come again. Towards the house*
466 *Together we returned & she enquired*
467 *If I had any hope. But for her babe*
468 *And for her little friendless Boy she said*
469 *She had no wish to live that she must*
die
470 [*180*] *Of sorrow—Yet I saw the idle loom*
471 *Still in its place. His sunday garments*
hung

---

457 It seemed the
460 root,
461 sheep—
462 arms,
463 And, tree,
466 returned,
467 Babe
469 live,
470 sorrow. Yet
471 hung *next to margin, del to* hung

---

470 The number is on the facing 38v; because of the misfolded gathering (see the note to 395/396 on 35r), it is here out of sequence and originally stood opposite l. 401 on 35r. In the misfolded gathering, no number faced this page.

40

Upon the self-same nail his very staff
Stood undisturbed behind the door. and when
I passed this way beaten by autumn wind
20 She told me that her little babe was dead
And she was left alone. That very time
I yet remember through the miry lane
She walked with me a mile when the bare trees
Trickled with foggy damps & in such sort
That any heart had ached to hear her begged
That whereso'er I went I still would ask
For him whom she had lost. ~~Five tedious~~ We parted then
Our final parting for from that time forth
Did many seasons pass ere I returned
Into this tract again. Five tedious years

472 *Upon the self-same nail—his very staff*
473 *Stood undisturbed behind the door, and when*
474 *I passed this way beaten by autumn wind,*
475 [*220*] *She told me that her little babe was*
dead
476 *And she was left alone. That very time*
477 *I yet remember through the miry lane*
walked
478 *She ~~went~~ with me a mile when the bare*
trees
479 *Trickled with foggy damps & in such sort*
480 *That any heart had ached to hear her*
begged
481 *That wheresoe'er I went I still would*
ask
-
482 *For him whom she had lost. ~~Five tedio~~*
We parted then
~~=ous years~~
Our final parting for from that time forth
Did many seasons pass ere I return'd
y
Into this tract again. Five tedious [?f] ears

472 *no dash*
474 way, Autumn winds,
476 time,
477 remember,

The draft at the foot of the page became part of the poem in MS. D (ll. 443–446), although it is not here included in the numbering. Another draft in WW's hand is on the facing 39v:

[?seven]
[?eight] seasons past
from the northern country
Ere I [?then] travelling [?~~far~~] into the north
And up amon the Heibrides return
Into this tract again

(41)

five tedious years
She lingered in unquiet widowhood
A wife, and widow. Needs must it have been
A sore heart-wasting. ~~[illegible]~~ I have heard
my friend
That in that broken arbour she would ~~[illegible]~~ sit
~~[illegible]~~
The idle length of half a sabbath day
There—when you see the toadstool's lazy head
And when a dog passed by she still would
quit
The shade & look abroad. On this old Bench
For hours she sate, & evermore, her eye
Was busy in the distance, shaping things
Which made her heart beat quick. Seest
thou that path?
The greensward now has broken its grey line
There, to & fro she paced through many a
day
Of the warm summer, from a belt of flax
That girt her waist spinning the long drawn
thread
With backward steps—Yet ever as there passed

40

482 *five tedious years*
483 *She lingered in unquiet widowhood*
484 *A wife, and widow. Needs must it have been*
485 *A sore heart-wasting. ~~Master!~~ I have heard*
my Friend
~~waste~~
486 *That in that broken arbour she would ~~sit~~*
(sit
~~lingering hours~~
487 *The idle length of half a sabbath day*
488 *There — where you see the toadstool's lazy head*
489 *And when a dog passed by she still would*
quit
490 *The shade & look abroad. On this old Bench*
491 *For hours she sate, & evermore, her eye*
492 *Was busy in the distance, shaping things*
493 *Which made her heart beat quick. Seest*
thou that path?
494 *The greensward now has broken its grey line*
495 [*140*] *There, to & fro she paced through many a*
day
496 *Of the warm summer, from a belt of flax*
497 *That girt her waist spinning the long-drawn*
thread
498 *With backward steps*—{*Y* / *yet ever as there passed*}

482–484 For him whom she had lost. Five tedious years
She lingered in unquiet widowhood a wife
And widow &c &c

The text of RC *in MS. B² ends here, and DW goes on:* you have the rest to the end of Margaret's story. There is much more about the Pedlar.

---

482 The placement of this half-line on the right, the skipped space at the bottom of 40^r, and the fact that leaf 41 begins a new gathering may mean that the original conclusion to *RC* on 41^r, 42^r, and 43^r was copied before part or all of what precedes it in MS. B. The paper, though, matches that in the rest of the manuscript.

487 The revision is deleted first in pencil, then in ink.

488 Originally separate or hyphenated, "toad" and "stool's" were later joined.

495 The number 140 on the facing 40^v, twenty lines after 220, is an error for 240. Also on 40^v is penciled "[?Bler]," seemingly in WW's hand; its significance, if any, is uncertain.

(42)

A man whose garments showed the Soldier's red
Or crippled Mendicant in Sailor's garb
The little Child who sate to turn the wheel
Ceased from his toil. & she with faltering voice
Expecting still to learn her husband's fate
Made many a fond enquiry & when they
Whose presence gave no comfort were gone by
Her heart was still more sad. And by yon gate
Which bars the traveller's road she often stood
And when a stranger horseman came the latch
Would lift. & in his face look wistfully
Most happy if from aught discovered there
Of tender feeling she might dare repeat
The same sad question. Meanwhile her poor hut
Sunk to decay, for he was gone whose hand,
At the first nippings of October frost,
Closed up each chink & with fresh bands of straw

160

499 *A man whose garment* {s/she} {o} *wed the Soldier's red*
500 *Or c[?l]* {r} *ippled Mendicant in Sailor's garb*
501 *The little Child who sate to turn the wheel*
502 *Ceased from his toil, & she with faltering voice*
503 *Expecting still to learn her husband's fate*
504 *Made many a fond inquiry & when they*
505 *Whose presence gave no comfort were gone*
by
506 *Her heart was still more sad. And by yon*
gate
507 *Which bars the traveller's road she often stood*
508 *And when a stranger horseman came the*
latch
509 *Would lift, & in his face look wistfully*
510 *Most happy if from aught dis-covered there*
511 *Of tender feeling she might dare repeat*
512 *The same sad question. Meanwhile her poor*
hut
513 *Sunk to decay, for he was gone whose hand,*
514 *At the first nippings of* {O/o} *ctober frost,*
515 [*160*] *Closed up each chink & with fresh bands of*
straw

499–515 *not in MS. B*[2]

---

515 The number 160 is on the facing 41^v; it is an error for 260; see the notes to ll. 495 and 528.

(43) lived
She cquered the green-grown thatch. And so she ~~sate~~
Through the long winter, reckless & alone
Till this reft ~~hut~~ house, by frost & thaw, & rain
Was sapped, & when she slept the nightly damps
Did chill her breast, & in the stormy day
Her tattered clothes were ruffled by the wind
Even at the side of her own fire—yet still
~~She loved~~
She lov'd this wretched spot, nor would for worlds
Have parted hence, & still that length of road
And this rude bench one torturing hope en
Fast rooted at her heart ~~& ...~~ dearest! here
In sickness she remained, & (my friend) here she died
Last human tenant of these ruined walls

293
The End
273
285
~~146~~
521
491
~~660~~

lived
516 *Checquered the green-grown thatch. And so she^~~sate~~*
517 *Through the long winter, reckless & alone*
house
518 *Till this reft ~~hut~~, by frost & thaw, & rain*
519 *Was sapped, & when she slept the nightly*
damps
520 *Did chill her breast, & in the stormy day*
521 *Her tattered clothes were ruffled by the wind*
522 *Even at the side of her own fire—Yet still*
~~she loved~~
523 *She loved this wretched spot, nor would for*
worlds
524 *Have parted hence, & still that length of*
road
525 *And this rude bench one torturing hope en=*
-deared,
526 *Fast rooted at her heart & ~~Stranger~~! here*
my friend
527 *In sickness she remained, & here she died*
528 *Last human tenant of these ruined*
walls

{2 / 173}

The End

273
285
540
146

431
440

516–528 *not in MS. B²*

---

528 Here ends the original text of *RC* in MS. B. The number 273 is the total of lines in Part Two (but see the note to ll. 394–395 on 35[r]). This 273 was increased to 285 by the addition of 12 lines on 36[v]; these 285 lines plus 255 from Part One produce a poem of 540 lines. The 146, 431, and 440 are in pencil: 146 is the number of lines in the addendum; when the 285 lines in Part Two are added, the total comes to 431. The addition of lines on 51[v] (actually 8 but seemingly counted as 9) makes 440.

The old man ceased; he saw that I was moved
From that low bench rising instinctively
I turned away in weakness; and my heart
Went back into the tale which he had told
And when at last returning from my mind
And waking from the silence of my grief
I looked around, the cottage and the elms
The road the pathway and the garden wall
Which old & loose & mossy o'er the road
Hung bellying, all appeared I know not how
But to some eye within me, all appeared
Colours & forms of a strange discipline
The trouble which they sent into my thought
Was sweet, I looked and looked again, & long
seemed a better and a wiser man.

this spot

The door the pathway and the garden walls
And when ~~the~~ at length the the silence of my
By some irregular fancy from within
Or by some chance . impulse from without
Was first disturbed I looked around the
~~The door the pathway and the garden~~

I well remember what I felt the road
The door the pathway and the garden wall

The old man ceased; he saw that I was moved 1
From that low bench rising instinctively 2
I turn'd away in weakness; and my heart 3
Went back into the tale which he had told 4
brought back own
And when at last returning from my^mind 5
And waking from the silence of my grief
I lookd around, the cottage and the elms 6
The road the pathway and the garden wall 7
Which old & loose & mossy oer the road 8
Hung bellying, all appeared I know not how 9
But to some eye within me, all appeared 10
Colours & forms of a strange discipline 11
The trouble which they sent into my thought 12
Was sweet, I lookd and looked again, & to myself 13
I seemed a better and a wiser man. 14

[?road ?&]
the seat 15
The door the pathway and the garden walls 16
And when ~~the~~ at length the silence of my grief 17
By some irregular fancy from within 18
Or by some chance impression from without 19
tu
Was first dist {rbed—I looked around the road 20
~~The door the pathway and the garden wall~~ 21
and then
I well remember what I felt the road 22
{T
The door {the pathway and the garden wall 23

Here, continuing onto 45ʳ, WW makes three attempts—all rejected—to provide a more optimistic conclusion to the original *RC*.

I turned to the old man & said my friend (44)
Your words have consecrated many things
And for the tale which you have told I think
I am a better and a wiser man

How sweetly breathes the air it breathes most sweet
And my heart feels it how divinely green
Are yon huge clouds how lovely are these elms
That shew themselves with all their verdant leaves
And all the myriad veins of those green leaves
A summer prospect [illegible] by the leaves
The very sunshine spread upon the [illegible]
Is transhaped [illegible] The old man

I turned to the old man, & said my friend 1
Your words have consecrated many things 2
And for the tale which you have told I think 3
I am a better and a wiser man 4

How sweetly breathes the air it breathes 5
most sweet
And my heart feels it how divinely fair 6
Are yon huge clouds how lovely are these 7
elms
That shew themselves with all their verdant 8
leaves
And all the myriad veins of those green 9
leaves
A luminous prospect [?silvered] by the sun 10
d }
The very sunshine spread upon the [?]} ust 11
Is beautified 12
The old m
[?in ?mai]

A stub, with no ink visible on it, stands between 43v and 45r. The modern pencil numbers visible at the upper right-hand corner of this and subsequent rectos omit this stub in the count of leaves.

Not useless do I deem (45)
These quiet sympathies with things that hold
An inarticulate language for the man
Once taught to love such objects as excite
No morbid passions no disquietude
No vengeance & no hatred needs must feel
The joy of that pure principle of love
So deeply that unsatisfied with aught
Less pure & exquisite he cannot choose
But seek for objects of a kindred love
In fellow-natures & a kindred joy
Accordingly he by degrees perceives
His feelings of aversion softened down
A holy tenderness pervade his frame
His sanity of reason not impaired
Say rather all his thoughts now flowing clear
From a clear fountain flowing he looks round
He seeks for good & finds the good he seeks

[D, 67v]

Not useless do I deem 1
These quiet sympathies with things that 2
hold
An inarticulate language for the ~~*heart*~~ 3
man
O}
T}*nce taught to love such objects as excite* 4
No morbid passions no disquietude 5
No vengeance & no hatred needs must feel 6
The joy of that pure principle of love 7
So deeply that unsatisfied with aught 8
Less pure & exquisite he cannot choose 9
But seek for objects of a kindred love 10
In fellow-natures & a kindred joy 11
Accordingly he by degrees perceives 12
His feelings of aversion softened down 13
A holy tenderness pervade his frame 14
His sanity of reason not impaired 15
h}
Say rather all [?*t*]}*is thoughts now* 16
flowing clear
From a clear fountain flowing he looks 17
round
He seeks for good & finds the good he ~~*see*~~ 18
seeks

The beginning of the addendum draws on drafts from the Alfoxden Notebook, 20v. Part of the addendum (46r–52r) eventually became *Excursion*, IV, 1207–1298 (*PW*, V, 148–150).

2 When STC copied out the first eighteen lines of the addendum in a letter to his brother (ca. 10 March 1798 [*STCL*, I, 397–398]), the opening of his second line read "These shadowy Sympathies." The variant might be STC's own, or he might have been copying from drafts preceding MS. B (see p. 21, above).

18 Deletion by erasure.

Till execration & contempt are things (46)
He only knows by name & if he hears
From other mouths
The language which they speak ~~he is~~
He is compassionate & has no ~~contempt~~ thought
No feeling which can overcome his love

And further, ~~by~~ contemplating these forms
In the relations which they bear to man
We shall discover what a power is theirs
To stimulate our minds, & multiply
The spiritual presences of absent things
Then weariness shall cease. We shall acquire
The habit by which sense is made
Subservient still to moral purposes
A vital essence, & a saving power
Nor shall we meet an object but may read
Some sweet & tender lesson to our minds
Of human suffering or of human joy
All things shall speak of man & we shall read

[D, 67v]

Till execration & contempt are things 1
He only knows by name & if he hears 2
From other mouths
[20] ^*The language which they speak* ~~*he is compassionate*~~ 3
He is compassionate & has no thought 4
No feeling which can overcome his love 5
And further, {·} {*By* / [*?by*]} *contemplating these forms* 6
In the relations which they bear to man 7
We shall discover what a power is theirs 8
T{*o* / [?]} *stimulate our minds, & multiply* 9
The spiritual presences of absent things 10
Then weariness shall cease. We shall 11
acquire
The habit by which sense is made 12
Subservient still to moral purposes 13
A vital essence, & a saving power 14
Nor shall we meet an object but may read 15
Some sweet & tender lesson to our minds 16
or
Of human suffering ~~&~~ *of human joy* 17
All things shall sp{*e* / [*?a*]}*ak of man & we shall read* 18

3 The penciled number 20 is on the facing 46v. The addendum is numbered in twenties throughout in pencil.

(47)

Our duties in all forms & general laws
And local accidents shall tend alike
To quicken & to rouze & give the will
And power which by a chain of good
Shall link us to our kind. No naked hearts
No naked minds shall then be left to mourn
The burthen of existence. Science then
Shall be a precious visitant; & then
And only then be worthy of her name
For then her heart shall kindle her dull eye
Dull & inanimate no more shall hang
Chained to its object in brute slavery
But better taught & mindful of its use
Legitimate & its peculiar power
While with a patient interest it shall watch

[D, 68r]

Our duties in all forms & general laws 1
And local accidents shall tend alike 2
To quicken & to rouze & give the will 3
And power which by a chain of 4
good
[40] *Shall link us to our kind. No naked* 5
hearts
No naked minds shall then be left 6
to mourn
The burthen of existence. Science then, 7
Shall be a precious visitant; & then 8
And only then be worthy of her name 9
For then her heart shall kindle 10
her dull eye
~~*Her dull eye, dull & inanimate*~~ 11
D
[?N]} *ull ~~& inanimate~~ no more shall hang* 12
Chained to its object in brute slavery 13
But better taught & mindful of its 14
use
Legitimate & its peculiar power 15
While with a patient interest it shall 16
watch

5 The penciled number 40 is on the facing 47v.
12 The line drawn under "& inanimate" appears to be related to the deletion of l. 11.

46

The princepes of things & serve the cause
Of order & distinctness not for this
Shall it forget that its most noble
end
Its most illustrious province must
be found
In ministering to the excursive power
Of intellect & thought. So build we up
The being that we are. For was it meant
That we should pore & dwindle as we
pore
For ever dimly pore on things minute
On solitary objects, still beheld
In disconnection dead & spiritless
And still dividing & dividing still
Break down all grandeur still un-
-satisfied
With our unnatural toil while littleness
May yet become more little. Waging
thus

[D, 68r]

The processes of things & serve the cause 1
Of order & distinctness, not for this 2
Shall it forget that its most noble 3
end
Its most illustrious province must 4
be found
In ministering to the excursive power 5
Of intellect & thought. So build we up 6
The being that we are. For was it meant 7
That we should pore & dwindle as we 8
pore
For ever dimly pore on things minute 9
[*60*] *On solitary objects, still beheld* 10
In disconnection dead & spiritless 11
And still dividing & dividing still 12
Break down all grandeur still un= 13
-satisfied
With our unnatural toil while littleness 14
May yet become more little. Waging 15
thus

---

10 The penciled number 60 is on the facing 48v.

An impious warfare with the very life
Of our own souls. Or was it ever meant
That this majestic imagery the clouds,
The ocean & the firmament of heaven
Should lie a barren picture on the mind
Never for ends of vanity & pain
And sickly wretchedness were we endued
Amid this world of feeling & of life
With apprehension, reason, will & thought
Affections, organs, passions. Let us rise
From this oblivious sleep, these fretful dreams
Of feverish nothingness. Thus disciplined
All things shall live in us & we shall live
In all things that surround us. This I deem
Our tendency, & thus shall every day

[D, 68v]

An impious warfare with the very life 1
Of our own souls. Or was it ever meant 2
je
That this ma[?gi] stic imagery the clouds, 3
The ocean & the firmament of heaven 4
Should lie a barren picture on the 5
mind
Never for ends of vanity & pain 6
~~A~~ *And sickly wretchedness were we endued* 7
Amid this world of feeling & of life 8
r
With app[?] ehension, reason, will & 9
thought
Affections, organs, passions. Let us rise 10
From this oblivious sleep, these fretful 11
dreams
Of feverish nothingness. Thus disciplined 12
All things shall live in us & we shall 13
live
[?*n*]
d
In all things that surrou [?*n*]*d us. This I deem* 14
[*80*] *Our tendency, & thus shall every day* 15

7 Deletion by erasure.
11 DW crossed the "l" in "sleep."
15 The penciled 80 is on the facing 49v.

50

Enlarge our sphere of pleasure & of pain
For thus the senses & the intellect ~~Shall~~
Shall each to each supply a mutual aid
Invigorate and sharpen & refine ~~each other~~
each other
With a power that knows no bound
And forms & feelings acting thus, & thus
Reacting, they shall each acquire &
A living spirit & a character
Till then unfelt & each be multiplied
With a variety that knows no end
Thus deeply drinking in the soul of thi
We shall be wise perforce & we sha
mo
From
~~By~~ strict necessity along the path
Of order & of good. Whate'er we see
Whate'er we feel by agency direct
Or indirect shall tend to feed & nurse
Our faculties & raise to loftier heights

[D, 68v]

Enlarge our sphere of pleasure & of pain 1
For thus the senses & the intellect ~~shall~~ 2
Shall each to each supply a mutual aid 3
Invigorate and sharpen & refine ~~each other~~ 4
Each other
^*With a power that knows no bound* 5
And forms & feelings acting thus, & thus 6
Reacting, they shall each acquire X 7
A living spirit & a character 8
Till then unfelt & each be multiplied 9
With a variety that knows no end 10
Thus deeply drinking in the soul of things 11
We shall be wise perforce & we shall 12
move
From
~~*By*~~^*strict necessity along the path* 13
Of order & of good. Whate'er we see 14
Whate'er we feel by ageny direct 15
t
Or indirect shall tend f o feed & nurse 16
Our faculties & raise to loftier heights 17

---

7 The mark perhaps indicates this line's metrical deficiency.
15 DW's "ageny" is an obvious miswriting for "agency."

The old man ceas'd. he saw that I was mov'd;
From that low bench rising instinctively
I turn'd away in weakness, for my heart
Was heavy with the tale which he had told
I stood and leaning o'er the garden gate
Retrac'd that womans story & it seem'd
To comfort me while with a brothers love
I bless'd [illegible] in the impotence of grief
At length upon the hut I fix'd my eyes
Fondly & trac'd ~~over a~~ with milder interest

[D, 493–502; E, 838–847]

The old man ceas'd. he saw that I was moved, 1
From that low bench rising instinctively 2
[?~~Fr~~] I turn'd away in weakness, for my heart 3
Was heavy with the tale which he had told 4
I stood and leaning oer the garden gate 5
Retraced that womans story & it seemed 6
To comfort me while with a brothers love 7
I bless'd him{er} in the impotence of grief 8
A[?nd]{t} length upon the hut I fix'd my eyes 9
Fondly & tracd [viewd] with milder inter 10

This draft was meant for insertion at the horizontal line below l. 12 on 52^r. These ten lines add eight to what is on the recto, but they were seemingly counted as nine in the totaling of the addendum's lines on 43^r.

The penciled number 100, visible at the upper right of the photograph, refers to the text on 52^r.

(51)

Our intellectual soul. The old man ceased
The words he uttered shall not pass away
100 They had sunk into me. but not as sounds
To be expressed by visible characters
For while he spake my spirit had obeyed
The presence of his eye, my ear had drunk
The meanings of his voice. He had discoursed
Like one who in the slow & silent works
The manifold conclusions of his thought
Had brooded till Imagination's power
Condensed them to a passion whence she drew
Herself, new energies, resistless force
Yet still towards the cottage did I turn
Fondly & trace with nearer interest
That secret spirit of humanity
Which 'mid the calm oblivious tendencies
Of nature, 'mid her plants, her weeds & flowers

[D, 69^r, 502–505; E, 846–850]

Our intellectual soul. The old man ceased 1
The words he uttered shall not pass away 2
[*100*] *They had sunk into me, but not as* 3
sounds
To be expressed by visible characters 4
For while he spake my spirit had 5
obeyed
The presence of his eye, my ear had drunk 6
The meanings of his voice. He had dis= 7
=coursed
Like one who in the slow & silent works 8
The manifold conclusions of his thought 9
Had brooded till Imagination's power 10
Condensed them to a passion whens{c/e} 11
she drew
Herself, new energies, resistless force 12

Yet still towards the cottage did I turn 13
Fondly & trace with nearer interest 14
That secret spirit of humanity 15
Which 'mid the calm oblivious tendencies 16
Of nature, 'mid her plants, her weeds 17
& flowers

---

3 The penciled number 100 is on the facing 51^v.
12/13 The horizontal line indicates either the place of insertion for the draft on 51^v or the stopping point in copying part of the addendum into MS. D—or perhaps both.

(52)

And silent overgrowings still survived
The old man seeing this, resumed & said
My Friend, enough to sorrow have you given
The purposes of wisdom ask no more
Be wise & chearful, & no longer read
The forms of things with an unworthy eye
She sleeps in the calm earth & peace is here
I well remember that those very plumes
Those weeds & the high spear-grass on that wall
By mist & silent rain-drops silver'd o'er
~~And then on~~
As once I passed did to my heart convey
So still an image of tranquillity
So calm & still and looked so beautiful
Amid the uneasy thoughts which filled my mind
That what we feel of sorrow & despair
From ruin & from change & all the grief

[D, 506–521; E, 851–866]

And silent overgrowings still survived 1
The old man seeing this, resumed & said 2
My Friend, enough to sorrow have you 3
given
The purposes of Wisdom ask no more 4
Be wise & chearful, & no longer read 5
[*120*] *The forms of things with an unworthy* 6
eye
She sleeps in the calm earth & peace is 7
here
I well remember that those very plumes 8
Those weeds & the high spear-grass 9
on that wall
By mist & silent rain-drops silvered 10
o'er
~~*And this* [?*o*]~~ 11
As once I passed did {*to* / *m* *my heart* 12
convey
So still an image of tranquillity 13
So calm & still and looked so beautiful 14
Amid the uneasy thoughts which 15
filled my
mind
That what we feel of sorrow & despair 16
From ruin & from change & all the 17
grief

---

6 The penciled number 120 is on the facing 52v.

The passing shews of being leave behind
Appeared an idle dream that could not live
Where meditation was. I turned away
And walked along my ~~path~~ road in happiness

He ceased, & now the sun declining shot
A slant & mellow radiance which began
To fall upon us where ~~within the shade~~ beneath the trees
We sate on that low bench, & now we felt,
Admonished thus, the sweet hour coming on
A linnet warbled from those lofty elms
A thrush sang loud; and other melodies
At distance heard, peopled the milder air.
The old man rose & hoisted up his load
Together casting then a farewell look
Upon those silent walls we ~~turned away~~ left the shade
~~And pleasantly did we pursue our road~~
And cheerfully pursued our evening way

[D, 522–538; E, 867–883]

The passing shews of being leave behind 1
Appeared an idle dream that could not 2
live
ta
Where medi[?at]tion was I turned away 3
road
And walked along my ~~path~~ in 4
happiness
He ceased, & now the sun declining shot 5
A slant & mellow radiance which began 6
beneath the trees
To fall upon us where ~~within the shade~~ 7
We sate on that low bench, & now we 8
felt,
Admonished thus, the sweet hour coming 9
on
[*140*] *A linnet warbled from those lofty elms* 10
A thrush sang loud; and other melodies 11
At distance heard, peopled the milder 12
air.
The old man rose & hoisted up his load 13
Together casting then a farewell look 14
left the shade
Upon those silent walls we ~~turned away~~ 15
~~chearfull pursued our road [?]~~
[*146*] ~~*And pleasantly did we pursue our road*~~ 16
And chearfully pursued our evening
way

The numbers 140 and 146, both in pencil, are on the facing 53v. The 146 seems to have been entered before correction of the final line.

[D, 66r]

Oh twas a pleasant thing to hear these tales
Of   which he had seen to hear [?him ?teach]
Wisdom by [?painting] as he did
The manners & the passions

That softens all its forms and
                                        [?melts ?]
    [?smooths ?]   [?]
        [?]
Into a gentle prospect that appears
[? ?earthly]

This page, much discolored and stained, served as the outside back cover of the notebook until recent restoration. Pages between 54r and 56v are blank.

The first four lines are in ink, the next three in pencil. The ink draft is related to MS. B, 17v, ll. 18–22.

At the bottom, upside down and in ink, is the following:

3 |130
   43

3 13[?0]
       4
   430
   [?4]
    2[?76]

Although the numbers may have nothing to do with *RC*, the possible 276 is interesting because that may have been the length of *The Pedlar*, 1802, at one stage (see the note to l. 35 in the transcription of MS. D, 46v, below).

MS. D

Like the *Christabel* Notebook, *Ruined Cottage* MS. D (DC MS. 16) is one of Dorothy's pocket notebooks, with a red leather cover and a flap for closure. Fifty-nine leaves, 12.3 centimeters wide by 19.5 centimeters high, are intact: 1, 4–7, 10–12, 28–34, 39–69, 74–82, and 87–90. Only stubs are left at 2–3, 8–9, 13–27, 35–38, 70–73, and 83–86. Little of the watermark is visible, but it may be a fleur-de-lys; the white laid paper has chain lines 2.3 centimeters apart. A complete list of the poems copied into this notebook may be found in *Chronology*: *EY*, pp. 325–328. The dating of *Ruined Cottage* MS. D is discussed on pp. 22–28, above; the manuscript includes material dating from 1799, 1801–1802, and—possibly—1809–1812.

In 1799, the Pedlar's history and most of the addendum were taken out of *The Ruined Cottage* as it stood in MS. B: Dorothy copied the more compact poem onto leaves 46^r to 56^r of MS. D. (Editorial line numbers in the left-hand margins of transcriptions of these leaves indicate corresponding lines in the MS. D reading text.) Dorothy then wrote out lines from the Alfoxden Notebook—"In storm and tempest"—as a "Fragment," beginning on 56^v and continuing on the top of 57^r. After leaving several blank pages, she transcribed on 60^r to 67^r the surplus passages about the Pedlar. That part of the original MS. B addendum not previously used in MS. D ("Not useless do I deem") followed on leaves 67^v to 69^r.

In late December 1801 Wordsworth returned to MS. D to create a new poem from the overflow Pedlar lines. Pencil drafts on 49^v and 59^v are probably the earliest work from this stage, along with pencil lines on 57^r to 59^r now erased (the erased pencil remains illegible even after infrared photography). Then William and Dorothy copied out the beginning of *The Pedlar*, 1802, writing over the erased pencil lines. Their line numbers link this fair copy with the original 1799 text and with a later 1802 passage (on 64^v). Dorothy's journal entries in January and February 1802 record extensive work on this new poem, and MS. D contains several levels of revision. Although it is not possible now to untangle these reshufflings and revisions completely (related manuscripts do not survive), the Wordsworths' numbering enables one to read most of an early state of *The Pedlar*, 1802, and italicized editorial numbers in the left-hand margins of 57^r to 66^r help to reconstruct this state partially. At line 233 on 66^r, the text probably jumped to another sheet, now lost; since Dorothy described this poem as 280 lines long in July 1802 (*Journals*, p. 146), as many as four dozen lines may be missing from the MS. D text. Transcription of these fair-copy additions in 1801–1802 is not set in reduced type; notes distinguish earlier from later work. Bracketed line numbers above transcriptions of the 1799 Pedlar overflow and *The Pedlar*, 1802, show corresponding lines from MS. E. To make possible reference to lines in the MS. D addendum (60^r–67^r) that are not used in *The Pedlar*, 1802, line numbers in the right-hand margin are serially assigned on the transcription of each leaf.

Between about December 1809 and March 1812, Mary Wordsworth copied what once was *The Ruined Cottage* as part of *Excursion* MS. P (DC MS. 71; *Chronology: MY*, pp. 22, 675–685); the number of variants between MS. P and the immediately preceding MSS. E, E^2, and M suggests the possibility of an intervening manuscript, now lost. In addition, the opening of MS. P is more closely related to MS. D than to MSS. E, E^2, and M. An X to the right of line 24 on MS. D, 46^v, may indicate the termination of use of that manuscript as a copying source for *Excursion* MS. P or for a now lost manuscript that preceded it; some of the revisions in lines 1–24 of MS. D may therefore have been made as late as 1809–1812.

Unlike earlier *Ruined Cottage* manuscripts, MS. D has been revised by erasure. Notes to lines with these erasures give the reading of the preceding MS. B, with any visible letters set in boldface type in the notes.

(MS. D) 45

The Ruined Cottage
1st Part

'Twas summer & the sun was mounted high
Along the south the uplands feebly glared
Through a pale steam, & all the northern downs
In clearer air ascending shewed far off,
Their surfaces with shadows dappled o'er
Of deep embattled clouds: far as the sight
Could reach those many shadows lay in spots
Determined & unmoved, with steady beams
Of clear & pleasant sunshine interposed
Pleasant to him who on the soft cool moss
Extends his careless limbs along the root
Of some huge oak whose aged branches make
A twilight of their own, a dewy shade
Where the wren warbles while the dreaming man
Half-conscious of that soothing melody
With side-long eye looks out upon the scene
By those impending branches made more soft
More soft and distant. Other lot was mine
Across a bare wide Common I had toiled
With languid feet which by the slippery ground
Were baffled still, & when I stretched myself
On the brown earth my limbs from very heat
The heat of ... [illegible]

The Ruined Cottage
1st Part

1 *'Twas summer & the sun was mounted high*
2 *Along the south the uplands feebly glared*
but
3 *Through a pale steam, & all the northern downs*
4 *In clearer air ascending shewed far off*
5 *Their surfaces with shadows dappled o'er*
6 *Of deep embattled clouds: far as the sight*
7 *Could reach those many shadows lay in spots*
8 *Determined & unmoved, with steady beams*
9 *Of clear & pleasant sunshine interposed*
10 *Pleasant to him who on the soft cool moss*
along the front
[? ?] the mouth
11 *Extends his careless limbs ~~beside~~ the root*
[?cave] rocky [?] boughs diffuse
12 *Of some huge oak whose ~~aged branches make~~*
13 *A twilight of their own, a dewy shade*
14 *Where the wren warbles while the dreaming man*
15 *Half-conscious of that soothing melody*
16 *With side-long eye looks out upon the scene*
at covert
17 *By th{ose impending ~~branches~~ made more soft*
low
18 *More ~~soft~~ and distant. Other lot was mine*
Yet did I look that day for livelier joy
19 *Across a bare wide Common I had toiled*
20 20 *With languid feet which by the slipp'ry ground*
nor could my weak arm disperse
21 *Were baffled still, & when I stretched myself*
22 *On the brown earth my limbs from very heat*
The host of insects gathering round my face

The penciled numbers visible in the upper corners of this and following photographs of rectos—and the designation as MS. D at upper left here—are of recent origin.

10 The erased word may be the MS. B reading: "grass."

17/18 low] In pencil.

20 The penciled line number is a later addition, associated with the number opposite l. 35 on 46v; see the note there and on 56r.

Could find no rest nor my weak arm disperse
The insect host which of insects gathered round my face
And joined their murmurs to the tedious noise
Of seeds of bursting gorse that crackled round
I rose and turned towards a group of trees
Which midway in that level stood alone
And thither come at length beneath a shade
Of clustering elms that sprang from the same root
I found a ruined house four naked walls
That stared upon each other. I looked round
And near the door I saw an aged Man
Alone, and stretched upon the cottage bench
An iron-pointed staff lay at his side
With instantaneous joy I recognized
That pride of nature & of lowly life
The venerable Armytage, a friend
As dear to me as is the setting sun *
He lay, his pack of rustic merchandize
Pillowing his head — I guess he had no thought
Of his way-wandering life. His eyes were shut
The shadows of the breezy elms above
Dappled his face. With thirsty heat oppress'd
At length I hailed him glad to see his hat
Bedewed with water-drops, as if the brim
Had newly scoop'd a running stream. He rose
And pointing to a sun-flower bade me climb
The wall where that same gaudy flower
Looked out upon the road. It was a plot
Of garden-ground, now wild its matted weeds
Marked with the steps of those whom as they pass'd

* Turn to the beginning

23 *Could find no rest nor my weak arm disperse*
of insects ing
24 *The ~~insect~~ host ~~which~~ gathered round my face* X
25 ~~*And joined their murmurs to the tedious noise*~~
26 *Of seeds of bursting gorse that crackled round*
27 *I rose and turned towards a group of trees*
28 *Which midway in that level stood alone,*
29 *And thither come at length beneath a shade*
30 *Of clustering elms that sprang from the same root*
31 *I found a ruined* house four naked *walls*
32 *That stared upon each other. I looked round*
33 *And near the door I saw an aged Man*
34 *Alone, and stretched upon the cottage bench*
35 *An iron-pointed staff lay at his side*
36 *With instantanious joy I recognized*
37 *That pride of nature & of lowly life*
38 *The venerable Armytage, a friend*
39 *As dear to me as is the setting sun**
44 *He lay, his pack of rustic merchandize*
45 *Pillowing his head—I guess he had no thought*
46 *Of his way-wandering life. His eyes were shut*
47 *The shadows of the breezy elms above*
48 *Dappled his face. With thirsty heat oppress'd*
49 At length I hailed him glad to see *his hat*
50 *Bedewed with water-drops, as if the brim*
51 *Had newly scoop'd a running stream. He rose*
52 *And pointing to a sun-flower bade me climb*
53 *The wall where that same gaudy flower*
54 *Looked out upon the road. It was a plot*
run
[?]
55 *Of garden-ground, ~~now~~ wild its matted weeds*
56 *Marked with the steps of those whom as they pass'd*

276
35
311

* *Turn to the beginning* [?ran ?run ?wild]

---

24 About the X to the right of this line, see the MS. D headnote.

31 The erased words are possibly the MS. B reading: "Cottage, **f**our c**lay**."

34–37 The lines were copied from the corrected version in MS. B, 26v; the erased lines may be from MS. B, 3v and 4r:

Stretched on a bench an iro**n**-pointe**d** st**aff**
Lay at his side with instantaneous joy
I view'd him for I recognized my **friend**
That pride of **nature** & of lowl**y** life

35 Since *The Pedlar* was about 280 lines long in July 1802, this sum may refer to an intended reinsertion of a description of the Pedlar's character here sometime between 1802 and the copying of MS. E. See also the note to the numbers on 56r.

38 The erased word may be the MS. B reading: "man."

39 The asterisk refers to DW's instruction at the bottom of the page. DW inadvertently skipped ll. 40–43 and copied them on 45v:

40 two days before
41 We had been fellow-travellers I knew
42 That he was in this neighbourhood and now
43 Delighted found him here in the cool shade
44 He lay, his pack &c

A photograph of 45v is in *SPP*, p. 204.

The goose-berry trees that shot in long lank slips
Or currants hanging from their leafless stems
In scanty strings had tempted to o'erleap
The broken wall. Within that cheerless spot
Where two tall hedgerows of thick alder boughs
Joined in a damp cold nook I found a well
Half covered up with willow flowers & grass
I slaked my thirst & to the shady bench
Returned & while I stood unbonneted
To catch the motion of the cooler air
The old Man said "I see around me here
Things which you cannot see, we die, my Friend
Nor we alone but that which each man loved
And prized in his peculiar nook of earth
Dies with him or is changed, & very soon
Even of the good is no memorial left
The Poets in their elegies & songs
Lamenting the departed call the groves
They call upon the hills & streams to mourn
And senseless rocks, nor idly; for they speak
In these their invocations with a voice
Obedient to the strong creative power
Of human passion. Sympathies there are
More tranquil yet perhaps of kindred birth
That steal upon the meditative mind
And grow with thought. Beside yon spring I stood
And eyed its waters till we seemed to feel

57 *The goose-berry trees that shot in long lank slips*
58 *Or currants hanging from their leafless stems*
59 *In scanty strings had tempted to o'erleap*
60 *The broken wall. Within that cheerless spot*
alder
61 *Where two tall hedgerows of thick ~~willow~~ boughs*
62 *Joined in a damp cold nook I found a well*
cover'd up with willow-flowers & grass
{~~with willow flowers & weeds~~
63 *Half-~~choked~~* {
64 *I slaked my thirst & to the shady bench*
R
65 [*?I*]} *eturned & while I stood unbonneted*
66 *To catch the* motion of the cooler air
{here
67 *The old Man said "I see around me* {
68 *Things which you cannot see, we die, my Friend*
69 *Nor we alone, but that which each man loved*
70 *And prized in his peculiar nook of earth*
71 *Dies with him or is changed, & very soon*
72 *Even of the good is no memorial left*
73 *The Poets in their elegies & songs*
74 *Lamenting the departed call the groves*
75 *They call upon the hills & streams to mourn*
76 *And senseless rocks, nor idly: for,* they speak
77 In these their invocations with a voice
78 *Obedient to the strong creative power*
79 *Of human passion. Sympathies there are*
80 *More* tranquil *yet* perhaps *of* *kindred birth*
81 *That steal upon the meditative mind*
82 *And grow with thought. Beside yon spring I stood*
83 *And eyed its waters till we seemed to feel*
I entered & within

---

63 with willow flowers & weeds] In pencil, but deleted in ink.
64–66 A related draft is on 91ʳ (see Transcriptions of Additions to MS. D, below).
66 The erased words may be the MS. B reading: "current **of** the breez**y** air."
76–77 The erased words may be the MS. B reading: "inspired / **By** no fallacious oracle the**y** speak."
80 There is an erasure between "of" and "kindred." In MS. B, the line reads: "More mild, yet haply of a kindred birth."

One sadness they & I. For them a bond
Of brotherhood is broken: time has been
When every day the touch of human hand
Disturbed their stillness, & they ministered
To human comfort. When I stooped to drink
~~[illegible]~~
~~A spider's web~~ hung to the water's edge
~~Upon the slimy~~ foot-stone, I espied
~~And on the wet & slimy foot-stone lay~~
~~The the useless fragments of a~~ ~~cup~~
The useless fragment of a wooden bowl
It moved my very heart. The day has been
When I could never pass this road but she
Who lived within these walls when I appeared
A daughter's welcome gave me & I loved her
As my own child. O Sir! the good die first
And they whose hearts are dry as summer dust
Burn to the socket. Many a passenger
Has blessed poor Margaret for her gentle looks
When she upheld the cool refreshment drawn
From that forsaken spring, & no one came
But he was welcome no one went away
But that it seemed she loved him. She is dead
The worm is on her cheek, & this poor hut
Stripp'd of its outward garb of houshold flowers
Of rose & sweet-briar offers to the wind
A cold bare wall whose earthy top is tricked
With weeds & the rank spear-grass. She is dead
And nettles rot & adders sun themselves
Where we have sate together while she nurs'd

84 *One sadness they & I. For them* a *bond*
85 *Of brotherhood is broken: time has been*
86 *When every day the touch of human hand*
87 *Disturbed their stillness, & they ministered*
88 *To human comfort. When I stooped to drink*
~~*At that deserted well a spider's web*~~
89 ~~A spider's web~~ ~~*hung to the water's edge*~~
Upon the slimy footstone I espied
90 ~~*And on the wet & slimy foot-stone, lay*~~
{[?~~And~~]
{[?] ~~The slimy footstone I espied~~
91 *The useless fragment of a wooden bowl*
92 *It moved my very heart. The day has been*
93 *When I could never pass this road but she*
94 *Who lived within these walls when I appeared*
95 *A daughter's welcome gave me & I loved her*
96 *As my own child. O Sir! the good die first*
97 *And they whose hearts are dry as summer dust*
98 *Burn to the socket. Many a passenger*
99 *Has blessed poor Margaret for her gentle looks*
100 *When she upheld the cool refreshment drawn*
101 *From that forsaken spring, & no one came*
102 *But he was welcome no one went away*
103 *But that it seemed she loved him. She is dead*
104 *The worm is on her cheek, & this poor hut*
105 *Stripp'd of its outward garb of houshold flowers*
106 *Of rose & sweet-briar offers to the wind*
107 *A cold bare wall whose earthy top is tricked*
108 *With weeds & the rank spear-grass. She is dead*
109 *And nettles rot & adders sun themselves*
110 *Where we have sate together while she nurs'd*

---

84 The space available for the erased word suggests that it may be "the."
89 The erased words are probably the MS. B reading: "**A**cross its mou**th**."
103b–108a The deletion mark is in pencil.

Her infant at her breast. The unshod Colt 49
The [houseless] ~~wandring~~ heifer and the Potter's ass
Find shelter now within the chimney-wall
Where I have seen her evening hearth-stone blaze
And through the window spread upon the road
Its chearful light.—You will forgive me Sir
But often on this cottage do I muse [sometimes]
As on a picture till my wiser mind
Sinks, yielding to the foolishness of grief.
She had a husband, an industrious man
Sober and steady I have heard her say
That he was up and busy at his loom
In summer ere the mower [was at work] ~~scythe had swept~~
The dewy grass, & in the early spring
Ere the last star had vanished. They who passed
At evening from behind the garden-fence
Might hear his busy spade which he would ply
After his daily work till the day-light
Was gone & every leaf & flower were lost
In the dark hedges. So they pass'd their days
In peace & comfort & two pretty babes
Were their best hope next to the God in Heaven.
— You may remember, now some ten years gone
Two blighting seasons when the fields were left
With half a harvest it pleased heaven to add
A worse affliction in the plague of war
A happy land was stricken to the heart
'Twas a sad time of sorrow & distress

111 *Her infant at her breast. The* unshod *Colt*
homeless
112 *The* wandring *heifer and the Potter's ass*
113 *Find shelter now within the chimney-wall*
114 *Where I have seen her evening hearth-stone blaze*
115 *And through the window spread upon the road*
116 *Its chearful light—You will forgive me Sir*
sometimes
117 But often on this cottage do I muse
118 As on a picture till my wiser mind
119 Sinks, yielding to the foolisness of grief.
120 *She had a husband, an industrious man*
121 *Sober and steady I have heard her say*
122 *That he was up and busy at his loom*
was abroad
123 *In summer ere the mower'~~s scythe had swept~~*
Among the grass
124 *The dewy grass, & in the early spring*
125 *Ere the last star had vanished. They who pass'd*
126 *At evening from behind the garden-fence*
127 *Might hear his busy spade which he would ply*
128 *After his daily work till the day-light*
129 *Was gone & every leaf & flower were lost*
130 *In the dark hedges. So they pass'd their days*
131 *In peace & comfort, & two pretty babes*
132 *Were their best hope next to the God in Heaven*
133 *—You may remember, now some ten years*
gone
134 *Two blighting seasons when the fields were left*
135 *With half a* harvest *it pleased heaven to add*
136 *A worse affliction in the plague of war*
137 *A happy land was stricken to the heart*
138 *'Twas a sad time of sorrow & distress*

---

111 The erased word may be the MS. B reading: "wild."
112 The erased word may be the MS. B reading: "unstalled."
117–119 Two ink dots before ll. 117 and 119 suggest that DW may have here counted a two-line gap in her numbering; since WW filled the gap in three lines, Part One has 198 lines rather than the 197 DW wrote on 49v.
123–124 The revisions are in pencil, although the deleting line in 123 is in ink.
135 The erased word may be the deleted reading in MS. B: "tillage."

A wanderer among the cottages
I with my pack of winter raiment saw
The hardships of that season many rich
Sunk down as ~~in~~ a dream among the poor
And of the poor did many cease to be
And their place knew them not. Meanwhile abridg'd
Of daily comforts, gladly reconciled
To numerous self-denials, Margaret
Went struggling on through those calamitous years
With chearful hope but ere the second autumn
A fever seized her husband. In disease
He lingered long, & when his strength returned
He found the little he had stored to meet
The hour of accident or crippling age
Was all consumed. As I have said 'twas now
A time of trouble, shoals of artisans
Were from their daily labour turned away
from public
~~To~~ ~~[illegible]~~ ~~for~~ bread ~~on~~ ~~[illegible]~~ charity
~~[illegible]~~
They & their wives & children, happier far
~~[illegible]~~
Could they have lived as do the little birds
That peck along the hedges or the kite
That makes her dwelling in the mountain rocks
Ill fared it now with Robert, he who dwelt
In this ~~poor~~ cottage, at his door he stood
And whistled many a snatch of merry tunes
That had no mirth in them, or with his knife
Carved uncouth figures on the heads of sticks
at this time

139 *A wanderer among the cottages*
140 *I with my pack of winter raiment saw*
141 *The hardships of that season many rich*
{*in*
142 *Sunk down as* {*a a dream among the poor*
143 *And of the poor did many cease to be*
144 *And their place knew them not. Meanwhile abridg'd*
145 *Of daily comforts, gladly reconciled*
146 *To numerous self-denials, Margaret*
147 *Went struggling on through those calamitous years*
148 *With chearful hope but ere the second* autumn
149 *A fever seized her husband. In disease*
150 *He lingered long, & when his strength returned*
151 *He found the little he had stored to meet*
152 *The hour of accident or crippling age*
153 *Was all consumed. As I have said 'twas now*
154 *A time of trouble, shoals of artisans*
155 *Were from their daily labour turned away* [?tracking] [?trooping]
{~~beg~~
{seek ~~their~~ from publi
156 ~~*To*~~ ~~*hang for*~~ *bread* ~~*on*~~ ~~*parish*~~ *charity*
To seek their /
157 *They & their wives & children, happier far*
~~So sometimes have I said within myself~~
~~When I have met them [?working] in the way~~
158 *Could they have lived as do the little birds*
159 *That peck along the hedges or the kite*
160 *That makes her dwelling in the mountain rocks'*
161 *Ill fared it now with Robert, he who dwelt*
here
162 *In this* ~~*poor*~~ *cottage, at his door he stood*
163 *And whistled many a snatch of merry tunes*
164 *That had no mirth in them, or with his knife*
165 *Carved uncouth figures on the heads of sticks*
at this time

---

142 The ink stroke between "in" and "a" looks like an abortive beginning of the "d" on "dream."
148 The erased word may be the MS. B reading: "spring."
156 The mark between "on" and "parish" may point to the correction above the line.

51

Then idly sought about through every nook
Of house or garden any casual task
Of use or ornament & with a strange
Amusing but uneasy novelty
He blended where he might the various tasks
Of summer, autumn, winter & of spring
But this endured not, his good humour soon
Became a weight in which no pleasure was
And poverty brought on a petted mood
And a sore temper day by day he drooped
And he would often leave his home & to the town
Without an errand would he turn his steps
Or wander here & there among the fields
One while he would speak lightly of his babes
And with a cruel tongue, at other times
He ~~toss'd them with a false unnatural joy~~
~~played with them with freaks of merriment~~
And 'twas a piteous thing to see the looks
Of the poor innocent children. "Every smile"
Said Margaret to me here beneath these trees
Made my heart bleed. At this the old Man paus'd
And looking up to those enormous elms
He said 'tis now the hour of deepest noon
At this still season of repose & peace
This hour when all things which are not at rest
Are chearful, while this multitude of flies
~~With~~
With

166 *Then idly sought about through every nook*
167 *Of house or garden any casual task*
168 *Of use or ornament & with a strange*
169 *Amusing but uneasy novelty*
170 *He blended where he might the various tasks*
171 *Of summer, autumn, winter & of spring*
172 *But this endured not, his good-humour soon*
173 *Became a weight in which no pleasure was*
174 *And poverty brought on a petted mood*
175 *And a sore temper day by day he drooped*
often ft
176 *And ~~he would~~ leave his home & to the town*
177 *Without an errand would he turn his steps*
178 *Or wander here & there among the fields*
179 *One while he would speak lightly of his babes*
180 *And with a cruel tongue, at other times*
tossd them with a false unnatural joy
181 *He ~~played with them wild freaks of merriment~~*
182 *And 'twas a piteous thing to see the looks*
183 *Of the poor innocent children. "Every smile"*
184 *Said Margaret to me here beneath these trees*
185 *Made my heart bleed. At this the old Man*
paus'd
186 *And looking up to those enormous elms*
187 *He said 'tis now the hour of deepest noon*
188 *At this still season of repose & peace*
189 *This hour when all things which are not at rest*
190 *Are chearful, while this multitude of flies*
~~With~~
He tossd them with a false unnatural
joy
With

---

176 The deleting line and the revisions are in pencil.
181 The revision is in pencil, but the deleting line is in ink.
190 The pencil draft below the line is a revision of l. 181. Both "With"s are in ink.

melody

Why should a tear be in an old mans eye
Why should we thus with an untoward mind
And in the weakness of humanity
From natural wisdom turn our hearts away
To natural comfort shut our eyes & ears
And feeding on disquiet thus disturb
The calm of Nature with our restless thoughts

197

End of the first Part

Is filling all the air with
191 ~~*Fills all the air with happy*~~ *melody*
192 *Why should a tear be in an old man's eye*
193 *Why should we thus with an untoward mind*
194 *And in the weakness of humanity*
195 *From natural wisdom turn our hearts away*
196 *To natural comfort shut our eyes & ears*
197 *And feeding on disquiet thus disturb*
198 *The calm of Nature with our restless thoughts*
197

End of the first Part

I have heard thee say
{of
all {us us that
That we are poets, that all [?livin ?men]
Are poets better far than they believe
Or know of
Glad were both at meeting thus [?ag]
have some happy [?times/?hours]
In the especial goodness of good hearts
As [?a ?natural ?doctrine]

---

198 About the discrepancy between DW's count and the editorial line number, see the note to ll. 117–119 on 48^r.

WW's draft beginning at the middle of the page is in pencil. Like the draft on 59^v, it is probably 1801–1802 work toward a separate poem about the Pedlar; both passages are concerned with the meeting of the poet and pedlar which would lead into the Pedlar's history.

53

Second Part

He spake with somewhat of a solemn tone
But when he ended there was in his face
Such easy chearfulness, a look so mild
That for a little time it stole away
All recollection and that simple tale
Passed from my mind like a forgotten sound
A while on trivial things we held discourse
To me soon tasteless. In my own despite
I thought of that poor woman as of one
Whom I had known & loved. He had rehearsed
Her homely tale with such familiar power
With such a [illegible] countenance, an eye
So busy that the things of which he spake
Seemed present & attention now relaxed
There was a heartfelt chillness in my veins
I rose & turning from that breezy shade
Went out into the open air & stood
To drink the comfort of the warmer sun
Long time I had not stayed ere looking round
20 Upon that tranquil ruin I returned
And begged of the old man that for my sake
He would resume his story. He replied
It were a wantonness & would demand
Severe reproof, if we were men whose hearts
Could hold vain dalliance with the misery
Even of the dead contented thence to draw
A momentary pleasure never marked

Second Part

199 *He spake with somewhat of a solemn tone*
200 *But when he ended there was in his face*
201 *Such easy chearfulness, a look so mild*
202 *That for a little time it stole away*
203 *All recollection and that simple tale*
204 *Passed from my mind like a forgotten sound*
205 *A while on trivial things we held discourse*
206 *To me soon tasteless. In my own despite*
207 *I thought of that poor woman as of one*
208 *Whom I had known & loved. He had rehearsed*
209 *Her homely tale with such familiar power*
210 *With such a* {active} *countenance, an eye*
211 *So busy that the things of which he spake*
212 *Seemed present & attention now relaxed*
213 *There was a heartfelt chillness in my veins*
214 *I rose & turning from that breezy shade*
215 *Went out into the open air & stood* ~~*to drink*~~
216 To drink the comfort of the warmer sun
217 *Long time I had not stayed ere looking round*
218 20 *Upon that tranquil ruin I returned*
219 *And begged of the old man that for my sake*
220 *He would resume his story. He replied*
221 *It were a wantonness & would demand*
222 *Severe reproof, if we were men whose hearts*
223 *Could hold vain dalliance with the misery*
224 *Even of the dead contented thence to draw*
225 *A momentary pleasure never marked*

---

210 active] In pencil.
212 MS. B reads as here, with the exception of a comma after the ampersand; the reason for the erasure is unclear.
215 Deletion by erasure.
216 The erasure corrected an error copied from MS. B (28r, 273–274). The erased line probably read: "The comfort of the warmer sun."

By reason, barren of all future good
But we have known that there is often found
In mournful thoughts, & always might be found
A power to virtue friendly were't not so
I am a dreamer among men indeed
An idle dreamer. 'Tis a common tale
By moving accidents uncharactered
A tale of silent suffering hardly clothed
In bodily form, & to the grosser sense
But ill adapted, scarcely palpable
To him who does not think. But at your bidding
I will proceed.
While thus it fared with them
40 To whom this cottage till that hapless year
Had been a blessed home it was my chance
To travel in a country far remote
And glad I was when, halting by yon gate
That leads from the green lane again I saw
These lofty elm-trees. Long I did not rest
With many pleasant thoughts I cheer'd my way
O'er the flat common. At the door arrived,
I knocked & when I entered with the hope
Of usual greeting Margaret looked at me
A little while then turned her head away
Speechless, & sitting down upon a chair
Wept bitterly. I wist not what to do *
~~at length she rose~~
Or how to speak to her. ~~Poor wretch~~. At last
She rose from off her seat – and then, oh Sir!
I cannot tell how she pronounced my name
or in what words to speak to her

226 *By reason, barren of all future good*
227 *But we have known that there is often found*
228 *In mournful thoughts, & always might be found*
229 *A power to virtue friendly were't not so*
230 *I am a dreamer among men indeed*
231 *An idle dreamer. 'Tis a common tale*
232 *By moving accidents uncharactered*
233 *A tale of silent suffering hardly clothed*
234 *In bodily form, & to the grosser sense*
t
235 *But ill adapp} ed, scarcely palpable*
desire
236 *To him who does not think. But at your bidding*
237 *I will proceed.*
While thus it fared with them
238 40 *To whom this cottage till that hapless year*
239 *Had been a blessed home it was my chance*
240 *To travel in a country far remote*
241 *And glad I was when, halting by yon gate*
a
242 *That leads from the green l[?]} ne, again I saw*
243 *These lofty elm-trees. Long I did not rest*
244 *With many pleasant thoughts I cheer'd my way*
245 *O'er the flat common. At the door arrived,*
246 *I knocked & when I entered with the hope*
247 *Of usual greeting Margaret looked at me*
248 *A little while then turned her head away*
249 *Speechless, & sitting down upon a chair*
250 *Wept bitterly. I wist not what to do* *
at length she rose
251 *Or how to speak to her. ~~Poor wretch! at last~~*
252 *She rose from off her seat—and then, oh Sir!*
253 *I cannot tell how she pronounced my name*
Or in what words to speak to her

---

236 desire] In pencil.
250 The asterisk is related to the following line's correction or to the line of revision at page foot; all three match in ink color.

55

With fervent love & with a face of grief
Unutterably helpless & a look
That seem'd to cling upon me she enquir'd
If I had seen her husband. As she spake
60 A strange surprize & fear came to my heart
Nor had I power to [illegible]

That he had disappeared, just two months gone
He left his house two wretched days had passed
And on the third by the first break of light
Within her casement full in view she saw
A purse of gold. "I trembled at the sight"
Said Margaret "for I knew it was his hand
That placed it there, & on that very day
By one, a stranger, from my husband sent
The tidings came that he had joined a troop
Of soldiers going to a distant land
He left me thus— Poor Man! he had not heart
To take a farewell of me, & he feared
That I should follow with my babes & sink
that wandering wretched
Beneath the misery of ~~a soldier's~~ life
This tale did Margaret tell with many tears
And when she ended I had little power
To give her comfort, & was glad to take
Such words of hope from her own mouth as served
80 To cheer us both but long we had not talked
Ere we built up a pile of better thoughts
And with a brighter eye she looked around

A letter [illegible] house [illegible]
Of [illegible] & found [illegible]
[illegible] & [illegible]

254 *With fervent love, & with a face of grief*
255 *Unutterably helpless & a look*
256 *That seem'd to cling upon me she enquir'd*
257 *If I had seen her husband. As she spake*
258 60 *A strange surprize & fear came to my heart*
259 Nor had I power to answer ere she told
260 *That he had disappeared; just two months gone*
261 *He left his house two wretched days had passed*
262 *And on the third by the first break of light*
263 *Within her casement full in view she saw*
264 *A purse of gold. "I trembled at the sight"*
265 *Said Margaret, "for I knew it was his hand*
266 *That placed it there,* & *on that very day*
267 *By one, a stranger, from my husband sent*
268 *The tidings came that he had joined a troop*
269 *Of soldiers going to a distant land*
270 *He left me thus— Poor Man! he had not heart*
271 *To take a farewell of me, & he feared*
272 *That I should follow with my babes, & sink*
that wandering wretched
273 *Beneath the misery of ~~a soldier's~~ life*
274 *This tale did Margaret tell with many tears*
275 *And when she ended I had little power*
276 *To give her comfort, & was glad to take*
277 *Such words of hope from her own mouth as*
serv'd
278 80 *To cheer us both but long we had not talked*
279 *Ere we built up a pile of better thoughts*
280 *And with a brighter eye she looked around*

[Left margin, written vertically:]
a Letter, such it seemed which sh forthwith
Opened, & found no writing but therein
Ten pounds in gold

259 Either WW's added line or a one-line gap is included in DW's numbering from 60 to 80.
263 Below "Within" the mark points to the draft written vertically in the left-hand margin; the lines contribute to MS. E (ll. 598–601).
266 The erased letters may have been "up."

As if she had been shedding tears of joy
We parted. It was then the early spring
I left her busy with her garden tools
And well remember o'er that fence she looked
And while I paced along the foot-way path
Called out & sent a blessing after me
With tender chearfulness & with a voice
That seemed the very sound of happy thoughts

I roved o'er many a hill & many a dale
With this my weary load, in heat & cold
Through many a wood, & many an open ground
In sunshine or in shade in wet or fair
Now blithe, now drooping as it might befal
My best companions now the driving winds
And now the "trotting brooks" & whispering trees
And now the music of my own sad steps
With many a short-lived thought that pass'd between
100 And disappeared. I came this way again
Towards the wane of summer when the wheat
Was yellow, & the soft & bladed grass
Sprang up afresh & o'er the hay-field spread
Its tender green. When I had reached the door
I found that she was absent. In the shade
Where now we sit I waited her return
Her cottage in its outward look appeared
As chearful as before; in any shew
Of neatness little changed but that I thought

281 *As if she had been shedding tears of joy*
282 *We parted. It was then the early spring*
283 *I left her busy with her garden tools*
284 *And well remember o'er that fence she looked*
285 *And while I paced along the foot-way path*
286 *Called out & sent a blessing after me*
287 *With tender chearfulness & with a voice*
288 *That seemed the very sound of happy thoughts.*
289 *I roved o'er many a hill & many a dale*
290 *With this my weary load, in heat & cold*
291 *Through many a wood, & many an open ground*
292 *In sunshine or in shade in wet or fair*
293 *Now blithe, now drooping as it might befal*
294 *My best companions, now the driving winds*
295 *And now the "trotting brooks" & whispering trees*
296 *And now the music of my own sad steps*
297 *With many a short-lived thought that pass'd between*
298 *100* *And disappeared. I came this way again*
299 *Towards the* wane *of summer when the wheat*
300 *Was yellow, & the soft & bladed grass*
301 *Sprang up afresh & o'er the hay-field spread*
302 *Its tender green. When I had reached the door*
303 *I found that she was absent. In the shade*
304 *Where now we sit I waited her return*
305 *Her cottage in its outward look appeared*
306 *As chearful as before; in any shew*
307 *Of neatness little changed but that I thought*

---

299 The erased word is no doubt "wa**i**n."

57

The honeysuckle crowded round the door
And from the wall hung down in heavier tufts ~~wreathes~~
And knots of worthless stone crop started out
Along the window's edge, & grew like weeds
Against the lower panes. I turned aside
And stroll'd into her garden. It was chang'd*
And, looking round, I saw the corner-stones
Till then unmark'd, on either side the door
With dull red stains discoloured & stuck o'er
With tufts & hairs of wool as if the sheep
That feed upon the commons thither came
Familiarly and found a couching-place
Even at her threshold – The ~~house~~-clock struck eight.
I turned & saw her distant a few steps
140 Her face was pale & thin her figure too
Was chang'd. As she unlocked the door she said
It grieves me you have waited here so long
But in good truth I've wandered much of late
And sometimes, to my shame I speak have need
Of my best prayers to bring me back again
While on the board she spread our evening meal
She told me she had lost her elder child
That he for months had been a serving-boy
Apprenticed by the parish. I perceive
You look at me and you have cause. Today
I have been travelling far, & many days
About the fields I wander knowing this
Only that what I seek I cannot find
And so I waste my time for I am changed

* Turn to the End

308 *The honeysuckle crowded round the door*
tufts
309 *And from the wall hung down in heavier* ~~*wreathes*~~
310 *And knots of worthless stone-crop started out*
311 *Along the window's edge, & grew like weeds*
312 *Against the lower panes. I turned aside*
313 *And stroll'd into her garden.—It was chang'd**
330 *And, looking round, I saw the corner-stones*
331 *Till then unmark'd, on either side the door*
332 *With dull red stains discoloured & stuck o'er*
a
333 *With tufts & hairs of wool [?]} s if the sheep*
334 *That feed upon the commons thither came*
335 *Familiarly and found a couching-place*
Close by
336 *Even at her threshold— The* house-*-clock struck*
eight
337 *I turned & saw her distant a few steps*
w
338 *140* *Her face &} as pale & thin her figure too*
339 *Was chang'd. As she unlocked the door she said*
340 *It grieves me you have waited here so long*
341 *But in good truth I've wandered much of late*
342 *And sometimes, to my shame I speak have need*
343 *Of my best prayers to bring me back again*
344 *While on the board she spread our evening meal*
345 *She told me she had lost her elder child*
346 *That he for months had been a serving-boy*
347 *Apprenticed by the parish. I perceive*
348 *You look at me and you have cause. Today*
349 *I have been travelling far, & many days*
350 *About the fields I wander knowing this*
351 *Only that what I seek I cannot find*
352 *And so I waste my time for I am changed*

* *Turn to the End*

---

313 The asterisk refers to "*Turn to the End" at the bottom of the page. DW inadvertently skipped sixteen lines here and copied them after the conclusion of the poem on 56r.

335 The erased line may be the MS. B reading: "As to a couchin**g-p**lace & nibble**d** their sides."

336 Close by] In pencil. The erased word is probably the MS. B reading: "**c**hurch." Although the first hyphen was not erased, a second one was added.

338 DW included in her count to 140 the sixteen lines omitted at l. 313.

347–351 The erased lines may be a revision of the original MS. B reading (some descenders do not match):

I am **changed**
And to myself said she have done much wr**ong**
And to this helpless infant. I have slept
Weeping & weeping I have waked my tears
Have flowed as if my body were not such

And to myself said she have done much wrong
And to this helpless infant. I have slept
Weeping, & weeping I have waked my tears
Have flow'd as if my body were not such
As others are & I could never die
150 But I am now in mind & in my heart
More easy, & I hope, said she that heaven
Will give me patience to endure the things
Which I behold at home. It would have grieved
Your very heart to see her. Sir I feel
The story linger in my heart. I fear
'Tis long & tedious but my spirit clings
To that poor woman so familiarly
Do I perceive her manner & her look
And presence, & so deeply do I feel
Her goodness that not seldom in my walks
A momentary trance comes over me
And to myself I seem to muse on one
By sorrow laid asleep or borne away
A human being destined to awake
To human life or something very near
To human life when he shall come again
For whom she suffered. Sir, it would have griev'd
Your very soul to see her evermore
Her eye-lids droop'd, her eyes were downward cast
160 And when she at her table gave me food
She did not look at me her voice was low
Her body was subdued. In every act

353 *And to myself, said she have done much wrong*
354 *And to this helpless infant. I have slept*
355 *Weeping, & weeping I have waked my tears*
such
356 *Have flow'd as if my body were not* ~~such as others are~~
357 *As others are, & I could never die*
358 *160* *But I am now in mind & in my heart*
~~have hope~~
359 *More easy, & I hope, said she that heaven* it is
ie feel a hope
360 *Will give me patei nce to endure the things*
361 *Which I behold at home. It would have grieved*
soul
362 *Your very heart to see her. Sir I feel*
363 *The story linger in my heart. I fear*
364 *'Tis long & tedious but my spirit clings*
365 *To that poor woman so familiarly*
366 *Do I perceive her manner, & her look*
367 *And presence, & so deeply do I feel*
368 *Her goodness that* not seldom in my walks
369 *A momentary trance comes over me*
370 *And to myself I seem to muse on one*
371 *By sorrow laid asleep or borne away*
372 *A human being destined to awake*
n
373 *To huma[?l] life or something very near*
374 *To human life when he shall come again*
375 *For whom she suffered. Sir, it would have griev'd*
376 *Your very soul to see her evermore*
377 *Her eye-lids droop'd, her eyes were downward cast*
378 *180* *And when she at her table gave me food*
379 *She did not look at me her voice was low*
380 *Her body was subdued. In every act*

---

356 Deletion by erasure.
362 soul] In pencil.
368 The erased words may be the MS. B reading: "a vision of the mind" (see MS. B, 36v).
373 Deletion by erasure.

Pertaining to her house affairs appeared 59
The careless stillness which a thinking mind
Gives to an idle matter—still she sighed
But yet no motion of the breast was seen
No heaving of the heart. While by the fire
We sate together sighs came on my ear
I knew not how, & hardly whence they came
I took my staff, & when I kissed her babe
The tears stood in her eyes. I left her then
With the best hope & comfort I could give
She thanked me for my will but for my hope
It seemed she did not thank me.
I returned

And took my rounds along this road again
Ere on its sunny bank the primrose flower
Had chronicled the earliest day of spring or
I found her sad and drooping; she had learnd
No tidings of her husband if he lived
200 She knew not that he lived if he were dead
She knew not he was dead she seemed the same
In person [?] appearance, but her house
Bespoke a sleepy hand of negligence
The floor was neither dry nor neat the hearth
Was comfortless
The windows too were dim & her few books
Which one upon the other heretofore
Had been piled up against the corner-panes
In seemly order, now with straggling leaves
[?] to which all outward things
Are like an idle matter

381 *Pertaining to her house-affairs appeared*
382 *The careless stillness which a thinking* mind
383 *Gives to an idle matter — still she sighed*
384 *But yet no motion of the breast was seen*
385 *No heaving of the heart. While by the fire*
386 *We sate together sighs came on my ear*
387 *I knew not how, & hardly whence they came*
388 *I took my staff, & when I kissed her babe*
389 *The tears* stood *in her eyes. I left her then*
390 *With the best hope & comfort I could give*
391 *She thanked me for my will, but for my*
hope
392 *It seemed she did not thank me.*
I returned
[?~~I~~ ?~~returned~~]
393 *And took my rounds along this road again*
394 *Ere on its sunny bank the primrose flower*
395 *Had chronicled the earliest day of spring*
;} [?]
396 *I found her sad and drooping* { *she had learn'd*
397 *No tidings of her husband if he lived*
398 *200* *She knew not that he lived if he were dead*
399 *She knew not he was dead she seemed*
the same
400 *In person ~~or~~ appearance, but her house*
401 *Bespoke a sleepy hand of negligence*
402 *The floor was neither dry nor neat the hearth*
403 *Was comfortless*
404 *The windows too were dim & her few books*
405 *Which one upon the other, heretofore*
406 *Had been piled up against the corner-panes*
407 *In seemly order, now with straggling leaves*
Self occupied to which all outward things
as
Are like an idle matter

382 For the erased word, MS. B has "mind" deleted to "soul."
389 The erased word was probably the MS. B reading: "**w**ere."
392 Deletion by erasure.
399 The erased words are doubtless the MS. B reading: "no**t** chan**ged**."
400 Deletion by erasure; the correction of l. 399 suggests that an ampersand should have been added.
WW's draft at the foot of this page was meant to replace l. 383a, as in MS. E.

Lay scattered here and there, open or shut
As they had chanced to fall. Her infant babe
Had from its mother caught the trick of grief
And sighed among its playthings. Once again
I turned towards the garden-gate & saw
More plainly still that poverty & grief
Were now come nearer to her the earth was hard
With weeds defaced & knots of withered grass
No ridges there appeared of clear black mould
No winter greenness of her herbs & flowers
220 It seemed the better part were gnawed away
Or trampled on the earth; a chain of straw
Which had been twisted round the tender stem
Of a young apple-tree lay at its root
The bark was nibbled round by truant sheep
Margaret stood near, her infant in her arms
And seeing that my eye was on the tree
She said I fear it will be dead & gone
Ere ~~Robert~~ come again. Towards the house
Together we returned & she inquired
If I had any hope. But for her Babe
And for her little friendless Boy she said
She had no wish to live that she must die
Of sorrow. Yet I saw the idle loom
Still in its place. His sunday garments hung
Upon the self-same nail, his very staff

408 *Lay scattered here and there, open or shut*
409 *As they had chanced to fall. Her infant babe*
410 *Had from its mother caught the trick of grief*
411 *And sighed among its playthings* {·/} {*O*/*once again*}
412 *I turned towards the garden-gate & saw*
413 *More plainly still that poverty & grief*
414 *Were now come nearer to her the earth was hard*
415 *With weeds defaced & knots of withered grass*
416 *No ridges there appeared of clear black mould*
417 *No winter greenness of her herbs & flowers*
418 *220* *It seemed the better part were gnawed away*
419 *Or trampled on the earth; a chain of straw*
420 *Which had been twisted round the tender stem*
421 *Of a young apple-tree lay at its root*
422 *The bark was nibbled round by truant sheep*
423 *Margaret stood near, her infant in her arms*
424 *And seeing that my eye was on the tree*
425 *She said I fear it will be dead & gone*
426 *Ere Robert come again. Towards the house*
427 *Together we returned & she inquired*
428 *If I had any hope. But for her* {*B*/*babe*}
honest
429 *And for her little friendless Boy she said*
430 *She had no wish to live that she must die*
her husbands
431 *Of sorrow. Yet I saw the idle loom*
432 *Still in its place. His sunday garments hung*
433 *Upon the self-same nail, his very staff*

---

431 her husbands] In pencil.

Stood undisturbed behind the door, and when 61
I passed this way beaten by Autumn winds
She told me that her little babe was dead
And she was left alone. That very time
240 I yet remember through the miry lane
She walked with me a mile, when the bare trees
Trickled with foggy damps, & in such sort
That any heart had ached to hear her begg'd
That where-soe'er I went I still would ask
For him whom she had lost. We parted then
Our final parting, for from that time forth
Did many seasons pass ere I returned
Into this tract again.

Five tedious years
From their first separation five long years
She lingered in unquiet widowhood
A wife & widow. Needs must it have been
A gnaw sore heart-wasting. I have heard, my friend
That in that broken arbour she would sit
The idle length of half a sabbath day
There, where you see the toadstool's lazy head
And when a dog passed by she still would quit
The shade & look abroad. On this old Bench
For hours she sate & evermore her eye
Was busy in the distance, shaping things
Which made her heart beat quick. Seest thou
that path?
you see that path
Now faint the grass has crept o'er its grey line

434 *Stood undisturbed behind the door, and when ~~I passed~~*
435 *I passed this way beaten by Autumn winds*
436 *She told me that her little babe was dead*
437 *And she was left alone. That very time*
438 240 *I yet remember through the miry lane*
439 *She walked with me a mile, when the bare trees*
440 *Trickled with foggy damps, & in such sort*
441 *That any heart had ached to hear her begg'd*
442 *That wheresoe'er I went I still would ask*
443 *For him whom she had lost. We parted then*
444 *Our final parting, for from that time forth*
445 *Did many seasons pass ere I returned*
446 *Into this tract again.*
Five tedious years
From their first separation five long years
447 *She lingered in unquiet widowhood*
448 *A wife & widow. Needs must it have been*
sad
449 *A sore heart-wasting. I have heard, my friend*
450 *That in that broken arbour she would sit*
451 *The idle length of half a sabbath day*
452 *There, where you see the toadstool's lazy head*
453 *And when a dog passed by she still would quit*
454 *The shade & look abroad. On this old Bench*
455 *For hours she sate, & evermore her eye*
456 *Was busy in the distance, shaping things*
457 *Which made her heart beat quick. Seest thou*
that path?
you see that path
Now faint the grass has crept oer its grey line

---

434 Deletion by erasure.
WW's draft at the foot of the page was incorporated in MS. E to replace ll. 457b–458 of MS. D.

262 The green-sward now has broken its grey line
There to and fro she paced through many a day
Of the warm summer from a belt of flax
That girt her waist spinning the long-drawn thread
With backward steps - Yet ever as there passed
A man whose garments shewed the Soldier's red
Or crippled Mendicant in Sailor's garb
The little child who sate to turn the wheel.
Ceased from his toil, & she with faltering voice
Expecting still to learn her husband's fate
Made many a fond inquiry, & when they
Whose presence gave no comfort were gone by
Her heart was still more sad. And by yon gate
Which bars the travellers road she often stood
And when a stranger horseman came the latch
Would lift & in his face look wistfully
Most happy if from aught discovered there
Of tender feeling she might dare repeat
The same sad question. Meanwhile her poor hut
Sunk to decay, for he was gone whose hand
280 At the first nippings of October frost
Closed up each chink & with fresh bands of straw
Chequered the green-grown thatch. And so she lived
Through the long winter reckless & alone
Till this reft house by frost, & thaw, & rain
Was sapped, & when she slept the nightly damps

458 *260* *The green-sward now has broken its grey line*
459 *There to and fro she paced through many a day*
460 *Of the warm summer from a belt of flax*
461 *That girt her waist spinning the long-drawn thread*
462 *With backward steps — Yet ever as there passed*
463 *A man whose garments shewed the Soldier's red*
464 *Or crippled Mendicant in Sailor's garb*
465 *The little child who sate to turn the wheel*
466 *Ceased from his toil, & she with faltering voice*
467 *Expecting still to learn her husband's fate*
468 *Made many a fond inquiry, & when they*
469 *Whose presence gave no comfort were gone by*
470 *Her heart was still more sad. And by yon gate*
[?crosses] the high way
471 *Which bars the traveller's road she often stood*
472 *And when a stranger horseman came the latch*
473 *Would lift, & in his face look wistfully*
474 *Most happy if from aught discovered there*
475 *Of tender feeling she might dare repeat*
476 *The same sad question. Meanwhile her poor hut*
477 *Sunk to decay, for he was gone whose hand*
478 *280* *At the first nippings of October frost*
479 *Closed up each chink & with fresh bands of straw*
480 *Chequered the green-grown thatch. And so she lived*
481 *Through the long winter reckless & alone*
482 *Till this reft house by frost, & thaw, & rain*
483 *Was sapped, & when she slept the nightly damps*

---

471 WW's revision is in pencil.

63

Did chill her breast, & in the stormy day
Her tattered clothes were ruffled by the wind
Even at the side of her own fire. Yet still
She loved this wretched spot, nor would for worlds
Have parted hence, & still that length of road
And this rude bench one torturing hope endeared
Fast rooted at her heart, & here, my friend
In sickness she remained, & here she died
Last human tenant of these ruined walls
Here Drummond
~~The old Man~~ ceased he saw that I was mov'd
From that low Bench, rising instinctively
I turned aside in weakness nor had power
To thank him for the tale which he had told
I stood and leaning o'er the garden gate
280 Reviewed that woman's sufferings & it seemed
To comfort me while with a brother's love
I blessed her in the impotence of grief
At length [illegible] the [illegible] feeling
Fondly, & traced with milder interest
That secret spirit of humanity
Which 'mid the calm oblivious tendencies
Of nature, 'mid her plants, her weeds & flowers
And silent overgrowings still survived
The old man seeing this, resumed & said
My Friend, enough to sorrow have you given
The purposes of wisdom ask no more
Be wise & chearful, & no longer read

484 *Did chill her breast, & in the stormy day*
485 *Her tattered clothes were ruffled by the wind*
486 *Even at the side of her own fire. Yet still*
487 *She loved this wretched spot, nor would for worlds*
488 *Have parted hence, & still that length of road*
489 *And this rude bench one torturing hope endeared*
490 *Fast rooted at her heart, & here, my friend*
491 *In sickness she remained, & here she died*
492 *Last human tenant of these ruined walls*
Here Drummon
493 ~~*The old Man*~~ *ceased he saw that I was mov'd*
494 *From that low Bench, rising instinctively*
495 *I turned a*side *in weakness* nor had power
496 To thank him for *the tale which he had told*
497 *I stood and leaning o'er the garden-gate*
498 *280* *Re*view*ed that Woman's* suff'rings & it seeme*d*
499 *To comfort me while with a brother's love*
er
500 *I blessed h*~~*im*~~ *in the impotence of grief*
501 *At length* ~~*upon*~~ *the* ~~*hut I fix'd my eyes*~~
feeling
502 *Fondly, & traced with* milder *interest*
503 *That secret spirit of humanity*
504 *Which 'mid the calm oblivious tendencies*
505 *Of nature, 'mid her plants, her weeds, & flowers*
506 *And silent overgrowings still survived*
507 *The old man seeing this, resumed & said*
508 *My Friend, enough to sorrow have you given*
509 *The purposes of wisdom ask no more*
510 *Be wise & chearful, & no longer read*

---

493 The correction to "Here Drummon[d]" probably postdates use of this name in *The Pedlar*, 1802. Since "Drummond" disappears by the time of the copying of MS. E, the revision may indicate that *The Pedlar*, 1802, was joined to *RC* sometime before the writing of MS. E (see p. 30, above).

495 For "aside," MS. B reads "away." The erasure under "nor had power" is probably the MS. B reading: "**f**or m**y** **h**ear**t**."

496 The erased words are probably the MS. B reading: "Was **h**eav**y** wit**h**."

498 The erased letters in the opening word were probably part of the MS. B reading: "Retraced." The MS. B reading for the erasure at the end of the line is "**st**ory and it seemed." DW accidentally repeats the number 280, which she had used at l. 478.

500 Deletion by erasure.

501 Deletion by erasure.

The forms of things with an unworthy eye
She sleeps in the calm earth & peace is here
I well remember that those very plumes
Those weeds & the high spear-grass on that wall
By mist and silent rain-drops silvered o'er
As once I passed did to my heart convey
So still an image of tranquillity
300 So calm, & still & looked so beautiful
Amid the uneasy thoughts which filled my mind
That what we feel of sorrow & despair
From ruin & from change & all the grief
The passing shews of being leave behind
Appeared an idle dream that could not live
Where meditation was. I turned away
And walked along my road in happiness

He ceased. By this the sun declining shot
A slant & mellow radiance which began
To fall upon us where beneath the trees
We sate on that low bench, & now we felt,
Admonished thus, the sweet hour coming on.
A linnet warbled from those lofty elms
A thrush sang loud, & other melodies
At distance heard, peopled the milder air
The old man rose & hoisted up his load.
Together casting then a farewell look
Upon those silent walls we left the shade

511 *The forms of things with an unworthy eye*
512 *She sleeps in the calm earth & peace is here*
513 *I well remember that those very plumes*
514 *Those weeds & the high spear-grass on that wall*
515 *By mist and silent rain-drops silver'd o'er*
516 *As once I passed did to my heart convey*
517 *So still an image of tranquillity*
518 *300* *So calm, & still, & looked so beautiful*
519 *Amid the uneasy thoughts which filled my mind*
520 *That what we feel of sorrow & despair*
521 *From ruin & from change & all the grief*
522 *The passing shews of being leave behind*
523 *Appeared an idle dream that could not live*
524 *Where meditation was. I turned away*
525 *And walked along my road in happiness*

526 *He ceased,* . By this *the sun declining shot*
527 *A slant & mellow radiance which began*
528 *To fall upon us where beneath the trees*
529 *We sate on that low bench, & now we felt,*
530 *Admonished thus, the sweet hour coming on*
531 *A linnet warbled from those lofty elms*
532 *A thrush sang loud, & other melodies*
533 *At distance heard, peopled the milder air*
534 *The old man rose & hoisted up his load.*
535 *Together casting then a farewell look*
536 *Upon those silent walls we left the shade*

---

518 DW's numbering error at l. 498 carries on; the number here should be 320.
521 The erased word is probably "grief," a copying error.
526 The erased words may be the MS. B reading: "**&** now."

319 And eere the stars were visible attain'd 65
A rustic inn, our evening resting-place.

The End

680
800

The unprofitable bindweed spread his bells
From side to side and with unwieldy wreaths
Had dragg'd the rose from its sustaining wall
And bent it down ~~to earth~~ [to the ground] the border tufts
120 Daisy and thrift and lowly camomile
And thyme had straggled out into the paths
Which they were used to deck. Ere this an hour
Was wasted back I turned my restless steps
And as I walked before the door it chanced
A stranger passed, and guessing whom I sought
He said that she was used to ramble far.
The sun was sinking in the west and now
I sate with sad impatience. From within
Her solitary infant cried aloud
The spot though fair seemed very desolate
The longer I remained more desolate
And looking round &c   I turn'd & look'd
Into her garden there was not an inch
Of untill'd earth but yet the place had lost
Its pride of neatness and appeared to lag
Behind the season, the trim border tufts
Daisy and thrift and lowly camomile
And thyme had straggled out into the paths
The unprofitable   it had lost, I thought
The pride of om——

537 *319* And e'ere the stars were visible attained
538 A rustic inn, our evening resting-place.

The End 630
800

---

314 *The unprofitable bindweed spread his bells*
315 *From side to side and with unwieldy wreaths*
316 *Had dragg'd the rose from its sustaining wall*
to the ground
317 *And bent it down to earth the border-tufts*
318 *120* *Daisy and thrift and lowly camomile*
319 *And thyme had straggled out into the paths*
320 *Which they were used to deck. Ere this an hour*
321 *Was wasted back I turned my restless steps*
322 *And as I walked before the door it chanced*
323 *A stranger passed, and guessing whom I sought*
324 *He said that she was used to ramble far.*
325 *The sun was sinking in the west and now*
326 *I sate with sad impatience. From within*
327 *Her solitary infant cried aloud*
328 *The spot though fair seemed very desolate*
329 *The longer I remained more desolate*
330 *And looking round &c*

I turn'd & stroll'd
Into her garden there was not an inch
Of untill'd earth but yet the place had lost
Its pride of neatness and appeared to lag
Behind the season, the trim border-tufts
Daisy and thrift and lowly camomile
And thyme had straggled out into the paths
The unprofitable [?:d] had lost, I thought
Its pride of [?summer]

---

537 The erased line may be the MS. B reading: "And chearfully pursued our evening way." The number 319 is an error for 339; see the note to l. 498.

The penciled 630 and 800 probably date from between 1802 and the writing of MS. E in 1803–1804. The 630 comes from the addition of 319 lines in Part Two to the 311 on 46v. The 800 is perhaps the approximate number of lines in the poem after *The Pedlar*, 1802, and the MS. D text were combined: Part One has 162 lines past the 311 on 46v, and 162 plus 311 plus 319 equal 792.

314–330 These lines were inadvertently omitted by DW in her copying on 52r.

WW's draft at the bottom of the page—related to MS. D, ll. 312–319—contributes to MS. E, ll. 649–654.

Perennial of the ancient hills; nor less 67
The changeful language of their countenance
Gave movement to his thoughts & multitude
With order & relation

A

Him had I seen the day before - alone
And in the middle of the public way
Standing to rest himself. His eyes were turn'd
Towards the setting sun while with that staff
Behind him fix'd he propp'd a long white pack
Which cross'd his shoulders: wares for them who live
In lonely villages, or straggling huts.
He stood, his back towards me but as soon
As I drew near to him great joy was ours
At this unthought of meeting. For the night
We parted nothing willingly, & now
He by appointment waited for me here
Beneath these elms it being our joint wish
To travel on together a few days.
-We were dear Friends: I from my childhood up
Had known him, in a nook of Furness Fells
At Hawkshead where I went to school 9 years
One room he had, the fifth part of a house
A place to which he drew from time to time
And found a kind of home or harbour there
-He was the best Old Man! and often I
Delight to recollect him, & his looks
And think of him & his affectionate ways
In that same ~~small~~ Town of Hawkshead where we dwelt
There was a little ~~girl~~ ~~fifty~~ ten years of age
But tiny for her years a pretty dwarf
Fair-hair'd, fair-fac'd, & though of stature small

[E, 24–45, 61–64]

[Pedlar Lines (Including *The Pedlar*, 1802)]

1 Him had I seen the day before—alone
2 And in the middle of the public way
3 *Standing to rest himself. His eyes were turn'd*
4 *Towards the setting sun, while with that staff*
5 *Behind him fix'd he propp'd a long white Pack*
6 *Which cross'd his shoulders: wares for them who live*
7 *In lonely villages, or straggling huts.*
8 *He stood, his back towards me but as soon*
9 *{A / as} I drew near to him great joy was ours*
10 *At this unthought-of meeting. For the night*
11 *We parted nothing willingly, & now*
12 *He by appointment waited for me here*
13 *Beneath these elms it being our joint wish*
14 *To travel on together a few days.*
15 —*We were dear Friends: I from my childhood up*
16 *Had known him, in a nook of Furness Fells*
17 *At Hawkshead where I went to school {9 / ten} years*
18 *One room he had, the fifth part of a house*
19 *A place to which he drew from time to time*
20 20 *And found a kind of home or harbour there*
21 —*He was the best {O / old} Man! and often I*
22 *Delight to recollect~~s~~ him, & his looks*
23 *And think of him, & his affectionate ways*
24 —*In that* ~~*small*~~ [same] *Town of Hawkshead where we dwelt*
25 *There was a little* ~~*Girl*~~ [~~maiden~~] [Girl] *ten years of age*
26 *But tiny for her years a pretty dwarf*
27 *Fair-hair'd, fair-fac'd, & though of stature small*

The four lines visible at the top of the photograph are the conclusion of "In storm and tempest," beginning on 56v and there labeled "Fragment" (this fragment is presented in Transcriptions of Additions to MS. D, below). In 1799, DW left blank the rest of 57r (after concluding "In storm and tempest") and skipped five pages before beginning the overflow passages about the Pedlar on 60r. Leaf 57r and these skipped pages were used by WW for pencil drafting, now erased and illegible, and were filled by WW and DW in late 1801–1802 with the beginning of the independent poem concerned solely with the Pedlar (see pp. 26–28, above). Italicized editorial numbers in the left-hand margin of this and subsequent pages identify lines included in the manuscript numbering of *The Pedlar*, 1802.

1 The penciled "A," visible in the photograph at the upper right of this line, is of recent origin. See the note to a similar "B" on 60r.

20 The number 20 is in pencil.

22 Deletion by erasure.

25 "Girl" in the base text is deleted in ink; the revision "maiden" is in ink but deleted in pencil, and the revision "Girl" is in pencil.

In [illegible] as forward as a lusty Child

~~This Girl [illegible] from his [illegible] return~~

~~[illegible] his [illegible] daily [illegible]~~

To play with the good Man & he was wont

To tell her stories of his early life

And often ~~have~~ I list'ned to their talk.

"Nay" would she answer him, unsaying thus

All he had said to her, "you never could

Be a poor ragged little Boy, and hir'd

As the poor Man you talk to herd Cattle

On a hill side for forty a year."

All which did to the Girl appear so strange

She could not credit it: & when she used

To doubt his words, as I remember well

Spite of himself the good Man smil'd & held

His hand up to his face to hide his smiles

Because he knew that if the little Girl

Once spied them, she would then be sure first doubt

That he was joking. She being thus perplex'd

He was far better pleas'd to sing to her

Scotch songs, sometimes, but oftener to repeat

Scotch poetry, old ballads, & old tales,

Love-Gregory, William Wallace & Rob Roy.

All this while she was sitting on a stool

Between his knees, & oft would she stand up

Upon her stool & coax him with a kiss

To tell her more ~~[illegible]~~ many a time would he

Cry over her & she would wonder why.

This, standing at his threshold have I seen

Yea many times, when he had little thought

That any one was near. And for myself

He lov'd me, out of many rosy Boys

Singled out me, as he in sport would say

60

[E, 65–95, 46–47]

28 *In heart as forward as a lusty Child*
29 *This Girl when from his Travels he return*
~~*Of*~~ [?] t ~~*to his Tenement this Girl would come*~~
30 *To his abiding place would daily come*
31 *To play with the good Man, & he was wont*
32 *To tell her stories of his early life*
33 *And* often have I listin'd to their talk.
34 "Nay—would she answer him," unsaying thus
35 All he had said to her, "you never could
36 Be a poor ragged little Boy, and hir'd
37 To the poor Man you talk to herd Cattle
38 On a hill-side for forty a year."
39 All which [?] d id to the Girl appear so strange
40
40 She could not credit it: & when she us'd
41 To doubt his words, as I remember well
42 Spite of himself the good Man smile & held
43 His hand up to his face to hide his smiles
44 Because he knew that if the little Girl
45 Once spi'd them, she would then be sure, past doubt,
46 That he was joking. She being thus perplex'd
47 He was far better pleas'd to sing to her
48 Scotch songs, sometimes, but oftener to repeat
49 Scotch poetry, old ballads, & old tales
50 Love-Gregory, William Wallace & Rob Roy.
51 All this while she was sitting on a stool
52 Between his knees, & oft would she stand up
53 Upon her stool & coax him with a kiss
many a time
54 To tell her more ~~& often-times~~ would he
55 Cry over her & she would wonder why
56 This, standing at his threshold have I seen
57 Yea many ~~a~~ time s, when he had little though t
58 That any one was near . — And for myself
59 He lov'd me, out of many rosy Boys
60 Singled out me, as he in sport would say
60

The lines on this page are written over WW's pencil drafting, now erased and illegible.

29–30 The position of the numbers 40 and 60 below shows that this correction is included in the numbering.

33–46a The vertical deleting stroke is in pencil (the X deleting ll. *33–36* is in ink).

37 WW omitted "of" between "talk" and "to"; "of" is included in MS. E, l. 73.

38 After "forty," WW omitted "pence"—the reading in MS. E, l. 74.

40 The number is in pencil. The placement of the number 60 at the bottom of the page aids in determining that the 40 refers to this line.

42 smile] The word should be "smiled."

60 The number is in pencil.

For my grave looks, too thoughtful for my years.
His name was Drummond:- the boon
Which he had told the Girl, truth it was, that he had been
A Herd-Callan for forty pence a year.
Among the hills of Perthshire he was born
His Father died when he was four years old & left three sons
And Patrick was the youngest of the three
His Mother married for a second Mate
A School-master who taught the Boys to read
And bred them up & gave them as he could
Needful instruction teaching them the ways
Of honesty & holiness severe
Patrick as soon as he was six years old
Stood as a Herd-Boy all the summer through
But in the winter months he duly went
To his Step-Fathers School that stood alone
Sole building on a mountain's dreary edge
Far from the sight of City spire or sound
Of minster clock. From that bleak tenement
He in the evening sometimes, to his home
In solitude returning saw the hills
Grow larger in the darkness all alone
Beheld the stars come out above his head
And travell'd through the wood with no one near
To whom he might confess the things he saw
He had small need of Books, &c
His history I from himself have heard
Full often after I grew up & he
Found in my heart a kindred heart to his. His father died

[E, 48, 99–109, 115–127, 157]

[?]
61 For my grave looks, too thoughtful for my years.
62 His name was Drummond:—~~true~~ the bare truth it was
63 Which he had told the Girl, that he had been
64 A Herd-Callan for forty pence a year.
Among the hills of Perthshire he was born
ere he was four years old
ere he was four years old & left
69 His Father died ~~& left~~^~~behind~~ three sons
70 And Patrick was the youngest of the three.
71 His Mother married for a second Mate
72 A School-master who taught the Boys to read
73 And bred them up & gave them as he could
74 Needful instruction teaching them the ways
75 Of honesty & holiness severe
a Herd boy was the summer through
76 Patrick ~~as soon as he was six years old~~
77 ~~Serv'd as a Herd-Boy all the summer~~ through
78 But in the winter-months he duly went
st}
79 To his Step-Fathers School that s{ood alone
80 Sole building on a mountain's dreary edge
80
81 Far from the sight of City spire or sound
82 Of minster clock. From this bleak tenement
many an evening to his distant
~~i~~}
83 He o{~~n the evening~~—~~sometimes, to~~ his home
ning
84 In solitude~~r~~ retur~~n'd &~~ saw the hills
85 Grow larger in the darkness all alone
86 Beheld the stars come out above his head
87 And travell'd through the wood
with no one near
[?~~With~~ ?~~n~~]
88 To whom he might confess the things he saw
89 *He had small need of Books &c*
65 *His history I from himself have heard*
66 *Full often after I grew up & he*
67 *Found in my heart as he would kindly say*
68 *A kindred heart to his. His father died*

The lines on this page are written over WW's pencil drafting, now erased and illegible.

64–69 The position of the number 80, in pencil, shows that DW's four-line addition at the bottom of the page precedes the numbering. The four lines should be added after either l. *64* or the following line, which would be included if the numbering preceded the correction in ll. *76–77*. DW's correction in l. *69* is associated with the inclusion of lines from the foot of the page; as corrected, l. *69* should read: "Ere he was four years old & left three sons."

76–77 The deletions and revision are in pencil, as are those in ll. *83–84* (with the exception of the "i" overwriting and the deletion by erasure of the terminal letter in "solituder").

89 The text of *The Pedlar*, 1802, here jumps to a nineteen-line passage from the 1799 overflow copying on 61r and 61v, which is included in the numbering from 80 on 58r to 120 on 58v. See the note to l. *107* on 58v.

Could never be forgotten.
Thus was he
Bred up among the fields & in a house
Virtuous & wanting little to the growth
Of a strong mind although exceeding poor
Pure livers were they all austere & grave
And fearing God the very children taught
Stern self respect, a reverence for God's word
And piety, scarce known on English land
And thus did Patrick gather when a Boy
Some gloomy notions which in later life
Would come to him at times but from his birth
He had a gracious nature genial blood
Flow'd in him & the region of the heart
Even from the first was sensitive & kind
Never had living man a gentler creed
For love was his & the pure joy of love
By sound diffus'd or by the breathing air
Or by the silent looks of happy things
Or flowing from the universal face
Of earth and sky. for he had early felt
The power of nature. Early had been taught
By his intense conceptions to receive
Deeply the lesson deep of love which he
Whom Nature by whatever means has taught
To feel intensely cannot but receive
He was a man of genius, & yet more
A man of science too roaming the hills

[E, 175, 110–114, 176–185, 238]

107 *Could never be forgotten.*
Thus was he
108 *Bred up among the fields, & in a house*
109 *Virtuous, & wanting little to the growth*
110 *Of a strong mind, although exceeding poor*
111 *Pure livers were they all—austere & grave*
112 *And fearing God the very children taught*
113 *Stern self respect, a reverence for God's word*
114 *And piety, scarce known on English land*
115 *And thus did Patrick gather when a Boy*
116 *Some gloomy notions which in later life*
117 *Would come to him at times but from his birth*
118 *He had a gracious nature, genial blood*
119 *Flow'd in him, & the region of the heart*
120 *Even from the first was sensitive & kind*
120
121 *Never had living man a gentler creed*
122 *For love was his, & the pure joy of love*
123 *By sound diffus'd or by the breathing air*
124 *Or by the silent looks of happy things*
125 *Or flowing from the universal face*
126 *Of earth and sky—for he had early felt*
127 *The power of nature early had been taught*
128 *By his intense conceptions to receive*
129 *Deeply the lesson deep of love which he*
130 *Whom Nature by whatever means has taught*
131 *To feel intensely cannot but receive*
132 *He was a man of genius, & yet more*
133 *A man of science too among the hills*

The lines on this page are written over WW's pencil drafting, now partially erased and illegible.
107 This line is the conclusion of the nineteen-line insert from the original 1799 copying (61^r and 61^v) into the 1802 work. DW's copying instruction for this insert is on 58^r at l. *89*, and the placement of 120 on 58^v shows that the passage was included in the numbering.
115–121 WW may have drawn on this passage for MS. E, ll. 344–359.
120 The number is in pencil.

While he was a hired Labourer tending herds
He gaz'd upon that mighty orb of day 71
The divine Milton Lore of different kind
His step father supplied, books that explaind

[E, 239–242]

134 *While he was a hired Labourer tending herds*
135 *He gaz'd upon that mighty orb of song*
136 *The divine Milton Lore of different kind*
137 *His Stepfather supplied, books that exp=*
=plaind

The lines on this page are written over WW's pencil drafting, now erased and illegible. The erased pencil writing continued for three or four lines below the ink overwriting.

137 After this line, the text of *The Pedlar*, 1802, jumps to a passage copied in 1799 and beginning at the last line on 62v.

The repetition of "amen," visible upside down on the photograph, was the Wordsworths' way—along with "m"—of breaking in a new pen.

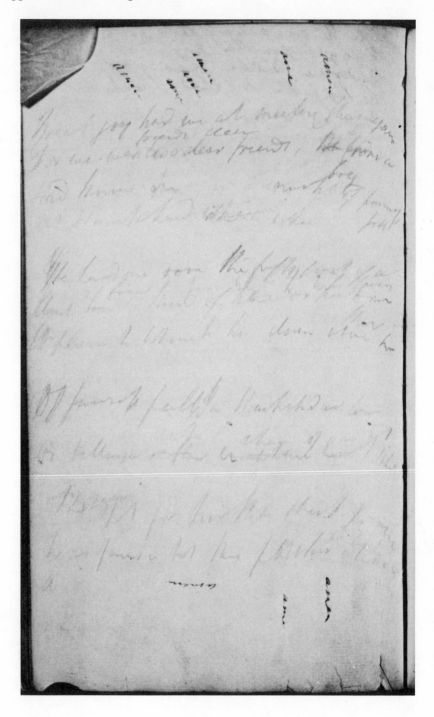

[E, 34–35, 40–45]

G}
I }reat joy had we at meeting thus again
friends dear {he {from
For we were two dear friends, {[?I] {[?had] a
boy

{me
Had known {him, in a nook of furness
fell

{ where
At Hawkshead {[?there] [?when]

{He
{[?&] had one room the fifth part of a
House

found from time to time
And had a kind of home or harbour
there
A place to which he drew [?when ?from]

{Of I }
{[?] furness fell [?]} n Hawkshd [? ?town]
[?call] where I was at School
Or Village rather [?it] where [?ten] ^

ten years
[?The/?That] spot for [?homespun ?shirt] & [?yarn]
[?to ?buy]
Was [?famous] but this [? ?]
[?A]

The lines are in pencil, no doubt the kind of drafting now erased and overwritten in ink from 57^r to 59^r.

This draft about the meeting of the poet and the Pedlar contributes to *The Pedlar*, 1802; see 57^r, ll. *15–20*.

On Hawkshead as a well-known eighteenth-century market for woolen yarn, see Henry Swainson Cowper, *Hawkshead* (London, 1899), pp. 269–270; and Thompson, pp. 20, 171.

In the third line, "in a" is smudged or partially erased.

B B

Him had I seen the day before—alone
And in the middle of the public way
Standing to rest himself. His eyes were turned
Towards the setting sun while with that staff
Behind him fixed he propp'd a long small white
Which crossed his shoulders: wares for pack them who love
In lonely villages or straggling huts
I knew him—he was born of lowly race
On Cumbrian hills & I have seen the tear
Stand in his luminous eye when he describes
The house in which his early youth was pass'd
And found I was no stranger to the spot
I loved to hear him talk of former days
And tell how when a child ere yet of age
To be a Shepherd he had learned to read
His bible in a school that stood alone
Sole building on a mountain's dreary edge
Far from the sight of city spire, or sound
Of Minster Clock. From that bleak tenement
He many an evening to his distant home
In solitude returning saw the hills
Grow larger in the darkness all alone
Beheld the stars come out above his head
And travell'd through the wood, with no one near
To whom he might confess the things he saw

[E, 24–30, 115–127]

Him had I seen the day before—alone 1
And in the middle of the public way 2
Standing to rest himself. His eyes were turned 3
Towards the setting sun while with that staff 4
small
Behind him fixed he propp'd a ~~long~~ white 5
pack
{them
Which crossed his shoulders: wares for {~~*maids*~~ 6
them
who live
In lonely villages or straggling huts 7
I knew him—he was born of lowly race 8
{*C*
On {*cumbrian hills, & I have seen the tear* 9
Stand in his luminous eye when he described 10
The house in which his early youth was pass'd 11
And found I was no stranger to the spot 12
I loved to hear him talk of former days 13
And tell how when a child ere yet of age 14
h}
To be a shepl{*erd he had learned to read* 15
t}
His bible in a school tha[?]{ *stood alone* 16
Sole building on a mountain's dreary edge 17
Far from the sight of city spire, or sound 18
Of Minster Clock. From that bleak tenement 19
,} sometimes in the [?evening]
He {*many an evening to his distant home* 20
sometimes
In solitude returnning saw the hills 21
Grow larger in the darkness all alone 22
Beheld the stars come out above his head 23
with no one near
And travell'd through the wood, ~~*no comrade near*~~ 24
To whom he might confess the things he saw 25

Here begin the overflow passages about the Pedlar copied in 1799.

The penciled "B," visible at the upper right-hand corner of the photograph, is of recent origin; see a matching "A" on 57r.

24 Deletion and revision are in pencil.

So the foundations of his mind were laid.
In such communion, not from terror free
While yet a child and long before his time
He had perceived the presence and the power
Of greatness & deep feelings had impressed
Great objects on his mind with portraiture
And colour so distinct that on his mind
They lay like substances & almost seemed
To haunt the bodily sense. He had received
A precious gift for as he grew in years
With these impressions would he still compare
All his ideal stores, his shapes & forms
And being still unsatisfied with aught
Of dimmer character he thence attained
An active power to fasten images
Upon his brain & on their pictured lines
Intensely brooded even till they acquired
The liveliness of dreams. Nor did he fail
While yet a child with a child's eagerness
Incessantly to turn his ear and eye
On all things which the rolling seasons brought
To feed such appetite nor this alone
Appeased his yearning. In the after day
Of boyhood, many an hour in caves forlorn

[E, 128–152]

So the foundations of his mind were laid. 1
In such communion, not from terror free 2
While yet a child and long before his time 3
He had perceived the presence and the power 4
Of greatness & deep feelings had impressed 5
Great objects on his mind with portraiture 6
And colour so distinct that on his mind 7
They lay like substances & almost seemed 8
To haunt the bodily sense. He had received 9
A precious gift for as he grew in years 10
With these impressions would he still compare 11
All his ideal stores, his shapes & forms 12
And being still unsatisfied with aught 13
Of dimmer character he thence attained 14
An active power to fasten images 15
Upon his brain & on their pictured lines 16
Intensely brood {ed / ing even till they acquired 17
The liveliness of dreams. Nor did he fail 18
While yet a child with a child's eagerness 19
Incessantly to turn his ear and eye 20
On all things which the rolling seasons brought 21
To feed such appetite nor this alone 22
Appeased his yearning. In the after day 23
Of boyhood, many an hour in caves forlorn 24

The deleting lines on this page are in pencil, with the exception of l. 17 (deletion by erasure).

75

And in the hollow depths of naked crags
He sate, & even in their fixed lineaments
Or from the power of a peculiar eye
Or by creative feeling overborne
Or by predominance of thought oppress'd
Even in their fixed & steady lineaments
He traced an ebbing and a flowing mind
Expression ever varying. ~~Thus informed~~
He ~~had small need of books for~~ many a tale
Traditionary round the mountains hung
And many a legend peopling the dark woods
Nourished Imagination in her growth
~~And gave the mind that apprehensive power~~
~~By which she is made quick to recognize~~
~~The moral properties & scope of things~~
[illegible]
But greedily he read & read again
What e'er the rustic Vicar's shelf supplied of books
The life and death of martyrs who sustain'd
Intolerable pangs, & here & there
A straggling volume torn & incomplete 100
Which left half-told the preternatural tale
Romance of giants, chronicle of fiends
Profuse in garniture of wooden cuts
Strange and uncouth dire faces, figures dire
Sharp-kneed, sharp-elbowed, & lean ankled too

[E, 153–173]

And in the hollow depths of naked crags 1
He sate, & even in their fixed lineaments 2
Or from the power of a peculiar eye 3
Or by creative feeling overborne 4
Or by predominance of thought oppress'd 5
Even in their fixed & steady lineaments 6
He traced an ebbing and a flowing mind 7
Expression ever-varying. ~~*Thus informed*~~ 8
89 ~~*He had small need of books for man*~~*y a tale*
90 *Traditionary round the mountains hung*
91 *And many a legend peopling the dark woods*
92 *Nourished Imagination in her growth*
93 ~~*And gave the mind that apprehensive power*~~
94 ~~*By which she is made quick to recognize*~~
95 ~~*The moral properties & scope of things*~~
This partly stood him in the stead
96 *But greedily he read & read again*
of books
97 *Whate'er the rustic Vicar's shelf supplied*
98 *The life and death of martyrs who sustain'd*
99 *Intolerable pangs, & here & there*
100 *A straggling volume torn & incomplete*
100
101 *Which left half-told the preternatural tale*
102 *Romance of giants, chronicle of fiends*
103 *Profuse in garniture of wooden cuts*
104 *Strange and uncouth, dire faces, figures dire*
105 *Sharp-knee'd, sharp-elbowed, & lean ankled too*

---

8 Deletion is in pencil.

89–107 This passage of 1799 copying was used in *The Pedlar*, 1802; see the note to l. *89* on 58^{r}. The deletion in l. *89* on 61^{r} is in ink; "for many a tale" completes l. *89* on 58^{r}.

93–95 The deleting marks are in pencil; the position of the number 100 shows that the numbering of *The Pedlar*, 1802, precedes the deletions.

95/96 In pencil, as is *96/97*.

100 The number is in pencil; it was added in 1802 when this passage (ll. *89–107*) was inserted at l. *89* on 58^{r}.

With long and ghostly shanks forms which once seen
Could never be forgotten. Things though low
Though low and humble not to be despised
By such as have observ'd the curious links
With which the perishable hours of life
Are bound together, and the world of thought
Exists and is sustained. Within his heart
Love was not yet nor the pure joy of love
By sound diffused or by the breathing air
Or by the silent looks of happy things
Or flowing from the universal face
Of earth and sky. But he had felt the power
Of nature and already was prepared
By his intense conceptions to receive
Deeply, the lesson deep of love, which he
Whom Nature, by whatever means, has taught
To feel intensely cannot but receive

Ere his ninth year he had been sent abroad
To tend his father's sheep such was his task
Henceforward till the later day of youth
Oh then what soul was his when on the tops
Of the high mountains he beheld the sun
Rise up and bathe the world in light. He looked
The ocean & the earth beneath him lay

[E, 174–193]

106 *With long and ghostly shanks, forms which once*
seen
107 *Could never be forgotten. Things though low*
Though low and humble not to be despised 3
By such as have observed the curious links 4
With which the perishable hours of life 5
Are bound together, and the world of thought 6
Exists and is sustained. Within his heart
Love was not yet nor the pure joy of love
By sound diffused or by the breathing air
Or by the silent looks of happy things 10
Or flowing from the universal face 11
Of earth and sky. But he had felt the power 12
Of nature and already was prepared 13
By his intense conceptions to receive 14
Deeply, the lesson deep of love, which he 15
Whom Nature, by whatever means, *has taught* 16
To feel intensely cannot but receive 17

Ere his ninth year he had been sent abroad 18
In summer to tend herds
To tend his father's sheep such was his task 19
Henceforward till the later day of youth 20
Oh then what soul was his when on the tops 21
Of the high mountains he beheld the sun 22
Rise up and bathe the world in light. He looked 23
The ocean & the earth beneath him lay 24

---

*107*a Here ends the passage of 1799 copying inserted into *The Pedlar*, 1802, at l. *89* on 58r. The text of the 1802 poem resumes at l. *107* on 58v.
*107*ff. Crossing out is in both pencil and ink.
21–24 The deleting X is in pencil.

In gladness and deep joy. The clouds were touched
And in their silent faces did he read 77
Unutterable love. Sound needed none
Nor any voice of joy: his spirit drank
The spectacle. Sensation, soul & form
All melted into him. They swallowed up
His animal being. In them did he live
And by them did he live. They were his life
In such access of mind, in such high hour
Of visitation from the living God
He did not feel the God: he felt his works.
Thought was not. In enjoyment it expired
Such hour by prayer or praise was unprofaned
He neither prayed, nor offered thanks or praise
His mind was a thanksgiving to the power
That made him. It was blessedness and love
A Shepherd on the lonely mountain-tops
Such intercourse was his and in this sort
Was his existence oftentimes possessed
Oh then how beautiful how bright appeared
The written promise; he had early learned
To reverence the volume which displays
The mystery the life which cannot die
But in the mountains did he feel his faith
There did he see the writing. All things there

[E, 194–217]

In gladness and deep joy. The clouds were touched 1
And in their silent faces did he read 2
Unutterable love. Sound needed none 3
Nor any voice of joy: his spirit drank 4
The spectacle. Sensation, soul & form 5
All melted into him. They swallowed up 6
His animal being. In them did he live 7
And by them did he live. They were his life 8
In such access of mind, in such high hour 9
Of visitation from the living God 10
He did not feel the God; he felt his works. 11
Thought was not: In enjoyment it expired 12
Such hour by prayer or praise was unprofan'd 13
He neither prayed, nor offered thanks or praise 14
His mind was a thanksgiving to the power 15
That made him. It was blessedness and love 16
A Shepherd on the lonely mountain-tops 17
Such intercourse was his and in this sort 18
Was his existence oftentimes possessed 19
Oh then how beautiful how bright appeared 20
The written promise; he had early learned 21
To reverence the volume which displays 22
The mystery the life which cannot die 23
But in the mountains did he feel his faith 24
There did he see the writing. All things there 25

The deleting X is in pencil.

Breathed immortality, revolving life
And greatness still revolving, infinite
There littleness was not, the least of things
Seemed infinite, & there his spirit shaped
Shaped her prospects nor did he believe — he saw
What wonder if his being thus became
Sublime & comprehensive low desires
Low thoughts had there no place, yet was his heart
Lowly; for he was meek in gratitude
Oft as he called to mind those ecstacies
And whence they flowed & from them he acquired
Wisdom which works through patience, thence he learn'd
In many a calmer hour of sober thought
To look on nature with an humble heart
Self-questioned where it did not understand
And with a superstitious eye of love.

Thus passed the time yet to the neighbouring town
He often went with what small overplus
His earnings might supply & brought away
The book which most had tempted his desires
While at the stall he read. Among the hills
He gazed upon that mighty orb of Song
The divine Milton. Lore of different kind
~~The annual savings of a toilsome life~~
The Schoolmaster supplied books that explain
The purer elements of truth involved

[E, 218–243]

Breathed immortality, revolving life 1
in
And greatness still revolving, infinite 2
There littleness was not, the least of things 3
Seemed infinite, & there his spirit shaped 4
Shaped her prospects,—nor did he believe—he saw 5
What *wonder if his being thus became* 6
Sublime & comprehensive low desires 7
Low thoughts had there no place, yet was his 8
heart
Lowly; for he was meek in gratitude 9
Oft as he called to mind those extacies 10
And whence they flowed; & from them he acquired 11
Wisdom which works through patience; thence 12
he learn'd
In many a calmer hour of sober thought 13
To look on nature with an humble heart 14
Self-questioned where it did not understand 15
And with a superstitious eye of love. 16
Thus passed the time yet to the neighbouring 17
town
He often went with what small overplus 18
His earnings might supply, & brought away 19
The book which most had tempted his desires 20
While at the stall he read. Among the hills 21
He gazed upon that mighty orb of Song 22
The divine Milton. Lore of different kind 23
~~*The annual savings of a toilsome life*~~, 24
step father
The ~~*Schoolmaster*~~ *supplied books that explain*~~*'d*~~ 25
138 *The purer elements of truth involved*

1–5 Deleted in pencil; DW's copying instruction, "in," is in ink.
24–25 Deletions and revision are in pencil, except for "'d," erased.
138 *The Pedlar*, 1802, continues here from l. *137* on 59r, incorporating lines copied in 1799.

79

In lines and numbers and by charm severe
Especially perceived where nature droops 140
And feeling is suppressed preserve the mind
Busy in solitude and poverty
And thus employed he many a time o'erlooked
The listless hours when in the hollow vale
Hollow and green he lay on the green turf
In lonesome idleness. What could he do?
Nature was at his heart and he perceived
Though yet he knew not how a wasting power
In all things which from her sweet influence
Might tend to wean him, therefore with her hues
Her forms & with the spirit of her forms
He clothed the nakedness of austere truth
While yet he lingered in the elements
Of science and among her simplest laws
His triangles they were the stars of heaven
The silent stars; his altitudes the crag
Which is the eagle's birth-place or some peak
Familiar with forgotten years which shews
[illegible] as with the token of the thought
~~Inscribed upon its bleak and visionary sides~~
Upon its bleak and visionary sides 160
The history of many a winter storm
Or obscure records of the path of fire
Yet with these lonesome sciences he still
Continued to amuse the heavier hours
Of solitude. ~~Yet not~~ the less he found Out
In cold relation, and the lifelessness

[E, 244–271]

139 *In lines and numbers and by charm severe*
140 *Especially perceived where nature droops* 140
141 *And feeling is suppressed preserve the mind*
142 *Busy in solitude and poverty*
143 *And thus employed he many a time o'erlooked*
144 *The listless hours when in the hollow vale*
145 *Hollow and green he lay on the green turf*
146 *In lonesome idleness. What could he do?*
147 *Nature was at his heart and he perceived*
148 *Though yet he knew not how a wasting power*
149 *In all things which from her sweet influence*
150 *Might tend to wean him, therefore with her hues*
151 *Her forms & with the spirit of her forms*
152 *He clothed the nakedness of austere truth*
153 *While yet he linger'd in the elements*

154 *Of si{c/s}ience and among her simplest laws*
155 *His triangles they were the stars of heaven*
oft did he take delight
156 *The silent stars; ~~his altitudes the crag~~*
To measure th'altitude of some tall crag
157 *Which is the eagle's birth-place or some peak*
158 *Familiar with forgotten years which shews*
as with the silence of the thought
159 *Inscribed ~~upon its bleak and visionary sides~~*
160 *Upon its bleak and visionary sides* 160
161 *The history of many a winter storm*
162 *Or obscure records of the path of fire*
163 *Yet with these lonesome sciences he still*
164 *Continued to amuse the heavier hours*
165 *Of solitude. ~~Yet not the less he found~~*
~~In cold relation and the lifelessness~~ | *out*

139/140 The mark visible near the left-hand margin in the photograph is offset from 62v.
140 The number is in pencil; it was added when this passage became part of *The Pedlar*, 1802. The preceding number for the new poem—120—is on 58v.
156–157 The deletion and revisions are in pencil.
160 The number 160—referring to *The Pedlar*, 1802—is in pencil.
165 The deleting marks here and in the following line are in pencil; the vertical stroke in the right-hand margin and DW's copying instruction are in ink. The text of *The Pedlar*, 1802, resumes at l. *165* on 64v.

Of truth by oversubtlety dislodged
From grandeur and from love an idle toy
The dullest of all toys. He saw in truth
A holy spirit and a breathing soul
He reverenced her and trembled at her look
When with a moral beauty in her face
She led him through the worlds. Out

But now before his twentieth year was pass'd
Accumulated feelings pressed his heart
With an encreasing weight, he was o'erpower'd
By nature and his spirit was on fire
With restless thoughts his eye became disturb'd
And many a time he wished the winds might rage
When they were silent: far more fondly now
Than in his earlier season did he love
Tempestuous nights the uproar & the sounds
That live in darkness: from his intellect
And from the stillness of abstracted thought
He sought repose in vain. I have heard him say
That at this time he scann'd the laws of light
Amid the roar of torrents where they send
From hollow clefts, up to the clearer air
A cloud of mist which in the shining sun
Varies its rainbow hues. But vainly thus
And vainly by all other means he strove
To mitigate the fever of his heart.

From Nature, & her overflowing soul
He had received so much that all his thoughts

Of truth by oversubtlety dislodged 1
From grandeur and from love, an idle toy 2
The dullest of all toys. He saw in truth 3
A holy spirit and a breathing soul 4
He reverenced her and trembled at her look 5
When with a moral beauty in her face 6
She led him through the worlds out 7

eighteenth
But now before his twentieth year was pass'd 8
Accumulated feelings pressed his heart 9
With an encreasing weight, he was o'erpower'd 10
By nature and his spirit was on fire 11
With restless thoughts—his eye became disturb'd 12
And many a time he wished the winds might rage 13
When they were silent: far more fondly now 14
Than in his earlier season did he love 15
Tempestuous nights the uproar & the sounds 16
That live in darkness: from his intellect 17
And from the stillness of abstracted thought 18
He sought repose in vain. I have heard him say 19
That a[?c]{t} this time he scann'd the laws of light 20
Amid the roar of torrents where they send 21
From hollow clefts, up to the clearer air 22
A cloud of mist which in the shining sun 23
Varies its rainbow hues. But vainly thus 24
And vainly by all other means he strove 25
To mitigate the fever of his heart. Turn to other paper 26

From Nature, & her overflowing soul 27
He had received so much that all his thoughts 28

The deleting lines on this page are all in pencil.

8–26 This passage, omitted in MS. E, is restored in MS. M, ll. 298–318.

The X, in pencil, at the beginning of l. 14 is of uncertain significance; it is probably related to a similar X to the right of l. 26, which is, however, in ink, matching the color of DW's copying instruction here and opposite l. 7. The "other paper" has not survived.

27 The nineteen-line passage beginning here and continuing on 64r becomes part of *Prelude* 1799 (II, 446–464).

81

Were steeped in feeling. He was only then
Contented, when with bliss ineffable
He felt the sentiment of being spread
O'er all that moves, & all that seemeth still
O'er all which lost beyond the reach of thought
And human knowledge to the human eye
Invisible yet liveth to the heart
O'er all that leaps & runs & shouts & sings
Or beats the gladsome air, o'er all that glides
Beneath the wave, yea in the wave itself
And mighty depth of waters. Wonder not
If such his transports were for in all things
He saw one life & felt that it was joy
One song they sang and it was audible
Most audible then when the fleshly ear,
O'ercome by grosser prelude of that strain,
Forgot its functions, & slept undisturbed.
These things he had sustained in solitude
Even till his bodily strength began to yield
Beneath their weight. The mind within him burnt
And he resolved to quit his native hills.
The Father strove to make his son perceive
As clearly as the old man did himself
With what advantage he might teach a school
In the adjoining village. But the youth
Who of this service made a short essay
Found that the wanderings of his thought were then

[E, 279–283]

Were steeped in feeling. He was only then 1
Contented, when with bliss ineffable 2
He felt the sentiment of being, spread 3
O'er all that moves, & all that seemeth still 4
O'er all which lost beyond the reach of thought 5
And human knowledge to the human eye 6
Invisible, yet liveth to the heart 7
O'er all that leaps & runs, & shouts, & sings 8
Or beats the gladsome air, o'er all that glides 9
Beneath the wave, yea in the wave itself 10
And mighty depth of waters. Wonder not 11
If such his transports were for in all things 12
He saw one life & felt that it was joy 13
One song they sang and it was audible 14
Most audible then when the fleshly ear, 15
O'ercome by grosser prelude of that strain, 16
Forgot its functions, & slept undisturbed. 17
These things he had sustained in solitude 18
Even till his bodily strength began to yield 19
Beneath their weight. The mind within him
burnt 20
And he resolved to quit his native hills. 21
The Father strove to make his son perceive 22
As clearly as the old man did himself 23
With what advantage he might teach a school 24
In the adjoining village. But the youth 25
Who of this service made a short essay 26
Found that the wanderings of his thought were
then 27

1–17 The deleting X is in pencil.

A misery to him that he must resign
A task he was unable to perform

Of solitude but now the time was come
When [illegible] began
Began to think about his way of life
In future, and his worldly maintenance
His mother strove to make her son perceive
With what advantage he might teach a school
In the adjoining village. But the youth
Who of this service made a short essay
Found that the wanderings of his thought were then
A misery to him, that he must resign
A task he was unable to perform.
His eldest brother elder than himself [illegible]
For years had travell'd southward long before
To carry up & down a Pedlars Pack
In England where he traffick'd at that time
Wealthy & prosperous. [illegible]
Said Patrick "I am strong and can bear
A load with ease the weight of [illegible]
This place long time has been his favourite
He ask'd his Mother's blessing, & with tears
Thank'd the good Man his second father, ask'd
Of him his parental blessings & affirmed
This lowly occupation. The good Priest
Offer'd up prayers & bless'd him but with the heart's
Forboding evil. From his native hills

in the high way [illegible]
Upon his back

[E, 284–285, 271–299]

A misery to him that he must resign P 1
A task he was unable to perform — 2

Of
165 *~~In~~ solitude but now the time was come*
growing up to manhood he began
166 *When ~~he, approaching fast to man's Estate~~*
{~~To~~ future
167 *~~Began~~ {to think about his ^ ~~way~~ of life*
168 *~~In future, and his worldly maintenance~~*
169 *His Mother strove to make her Son perceive*
170 *With what advantage he might teach a School*
171 *In the adjoining Village. But the Youth*
172 *Who of this service made a short essay*
{thought
173 *Found that the wanderings of his {[?] were then*
174 *A misery to him, that he must resign*
175 *A task he was unable to perform.*
had a
176 *His ~~eldest~~ ^ Brother, elder than himself*
who long before had left his home
177 *Six years ~~had travell'd southward long before~~*
178 *To carry up & down a Pedlars Pack*
{fficked
179 *In England where he tra{ded at that time*
180 *Healthy & prosperous.— "~~I to him will~~ go,"*
Patrick was resolved 180
181 *~~Said Patrick "I am stout as he, can bear~~*
To toil in the same calling & in truth
182 *~~A Load with ease the weight of twenty stone~~*
183 *This plan, long time, had been his favorite*
{M he thought
184 *He ask'd his {mother's blessing, ~~&~~ with tears*
185 *Thank'd the good Man, his second father, askd*
Pedlar *set forth*
186 *From him parental blessings, & assum'd*
A Traveller bound to England
187 *~~This lowly occupation~~. The good Pair*
188 *Offe'r'd up prayers & blessed him but with hearts*
189 *Foreboding evil. From his native hills*

[?pack]
in the high way, while walking [?with ?a]
Upon his back

WW's large penciled "P" may indicate a place where an addition, perhaps ll. *165–189* below, should be included.

165–189 In 1802, DW wrote these lines in a gap left in her 1799 copying. The text of *The Pedlar*, 1802, continues from l. *165* on 63r.

166–189 All deleting lines, revisions, and carets are in pencil, with the exception of "thought" in l. *173* and "Mother" in l. *184*.

180 The 180, in pencil, continues the numbering of *The Pedlar*, 1802; the number 160 is on 63r.

180–182 On the revision, see the note to l. *201* on 65r.

185/186 Pedlar] Perhaps an alternate for "Traveller" below.

189 This line leads into l. *190* on 65r.

WW's draft at the bottom of the page is in pencil.

83

He asked his father's blessing and assumed
This lowly occupation. The old man
Blessed him & prayed for him yet with a heart
Forboding evil. From his native hills
He wandered far; much did he see of men
Their manners, their enjoyments and pursuits
Their passions and their feelings, chiefly those
Essential and eternal in the heart
Which 'mid the simpler forms of rural life
Exist more simple in their elements
And speak a plainer language. ~~Many a year~~ He was now
In gathering wealth he had an easy [illegible]
~~Of lonesome meditation & impelled~~
That never could refuse, whoever ask'd
~~By curious thought, he was content to toil~~
To needed, & when for disparagers [illegible]
~~In this poor calling which he now pursued~~
With [illegible] about themselves & selfish [illegible]
~~From habit and necessity.~~ He walked
The [illegible] little thought
Among the impure haunts of vulgar men
Unstained; the talisman of constant thought
And kind sensations in a gentle heart
Preserved him; every shew of vice to him
Was a remembrancer of what he knew
Or a fresh seed of wisdom, or produced
That tender interest which the virtuous feel
Among the wicked, which when truly felt
May bring the bad man nearer to the good
But, innocent of evil, cannot sink
The good man to the bad. Among the woods
A lone enthusiast, & among the hills

[E, 294–307]

He asked his father's blessing and assumed 1
This lowly occupation. The old man 2
Blessed him & prayed for him yet with a heart 3
Forboding evil. From his native hills 4

190 *He wandered far, much did he see of ma{e n}*
191 *Their manners, their enjoyments and pursuits*
192 *Their passions and their feelings, chiefly those*
193 *Essential and eternal in the heart*
194 *Which 'mid the simpler forms of rural life*
195 *Exist more simple in their elements*
He was slow
196 *And speak a plainer language. ~~Many a year~~*
197 *In gathering wealth he had an open hand*
~~Of lonesome meditation & impelled~~
198 *That never could refuse whoever ask'd*
~~By curious thought he was content to toil~~
bot
199 *Or needed, & when his old parents [?eac]{h*
~~In this poor calling which he now pursued~~
200 *Were dead about himself & selfish cares*
~~From habit and necessity~~: ~~He walked~~
[201] *He took but little thought*
Among the impure haunts of vulgar men 16
Unstained; the talisman of constant thought 17
And kind sensations in a gentle heart 18
Preserved him; every shew of vice to him 19
Was a remembrancer of what he knew 20
Or a fresh seed of wisdom, or produced 21
That tender interest which the virtuous feel 22
Among the wicked, which when truly felt 23
May bring the bad man nearer to the good 24
But, innocent of evil, cannot sink 25
[?]
In
[201] *The good man to the bad. Among the woods*
200
202 *A lone enthusiast, & among the hills*

The original 1799 copying resumes on this page, after the gap—filled in 1802—which DW left on 64v.

1–4 Deleted in ink that matches the color of DW's 1802 addition on 64v and her revisions (ll. *196–201a*), below. The text of *The Pedlar*, 1802, continues from the bottom of 64v to l. *190* here, dovetailing 1802 work with 1799 copying.

196–201a The horizontal deleting lines are in ink but "He walked" in *200/201* is also deleted in pencil. These ink deleting lines—and the interlinings here—match the ink color of the 1802 passage on 64v. After the numbering of *The Pedlar*, 1802, ll. *196–201a* were deleted with vertical pencil strokes; the X's deleting the next ten and one-half lines are in pencil and ink.

201 The line of 1802 revision at the middle of the page connects with the half-line of 1799 fair copy at the bottom. The revision "In" and the number 200 are in pencil. The count from 180 on 64v to 200 is quite complicated; the revisions at ll. *180–182* on 64v may precede the numbering (although part of that correction appears to be written over the 180) or WW may have miscounted. The editorial numbers in the left-hand margins are now one higher than those in the manuscript numbering of *The Pedlar*, 1802.

Itinerant in this labour he had passed
The better portion of his time, & there
From day to day had his affections breathed
The wholesome air of nature there he kept
In solitude and solitary thought
So ~~pleasant were those comprehensive views~~
His mind in a just equipoise of love
Serene it was, unclouded by the cares
Of ordinary life unvexed unwarped
By partial bondage. In his steady course
No piteous revolutions had he felt
No wild varieties of joy or grief
Unoccupied by sorrow of its own
His heart lay open ~~and by nature~~ tuned
~~And constant disposition of his thoughts~~
~~To sympathy with man~~ he was alive
To all that was enjoyed where'er he went
And all that was endured, and in himself
Happy, & quiet in his chearfulness
He had no painful pressure from within
Which made him turn aside from wretchedness 220
With coward fears. He could afford to suffer
With those whom he saw suffer. Hence it was
That in our best experience he was rich
And in the wisdom of our daily life
For hence ~~minutely~~ In his various rounds
He had observed the progress and decay
Of many minds of minds and bodies too

[E, 308–334]

203 *Itinerant in this labour he had passed*
204 *The better portion of his time, & there*
205 *From day to day had his affections breathed*
206 *The wholesome air of nature, there he kept*
207 *In solitude and solitary thought*
208 *So ~~pleasant were those comprehensive views~~*
209 *His mind in a just equipoise of love*
210 *Serene it was, unclouded by the cares*
211 *Of ordinary life unvexed unwarped*
212 *By partial bondage. In his steady course*
213 *No piteous revolutions had he felt*
214 *No wild varieties of joy or grief*
215 *Unoccupied by sorrow of its own*
[216] *His heart lay open ~~and by nature~~ tuned*
~~And constant disposition of his thoughts~~
{&
[216] *~~To sympathy with man~~* { *he was alive*
217 *To all that was enjoyed where'er he went*
218 *And all that was endured, and in himself*
219 *Happy; & quiet in his chearfulness*
220 *He had no painful pressure from within*
221 *Which made him turn aside from wretchedness* 220
222 *With coward fears. He could afford to suffer*
223 *With those whom he saw suffer. Hence it was*
224 *That in our best experience he was rich*
225 *And in the wisdom of our daily life*
{For {minutely
{A[?] hence {[?his]
226 *In his various rounds*
227 *He had observed the progress and decay*
228 *Of many minds of minds and bodies too*

---

216 The added ampersand is in pencil.
221 The number 220 is in pencil. For there to be twenty lines from the preceding number 200 in *The Pedlar*, 1802 (see the note to l. *201* on 65r), the deletion at l. *216* would have to precede the numbering and the deletion of l. *208* would have to follow it.

85

The history of many families
And how they prospered, how they were o'erthrown
By passion or mischance or ~~such~~ by misrule
Among the unthinking masters of the earth
Which ~~As~~ makes the nations groan [illegible]
One whom you could not pass without remark
If you had met him on a rainy day
You would have stopped to look at him. Robust
Active and nervous was his gait his limbs
And his whole figure breathed intelligence
His body tall and shapely shewed in front
A faint line of the hollowness of age
Or rather what appeared the curvature
Of toil his head looked up steady and fixed
Age had compressed the rose upon his cheek
Into a narrower circle of deep red
But had not tamed his eye which under brows
Of hoary grey had meanings which it brought
From years of youth which like a being made
Of many beings he had wondrous skill
To blend with meanings of the years to come
Human, or such as lie beyond the grave
Long had I loved him. Oh it was most sweet
To hear him teach in unambitious style
Reasoning and thought by painting as he did
The manners and the passions. Many a time
He made a holiday and left his ~~pack~~ toil

[E, 335–339, 363–374, 51–52]

229 *The history of many families*
230 *And how they prospered, how they were o'erthrown*
by
231 *By passion or mischance or ~~such~~ ^ misrule*
232 *Among the unthinking masters of the earth*
Which *As I [?never ?had]*
233 *~~As~~ ^ makes the nations groan.* | X *He was a man*
Whom no one could have passd [*?as*]
One whom you could not pass without remark 6
&c

i
If you had met him in a ra[?]ny day 7
You would have stopped to look at him. Robust 8
Active and nervous was his gait his limbs 9
And his whole figure breathed intelligence 10
His body tall and shapely shewed in front 11
A faint line of the hollowness of age 12
Or rather what appeared the curvature 13
Of toil, his head looked up steady and fixed 14
Age had compressed the rose upon his cheek 15
Into a narrower circle of deep red 16
But had not tamed his eye ~~which under brows~~ 17
Of hoary grey had meanings which it brought 18
From years of youth which like a being made 19
Of many beings he had wondrous skill 20
To blend with meanings of the years to come 21
Human, or such as lie beyond the grave 22
, how sweet it was
Long had I loved him. X *Oh!* *it was most sweet* 23
To hear him teach in unambitious style 24
Reasoning and thought by painting as he did 25
The manners and the passions. Many a time 26
load
He made a holiday and left his ~~pack~~ 27

The deleting X's on this page are in pencil.

233 With the exception of the first word, the revisions and marks above and below this line are all in pencil. The X may refer to a similar X in l. 23 below; *The Pedlar*, 1802, may once have jumped to that point and included subsequent uncanceled lines, but there is no further pencil numbering in the manuscript. Perhaps WW's large "P" indicates that the conclusion of *The Pedlar*, 1802, was on a different sheet, with the doubtful readings above and below l. *233* giving opening words that unfortunately do not correspond to a part of the poem now surviving (see p. 27, above). Lines known to be included in *The Pedlar*, 1802, end here.

13 Erasure, perhaps of a comma, after "rather."

17 Deletion in pencil.

23 The exclamation point has been erased to leave what is probably intended as a comma.

27 The erasure after "pack" may be of "behind"—the beginning of the following line on 66v.

Behind, and we two wandered through the hills
A pair of random travellers. His eye
Flashing poetic fire he would repeat
other minstrelsy
The songs of Burns or many a ditty wild
Which he had fitted to the moorland harp
His own sweet verse, and as we trudged along
Together did we make the hollow grove
Ring with our transports.

What though he was
though he was untaught
In the dead lore of schools undisciplined
Why should he grieve! He was a chosen son
He yet retained an ear which deeply felt
The voice of Nature in the obscure wind
The sounding mountain and the running stream.
From deep analogies by thought supplied
Or consciousnesses not to be subdued
To every natural form, rock, fruit, and flower
Even the loose stones that cover the highway
He gave a moral life he saw them feel

[E, 53–60]

Behind, and wa{e} two wandered through the hills 1
A pair of random travellers. His eye 2
Flashing poetic fire he would repeat 3
other minstrelsy
The songs of Burns or many a ditty wild 4
Which he had fitted to the moorland harp 5
His own sweet verse, and as we trudged along 6
Together did we make the hollow grove 7
Ring with our transports. 8a

What though he was
though he was untaught 8b
In the dead lore of schools undisciplined 9
Why should he grieve? He was a chosen Son 10
He yet retained an ear which deeply felt 11
The voice of Nature in the obscure wind 12
The sounding mountain and the running stream 13
From deep analogies by thought supplied 14
Or consciousnesses not to be subdued 15
To every natural form, rock, fruit, and flower 16
Even the loose stones that cover the highway 17
He gave a moral life he saw them feel 18

There is no obvious reason for the gap left on this page. The lines at the bottom—the passage continues on 67r—eventually became part of *Prelude* (III, 82, 122–127, 141–147, 156–167); see *M of H*, p. 167, n. 1.

4 The correction is in pencil, as are the revision of l. 8b and the deleting **X** across the bottom paragraph.

87

Or linked them to some feeling. In all shapes
He found ~~the presence~~ a secret and mysterious ~~[illegible]~~ soul
~~A fragrance & a spirit of strange meaning.~~
[illegible]
~~Though poor in outward shew~~ he was most rich
He had a world about him—'twas his own
He made it—for it only lived to him
And to the God who looked into his mind
Such sympathies would often bear him far
In outward gesture & in visible look
Beyond the common seeming of mankind
Some called it madness such it might have been
But that he had an eye which evermore
Looked deep into the shades of difference
As they lie hid in all exterior forms
Near or remote, minute or vast, an eye
Which from a stone, a tree, a withered leaf
To the broad ocean and the azure heavens
Spangled with kindred multitudes of stars
Could find no surface where its power might sleep
Which spake perpetual logic to his soul
And by an unrelenting agency
Did bind his feelings even as in a chain

Or linked them to some feeling. In all shapes 1
the presence of a living soul
He found a secret and mysterious soul 2
~~*A fragrance & a Spirit of strange meaning*~~, 3
Unknown unthought [?of] yet I
~~*Though poor in outward shew*~~ *he was most rich* 4
He had a world about him—'twas his own 5
He made it—for it only lived to him 6
And to the God who looked into his mind 7
Such sympathies would often bear him far 8
In outward gesture & in visible look 9
Beyond the common seeming of mankind 10
Some called it madness—such it might have been 11
But that he had an eye which evermore 12
Looked deep into the shades of difference 13
As they lie hid in all exterior forms 14
Near or remote, minute or vast, an eye 15
Which from a stone, a tree, a withered leaf 16
To the broad ocean and the azure heavens 17
Spangled with kindred multitudes of stars 18
Could find no surface where its power might sleep 19
Which spake perpetual logic to his soul 20
And by an unrelenting agency 21
Did bind his feelings even as in a chain 22

The deleting X is in pencil. The lines here were used in *Prelude*; see the note to 66v.

The Ruined Cottage

Transcriptions of Additions to MS. D

Additions to MS. D

[Inside front cover]

habitual [?wanderings]
And now she saw a road before them & a wain
He [?lovd] the [? ?]
But by [?his] [? ?]
B
[?] y loneliness, & goodness & kind deeds
The vigour of his [?conduct ?oersoothed]
His fears & gloomy thoughts & this [?so ?much]
That
[?Th]

I did not speak & now

or
had sate beside him for an hour ~~&~~ [?more]
Upon this Bench unnotic'd & [?unheard]

[56ᵛ]

Fragment

In storm and tempest and beneath the beam 1
Of quiet moons and there 2
Whate'er there is of power in sound 3
To breathe an elevated mood, by form 4
Or image unprofan'd there would he stand 5
Beneath some rock listening to sounds that are 6
The ghostly language of the ancient earth 7
Or make their dim abode in distant winds 8
Thence did he drink the visionary power 9
I deem not profitless these fleeting moods 10
Of shadowy exaltation, not for this 11
That they are kindred to our purer mind 12
And intellectual life but that the soul 13

Inside front cover In the first passage, the ink has washed away from the center. The first three lines are related to *ASP* (*SPP*, p. 207), but "habitual [?wanderings]" and the rest of this draft contribute to MS. E, ll. 350–355. The second passage, scrawled in pencil, probably by DW, is written vertically over lines for *Prelude*, III (see *Chronology: MY*, pp. 632–633). The *RC* lines contribute to MS. E, ll. 380–382.

56ᵛ The fragment "In storm and tempest," continuing onto 57ʳ, was developed from drafts in the Alfoxden Notebook (20ʳ and 20ᵛ) related to WW's conception of the Pedlar. The lines were not used in MS. B but were copied into MS. D on pages between *RC* and the 1799 Pedlar addendum. By late 1799, ll. 1–20 of the fragment were used in the two-part *Prelude* (II, 352–371); ll. 22–27 on 56ᵛ and ll. 1–4 on 57ʳ contribute to *Prelude*, VII, 720–729.

Remembering how she felt, but what she felt 14
Remembering not, retains an obscure sense 15
Of possible sublimity at which 16
With growing faculties she doth aspire 17
With faculties still growing, feeling still 18
That whatsoever point they gain there still 19
Is something to pursue. But from these haunts 20
Of lonesome nature he had skill to draw 21
A better and less transitory power 22
An influence more habitual. To his mind 23
The mountain's outline, & its steady form 24
Gave simple grandeur, & its presence shaped 25
The measure & the prospect of his soul 26
To majesty, such virtue had the forms 27

[57r]

Perennial of the ancient hills; nor less 1
The changeful language of their countenance 2
Gave movement to his thoughts & multitude 3
With order & relation 4

[67v]

Not useless do I deem 1
These quiet sympathies with things that hold 2
An inarticulate language for the man 3
Once taught to love such objects as excite 4
No morbid passions no disquietude 5
No vengeance and no hatred needs must feel 6
The joy of that pure principle of love 7
So deeply that unsatisfied with aught 8
Less pure and exquisite he cannot chuse 9
But seek for objects of a kindred love 10
In fellow-natures and a kindred joy 11
Accordingly he by degrees perceives 12
His feelings of aversion softened down 13
A holy tenderness pervade his frame 14
His sanity of reason not impaired 15
Say rather all his thoughts now flowing clear 16
From a clear fountain flowing he looks round 17
He seeks for good and finds the good he seeks 18
Till execration and contempt are things 19
He only knows by name and if he hears 20
From other mouth the language which they speak 21

67v After copying the Pedlar overflow into MS. D in 1799, DW transcribed on 67v–69r the omitted part of the MS. B addendum. The lines do not appear in MSS. E or M; they eventually became *Excursion*, IV, 1207–1298 (*PW*, V, 148–150). In l. 1, DW began "Not useless" next to the left margin, erased it, and started again in the middle of the line.

He is compassionate and has no thought 22
No feeling which can overcome his love 23
And further, by contemplating these forms 24
In the relations which they bear to man 25
We shall discover what a power is theirs 26
To stimulate our minds, and multiply 27

[68r]

The spiritual presences of absent things 1
i
Then weary{ness will cease— We shall acquire 2
The habit by which sense is made 3
Subservient still to moral purposes 4
A vital essence and a saving power 5
Nor shall we meet an object but may read 6
Some sweet and tender lesson to our minds 7
Of human suffering or of human joy 8
All things shall speak of man and we shall read 9
Our duties in all forms, and general laws 10
And local accidents shall tend alike 11
To quicken and to rouze, and give the will 12
benefits
And power which by a chain of ~~*good*~~ 13
man
Shall link us to our kind. No naked hearts 14
No naked minds shall then be left to mourn 15
The burthen of existence. Science then 16
Shall be a precious visitant, and then godlike 17
And only then be worthy of her name 18
For then her heart shall kindle her dull eye 19
Dull and inanimate no more shall hang 20
Chained to its object in brute slavery 21
But better taught and mindful of its use 22
Legitimate, and its peculiar power 23
While with a patient interest it shall watch 24
The processes of things, and serve the cause 25
Of order and distinctness, not for this 26
Shall it forget that its most noble end 27
Its most illustrious province must be found 28
In ministering to the excursive power 29

[68v]

Of Intellect and thought. So build *we up* 1
The being that we are. For was it meant 2
That we should pore & dwindle as we pore 3
Forever dimly pore on things minute 4

68r 17 godlike] Probably an alternate for "precious."

On solitary objects still beheld 5
In disconnection dead and spiritless 6
And still dividing, and dividing still 7
Break down all grandeur still unsatisfied 8
With our unnatural toil while littleness 9
May yet become more little waging thus 10
An impious warfare with the very life 11
Of our own souls X Or was it ever meant 12
That this majestic imgery, the clouds 13
The ocean, and the firmament of heaven 14
Should lie a barren picture on the mind? 15
Never for ends of vanity and pain 16
And sickly wretchedness were we endued 17
Amid this world of feeling and of life 18
With apprehension, reason, will and thought 19
Affections, organs, passions. Let us rise 20
From this oblivious sleep, these fretful dreams 21
Of feverish nothingness. Thus disciplined 22
All things shall live in us, and we shall live 23
In all things that surround us. This I deem 24
Our tendency & thus shall every day 25
Enlarge our sphere of pleasure & of p{ower / *ain*} 26
Fa{*o*} *r thus the senses and the intellect* 27
Shall each to each supply a mutual aid 28

[69r]

Invigorate and sharpen and refine 1
low and high to comprehend force
Each other with ~~a power that knows no bound~~ 2
Minute & vast with ever growing [?~~sway~~] sway
And forms & feelings acting thus, & thus 3
Reacting they shall each acquire 4
A living spirit & a character 5
Till then unfelt, & each be multiplied 6
With a variety that knows no end 7
Thus deeply drinking in the soul of things 8
We shall be wise perforce, and we shall move 9
From strict necessity along the path 10
Of order and of good. Whate'er we see 11
Whate'er we feel by agency direct 12
Or indirect shall tend to feed and nurse 13
Our faculties and raise to loftier height 14
Our intellectual soul. The old man ceased 15
The words he uttered shall not pass away 16

68v 12 The significance of the X is unclear.
13 imgery] An obvious miswriting for "imagery."

They had sunk into me but not as sounds 17
To be expressed by visible characters 18
mind & heart
For while he spake my ~~spirit had~~ obeyed 19
The presence of his eye, my ear ~~had~~ drunk 20
in
The meanings of his voice. He had discoursed 21
slow & patient X
Like one who in the^silent works 22
The manifold conclusions of his thought 23
Had brooded till Imagination's power 24
Condensed them to a passion whence she drew 25
Herself new energies, resistless force. 26

[91r]

drank
I slake and soon to the shady bench
I had returned while with uncover'd head
I stood to catch the motion [?of ?&c]

69r 21 The symbol—and possibly the X—refer to a draft in WW's hand on 74r intended for insertion here:

Like one whom Time & Nature have made wise
Gracing his language with authority
Which hostile Spirits silently allow
{O
Like {one

91r This draft—a revision of ll. 64–66 from MS. D, 47r—contributes to MS. E, ll. 402–404.

The Pedlar

Reading Text of MS. E (1803–1804), with Variant Readings from MS. E and from *Peter Bell* MS. 2 in an *Apparatus Criticus*

Transcriptions of MS. M (1804), with Variant Readings from MS. E^2 in an *Apparatus Criticus*

MSS. E, E², and M

MS. E (DC MS. 37), dating from between late November 1803 and about 6 March 1804, is described on pp. 30–34, above. Dorothy copied into this manuscript the earliest complete text of *The Pedlar* (the title the Wordsworths now assigned to the combined stories of Margaret and the Pedlar). This manuscript is relatively uncomplicated, and it is here presented as an edited reading text according to the principles set down in Editorial Procedure, above; it is preceded by a specimen photograph of the opening page. An *apparatus criticus* gives manuscript variants—chiefly differences resulting from editorial expansion of "&" and alteration of the punctuation, and from Wordsworth's revisions for MSS. E² and M. A 1799 draft from *Peter Bell* MS. 2 (DC MS. 33) contributes to MS. E, lines 445–451, and it is also included in the *apparatus criticus*. Variants recorded in the *apparatus criticus* are in Dorothy's hand and in ink, unless otherwise noted. The MS. E reading text, facing a transcription of MS. M, has bracketed line references to the MS. D reading text to facilitate comparison of *The Ruined Cottage* and *The Pedlar*; MS. E line numbers are supplied by the editor.

Beginning about 6 March 1804, Dorothy copied *The Pedlar* as part of the collection of Wordsworth's unpublished poems (MS. M, DC MS. 44) sent to Coleridge by 18 March for him to take to Malta. MS. M is a homemade notebook, formed of sheets of paper (watermarked with an image of Britannia in a crowned oval, with the date 1802 at the bottom inside the oval—see the photograph on p. 31, above—and countermarked C HALE) folded to make leaves about 10.7 centimeters wide by 16.9 centimeters high; chain lines appear at intervals of 2.65 centimeters. Paper watermarked with a crowned heraldic device, containing the word LIBERTAS, over AMP and countermarked VORNO is also in the notebook (cf. Edward Heawood, *Watermarks* [Hilversum, 1950], no. 781). A similar watermark appears in the W. A. Churchill Collection (British Library Add. MS. 44863, ff. 45–46) on a 1793 document written in Italian. This azure, laid AMP/VORNO paper, with chain lines 2.7 centimeters apart, was probably added to the notebook by Coleridge or his binder. MS. M opens with a four-leaf gathering of the AMP/VORNO paper. The first two leaves of the next gathering (once consisting of eight leaves, formed from two sheets of the C HALE paper) are missing; the second of the missing leaves contained the opening of *The Pedlar*, which now begins at line 51 on leaf 7ʳ (see the photograph of leaf 7ʳ of MS. M, below). Dorothy began *The Pedlar* on the second leaf because she was recopying MS. E² (seven leaves and a stub) to dovetail with the already written second gathering of MS. M (see p. 33, above).

The rest of *Pedlar* MS. M is written on a gathering of eight leaves and a bifolium of the C HALE paper. A single leaf (no. 23)—its color and chain line intervals suggest that it is the AMP/VORNO paper, although no watermark shows—divides *The Pedlar* from the following section of Wordsworth's sonnets. A complete list of the remaining contents of MS. M may be found in *Chronology: MY*, pp. 619–622. Coleridge must at one time have stuck gatherings together with red sealing wax; surviving traces of this wax appear in the *Pedlar* section between leaves 12 and 13, 20 and 21, 22 and 23, and 23 and 24.

MS. M is presented here in transcription to enable the reader to see the exact text that the Wordsworths sent to Coleridge. Since the first page of text is missing from MS. M, lines 1–50 are transcribed from MS. E^2 (described on p. 32, above), which once was the opening gathering of MS. M. From line 51 to its stopping place at line 363, MS. E^2 variants of the numbered base-text lines in MS. M are given in an *apparatus criticus*; variants are in Dorothy's hand and in ink, unless otherwise noted. Although revisions in Dorothy's hand in MS. E^2—often written over an erasure in accordance with her brother's penciled instructions—are copied as parts of the base text of the later MS. M, Wordsworth's ink revisions are not (two revisions in Wordsworth's ink in MS. E^2 also appear as revisions in MS. M; see the transcription of MS. M, ll. 193 and 323, and the *apparatus criticus*). Since MSS. E^2 and M were intended to be neat manuscripts for Coleridge, most of Wordsworth's ink revisions were probably made after the dispatch of MS. M by 18 March 1804. Revisions on MS. M were probably made after Coleridge's return from Malta in the summer of 1806, possibly as late as December 1809 to March 1812, when *The Pedlar* became part of *Excursion* MS. P (*Chronology: MY*, pp. 22, 675–685). Editorial line numbers in the left-hand margins include revisions in Dorothy's hand (one exception occurs, at ll. 690–691, where Wordsworth's revision is taken as preceding 18 March); the numbered text thus approximates the state of the poem sent to Coleridge in 1804. In the right-hand margins, within brackets, are matching line numbers from MS. E. When a reading beneath an erasure is uncertain, notes record what is in the immediately preceding manuscript, with any visible letters presented in boldface type.

426
160
353
939 23

Part First.

123

'Twas summer– and the sun was mounted high.
Travelling on foot and distant from my home
Several days journey, over the flat Plain
Of a bare Common, I had toil'd along
With languid steps; & when I stretch'd myself
On the brown earth my limbs from very heat
Could find no rest, nor my weak arm disperse
The hosts of insects gathering round my face.
The time was hot, the place was shelterless;
And, rising, right across the open Plain
On to the spot I hasten'd whither I
Was bound that morning, a small group of Trees
Which midway on the Common stood alone
I made no second stop, and soon I reach'd
The spot that lay before me full in view.
It was a knot of clustering Elms that sprang
As if from the same root, beneath whose shade
I found a Ruin'd House, four naked walls
That star'd upon each other, I look'd round
In search of the Old Man whom I that morning
Had come to meet: he on the Cottage Bench
Was lying in the shade as if asleep;
An iron-pointed Staff lay at his side.

Pedlar MS. E, leaf 2r

For my grave looks, too thoughtful ...
Glad was I when he from his rounds ...
As I grew up it was my best delight
To be his chosen comrade. Many a time
He made a holiday and left his Pack
Behind, and we two wander'd through the ...
A Pair of random Travellers – we sate,
We walk'd; he pleas'd me with his sweet ...
Of things which he had seen, & oft times touch'd
Abstrusest matter, reasonings of the mind
Turn'd inwards, or, in other mood, he sang
Old songs, and sometimes, too, at my reque...
More solemn music which he in his you...
Had learn'd, religious anthems, sounds se...
And soft, and most refreshing to the hear...
In that same Town of Hawkshead w...
There was a little Girl, (and though, in truth,
This incident be something like a nook
Or pleasant corner which from my right path
Diverts me, yet I cannot pass it by)
There was a little Girl, ten years of age,
But tiny for her years, a pretty Dwarf,
Fair-hair'd, fair-fac'd, and, though of statu...
In heart as forward as a lusty child.
This Girl when from his travels he return'd,
To his abiding-place would daily come
To play with the good Man, and he was wont
To tell her stories of his early life,

Pedlar MS. M, leaf 7[r]

MS. E: Reading Text

The Pedlar

Part First.

'Twas summer—and the sun was mounted high.
Travelling on foot, and distant from my home
Several days journey, over the flat Plain
Of a bare Common I had toil'd along
[D, 20] With languid steps; and when I stretch'd myself 5
On the brown earth my limbs from very heat
Could find no rest, nor my weak arm disperse
The host of insects gathering round my face.
The time was hot, the place was shelterless;
[D, 27] And, rising, right across the open Plain 10
On to the spot I hasten'd whither I
Was bound that morning, a small group of Trees
Which midway on the Common stood alone.
I made no second stop, and soon I reach'd

The Pedlar] *no title*

Above and to the right of Part First. *are a column of penciled numbers* (426, 160, 353), *their sum* (939), *and* 123 *repeated twice. The first three numbers obviously refer to the lines in the three parts of* The Pedlar, *but seem to be later than MS. E. The revised state of MS. M comes closer to having the appropriate number of lines in each part. The significance of* 123 *is unclear.*

3 {P / plain}
4 Common,
5 and] &
8 host] hosts *a probable copying error, since the* s *on hosts is deleted at WW's instruction in MS.* E^2 *and MS. D has* host *in a similar context;* Excursion, *1814, reads* host
12–18 *on a pasted-over sheet; the original reading beneath the pastedown is as follows:*

Was bound that morning, a small group of {T / trees}
[?Which] midway on the Common stood alone
[? ? ? ? ? ?] Elms that sprang
As if from the same root beneath whose shade
I found a Ruin'd House, four naked walls

The last four lines of the original reading were erased, and DW wrote over the erased second and third lines:

Which midway on the Common stood alone
I made no second stop & soon I reach'd the port
Which lay before me full in view

When she noticed her error in placing the port *in her overwriting, DW must have decided on a pasteover.*
13 alone.] alone

For that part of the Fenwick note relating to *The Pedlar*, see Appendix II, below.

MS. M: Transcriptions

[E², 1ʳ]

~~*Part First.*~~

1 *'Twas summer and the sun was mounted high.*
2 *Travelling on foot, and distant from my home*
3 *Several days' journey, over the flat Plain*
4 *Of a bare Common I had toil'd along*
5 *With languid steps; and when I stretch'd myself* [E, 5]
6 *On the brown earth my limbs from very heat*
7 *Could find no rest; nor my weak arm disperse*
8 ~~s~~ *The hosts~~s~~ of insects gathering round my face.*
9 *The time was hot, the place was shelterless;*
10 *And, rising, right across the open Plain* [E, 10]
11 *On to the spot I hasten'd whither I*
12 *Was bound that morning, a small Group of Trees*
13 *Which midway on the Common stood alone.*

[?attaind]
had / gain'd
14 *I made no second stop, and soon* *I ~~reach'd~~*

As explained in the headnote, MS. M is missing its opening leaf of text; MS. E² (the original first gathering of MS. M) is thus transcribed up to l. 51.

Deletion by erasure of "Part First."

8 WW's deletion of the marginal "s" (now no longer visible in the MS after recent restoration) is in pencil; the "s" on "hosts" is erased.

14 The addition of "[?attaind]" is in pencil.

The Port that lay before me full in view. 15
[D, 30] It was a knot of clustering Elms that sprang
As if from the same root, beneath whose shade
I found a Ruin'd House, four naked walls
That star'd upon each other; I look'd round
In search of the Old Man whom I that morning 20
Had come to meet: he on the Cottage Bench
[D, 35] Was lying in the shade as if asleep;
An iron-pointed Staff lay at his side.
  Him had I seen the day before—alone
And in the middle of the public way 25
Standing to rest himself. His eyes were turn'd
Towards the setting sun, while, with that Staff
Behind him fix'd, he propp'd a long white Pack
Which cross'd his shoulders, wares for them who live
In lonely villages or straggling huts. 30
Thus with his face towards the setting sun
He stood in the high road, and I stopp'd short,
Half-wondering who the Man might be, but soon
As I came up to him, great joy was ours
At such unthought-of meeting. For the night 35
We parted, nothing willingly, and now
He by appointment waited for me here
Beneath these Elms, we having both a wish
To travel on together a few days.
  We were dear Friends: I from my childhood up 40
Had known him. In a nook of Furness Fells,

---

15 {P / port}
19 other,
20 {O / old}
21 *after* meet: *WW penciled an* X *and* [?&c] *marking a place where the text was altered before MS. E*[2] Bench,
23 *blot obliterates terminal punctuation, if any*
30 huts.] huts
31–32 *erased, overwritten* With slacker pace towards him I advanced *there are traces of two penciled lines in WW's hand; only the ending of the first is legible:* the Road
38 *after* wish *WW penciled a caret and* &c *marking a place expanded in MS. E*[2]
40 We *originally begun at left margin, then erased and indented* Friends,

---

24–374 The Pedlar is a combination of a packman with whom WW had conversations while a schoolboy; James Patrick, with whom Sara Hutchinson lived as a child; and what the poet fancied his "own character might have become in his circumstances." See the Fenwick note in Appendix II.

41 "Furness Fells" are the fells, or mountains, in the area from the river Duddon to the Leven, formerly in the county of Lancashire.

15 *The Port that lay before me full in view.* [E, 15]
16 *It was a knot of clustering Elms that sprang*
17 *As if from the same root beneath whose shade*
18 *I found a Ruin'd House, four naked walls*
19 *That star'd upon each other,* {.} {*G*} *glad I was*
20 ^ *And cast immediately my eyes about*
21 *In search of the Old Man whom I that morning* [E, 20]
22 *Had come to meet.* {;} {*t*} *This was the appointed place*
^ [?And ?cast ?my ?eyes] about immediately

[E², 1ᵛ]

23 *And here he was upon the Cottage Bench*
24 *Lying within the shade, as if asleep;*
25 *An iron-pointed Staff lay at his side.*
26 *Him had I seen the day before—alone*
27 *And in the middle of the public way* [E, 25]
28 *Standing to rest himself. His eyes were turn'd*
29 *Towards the setting sun; while with that Staff*
30 *Behind him fix'd he propp'd a long white Pack*
31 *Which cross'd his shoulders, wares for them who live*
32 *In lonely villages or straggling huts.* [E, 30]
33 *At sight of one thus standing in the road*
34 ^ *With slacker pace towards him I advanc'd,*
^ With slackend footsteps I advancd
35 ~~*Half wondering who the Man might*~~ *be, but soon*
36 *As I came up to him, great joy was ours*
37 *At such unthought-of meeting. For the night* [E, 35]
38 *We parted, nothing willingly, and now*
39 *He by appointment waited for me here*
sheler of these clustering elms.
40 *Beneath these*^~~*Elms, we having both a wish*~~
41 *To turn to profit this good hap, and be*
42 *Companions to each other a few days.*
43 *We were dear Friends: I from my Childhood up* [E, 40]
~~a~~ [?~~shelterd~~] a little town obscure,
44 *Had known him. In* ~~*the heart of Fur*~~*ness Fells*
hidden
Or market village ~~seated~~ in^a tract

---

19 The erased words may be the MS. E reading: "I loo**k**'d roun**d**."
20 The caret is in pencil and refers to a similar caret at page foot where there is a nearly illegible pencil line in WW's hand, draft for DW's interlining.
34 The carets are in pencil; they match a caret at page foot (after l. 49), where WW penciled the line he wished DW to insert.
40 WW mistakenly wrote "sheler" for "shelter."
44 The erased words may be the MS. E reading: "a nook."
44–45 The carets are in pencil. Traces of WW's pencil writing here are probably instructions for DW's revisions.

At Hawkshead, where I went to School nine years,
One Room he had, the fifth part of a house,
A place to which he drew from time to time
And found a kind of home or harbour there. 45
—He lov'd me, out of many rosy Boys
Singl'd out me, as he in sport would say,
For my grave looks, too thoughtful for my years.
Glad was I when he from his rounds return'd:
As I grew up, it was my best delight 50
To be his chosen comrade. Many a time
He made a holiday, and left his Pack
Behind, and we two wander'd through the hills,
A pair of random Travellers—we sate,
We walk'd, he talk'd about himself, or held 55
Abstruse discourses, reasonings of the mind
Turn'd inwards, or in other mood, he sang
Old songs, and sometimes, too, at my request,
Psalms and religious anthems, sounds sedate
And soft, and most refreshing to the heart. 60
In that same Town of Hawkshead where we dwelt

---

42 years,] years
46 *WW penciled* in *before this line, perhaps because erasures showing through from the other side—or the correction in l. 46 itself—might look like an intended deletion* out of many rosy *in DW's ink over erasure, itself then overwritten* from a swarm of (*WW, pencil*)
52 and] &
54 sate,] sate *WW's penciled* B *after* sate *marks where the text was expanded in MS.* E^2
55 *erased* *WW penciled one line above and one below; the one below may end in* touched
57 *after* sang *WW penciled* $_{\wedge}$C
61/62 and though in truth *continuing 62/63* This incident be something like a nook *continuing at page foot* Or pleasant Corner which from my right path / Diverts me yet I cannot pass it by (*WW, pencil*)

45 ~~*At Haw*~~*kshead, where my*^*school-boy days were*
^
pass'd

Of [?mountains]
ownd

46 *One Room he* ~~*had*~~, *the fifth part of a house,*
47 *A place to which he drew from time to time*
48 *And found a kind of home or harbour there.* [E, 45]
49 *—He lov'd me, from a swarm of rosy Boys*
^—At sight of one thus standing in the road

[E², 2^r]

50 *Singl'd out me, as he in sport would say,*

[M, 7^r]

51 *For my grave looks, too thoughtful for my* [ ]
52 *Glad was I when he from his rounds returnd*
53 *As I grew up it was my best delight* [E, 50]
54 *To be his chosen comrade. Many a time*
55 *He made a holiday and left his Pack*
56 *Behind, and we two wander'd through the Hills,*
57 *A Pair of random Travellers—we sate,* [E, 54]
58 *We walk'd; he pleas'd me with his sweet dis=*
=course
59 *Of things which he had seen, & oft-times touch'd*
60 *Abstrusest matter, reasonings of the mind*
61 *Turn'd inwards, or, in other mood, he sang* [E, 57]
62 *Old songs, and sometimes, too, at my reques*[ ]
63 *More solemn music, which he in his youth*
64 *Had learn'd, religious anthems, sounds sedate*
65 *And soft, and most refreshing to the heart.* [E, 60]
66 *In that same Town of Hawkshead where*
we dwelt

67 *There was a little Girl,* {(*and though, in truth,*
68 *This incident be something like a nook*

---

51 *in the gap* years.
52 Glad was *over erasure* return'd.
55 *del*
56 Behind, and we two *del to* On holydays *(WW)*
57 pair
59 oft times
62 request,
63 music,] music
67 though, in truth,] though in truth *the opening parenthesis may also be a later addition*
67–70 *del*

---

51 Transcription of MS. M now begins; variants for the remainder of MS. E² (corresponding to ll. 51–363) are shown in the *apparatus criticus*. The last word, "years," has been worn or cut away.

62 The "t" on "request" has worn away.

There was a little Girl, ten years of age,
But tiny for her years, a pretty dwarf,
Fair-hair'd, fair-fac'd, and though of stature small,
In heart as forward as a lusty child. 65
This Girl, when from his travels he return'd,
To his abiding-place would daily come
To play with the good Man, and he was wont
To tell her stories of his early life.
"Nay," would she answer him, unsaying thus 70
All he had said to her, "you never could
Be a poor, ragged little Boy, and hired
By the poor Man you talk of to tend cattle
On a hill-side, for forty pence a year."
All which did to the Girl appear so strange 75
She could not give it faith; and when she us'd
To doubt his words, as I remember well,
Spite of himself, the good Man smil'd, and held
His hand up to his face to hide his smiles
Because he knew that if the little Girl 80
Once spied them, she would then be sure, past doubt,
That it was but a story told in sport.
Seeing that she was thus perplex'd in mind,
He was far better pleas'd to sing to her
Scotch Songs, sometimes, but oftener to repeat 85
Scotch poetry, old Ballads, and old Tales—
Love Gregory, William Wallace, and Rob Roy.
All this while she was sitting on a stool
Between his knees; and oft did she stand up
Upon her stool, and coax him with a kiss 90
To tell her more, and, many a time, would he
Weep over her; and she would wonder why.
This, standing at his threshold, have I seen,
Yea many times, when he had little thought

---

64 and] & small,] small
is
69 his] her} *a copying error corrected* life.] life
72–74 *lines begin with quotation marks*
74 year"
78 and] &
82 told in *del to* framed for (*WW, pencil*)
84–98 *del with pencil and ink* **X**'s
86 Tales,
.
87 Roy,}

69 *Or pleasant corner which from my right path*
70 *Diverts me, yet I cannot pass it by*)}
71 *There was a little Girl, ten years of age,* [E, 62]
72 *But tiny for her years, a pretty Dwarf,*
73 *Fair-hair'd, fair-fac'd, and, though of stature small*
74 *In heart as forward as a lusty child.* [E, 65]
75 *This Girl, when from his travels he return'd,*
76 *To his abiding-place would daily come*
77 *To play with the good Man, and he was wont*
78 *To tell her stories of his early life,*

[7v]

79 *Nay, would she answer him, unsaying thus* [E, 70]
80 *All he had said to her, "you never could*
81 *Be a poor ragged little Boy, and hired*
82 *By the poor Man you talk of to tend cattle*
83 *On a hill side, for forty pence a year."*
84 *All which did to the Child appear so strange* [E, 75]
85 *She could not give it faith; and when she us'd*
86 *To doubt his words, as I remember well,*
87 *Spite of himself, the good Man smil'd, & held*
88 [ ]*is hand up to his face to hide his smiles,*
89 [ ]*ecause he knew that if the little Girl* [E, 80]
90 *Once spied them, she would then be sure, past doubt*
91 *That it was but a story fram'd in sport.* [E, 82]

---

70 by,)}
71 was a] wa *a copying error*
72 dwarf,
73 and,] &
77 and] &
79 Nay,] "Nay"
81 hir'd
82 cattle *del to* herds *(WW)*
83 side,] side year."] year"
86b–87a *del*
88 His hand
89 Because the little Girl *alt* his [?dwarf] *(WW)*
90 spied *del to* Did espi *(WW)* them,] them past doubt, *del*

---

79 The page has been trimmed at the top, so it is not possible to see if "Nay" once was enclosed in quotation marks (as in MSS. E and E²).
88 The opening "H" is torn away.
89 The opening "B" is torn away; DW began to write "he" with a "k."

That any one was near. He was, in truth, 95
The kindest-natur'd Man! and dearly I
Delight to recollect him, and his looks,
And think of him, and his affectionate ways.
His history I from himself have heard
Full often, after I grew up, and he 100
Found in my heart, as he would kindly say,
A kindred heart to his. Among the hills

---

96 *no hyphen*
99 I from himself have heard *del to* which he would thus in part (*WW, pencil*)
99/100 Tell to this Child I from himself have heard (*WW, pencil*)
100 Full often, *del to* Minutely (*WW, pencil*)
102 *after* his. *WW penciled two* H-*shaped marks indicating where the text was altered before MS.* E^2

92 *His History which he would thus in part*
93 *Tell to this Child I from himself have heard*
94 *Minutely, after I grew up, and he* [E, 100]
95 *Found in my heart, as he would kindly say,*
96 *A kindred heart to his. I was a Boy* [E, 102]
97 *When first he notic'd me, and I began*
98 *To love him, and to seek him, and rejoice*
99 *In the plain presence of his dignity.*
100 *Oh! many are the Poets that are sown*
101 *By nature, men endued with highest gifts,*
102 *The vision and the faculty divine,*
103 *Yet wanting the accomplishment of verse*
104 *And never being led by accident*

[8r]

105 *Or circumstance to take unto the height*
106 *By estimate comparative, at least,*
107 *The measure of themselves, live out their time*
108 *Husbanding that which they possess within*
109 *And go to the grave unthought of. Strongest minds*
110 *Are often those of which the noisy world*
111 *Hears least, else, surely, this Man had not left,*
112 *And sundry others, too, whom I have known*
113 *His graces unreveal'd and unproclaim'd.*
114 *Though born in low estate, and earning bread*
115 *By a low calling, yet this very Man*
116 *Was as the prime and choice of sterling minds:*
117 *I honor'd him, respected, nay rever'd.*
118 *And some small portion of his eloquent words,*
119 *The feeling pleasures of his loneliness,*

---

93 Child] [?little] Girl *then* [?little] *erased, overwritten* Child, *and* Girl *del*
95 say,] say
98 love him,] love him
102 divine,] divine
106 *added parentheses enclose the line*
107 themselves,] themselves
108 [?And] *erased* {H / husbanding} {t / what *with* w *erased*, which *inserted with a caret* *traces of illegible pencil writing here*
109 And *inserted in pencil (WW), then with caret in ink (DW)* Go
111 else, surely,] else surely left,] left
112 And sundry others too *del to* And others of like mold *(WW)*
113 His] Their *erased, overwritten* His
115 very Man *del to* mild good Man *(WW) with alt* he [?of ?whom ?I] *(WW), repeated* he of [?whom] I speak *(WW)*
116 Was as *del to* Rankd with *(WW)* minds.
117 honour'd
117/118 He was a light that shone before my youth *del in pencil and ink*
118 words,] words
119 loneliness,] loneliness
119–120 *WW's* 1 *before l.* 120 *and his* 2 *before l.* 119 *in MS.* E^2 *seem intended to reverse their order*

Of Perthshire he was born: his Father died
In poverty, and left three Sons behind.
[His] Mother married for a second mate 105
A Schoolmaster, who taught the Boys to read
And brought them up, and gave them as he could
Needful instruction, teaching them the ways
Of honesty and holiness severe.
A virtuous houshold, though exceeding poor, 110
Pure livers were they all, austere and grave
And fearing God, the very children taught
Stern self-respect, a reverence for God's word,
And piety scarce known on English Land.
From his sixth year the Boy of whom I speak 115
In summer tended cattle on the hills
But in the winter time he duly went
To his Step-father's School, that stood alone,
Sole Building on a mountain's dreary edge,
Far from the sight of city spire, or sound 120
Of minster clock. From that bleak tenement
He, many an evening, to his distant home
In solitude returning, saw the hills
Grow larger in the darkness, all alone
Beheld the stars come out above his head, 125
And travell'd through the wood with no one near
To whom he might confess the things he saw.
So the foundations of his mind were laid.
In such communion, not from terror free,
While yet a child, and long before his time 130

---

104 behind.] behind
105 His *added by WW in pencil in gap left by DW*
106 Schoolmaster,] Schoolmaster
108 teaching *del to* shewing (*WW, pencil*)
113 word,] word
126 wood] woods *a probable copying error since MSS. B, D,* and *M—and* Excursion, *1814—read* wood (*MS. E*[2] *reads* woods *with the* s *erased at WW's instruction*)

110–114 Cf. *Resolution and Independence*, ll. 97–98: "Such as grave Livers do in Scotland use, / Religious men, who give to God and man their dues" (*PW*, II, 238). Both passages date from 1802.

129 Like the Pedlar's, WW's own development—as described in *The Prelude*—was "Foster'd alike by beauty and by fear" (I, 306; see also I, 625–640, and XIII, 143–149).

120 *And something that may serve to set in view*
121 *The doings, observations, which his life*
122 *Had dealt with, I will here record in verse.*
123 *Among the Hills of Perthshire he was born*
124 *His Father, he being yet an Infant, died*
125 *In poverty, and left three Sons behind.*
126 *The Mother married for a second Mate* [E, 105]
127 *A Schoolmaster, who taught the Boys to read*
128 *And brought them up, & gave them, as he could,*
129 *Needful instruction, shewing them the ways*
130 *Of honesty and holiness severe.*

[8v]

131 *A virtuous houshold, though exceeding poor,* [E, 110]
132 *Pure livers were they all, austere and grave,*
133 *And fearing God, the very children taught*
134 *Stern self-respect, a reverence for God's word,*
135 *And piety scarce known on English Land.*
136 *From his sixth year, the Boy of whom I speak* [E, 115]
137 *In summer tended cattle on the Hills,*
138 *But in the winter time he duly went*
139 *To his Step-father's School that stood alone,*
140 *Sole Building on a Mountain's dreary edge,*
141 *Far from the sight of City Spire, or Sound* [E, 120]
142 *Of Minster Clock. From that bleak Tenement*
143 *He, many an evening, to his distant home*
144 *In solitude returning, saw the hills*
145 *Grow larger in the darkness, all alone*
146 *Beheld the stars come out above his head* [E, 125]
147 *And travell'd through the wood with no one near*
148 *To whom he might confess the things he saw.*
149 *So the foundations of his mind were laid.*
150 *In such communion, not from terror free,*
151 *While yet a Child, and long before his time,* [E, 130]

---

121 observations,] observations
123 born,
124 infant,
126 The] [?His] *erased, overwritten* The *(DW, following WW's penciled* The*)* mate
129 shewing them *del to* training them to *(WW)*
132 and grave,] & grave
134 word,] word
136 year,] year
139 School,
141 sound
142 clock. tenement
147 woods *with* s *erased, following WW's penciled left-hand-margin* s *del*
151 child, & time,] time

---

123 Terminal punctation, if any, is worn away.

He had perceiv'd the presence and the power
Of greatness, and deep feelings had impress'd
Great objects on his mind with portraiture
And colour so distinct that on his mind
They lay like substances and almost seem'd 135
To haunt the bodily sense. He had receiv'd
(Vigorous in mind by nature as he was)
A precious gift; for as he grew in years
With these impressions would he still compare
All his ideal stores, his shapes and forms; 140
And, being still unsatisfied with aught
Of dimmer character, he thence attain'd
An active power to fasten images
Upon his brain; and on their pictur'd lines
Intensely brooded, even till they acquir'd 145
The liveliness of dreams. Nor did he fail,
While yet a child, with a child's eagerness
Incessantly to turn his ear and eye
On all things which the moving seasons brought
To feed such appetite: nor this alone 150
Appeas'd his yearning. In the after day
Of boyhood, many a time in caves forlorn,
And in the hollow depths of naked crags
He sate; and even in their fix'd lineaments,

---

131 and] &
139/140 *WW penciled* X *and* [?Blank] *perhaps to indicate alteration of l. 140 before MS.* E^2
140 and forms;] & forms
147 child's] childs
151 yearning.] yearnings. *a probable copying error, since* yearning *is in MSS. B, D, and M—and in* Excursion, *1814* (*MS.* E^2 *reads* yearnings *with the* s *deleted*)
154–156 *erased, perhaps because lines corresponding to MS. M, 176–179* (*also in MS. D—see p. 343, above*), *were inadvertently omitted*

131–136 Similar passages appear in *The Prelude* (I, 614–624) and *The Borderers* (ll. 1808–1810; *PW*, I, 200).

152 *He had perceiv'd the presence and the power*
153 *Of greatness, and deep feelings had impress'd*
154 *Great objects on his mind, with portraiture*
155 *And colours so distinct that on his mind they lay*
156 *Like substances, and almost seem'd* [E, 135]

[9r]

157 *To haunt the bodily sense. He had receiv'd*
158 *(Vigorous in mind by nature, as he was)*
159 *A precious gift; for, as he grew in years,*
160 *With these inpressions would he still compare* [E, 139]
161 *All his Remembrances, thoughts, shapes, & forms.*
162 *And being still unsatisfied with aught*
163 *Of dimmer character, he thence attain'd*
164 *An active power to fasten images*
165 *Upon his brain, and on their pictur'd lines*
166 *Intensely brooded, even till they acquir'd* [E, 145]
167 *The liveliness of dreams. Nor did he fail,*
168 *While yet a child, with a child's eagerness*
169 *Incessantly to turn his ear and eye*
170 *On all things which the moving seasons brought*
171 *To feed such appetite: nor this alone* [E, 150]
172 *Appeas'd his yearning. In the after day*
173 *Of boyhood, many an hour in caves forlorn,*
174 *And in the hollow depths of naked crags*
175 *He sate, and even in their fix'd lineaments* [E, 154]
176 *Or from the power of a peculiar eye,*
177 *Or by creative feeling overborne,*
178 *Or by predominance of thought oppress'd,*
179 *Even in their fix'd and steady lineaments,*

---

155 colours distinct *with the* s *on* colours *erased and* so *squeezed in* *line ends with* mind
156 They lay like substances, &
157 receiv'd,
158 nature,] nature
159 for,] for years,] years
160 impressions
161 remembrances, shapes, & forms.] shapes and forms
162 And, *no erasure*
165 brain;
172 yearnings. *with* s *erased, following WW's penciled left-hand-margin* s *del*
173 an hour] a *with* n *added*, [?time] *erased, overwritten* hour
175 sate,] sate
176 eye,] eye
177 overborne,] overborne
178 oppress'd,] oppress'd
179 and] & lineaments,] lineaments

155–156 The concluding words of l. 155, "they lay," should have been copied at the beginning of l. 156. In l. 155, "colours" is an error for "colour."
160 DW mistakenly wrote "inpressions" for "impressions."
162 The erased word was probably "satisfied."
165 The comma may be written over a semicolon.
169 DW began "eye" with a false start, possibly with a capital "E."

He trac'd an ebbing and a flowing mind, 155
Expression ever varying.
Thus inform'd
He had small need of books; for many a Tale
Traditionary round the mountains hung;
And many a legend, peopling the dark woods,
Nourish'd Imagination in her growth 160
And gave the mind that apprehensive power
By which she is made quick to recognise
The moral properties and scope of things.
But greedily he read, and read again
Whate'er the Minister's old Shelf supplied, 165
The life and death of Martyrs who sustain'd
Intolerable pangs, and here and there
A straggling volume torn and incomplete
That left half-told the preternatural tale,
Romance of Giants, Chronicle of Fiends, 170
Profuse in garniture of wooden cuts,
Strange and uncouth, dire faces, figures dire,
Sharp-knee'd, sharp-elbow'd, and lean-ancled too,
With long and ghostly shanks, forms which once seen
Co[uld never be forgotten.]
In his heart 175
Love was not yet, nor the pure joy of love

---

167 *penciled* X*'s before and after* Intolerable pangs, *perhaps indicate the expansion made here before MS.* E^2
173 and] &
174 *line written over an erased copying error:* Forms which, once seen, could never be forgotten.
175 Could never be forgotten.] *in correcting her copying error (see the note to l. 174), DW here wrote only* Co Within his heart *erased and* In his heart *overwritten to make line metrical*

156–163 As a boy WW himself heard "tales traditionary," and "the first / Of those domestic tales" is related in *Michael*:

And hence this Tale, while I was yet a Boy
Careless of books, yet having felt the power
Of Nature, by the gentle agency
Of natural objects, led me on to feel
For passions that were not my own, and think
(At random and imperfectly indeed)
On man, the heart of man, and human life. [*PW*, II, 81]

Anne Tyson related such stories to WW at Hawkshead (see Thompson, pp. xv–xvi), tales sometimes "half as long as an ancient romance" (*Journals of Dorothy Wordsworth*, ed. Ernest de Selincourt [London, 1941], I, 309).

164–175 WW's reading was equally voracious; see Thompson, p. 344, and David Weiner, "Wordsworth, Books, and the Growth of a Poet's Mind," *JEGP*, 74 (1975), 209–220.

169 Cf. *Il Penseroso*, ll. 109–110; "Or call up him that left half told / The story of Cambuscan bold." Milton's couplet also appears on the reverse of a manuscript of the Prospectus (DC MS. 24) and as the epigraph for WW's modernization of the *Prioress's Tale* from its publication in 1820.

180 *He trac'd an ebbing and a flowing mind* [E, 155]
181 *Expression ever varying.*
Thus inform'd
182 *He had small need of books; for many a Tale*
183 *Traditionary round the mountains hung:*

[9^v]

184 *And many a legend peopling the dark wood's*
185 *Nourish'd Imagination in her growth* [E, 160]
186 *And gave the mind that apprehensive power*
187 *By which she is made quick to recognise*
188 *The moral properties and scope of things*
189 *But greedily he read and read again*
190 *Whate'er the Minister's old Shelf supplied,* [E, 165]
191 *The life and death of Martyrs who sustain'd*
192 *Intolerable pangs, the Records left*
times
193 *Of Persecution and the Covenant,*
Whose echo rings through Scotland to this hour
194 *That, like an echo, ring through Scotland still;*
195 *Nor haply was there wanting here and there*
196 *A straggling volume torn and incomplete*
197 *That left half-told the preternatural Tale,*
198 *Romance of Giants, Chronicle of Fiends,* [E, 170]
199 *Profuse in garniture of wooden cuts,*
200 *Strange and uncouth, dire faces, figures dire,*
201 *Sharp-knee'd, sharp-elbow'd, and lean-ancled*
too,
202 *With long & ghostly shanks, forms which once seen*
203 *Could never be forgotten.*
In his heart
X ~~Thus yielding to the majesty of fear~~
204 *Love was not yet, nor the pure joy of love,* [E, 176]

---

180 and] &
183 hung;
184 wood's] woods
190 supplied,] supplied
192 Records left] cruel times *traces of illegible pencil writing*
193 Persecution] {per / superstition *del to* persecution *(WW)* times *added in pencil (WW) without preceding comma*
194 That,] That echo,] echo
195 was there *alt* might be *(WW)*
200 dire,] dire
201 lean-ancl'd
202 &] and
204 love,] love

---

192 The erased words are probably the MS. E[2] reading: "crue**l** **t**imes."
193 The erasure is of the first nine letters of the MS. E[2] reading, "**s**uperst**i**tion." times] A later addition when the correction here and in l. 192 was made.
203/204 The **X** refers to the draft at the bottom of 9^v.

By sound diffus'd or by the breathing air,
Or by the silent looks of happy things,
Or flowing from the universal face
Of earth and sky. But he had felt the power 180
Of Nature, and already was prepar'd,
By his intense conceptions, to receive
Deeply the lesson deep of love, which he
Whom Nature, by whatever means, has taught
To feel intensely cannot but receive. 185
From early childhood, even, as I have said,
From his sixth year, he had been sent abroad
In summer to tend herds: such was his task
Thenceforward till the later day of youth.
Oh! then what soul was his when on the tops 190
Of the high mountains he beheld the sun
Rise up, and bathe the world in light. He look'd;
The ocean and the earth beneath him lay
In gladness and deep joy. The clouds were touch'd,
And in their silent faces did he read 195
Unutterable love. Sound needed none,
Nor any voice of joy: his spirit drank
The spectacle. Sensation, soul, and form
All melted into him: they swallow'd up
His animal being: in them did he live 200
And by them did he live. They were his life.
In such access of mind, in such high hour
Of visitation from the living God,
Thought was not. In enjoyment it expir'd.

---

187 year,] year
196 none,] none
203 God,] God

190–211 The Pedlar's sunrise experiences are described in terms similar to WW's account of the dedication walk in *The Prelude* (IV, 315–345).

205 *By sound diffus'd, or by the breathing air,*
206 *Or by the silent looks of happy things*
207 *Or flowing from the universal face*
208 *Of earth and sky. But he had felt the power* [E, 180]
209 *Of nature, and already was prepar'd*
X Where fear sate thus a cherished Visitant
a milder Spirit yet had found no place
Love yet was wanting the pure joy of love

[10r]

210 *By his intense conceptions to receive*
211 *Deeply, the lesson deep of love, which he*
212 *Whom Nature, by whatever means, has taught*
213 *To feel intensely cannot but receive.* [E, 185]
214 *From early childhood, even, as I have said,*
215 *From his sixth year, he had been sent abroad*
216 *In summer, to tend herds: such was his task*
217 *Henceforward till the later day of youth.*
218 *Oh! then what soul was his when on the tops* [E, 190]
219 *Of the high mountains he beheld the sun*
220 *Rise up, and bathe the world in light. He look'd;*
221 *The ocean and the earth beneath him lay*
222 *In gladness and deep joy. The clouds were touch'd*
223 *And in their silent faces did he read* [E, 195]
224 *Unutterable love. Sound needed none,*
225 *Nor any voice of joy: his spirit drank*
226 *The spectacle; sensation, soul, and form*
227 *All melted into him; they swallow'd up*
228 *His animal being: in them did he live,* [E, 200]
229 *And by them did he live: they were his life,* {.
230 *In such access of mind, in such high hour*
231 *Of visitation from the living God*
232 *Thought was not. In enjoyment it expir'd.*
Ah what would then have servd how needless [?there]

---

205 air,] air
206 things,
209 Nature,
211 Deeply,] Deeply love,] love
215 year,] year
216 summer,] summer
217 {Th H}enceforward
226 spectacle,
227 him:
228 live,] live

---

207 After "face," a miswriting—"of earth & sky"—is erased.
231–235 For revisions of these lines, see drafts on MS. M, 1v and 2r, in Transcriptions of Additions to MSS. E and M, below.

Such hour by prayer or praise was unprofan'd; 205
He neither pray'd, nor offer'd thanks or praise;
His mind was a thanksgiving to the Power
That made him: it was blessedness and love.
A Herdsman on the lonely mountain tops,
Such intercourse was his, and in this sort 210
Was his existence oftentimes possess'd.
Oh! then, how beautiful, how bright appear'd
The written promise! He had early learn'd
To reverence the Volume which displays
The mystery, the life which cannot die: 215
But in the mountains did he *feel* his faith:
There did he see the writing. All things there
Breath'd immortality, revolving life,
And greatness still revolving; infinite.
There littleness was not; the least of things 220
Seem'd infinite, and there his spirit shap'd
Her prospects, nor did he *believe*, he saw.
What wonder if his being thus became
Sublime and comprehensive! Low desires,
Low thoughts had there no place; yet was his mind 225
Lowly; for he was meek in gratitude
Oft as he call'd to mind those ecstasies
And whence they flow'd, and from them he acquir'd

---

213 promise: !} he
214 To reverence the Volume which *over erasure*
216 *feel*] *double underlining*
224 and] & desires,] desires

233 ~~*Such hour by prayer or praise was unprofan'd;*~~ [E, 205]
The imperfect offices of prayer & praise
234 *His mind was a thanksgiving to the* {*P* / *power*}
235 *That made him: it was blessedness and love.*
236 *A Herdsman on the lonely mountain tops,*
237 *Such intercourse was his, & in this sort* [E, 210]
238 *Was his existence oftentimes possess'd*
239 *Oh! then how beautiful, how bright appear'd*

[10^v]

240 *The written Promise! he had early learn'd*
241 *To reverence the Volume which displays*
242 *The mystery, the life which cannot die:* [E, 215]
243 *But in the mountains did he feel his faith.*
244 *There did he see the writing. All* {*things there*}
245 *Breath'd immortality, revolving life,*
246 *And greatness still revolving: infinite.*
247 *There littleness was not; the least of things* [E, 220]
248 *Seem'd infinite, and there his spirit shap'd*
249 *Her prospects, nor did he believe, he saw.*
250 *What wonder if his being thus became*
251 *Sublime and comprehensive! Low desires,*
252 *Low thoughts had there no place, yet was his mind* [E, 225]
253 *Lowly; for he was meek in gratitude*
254 *Oft as he call'd to mind those ecstasies*
255 *And whence they flow'd, and from them he acquir'd*

---

234 Power
234–235 *over these lines* in MS. E² *WW penciled a large P, which usually indicates a revision on another sheet of paper; the reference is possibly to drafts added in MS. M, 1^v and 2^r (see Transcriptions of Additions to MSS. E and M, below)*
236 *no erasure* tops,] tops
237 &] and
238 possess'd.
240 promise!
243 faith:
244 *no erasure* All things there
245 *no erasure*
246 revolving, infinite, *then comma del to period*
248 shap'd *later addition, when copying error in l. 249 was noticed*
249 Her prospects,] Shap'd her pr *erased, overwritten* Her prospects, believe,
252 place;
254 ecstasies,
255 and] &

243–245 The erasures are of a miswriting, beginning after "faith" in l. 243:
All
Thin**gs** here **b**reath'**d** immorta**lity**
Revolving life and
In l. 244, "things there" was added as part of the correction after the erasure.
249 DW began "saw" with a false start, perhaps a "w."

Wisdom which works through patience; thence he learn'd,
In many a calmer hour of sober thought, 230
To look on nature with an humble heart,
Self-question'd where it did not understand,
And with a superstitious eye of love.
Thus pass'd the time; yet to the neighbouring Town
He often went with what small overplus 235
His earnings might supply; and brought away
The book which most had waken'd his desires
While at the stall he read. Among the hills
He gaz'd upon that mighty Orb of Song,
The divine Milton. Lore of different kind, 240
The annual savings of a toilsome life,
His Step-father supplied; books that explain
The purer elements of truth, involv'd
In lines and numbers, and by charm severe,
Especially perceiv'd where nature droops 245
And feeling is suppress'd, preserve the mind
Busy in solitude and poverty.
And, thus employ'd, he many a time o'erlook'd
The listless hours, when in the hollow vale,
Hollow and green, he lay on the green turf 250
In lonesome idleness. What could he do?
Nature was at his heart; and he perceiv'd,
Though yet he knew not how, a wasting power
In all things which from her sweet influence
Might tend to wean him. Therefore with her hues, 255
Her forms, and with the spirit of her forms,
He cloth'd the nakedness of austere truth.
While yet he linger'd in the elements

---

229 patience,
230 thought,] thought
233 *a penciled* **X** *after* love. *is of uncertain significance*
237 *for* waken'd *MSS. B, D, and M—and* Excursion, *1814—read* tempted (*MS. E*[2] *reads* waken'd)
242 explain] explain'd *with* 'd *del in pencil—a copying error corrected, since MSS. B and M—and* Excursion, *1814—read* explain (*MSS. D and E*[2] *read* explain'd *with* 'd *erased*)
255 hues,] hues
256 of her forms,] of her forms
257 truth:

240–271 "Geometric science" also appealed to WW, and he and the Pedlar both found solace in it (*Prelude*, V, 64–68; VI, 135–159, 178–187).
254 Cf. *Paradise Lost*, VII, 374–375: "The *Pleiades* before him danc'd / Shedding sweet influence."

256 *Wisdom which works through patience, thence he learn'd*
257 *In many a calmer hour of sober thought* [E, 230]
258 *To look on nature with an humble heart*
259 *Self-question'd where it did not understand,*
260 *And with a superstitious eye of love.*
261 *Thus pass'd the time; yet to the neighbouring Town*
262 *He often went with what small overplus* [E, 235]
263 *His earnings might supply, and brought away*
264 *The book which most had tempted his desires*
265 *While at the Stall he read. Among the hills*
266 *He gaz'd upon that mighty Orb of Song,*
267 *The divine Milton. Lore of different kind,* [E, 240]
268 *The annual savings of a toilsome life,*
269 *His Step-father supplied, books that explain*

[11r]

270 *The purer elements of truth, involv'd*
271 *In lines and numbers, and by charm severe,*
272 *Especially perceiv'd where nature droops* [E, 245]
273 *And feeling is suppress'd, preserve the mind*
274 *Busy in solitude and poverty*
275 *And, thus employ'd, he many a time o'erlook'd*
276 *The listless hours when in the hollow vale,*
277 *Hollow and green, he lay on the green turf* [E, 250]
278 *In pensive idleness. What could he do,*
279 *With blind endeavours, in that lonesome life*
280 *Thus thirsting daily? Yet, still uppermost,*
281 *Nature was at his heart, as if he felt,*
282 *Though yet he knew not how, a wasting power*
283 *In all things which from her sweet influence*
284 *Might tend to wean him. Therefore with her hu[ ]* [E, 255]
285 *Her forms, and with the spirit of her forms*
286 *He cloth'd the nakedness of austere truth.*
287 *While yet he linger'd in the elements*

---

256 through] by patience *erased, overwritten* through
257/258 *at this point in MS. E² a leaf has been torn out; although the stub shows traces of a few unidentifiable letters, the text is not interrupted*
262 often *del to* sometimes *(WW)*
263 and] &
264 tempted] waken'd
269 explain'd *with* 'd *del in pencil and erased*
278 *terminal question mark erased and comma overwritten*
278/279 The weight of genius was upon his mind, *del in pencil and ink*
280 Thus *over erasure* thirsting, *with* ing *over erasure and comma erased* {? / daily,} {Y / yet,} *traces of illegible pencil writing*
284 hues

---

284 The last two letters of "hues" are worn away.

Of science, and among her simplest laws,
His triangles, they were the stars of Heaven, 260
The silent stars: oft did he take delight
To measure th'altitude of some tall crag
Which is the eagle's birth-place, or some peak
Familiar with forgotten years, which shews
Inscrib'd, as with the silence of the thought, 265
Upon its bleak and visionary sides
The history of many a winter storm,
Or obscure records of the path of fire.
Yet with these lonesome sciences he still
Continued to amuse the heavier hours 270
Of solitude.

And thus his time pass'd on
In dreams, in study, and in ardent thought,

---

259 science,] science laws,] laws
260 Heaven,] Heaven
263 eagles
268 Or] And *a probable copying error, since MSS. B, D, and M—and* Excursion, *1814—read* Or *(MS. E*[2] *has* And *erased and* Or *overwritten)*
269–271 *erased*

288 *Of science, and among her simplest laws,*
289 *His triangles they were the stars of Heaven,* [E, 260]
290 *The silent stars: oft did he take delight*
291 *To measure th' altitude of some tall crag*
292 *Which is the eagle's birth-place, or some peak*
293 *Familiar with forgotten years which shews*
294 *Inscrib'd, as with the silence of the thought* [E, 265]

[11v]

295 *Upon its bleak and visionary sides*
296 *The history of many a winter storm,*
297 *Or obscure records of the path of fire.* [E, 268]
298 *And thus before his eighteenth year was gone*
299 *Accumulated feelings press'd his heart*
300 *With an encreasing weight: he was o'erpow'r'd*
301 *By his own nature, by the turbulence*
302 *Of his own heart, by mystery, and hope,*
303 *And the first virgin passion of a mind*
304 *Communing with the glorious universe*
305 *Full often wish'd he that the winds might rage*
306 *When they were silent; far more fondly now*
307 *Than in his earlier season did he love*
308 *Tempestuous nights, the uproar and the sounds*
309 *That live in darkness: from his intellect,*
310 *And from the stillness of abstracted thought,*
311 *He sought repose in vain. I have heard him say*
312 *That at this time he scann'd the laws of light*
313 *Amid the roar of torrents, where they send*
314 *From hollow clefts up to the clearer air*
315 *A cloud of mist which in the shining sun*
316 *Varies its rainbow hues. But vainly thus,*

[12r]

317 *And vainly by all other means he strove*
318 *To mitigate the fever of his heart.*
319 *In dreams, in study and in ardent thought* [E, 272]

---

288 and] & laws,] laws
293 years,
294 thought,
297 Or] And *erased, overwritten* Or *(DW, following WW's penciled* Or *and caret)*
298 thus,
300 weight:] load *erased, overwritten* weight: *(DW, following WW's penciled* weight*)*
301 turbulence] turbulen{ce / t [?force] *with* t *and* [?force] *erased*
302 heart,] [?mind] *erased, overwritten* heart, *(DW, following WW's penciled* heart*)* mystery, and hope,] mystery & hope
309 intellect,] intellect
310 thought,] thought
313 torrents,] torrents
317–318 *over these lines WW penciled a large* P, *which usually indicates a revision on another sheet of paper*
318/319 And thus from month to month his time pass'd on *del in pencil and ink*
319 *no paragraph* *del of 318/319 continues onto* In dr *probably by error* study,

He wanting much perhaps, but gaining more,
Breathing a piercing air of poverty
And drinking of the Well of homely life. 275
And now, growing up to manhood, he began
To think about his future life, and how
He best might earn his worldly maintenance.
His Mother strove to make her Son perceive
With what advantage he might teach a School 280
In the adjoining Village; but the Youth,
Who of this service made a short essay,
Found that the wanderings of his thought were then
A misery to him, that he must resign
A task he was unable to perform. 285
He had a Brother elder than himself
Six years who, long before, had left his home
To journey up and down with Pedlar's wares
In England where he traffick'd at that time,
Healthy and prosperous. "What should hinder now," 290
Said he within himself, "but that I go
And toil in the same calling?" And, in truth,
This plan, long time, had been his favorite thought.

---

273 more,] more
281 Youth,] Youth
282 essay,] essay
283 were then *added when error in l. 284 corrected*
284 *first six words written over* Were then a misery to him *a copying error erased*
292 "And

320 *Thus, even from childhood upward, was he rear'd,*
321 *Doubtless in want of much, yet gaining more,*
322 *Breathing a piercing air of poverty,*
from
323 *And drinking of the Well of homely life.* [E, 275]
brought
324 *And now, ~~drawing~~ near to manhood, he began*
upon lifes future course
325 *To think ~~about his future years~~, and how*
326 *He best might earn his worldly maintenance.*
327 *His Mother strove to make her Son perceive*
328 *With what advantage he might teach a School* [E, 280]
329 *In the adjoining Village; but the Youth,*
330 *Who of this service made a short essay*
331 *Found that the wanderings of his thought were then*
332 *A misery to him, that he must resign*
333 *A task he was unable to perform.* [E, 285]
334 *He had a Brother elder than himself*
335 *Six years, who, long before, had left his home*
far & wide
336 *To journey ~~up and down~~ with Pedlar's Wares*
337 *In England, where he traffick'd at that time,*
338 *Healthy and prosperous. "What should hinder now,"*
339 *Said he within himself, "but that I go* [E, 291]

[12v]

340 *And toil in the same calling?" And, in truth,*
341 *This plan, long time had been his favorite thought*

---

320 *interlined by DW in MS. E²; traces of WW's pencil writing here* Thus,] Thus upward,] upward rear'd,] reared
321 He wanting much perhaps, but gaining more, *first five words del by erasure to* Though doubtless wanting much yet *then* Though *del*, in *added*, ing *of* wanting *del*, of *added by DW, following WW's penciled instruction at page foot:* doubtless in want of much *traces of WW's pencil writing below line*
323 *first* of *del to* from *(WW)*
324 drawing near] growing up
325 years,] life, *alt* course *in WW's pencil erased, then entire line del*
326 *del to* To take in thought his future livelihood *(WW)*
329 Youth,] Youth
334 Brother, o{e/l}der *DW, following WW's penciled* e/
336 wares
337 time,] time
341 time,

---

320 A comma after "childhood" was erased.
321 The first erasure is probably of the uncorrected MS. E² reading: "**Though** doubt**l**ess." An "**ing**" once attached to "want" is erased.
324 The first three letters of the MS. E² reading—"**g**rowing"—are erased; the erased word under "near" was probably "up."
325 The erasure is probably of the MS. E² reading: "**l**ife."

He ask'd his Mother's blessing; he with tears
Thank'd the good Man, his second Father, ask'd 295
From him paternal blessings, and set forth,
A Traveller bound to England. The good Pair
Offer'd up prayers, and bless'd him; but with hearts
Foreboding evil. From his native Hills
He wander'd far: much did he see of men, 300
Their manners, their enjoyments, and pursuits,
Their passions, and their feelings, chiefly those
Essential and eternal in the heart,
Which, 'mid the simpler forms of rural life,
Exist more simple in their elements 305
And speak a plainer language. In the woods,
A lone enthusiast, and among the fields,
Itinerant in this labour, he had pass'd
The better portion of his time; and there
From day to day had his affections breath'd 310
The wholesome air of nature; there he kept,
In solitude and solitary thought,
His mind in a just equipoise of love.
Serene it was, unclouded by the cares
Of ordinary life, unvex'd, unwarp'd 315
By partial bondage. In his steady course
No piteous revolutions had he felt,
No wild varieties of joy or grief;
Unoccupied by sorrow of its own,
His heart lay open; and, by Nature tun'd 320
And constant disposition of his thoughts
To sympathy with man, he was alive
To all that was enjoy'd where'er he went

---

296 forth,] forth
298 and] &
301 and pursuits,] & pursuits
303 heart,] heart
304 life,] life
309 and] &
313 love.] love

---

300 For WW's note to this line in *The Excursion*, see pp. 479–480, below.

302–306 Cf. Preface to *Lyrical Ballads* (1800): "Low and rustic life was generally chosen because in that situation the essential passions of the heart find a better soil in which they can attain their maturity, are less under restraint, and speak a plainer and more emphatic language" (*The Prose Works of William Wordsworth*, ed. W. J. B. Owen and Jane Worthington Smyser [Oxford, 1974], I, 124).

342 *He ask'd his Mother's blessing, did with tears*
343 *Thank the good Man, his second Father, ask'd* [E, 295]
344 *From him paternal blessings, and set forth*
345 *A Traveller bound to England. The good Pair*
346 *Offer'd up prayers, and bless'd him; but with hearts*
347 *Foreboding evil. From his native Hills*
348 *He wander'd far: much did he see of men,* [E, 300]
349 *Their manners, their enjoyments and pursuits,*
350 *Their passions and their feelings, chiefly those*
351 *Essential and eternal in the heart*
352 *Which, 'mid the simpler forms of rural life,*
353 *Exist more simple in their elements,* [E, 305]
354 *And speak a plainer language. In the woods,*
355 *A lone enthusiast, and among the fields,*
356 *Itinerant in this labour, he had pass'd*
357 *The better portion of his time; and there*
358 *From day to day had his affections breath'd* [E, 310]
359 *The wholesome air of nature; there he kept,*
360 *In solitude and solitary thought*
361 *His mind in a just equipoise of love,* { . ,}
362 *Serene it was, unclouded by the cares*
363 *Of ordinary life, unvex'd, unwarp'd* [E, 315]

[13r]

364 *By partial bondage. In his steady course*
365 *No piteous revolutions had he felt,*
366 *No wild varieties of joy or grief;*
367 *Unoccupied by sorrow of its own*
368 *His heart lay open; and, by Nature tun'd* [E, 320]
369 *And constant disposition of his thoughts*
370 *To sympathy with man, he was alive*
371 *To all that was enjoy'd where'er he went*

---

342 did] he *erased, overwritten* did *(DW, following WW's penciled* did*)*
343 Thank'd *with* 'd *del in pencil, then erased*
344 blessings,] blessings
349 enjoyments,
361 love.
363 *MS. E² ends here*

---

361 It is not clear whether the added dot was intended to convert the comma into a period or a semicolon.

And all that was endur'd; and in himself
Happy, and quiet in his chearfulness, 325
He had no painful pressure from without
Which made him turn aside from wretchedness
With coward fears. He could afford to suffer
With them whom he saw suffer. Hence it was
That in our best experience he was rich, 330
And in the wisdom of our daily life:
For hence minutely in his various rounds
He had observ'd the progress and decay
Of many minds, of minds and bodies too,
The history of many families, 335
And how they prosper'd; how they were o'erthrown
By passion or mischance, or such misrule
Among the unthinking Masters of the earth
As makes the nations groan. Pure from taint
Of worldly-mindedness or anxious care, 340
Observant, studious, thoughtful, and refresh'd
By knowledge gather'd up from day to day,
Thus had he liv'd a long and innocent life.
The Scottish Church, both on himself and those
With whom, from childhood, he grew up, had held 345
The strong hand of her purity; and still

---

324 endur'd,
326 without] *a possible copying error, since MSS. B and D read* within*; MS. M and* Excursion, *1814, read* without
329 them] *a possible copying error, since* those *is in MSS. B and D and in* Excursion, *1814*; *MS. M reads* them
330 rich,] {rich / [?wise] *(WW)*
336 o'er thrown
338 Masters] Rulers *del to* Masters *(WW); a probable copying error corrected, since* Masters *is in MSS. B, D, M, and in* Excursion, *1814*
339 groan.] *original punctuation (perhaps a semicolon) erased and period overwritten* *last three words erased, overwritten* Untouch'd by *(WW, pencil)*
340–343 *erased*
341 and] &
344 Church,] Church and] &

328–329 Cf. *The Tempest*, I, ii, 5–6: "O, I have suffer'd / With those that I saw suffer." Helen Darbishire refers to WW's comment about STC: "It was poor dear Coleridge's constant infelicity that prevented him from being the poet that Nature had given him the power to be. He had always too much personal and domestic discontent to paint the sorrows of mankind. He could not 'afford to suffer / With those whom he saw suffer'" (I quote from *Barron Field's Memoirs of Wordsworth*, ed. Geoffrey Little [Sydney, Australia, 1975], p. 100). She also points out WW's statement in *The Prelude* (X, 870–872) that he felt himself to be "withal / A happy man, and therefore bold to look / On painful things" (*PW*, V, 412–413).

372 *And all that was endur'd* ;} *and in himself*
373 *Happy, and quiet in his chearfulness,* [E, 325]
374 *He had no painful pressure from without*
375 *Which made him turn aside from wretchedness*
376 *With coward fears. He could afford to suffer*
377 *With them whom he saw suffer. Hence it was*
378 *That in our best experience he was rich* [E, 330]
379 *And in the wisdom of our daily life:*
380 *For hence minutely in his various rounds*
381 *He had observ'd the progress and decay*
382 *Of many minds, of minds and bodies too,*
383 *The history of many families,* [E, 335]
384 *And how they prosper'd; how they were o'erthrown*
385 *By passion or mischance, or such misrule*
386 *Among the unthinking Masters of the earth*

387 *As makes the Nations groan* .} *Untouch'd by taint*
388 *Of worldly mindedness or anxious care* [E, 340]
389 *Observant, studious, thoughtful, and refresh'd*

[13^{v}]

390 *By knowledge gather'd up from day to day*
391 *Thus had he liv'd a long and innocent life.*
392 *The Scottish Church both on himself, & those*
393 *With whom from childhood he grew up, had held* [E, 345]
394 *The strong hand of her purity; and still*

372 The original punctuation after "endur'd" is erased and a semicolon added in pencil.
374 Perhaps "without" is an error for "within," the reading in MSS. B and D; all lifetime *Excursion* editions read "without."
387 The original punctuation after "groan" was obliterated when a word, possibly "Untouch'd," was erased.

Had watch'd him with an unrelenting eye.
This he remember'd in his riper years
With gratitude and reverential thoughts.
But by the native vigour of his mind, 350
By his habitual wanderings out of doors,
By loneliness, and goodness, and kind works,
Whatever in his childhood, or in youth,
He had imbib'd of fear or darker thought
Was melted all away: so true was this 355
That sometimes his religion seem'd to me
Self-taught, as of a dreamer in the woods.
—And, surely, never did there live on earth
A man of sweeter temper. Birds and beasts,
He lov'd them all, chickens and houshold dogs, 360
And to the kitten of a neighbour's house
Would carry crumbs and feed it.
Poor and plain
Was his appearance; yet he was a man
Whom no one could have pass'd without remark;
Active and nervous was his gait; his limbs 365
And his whole figure breath'd intelligence.
Age had compress'd the rose upon his cheek
Into a narrower circle of deep red
But had not tam'd his eye, which, under brows
Shaggy and grey, had meanings which it brought 370
From years of youth, which, like a being made
Of many beings, he had wondrous skill
To blend with knowl[edge] of the years to come,
Human or such as lie beyond the grave.

End of Part First.

---

349 thoughts.] thoughts
352 & kind
357 in] {of / in *(?WW)*; of *alt* in *in MS. M*; in *in* Excursion, *1814*
359 and] &
360 and] &
362 crumbs *del to* milk *(WW)* & feed
365 and] &
367 {freshness of his / rose upon his *(WW, pencil)*
367–368 *erased, with traces of three or four illegible pencil lines in WW's hand*
373 knowledge] *DW did not write the last four letters; MS. M and* Excursion, *1814, read* knowledge

---

365 WW uses "nervous" in the sense of "vigorous" or "strong" (*OED*).

395 *Had watch'd him with an unrelenting eye.*
396 *This he remember'd in his riper years*
397 *With gratitude and reverential thoughts.*
398 *But by the native vigour of his mind,* [E, 350]
399 *By his habitual wanderings out of doors,*
400 *By loneliness, and goodness, and kind works,*
401 *Whatever in his childhood or in youth*
402 *He had imbib'd of fear or darker thought*
403 *Was melted all away: so true was this* [E, 355]
404 *That sometimes his religion seem'd to me*
in
405 *Self-taught, as of a dreamer of the woods.*
406 ——*And surely never did there live on earth*
407 *A man of sweeter temper. Birds and beasts,*
408 *He lov'd them all, chickens and houshold dogs,* [E, 360]
409 *And to the kitten of a neighbour's house*
410 *Would carry crumbs and feed it.*
Poor and plain
411 *Was his appearance, yet he was a man*
412 *Whom no one could have pass'd without*
remark
413 *Active and nervous was his gait; his limbs* [E, 365]
414 *And his whole figure breath'd intelligence.*
415 *Age had compress'd the freshness of his cheek*
416 *Into a narrower circle of deep red*

[14r]

417 *But had not tam'd his eye, which under brows*
418 *Shaggy and grey, had meanings which it brought* [E, 370]
419 *From years of youth, which, like a being made*
420 *Of many beings he had wondrous skill*
421 *To blend with knowledge of the years to come*
422 *Human, or such as lie beyond the grave.*

---

416 The word "deep" was corrected by erasure from "deeper," or possibly "deepest"; there appear to be two pencil strokes marking the place for erasure.

Part Second

Such was, in brief, the history of my Friend: 375
So was he fram'd. Now on the Bench he lay
And of his Pack of merchandise had made
A pillow for his head: his eyes were shut;
[D, 47] The shadows of the breezy elms above
Dappl'd his face. He had not heard my steps 380
As I approach'd; and near him did I sit
Unnotic'd in the shade some minutes' space;
At length I hail'd him, seeing that his hat
[D, 50] Was wet with water-drops, as if the brim
Had newly scoop'd a running stream. He rose; 385
And ere the joyful greeting which we had
Was ended, "'Tis a burning day," said I,
"My lips are parch'd with thirst; but you, I see,
Have somewhere found relief." He at the word,
Pointing towards a sweet-briar, bade me climb 390
The fence hard by, where that same slender shrub
Look'd out upon the road. It was a plot
[D, 55] Of garden ground run wild, its matted weeds
Mark'd with the steps of those whom, as they pass'd,
The gooseberry trees that shot in long lank slips 395
Or currants, hanging from their leafless stems
In scanty strings, had tempted to o'erleap
[D, 60] The broken wall. I look'd about; and there,
Where two tall hedgerows of thick alder boughs
Join'd in a damp cold nook, I found a Well 400
Half cover'd up with willow flowers and grass;
I slak'd my thirst; and soon as to the Bench
[D, 65] I had return'd, while with uncover'd head
I stood, to catch the motion of the air,

---

378 shut;] shut
382 minutes
385 newly] lately *del to* newly *(WW, pencil); a probable copying error corrected, since MSS. B, D, and M—and* Excursion, *1814—read* newly
386 joyful *del to* pleasant *(WW, pencil)*
387 "'Tis] 'Tis
388 see,] see
389 "Have He *inserted with caret* {a / At *with* A *erased*}
391 same *erased, overwritten* tall *(?WW)*
394 pass'd,] pass'd
401 and] &
402 I slak'd *del and inserted with caret after* thirst; *(WW, pencil)*
404 air,] air

423 *Such was, in brief, the history of my Friend:* [E, 375]
424 *So was he fram'd. Now on the Bench he lay*
425 *And of his Pack of Merchandise had made*
426 *A pillow for his head: his eyes were shut;*
427 *The shadows of the breezy elms above*
~~the sound~~
428 *Dappled his face. He had not heard my steps* [E, 380]
Of
~~My my approaching steps~~
429 *As I approach'd; and near him did I sit*
430 *Unnotic'd in the shade some minute's space,* }
431 *At length I hail'd him, seeing that his hat*
moist
432 *Was ~~wet~~ with water-drops, as if the brim*
433 *Had newly scoop'd a running stream. He rose,* [E, 385]
that ensued
434 *And ere the pleasant greeting ~~which we had~~*
435 *Was ended, "'Tis a burning day," said I,*
guess
436 *"My lips are parch'd with thirst; but you, I ~~see~~*
437 *Have somewhere found relief." He, at the word,*

[14v]

438 *Pointing towards a sweet-briar, bade me climb* [E, 390]
439 *The fence hard by, where that tall slender shrub*
440 *Look'd out upon the road. It was a plot*
441 *Of garden-ground run wild, its matted weeds*
442 *Mark'd with the steps of those whom, as they*
pass'd,
443 *The gooseberry trees that shot in long lank slips* [E, 395]
444 *Or currants hanging from their leafless stems*
445 *In scanty strings, had tempt'ed to o'erleap*
446 *The broken wall. I look'd about, and there,*
447 *Where two tall hedge-rows of thick alder boughs*
448 *Join'd in a damp cold nook, I found a Well,* [E, 400]
449 *Half cover'd up with willow flowers & grass;*
1 from the chearless spot
450 *I slak'd my thirst; and soon as to the Bench*
2
Withdrew, and while beside the shady Bench
451 *~~I had return'd while~~ with uncover'd head*
I yet was standing ∧
452 *~~I stood~~ to catch the motion of the air*
Intent ∧

---

425 A bold ink slash slants across the "P" in "Pack"—perhaps to make it lower case.
429 The phase "my approaching steps" was deleted by erasure.
450 WW's 1 and 2, and the wavy line, show that the revised reading should be "My thirst I slak'd."
451 A blot obliterates the punctuation, if any, after "return'd."

The Old Man spake, "I see around me here 405
Things which you cannot see: we die, my Friend,
Nor we alone, but that which each Man lov'd
[D, 70] And priz'd in his peculiar nook of earth
Dies with him, or is chang'd; and very soon
Even of the good is no memorial left. 410
The Poets in their elegies and songs,
Lamenting the departed, call the groves,
[D, 75] They call upon the hills and streams to mourn,
And senseless rocks; nor idly; for they speak,
In these their invocations, with a voice 415
Obedient to the strong creative power
Of human passion. Sympathies there are
[D, 80] More tranquil, yet perhaps of kindred birth,
That steal upon the meditative mind
And grow with thought. Beside yon Spring I stood, 420
And ey'd its waters till we seem'd to feel
One sadness, they and I. For them a bond
[D, 85] Of brotherhood is broken: time has been
When every day the touch of human hand
Disturb'd their stillness, and they minister'd 425
To human comfort. When I stoop'd to drink,
[D, 90] Upon the slimy foot-stone, I espied
The useless fragment of a wooden bowl;
It mov'd my very heart. The day has been
When I could never pass this road but she 430
Who liv'd within these walls, when I appear'd,
[D, 95] A daughter's welcome gave me, and I lov'd her
As my own child. O Sir! the good die first,

---

405 {O / old}
412 groves,] groves
413 and] & *WW's number 2 below* hills *and his* 1 *below* streams *probably indicate an intended reversal in order*
418 birth,] birth
421 water{s} *addition agrees with MSS. D and M*
425 *alt* Dislodgd the natural sleep that binds them up / In mortal stillness & they minister'd *(WW, pencil)*
429 my very] me to the *del to* my very *(WW, pencil)*; *a probable copying error corrected, since MSS. B, D, and M read* my very day *del to* time *(WW, pencil)*
431 walls,] walls appear'd,] appear'd

426–428 See the note to ll. 140–145 of the MS. B Reading Text, above.
433b–435a STC quoted these lines in *The Friend*, 25 January 1810 (*The Friend*, ed. Barbara E. Rooke [Princeton, N. J., 1969], II, 292).

453 *The Old Man spake, "I see around me here* [E, 405]
454 *Things which you cannot see: we die, my Friend,*
455 *Nor we alone, but that which each man lov'd*
456 *And priz'd in his peculiar nook of earth*
457 *Dies with him, or is chang'd; and very soon*
458 *Even of the good is no memorial left.* [E, 410]
459 *The Poets in their elegies and songs,*
460 *Lamenting the departed, call the groves,*
461 *They call upon the hills and streams to mourn*
462 *And senseless rocks; nor idly; for they speak*
463 *In these their invocations, with a voice* [E, 415]

[15r]

464 *Obedient to the strong creative power*
465 *Of human passion. Sympathies there are*
466 *More tranquil, yet perhaps of kindred birth*
467 *That steal upon the meditative mind*
468 *And grow with thought. Beside yon Spring I stood,*
469 *And ey'd its waters till we seem'd to feel* [E, 421]
470 *One sadness, they and I. For them a bond*
471 *Of brotherhood is broken: time has been*
472 *When every day the touch of human hand*
473 *Dislodg'd the natural sleep that binds them up*
474 *In mortal stillness, and they minster'd*
Stooping down [deleted]
475 *To human comfort.* ~~*When I stoop'd*~~ *to drink* [E, 426]
476 *Upon the slimy foot-stone I espied*
477 *The useless fragment of a wooden bowl;*
Green with the moss of yearts, a sight it was
478 ~~*It mov'd my very heart.*~~ {~~For~~ / ~~*The time ha*~~} {~~th~~ / ~~*s been*~~}
It moved my heart, recalling former times
479 *When I could never pass this road but she* [E, 430]
480 *Who liv'd within these walls, when I appear'd,*
481 *A daughter's welcome gave me, & I lov'd her*
482 *As my own child. O Sir! the good die first,*

---

474 DW mistakenly wrote "minster'd" for "minister'd."
477/478 WW mistakenly wrote "yearts" for years."

	And they whose hearts are dry as summer dust	
	Burn to the socket. Many a passenger	435
	Has bless'd poor Margaret for her gentle looks	
[D, 100]	When she upheld the cool refreshment, drawn	
	From that forsaken Spring; and no one came	
	But he was welcome, no one went away	
	But that it seem'd she lov'd him. She is dead,	440
	Forgotten in the quiet of the grave.	
	I speak of a poor Woman who dwelt here:	
	This Cottage was her home, and she the best	
	Of many thousands who are good and poor.	
	She was a Woman of a steady mind,	445
	Tender and deep in her excess of love,	
	Not speaking much, pleas'd rather with the joy	
	Of her own thoughts: by some especial care	
	Her temper had been fram'd as if to make	
	A being who by adding love to peace	450
	Might live on earth a life of happiness.	
[D, 120]	She had a Husband, an industrious Man,	
	Sober and frugal; I have heard her say	
	That he was up, and busy at his loom	
	In summer ere the mower was abroad	455
	Among the grass, and in the early spring	
[D, 125]	Ere the last star had vanish'd. They who pass'd	
	At evening, from behind the garden fence	
	Might hear his busy spade, which he would ply	
	After his daily work till the day-light	460

436 Ha{th / s} *(WW, pencil)* Margaret] Margeret
442 here:] here
443 Her name was Margaret [? ?], the best *all but* the best *erased, overwritten* This Cottage was her home & she the *(WW, pencil)*
445–451 *A draft for these lines, in WW's hand, probably written in Goslar, appears in* Peter Bell *MS. 2 (DC MS. 33) on 50*^{v} *(the MS is described in* Prelude *1799*, p. 161*)*:

she was of quiet mood
Tender and deep in her excess of love
Not speaking much pleased rather with the joy
Of her own heart. By some especial care
Her temper had been framed as if to make
A being who by adding love to peace
Should live on earth a life of happiness.
Her person & her face
Were homely such as none who pass her by
Would have remembered yet when she was seen
In her own dwelling place a grace was hers
And Beauty which beginning from without
Fell back on her with sanctifying power.

450 peace,
460 day-light] day light

483 *And they whose hearts are dry as summer dust*
484 *Burn to the socket. Many a passenger* [E, 435]
485 *Hath bless'd poor Margaret for her gentle looks*
486 *When she upheld the cool refreshment, drawn*
487 *From that forsaken Spring; & no one came*
488 *But he was welcome; no one went away*
489 *But that it seem'd she lov'd him. She is dead,* [E, 440]
490 *Forgotten in the quiet of the grave.*

[15v]

491 *I speak of a poor Woman who dwelt here*
492 *This Cottage was her home, and she the best*
493 *Of many thousands who are good and poor.*
494 *She was a Woman of ~~as~~ steady mind* [E, 445]
495 *Tender and deep in her excess of love,*
496 *Not speaking much, pleas'd rather with the joy*
497 *Of her own thoughts: by some especial care*
498 *Her temper had been fram'd as if to make*
499 *A being who by adding love to peace,* [E, 450]
500 *Might live on earth a life of happiness.*
Her wedded Partner lack'd not on his side
{The {umble worth that satisfied {her heart
501 {*She h* {*ad a Husband, an industrious* [?*Man,*]
Frugal, affectionate, {sober~~er~~ / [?], ~~[?]~~ {[~~?and~~] / [?] {[~~?therewith~~] / [?]
502 ~~*Sober and frugal*~~ .} *I have heard her say*
Keenly industrious ^
503 *That he was up, and busy at his loom*
504 *In summer ere the mower was abroad* [E, 455]
505 *Among the grass, and* {oft / *in* ~~*the*~~ ^in *early spring*
506 *Ere the last star had vanish'd.* .} {— *They who pass'd*
507 *At evening, from behind the garden fence*
508 *Might hear his busy spade which he would* *ply*
509 *After his daily work, till the day-light* [E, 460]

and therewith

---

490 A short penciled line, of uncertain significance, is drawn at the foot of the page.
494 Deletion by erasure.
501 After the first two words, DW's base line is erased.

Was gone, and every leaf and flower were lost
[D, 130] In the dark hedges. So they pass'd their days
In peace and comfort, and a pretty Boy
Was their best hope, next to the God in Heaven.
Some twenty years ago, but you, I think, 465
Can scarcely bear it now in mind, there came
Two blighting seasons, when the fields were left
[D, 135] With half a harvest. It pleas'd Heaven to add
A worse affliction in the plague of war:
A happy Land was stricken to the heart; 470
'Twas a sad time of sorrow and distress:
A wanderer among the cottages,
[D, 140] I, with my Pack of winter raiment, saw
The hardships of that season: many rich
Sank down, as in a dream, among the poor, 475
And of the poor did many cease to be
And their place knew them not. Meanwhile, abridg'd
[D, 145] Of daily comforts, gladly reconcil'd
To numerous self-denials, Margaret
Went struggling on through those calamitous years 480
With chearful hope: but ere the second autumn
A fever seiz'd her Husband. In disease
[D, 150] He linger'd long; and when his strength return'd
He found the little he had stor'd to meet
The hour of accident, or crippling age, 485
Was all consum'd. Two children had they now,
One newly born. As I have said, it was
A time of trouble; shoals of artisans
[D, 155] Were from their daily labour turn'd away
To seek their bread from public charity, 490

---

461 & flower
463 & comfort,
464 Heaven.] Heaven
466 Can *alt* Will *(WW)*
473 saw *possibly added when error in l. 474 corrected*
474 {The / Sa}
475 poor,] poor
485 age,] age
486 {c / Children}
490 charity,] charity

---

477 See the note to l. 196 of the MS. B Reading Text, above.

510 *Was gone, and every leaf and flower were lost*
511 *In the dark hedges. So they ~~pass'd~~ their days*
were
spent
512 *In peace and comfort, and a pretty Boy*
513 *Was their best hope next to the God in Heaven.*
514 *Some twenty years ago, but you, I think,* [E, 465]
515 *Can scarcely bear it now in mind, there came*
516 *Two blighting seasons when the fields were left*
517 *With half a harvest. It pleas'd Heaven to add*

[16r]

518 *A worse affliction in the plague of war:*
519 *A happy Land was stricken to the heart;* [E, 470]
520 *'Twas a sad time of sorrow and distress:*
521 *A wanderer among the cottages,*
522 *I, with my Pack of winter raiment, saw*
:}
523 *The hardships of that season,} many rich*
524 *Sank down, as in a dream, among the poor,* [E, 475]
525 *And of the poor did many cease to be*
526 *And their place knew them not. Meanwhile,*
abridg'd
527 *Of daily comforts, gladly reconcil'd*
528 *To numerous self-denials, Margaret*
529 *Went struggling on through those calamitous*
years
530 *With chearful hope: but ere the second autumn* [E, 481]
Her husband to a sick bed was confined
531 ~~*A fever seiz'd her Husband.*~~ *In disease*
Labouring with perilous fever. ^
532 *He linger'd long; & when his strength return'd*
533 *He found the little he had stor'd to meet*
534 *The hour of accident or crippling age* [E, 485]
535 *Was all consum'd. Two children had they now,*
536 *One newly born. As I have said, it was*
537 *A time of trouble; shoals of artisans*
adrift
538 *Were from their daily labour turn'd ~~away~~*
539 *To seek their bread from publick charity,* [E, 490]

They and their wives and children—happier far
Could they have liv'd as do the little birds
That peck along the hedges, or the kite
[D, 160] That makes his dwelling on the mountain rocks.
Ill far'd it now with Robert, he who dwelt 495
Here in this Cottage. At his door he stood
And whistl'd many a snatch of merry tunes
That had no mirth in them; or with his knife
[D, 165] Carv'd uncouth figures on the heads of sticks,
Then idly sought about through every nook 500
Of house or garden any casual task
Of use or ornament, and with a strange,
Amusing but uneasy novelty
[D, 170] He blended, where he might, the various tasks
Of summer, autumn, winter, and of spring. 505
But this endur'd not; his good-humour soon
Became a weight in which no pleasure was,
And poverty brought on a petted mood
[D, 175] And a sore temper: day by day he droop'd,
And he would leave his home, and to the Town 510
Without an errand would he turn his steps
Or wander here and there among the fields.
One while he would speak lightly of his Babes
[D, 180] And with a cruel tongue: at other times
He toss'd them with a false, unnatural joy: 515
And 'twas a rueful thing to see the looks
Of the poor innocent Children. 'Every smile,'
Said Margaret to me, here, beneath these Trees,

---

491 children,
er}
494 his} *(?WW)*; her *in MSS. A, B, and D*; his *in MS. M and* Excursion, *1814 and 1820*; her *from edition of 1827* rocks.] rocks
495 dwelt *del to* liv'd *(WW, pencil)*
499 sticks,] sticks
501 garden, task *erased, overwritten* work *(WW, pencil)*
502 strange,] strange
509 droop'd,] droop'd
512 and] &
513 he would *alt* did he *(WW)*
515 joy:] joy
517 "Every smile,"
re}
518 hear},

491–493 See the note to ll. 210–211 of the MS. B Reading Text, above.

540 *They and their wives and children, happier far*
541 *Could they have liv'd as do the little birds*
542 *That peck along the hedges, or the kite*
543 *That makes his dwelling on the mountain rocks.*
dwelt
544 *Ill far'd it now with Robert, he who ~~liv'd~~* [E, 495]
545 *Here in this Cottage. At his door he stood*
546 *And whistled many a snatch of merry tunes*

[16v]

547 *That had no mirth in them; or with his knife*
548 *Carv'd uncouth figures on the heads of sticks,*
549 *Then idly sought about through every nook* [E, 500]
In
550 *~~Of~~ house or garden any casual work*
551 *Of use or ornament, and with a strange*
552 *Amusing, but uneasy novelty*
553 *He blended, where he might, the various tasks*
554 *Of summer, autumn, winter and of spring.* [E, 505]
555 *But this endur'd not; his good-humour soon*
556 *Became a weight in which no pleasure was*
557 *And poverty brought on a petted mood*
558 *And a sore temper: day by day he droop'd,*
559 *And he would leave his home, and to the Town* [E, 510]
direct
560 *Without an errand would he turn his steps*
561 *And wander here and there among the fields.*
562 *One while he would speak lightly of his Babes*
563 *And with a cruel tongue: at other times*
564 *He toss'd them with a false unnatural joy* [E, 515]
565 *And 'twas a rueful thing to see the looks*
566 *Of the poor innocent Children. "Every smile"*
567 *Said Margaret to me, here, beneath these*
trees,

[D, 185] 'Made my heart bleed.'"
At this the Old Man paus'd
And, looking up to those enormous Elms, 520
He said, "'Tis now the hour of deepest noon.
At this still season of repose and peace,
This hour when all things which are not at rest
[D, 190] Are chearful; while this multitude of flies
Is filling all the air with melody; 525
Why should a tear be in an old Man's eye?
Why should we thus with an untoward mind,
And in the weakness of humanity,
[D, 195] From natural wisdom turn our hearts away,
To natural comfort shut our eyes and ears 530
And, feeding on disquiet, thus disturb
The calm of nature with our restless thoughts?"

End of Part Second.

Part Third.

He spake with somewhat of a solemn tone:
[D, 200] But when he ended there was in his face
Such easy chearfulness, a look so mild 535
That for a little time it stole away
All recollection, and that simple Tale
Pass'd from my mind like a forgotten sound.
[D, 205] A while on trivial things we held discourse,
To me soon tasteless. In my own despite 540
I thought of that poor Woman, as of one
Whom I had known and lov'd. He had rehears'd
Her homely Tale with such familiar power,
[D, 210] With such an active countenance, an eye

---

519 "Made bleed."
521 "'tis noon,
522 peace,] peace
525 melody;] melody
526 {o / Old *with* O *erased*}
528 humanity,] humanity
529 away,] away
532 thoughts."
532/533 [?Third] *erased, preceding* Part Third.
533 tone:] tone
539 discourse,] discourse
543 power,] power

568 *"Made my heart bleed."*
At this the Old Man paus'd
569 *And, looking up to those enormous Elms,* [E, 520]
570 *He said, " 'tis now the hour of deepest noon.*
571 *At this still season of repose and peace*
572 *This hour when all things which are not at*
rest
573 *Are chearful; while this multitude of flies*

[17r]

574 *Is filling all the air with melody* [E, 525]
575 *Why should a tear be in an old Man's eye?*
576 *Why should we this with an untoward mind*
577 *And in the weakness of humanity*
578 *From natural wisdom turn our hearts away,*
579 *To natural comfort shut our eyes and ears* [E, 530]
580 *And, feeding on disquiet, thus disturb*
581 *The calm of nature with our restless thoughts.*

---

582 *He spake with somewhat of a solemn tone*
583 *But when he ended there was in his face*
584 *Such easy chearfulness, a look so mild* [E, 535]
585 *That for a little time it stole away*
586 *All recollection, and that simple Tale*
587 *Pass'd from my mind like a forgotten sound*
588 *A while on trivial things we held discourse,*
589 *To me soon tasteless. In my own despite* [E, 540]
590 *I thought of that poor Woman as of one*
591 *Whom I had known and lov'd. He had rehears'd*
592 *Her homely Tale with such familiar power,*
593 *With such an active countenance, an eye*

---

576 DW mistakenly wrote "this" for "thus."

So busy, that the things of which he spake 545
Seem'd present; and, attention now relax'd,
There was a heartfelt chillness in my veins.
I rose; and, turning from that breezy shade,
[D, 215] Went out into the open air, and stood
To drink the comfort of the warmer sun. 550
Long time I had not stay'd, ere, looking round
Upon that tranquil Ruin, I return'd
And begg'd of the Old Man that for my sake
[D, 220] He would resume his story. He replied,
"It were a wantonness and would demand 555
Severe reproof if we were men whose hearts
Could hold vain dalliance with the misery
Even of the dead; contented thence to draw
[D, 225] A momentary pleasure, never mark'd
By reason, barren of all future good. 560
But we have known that there is often found
In mournful thoughts, and always might be found,
A power to virtue friendly; wer't not so,
[D, 230] I am a dreamer among men, indeed
An idle dreamer. 'Tis a common Tale, 565
An ordinary sorrow of Man's life,
A Tale of silent suffering, hardly cloth'd
In bodily form, and to the grosser sense
[D, 235] But ill adapted, scarcely palpable
To him who does not think; but at your bidding 570
I will proceed.
While thus it far'd with them
To whom this Cottage till those hapless years
Had been a blessed home, it was my chance

551 round,
554 replied,] replied
562 and] & found,] found
563 so,] so
568 and] &
568b–570a *del to* but at your bidding now *(WW, pencil) and alt at page foot* and yet at your request *(WW, pencil)*
570 *WW added* now *in pencil after* bidding
573 home,] home

555–563a These lines, the first passage from the poem to be published, were quoted in *The Friend* for 16 November 1809 (Rooke, II, 172).

594 *So busy, that the things of which he spake* [E, 545]
595 *Seem'd present, and, attention now relax'd,*

[17v]

596 *There was a heartfelt chillness in my veins.*
597 *I rose, and, turning from that breezy shade,*
{forth
598 *Went* {*out into the open air, and stood*
599 *To drink the comfort of the warmer sun* [E, 550]
600 *Long time I had not stay'd, ere, looking round*
601 *Upon that tranquil Ruin, I return'd*
602 *And begg'd of the Old Man that for my sake*
603 *He would resume his story. He replied,*
604 *"It were a wantonness and would demand* [E, 555]
605 *Severe reproof if we were men whose hearts*
606 *Could hold vain dalliance with the misery*
607 *Even of the dead; contented thence to draw*
608 *A momentary pleasure, never mark'd*
609 *By reason, barren of all future good.* [E, 560]
610 *But we have known that there is often found*
611 *In mournful thoughts, and always might be found*
612 *A power to virtue friendly, were't not so*
613 *I am a dreamer among men, indeed*
614 *An idle dreamer. 'Tis a common Tale,* [E, 565]
615 *An ordinary sorrow of man's life,*
{*T*
616 *A* {*tale of silent suffering, hardly cloth'd*
617 *In bodily form. But without further bidding*
618 *I will proceed.*
While thus it far'd with them
619 *To whom this Cottage till those hapless years* [E, 572]
620 *Had been a blessed home it was my chance*

617 The erased words may be the revised MS. E reading: "at your bidd**ing** now."

[D, 240] To travel in a country far remote.
And glad I was when, halting by yon gate 575
That leads from the green lane, again I saw
These lofty Elm-trees. Long I did not rest:
With many pleasant thoughts I cheer'd my way
[D, 245] O'er the flat Common. At the door arriv'd,
I knock'd, and, when I enter'd with the hope 580
Of usual greeting, Margaret look'd at me
A little while, then turn'd her head away
Speechless, and, sitting down upon a chair,
[D, 250] Wept bitterly. I wist not what to do
Or how to speak to her. Poor Wretch! at last 585
She rose from off her seat—and then—O Sir!
I cannot tell how she pronounc'd my name:
With fervent love, and with a face of grief
[D, 255] Unutterably helpless, and a look
That seem'd to cling upon me, she inquir'd 590
If I had seen her Husband. As she spake
A strange surprize and fear came to my heart,
Nor had I power to answer, ere she told
[D, 260] That he had disappear'd just two months gone.
He left his House; two wretched days had pass'd, 595
And on the third by the first break of light,
Within her casement full in view she saw
A letter folded up, which she forthwith
Open'd, and found no writing, but therein
Pieces of money carefully [wrapp'd up], 600
Silver and gold. 'I trembl'd at the sight,'
[D, 265] Said Margaret, 'for I knew it was his hand
That plac'd it there; and on that very day,
By one, who from my Husband had been sent,
The tidings came that he had join'd a Troop 605

---

574 remote.] remote
583 chair,] chair
586 Sir!] Sir
588 and,
592 heart,] heart
596 light,] light
598 folded up, *erased, overwritten* as it seem'd *(WW, pencil)*
600 wrapp'd up,] wrapp'd up *over illegible erasure, first in WW's pencil, then DW's ink*
601 gold "I sight,"
602 "for it was his *alt* [?the ?authors] *(WW, pencil)*
603 That *erased, overwritten* That *(?DW, ink) del to* Which *(WW, pencil)*

600–601 See the note to l. 323 of the MS. B Reading Text, above.

621 *To travel in a country far remote*
622 *And glad I was, when, halting by yon gate* [E, 575]

[18r]

623 *That leads from the green lane, again I saw*
624 *These lofty Elm-trees. Long I did not rest:*
625 *With many pleasant thoughts I cheer'd my way*
626 *O'er the flat Common. At the door arriv'd,*
627 *I knock'd, and when I enter'd with the hope* [E, 580]
628 *Of usual greeting, Margaret look'd at me*
629 *A little while, then turn'd her head away*
630 *Speechless, and sitting down upon a chair,*
631 *Wept bitterly. I wist not what to do*
632 *Or how to speak to her. Poor Wretch! at last* [E, 585]
633 *She rose from off her seat, and then, O Sir!*
634 *I cannot tell how she pronounc'd my name:*
635 *With fervent love, and with a face of grief*
636 *Unutterably helpless and a look*
637 *That seem'd to cling upon me she inquir'd* [E, 590]
638 *If I had seen her Husband. As she spake*
639 *A strange surprize and fear came to my heart*
640 *Nor had I power to answer, ere she told*
641 *That he had disappear'd just two months gone.*
642 *He left his house; two wretched days had pass'd* [E, 595]
643 *And on the third, by the first break of light*
644 *Within her casement full in view she saw*
such
645 *A letter, ~~as~~^ it seem'd, which she forthwith*
646 *Open'd, and found no writing, but therein*
647 *Pieces of money carefully wrapp'd up,* [E, 600]
648 *Silver and gold, "I trembled at the sight"*
649 *Said Margaret "for I knew it was his hand*
650 *Which plac'd it there; and on that very day,*
651 *By one who from my Husband had been sent,*
652 *The tidings came that he had join'd a Troop* [E, 605]

---

630 A comma after "and" is erased.

Of Soldiers, going to a distant Land.
[D, 270] He left me thus—Poor Man! he had not heart
To take a farewell of me; and he fear'd
That I should follow with my Babes, and sink
Beneath the misery of that wandering life.' 610
This Tale did Margaret tell with many tears:
[D, 275] And when she ended I had little power
To give her comfort, and was glad to take
Such words of hope from her own mouth as serv'd
To cheer us both: but long she had not talk'd 615
Ere we built up a pile of better thoughts,
[D, 280] And with a brighter eye she look'd around
As if she had been shedding tears of joy.
We parted. It was then the early spring;
I left her busy with her garden tools; 620
And well remember, o'er that fence she look'd,
[D, 285] And, while I pac'd along the foot-way path,
Call'd out, and sent a blessing after me
With tender chearfulness, and with a voice
That seem'd the very sound of happy thoughts. 625
I rov'd o'er many a hill and many a dale
[D, 290] With this my weary load, in heat and cold,
Through many a wood and many an open ground,
In sunshine, or in shade, in wet or fair,
Now blithe, now drooping, as it might befal, 630
My best companions now the driving winds,
[D, 295] And now the 'trotting brooks' and whispering trees,
And now the music of my own sad steps,

---

610 life.'] life.
611 tears:] tears
616 thoughts,] thoughts
620 tools;] tools
621 look'd,] look'd
622 path,] path
623 out,] out
624 and] &
626 hill, &
627 cold,] cold
628 ground,] plain *erased, overwritten* ground *a probable copying error corrected, since* ground *is in MSS. D and M, and in* Excursion, *1814*
631 companions,
632 "trotting brooks"
633 steps,] steps

---

632 See the note to l. 295 of the MS. D Reading Text, above.

[18^v]

653 *Of Soldiers going to a distant Land.*
654 *He left me thus—Poor Man! he had not heart*
655 *To take a farewell of me; and he fear'd*
656 *That I should follow with my Babes, and sink*
657 *Beneath the misery of that wandering life."* [E, 610]
658 *This Tale did Margaret tell with many tears*
659 *And when she ended I had little power*
660 *To give her comfort, and was glad to take*
661 *Such words of hope from her own mouth as serv'd*
662 *To cheer us both: but long* , *she had not talk'd* [E, 615]
663 *Ere we built up a pile of better thoughts,*
664 *And with a brighter eye she look'd around*
665 *As if she had been shedding tears of joy.*
666 *We parted. It was then the early spring;*
667 *I left her busy with her garden tools;* [E, 620]
668 *And well remember, o'er that fence she look'd*
669 *And, while I pac'd along the foot-way path*
670 *Call'd out; and sent a blessing after me*
671 *With tender chearfulness, and with a voice*
672 *That seem'd the very sound of happy thoughts.* [E, 625]
673 *I rov'd o'er many a hill, and many a dale*
674 *With this my weary load, in heat and cold*
675 *Through many a wood, and many an open ground*
676 *In sunshine, or in shade, in wet or fair,*
Drooping, or ~~gay and~~ blithe of heart
677 ~~*Now blithe, now drooping,*~~ *as* ~~*it*~~ *might befal,* [E, 630]
678 *My best companions now the driving winds*
679 *And now the "trotting brooks," and whispering trees,*
680 *And now the music of my own sad steps,*

---

662 The added comma is in pencil.

With many a short-liv'd thought that pass'd between
And disappear'd. I came this way again 635
Towards the wane of summer, when the wheat
[D, 300] Was yellow, and the [soft] and bladed grass
Sprang up afresh, and o'er the hay-field spread
Its tender green. When I had reach'd the door
I found that she was absent. In the shade 640
Where now we sit I waited her return.
[D, 305] Her Cottage, in its outward look, appear'd
As chearful as before; in any shew
Of neatness little chang'd; but that I thought
The honeysuckle crowded round the door, 645
And from the wall hung down in heavier tufts;
[D, 310] And knots of worthless stone-crop started out
Along the window's edge and grew like weeds
Against the lower panes. I turn'd aside
And stroll'd into her garden. It appear'd 650
To lag behind the season, and had lost
Its trimness and its pride. The border tufts—
[D, 318] Daisy, and thrift, and lowly camomile
And thyme—had straggl'd out into the paths;
The bindweed with its bells, and cumbrous wreathes, 655
Had twin'd about her two small rows of peas
[D, 320] And dragg'd them to the earth. Ere this, an hour
Was wasted. Back I turn'd my restless steps,
And, as I walk'd before the door, it chanc'd
A Stranger pass'd, and, guessing whom I sought, 660
He said that she was us'd to ramble far.
[D, 325] The sun was sinking in the west; and now

---

636 summer,] summer
637 yellow, & soft] *an evident miswriting* fresh *was erased; the proper reading* soft *(as in MSS. B, D, and M—and* Excursion, *1814) was not added*
638 and] & hay-field] hay field
641 return.] return
643 before;] before,
647 stone-crop] stone crop
648 and] &
652 tufts,
653 & lowly
654 thyme, paths;] paths
655 and] & wreathes,] wreathes
658 steps,] steps
662 and] &

---

637 See the note to l. 358 of the MS. B Reading Text, above.

681 *With many a short-liv'd thought that pass'd between*
682 *And disappear'd. I came this way again* [E, 635]

[19r]

683 *Towards the wane of summer, when the wheat*
{*and the soft and bladed grass*
684 *Was yellow* {
685 *Sprang up afresh, and o'er the hay-field spread*
686 *Its tender green. When I had reach'd the door*
687 *I found that she was absent. In the shade* [E, 640]
688 *Where now we sate I waited her return.*

689 *Her Cottage wore its customary look*'}
690 *As chearful as before;* but that I thought
~~*Of neatness little chang'd; but that I thought*~~
691 *The honeysuckle crowded round the door* [E, 645]
692 *And from the wall hung down in heavier tufts,*
693 *And knots of worthless stonecrop started out*
694 *Along the window's edge and grew like weeds*
695 *Against the lower panes. I turn'd aside*
696 *And stroll'd into her garden. It appear'd* [E, 650]
697 *To lag behind the season, and had lost*
698 *Its pride of neatness. The twin border tufts,*
699 ~~*Daisy, and thrift, and lowly camomile*~~
700 ~~*And thyme, had straggled out into the paths;*~~
701 *The cumbrous bindweed with its wreaths and bells* [E, 655]
702 *Had twin'd about her two small rows of peas*
703 *And dragg'd them to the earth. Ere this an hour*
704 *Was wasted. Back I turn'd my restless steps*
705 *And, as I walk'd before the door it chanc'd*
706 *A Stranger pass'd, and guessing whom I sought* [E, 660]
707 *He said that she was us'd to ramble far.*
708 *The sun was sinking in the west; and now*

[Marginal draft, written vertically and deleted:]
P}
{Of} ride of neatness {B
{bright carnations, once
{superior
Prized for {pecul beauty and no less
For the peculiar pains which they required
Hung down their heads unpropp'd. The Border

---

684 DW left a gap after "yellow" (the line is defective in MS. E); WW penciled in the proper reading (traces survive), and DW then copied his addition in ink.

688 DW mistakenly wrote "sate" for "sit."

689 There is an erasure after "look"; in MS. E, this line reads: "Her Cottage, in its outward look, appear'd."

690 The erased words may be the MS. E reading: "in any shew." The appearance of WW's fair-copy, in-line revision and the neater than usual deletion of l. 690/691 suggest that his alteration may precede dispatch of MS. M to STC. The change here was made to avoid an echo of l. 698, as revised.

694 The erasure is of a copying error: "**And g**rew **lik**e weeds."

698 The erased words may be the MS. E reading: "trimness and its pride. The"; the X probably indicates where the marginal draft was to come in.

698–701 A revision is on 23r; see Transcriptions of Additions to MSS. E and M, below.

701 The erasure may be of the MS. E reading: "**b**indweed wi**th** its bells, & cumbrous wreathes."

I sate with sad impatience. From within
Her solitary Infant cried aloud.
The spot, though fair, seem'd very desolate, 665
The longer I remain'd more desolate.
[D, 330] And, looking round, I saw the corner stones,
Till then unnotic'd, on either side the door
With dull red [stains] discolor'd, and stuck o'er
With tufts and hairs of wool, as if the sheep 670
That fed upon the Common thither came
[D, 335] Familiarly, and found a couching-place
Even at her threshold. The house-clock struck eight;
I turn'd and saw her distant a few steps.
Her face was pale and thin, her figure too 675
Was chang'd. As she unlock'd the door she said,
[D, 340] 'It grieves me you have waited here so long,
But, in good truth, I've wander'd much of late
And sometimes, to my shame I speak, have need
Of my best prayers to bring me back again.' 680
While on the board she spread our evening meal
[D, 345] She told me she had lost her elder Child,
That he, for months, had been a Serving-boy,
Apprentic'd by the Parish. 'I perceive
You look at me, and you have cause. Today 685
I have been travelling far; and many days
[D, 350] About the fields I wander, knowing this
Only, that what I seek I cannot find.
And so I waste my time: for I am chang'd;
And to myself,' said she, 'have done much wrong, 690
And to this helpless Infant. I have slept
[D, 355] Weeping; and weeping I have wak'd; [my tears

---

666 desolate.] desolate
669 stains] stones *a copying error*; stains *is in MSS. B and D, and in* Excursion, *1814*
677 "It long,] long
680 again.'] again.
684 "I
685–698 *lines begin with double quotation marks*
689 chang'd;] chang'd
690 myself,'] myself 'have] have
692 wak'd; *DW mistakenly broke the line here*

667–673 See the note to ll. 388–394 of the MS. B Reading Text, above.

709 *I sate with sad impatience. From within*
710 *Her solitary Infant cried aloud.*
711 *The spot, though fair, seem'd very desolate,* [E, 665]
712 *The longer I remain'd more desolate*

[19^v]

713 *And, looking round, I saw the corner stones,*
714 *Till then unnotic'd, on either side the door*
715 *With dull red stones discolour'd, and stuck o'er*
716 *With tufts and hairs of wool, as if the sheep* [E, 670]
717 *That fed upon the Common thither came*
718 *Familiarly, and found a couching-place*
719 *Even at her threshold. The house-clock struck eight,*
720 *I turn'd, and saw her distant a few steps.*
721 *Her face was pale and thin, her figure too* [E, 675]
722 *Was chang'd. As she unlock'd the door, she said,*
723 *"It grieves me you have waited here so long*
724 *But, in good truth, I've wander'd much of late*
725 *And sometimes, to my shame I speak, have need*
726 *Of my best prayers to bring me back again.* [E, 680]
727 *While on the board she spread our evening meal*
728 *She told me, she had lost her elder Child,*
729 *That he, for months, had been a Serving-boy*
730 *Apprentic'd by the Parish. "I perceive*
731 *You look at me, and you have cause. Today* [E, 685]
732 *I have been travelling far, and many days*
733 *About the fields I wander, knowing this,*
734 *Only that what I seek I cannot find.*
735 *And so I waste my time: for I am chang'd*
736 *And to myself," said she "have done much wrong,* [E, 690]
737 *And to this helpless Infant. I have slept*
738 *Weeping, and weeping I have wak'd,* {*my tears*

715 Despite the copying of "stones" into both MSS. E and M, the sense calls for "stains"—the reading in MSS. B and D, and in the published *Excursion*.

728–730 A revision is on 23^r and 23^v; see Transcriptions of Additions to MSS. E and M, below.

738 The addition of "my tears," required when DW broke the line in the wrong place, is in pencil (?WW) traced over in ink (DW).

Have flow'd as if my body were not such]
As others are, and I could never die.
But I am now in mind and in my heart 695
More easy, and I hope,' said she, 'that Heaven
[D, 360] Will give me patience to endure the things
Which I behold at home.' It would have griev'd
Your very soul to see her. Sir, I feel
The Story linger in my heart; I fear 700
'Tis long and tedious, but my spirit clings
[D, 365] To that poor Woman: so familiarly
Do I perceive her manner and her look
And presence, and so deeply do I feel
Her goodness, that, not seldom, in my walks 705
A momentary trance comes over me;
[D, 370] And to myself I seem to muse on one
By sorrow laid asleep, or borne away,
A human Being destin'd to awake
To human life, or something very near 710
To human life, when he shall come again
[D, 375] For whom she suffer'd. Sir, it would have griev'd
Your very soul to see her: evermore
Her eyelids droop'd, her eyes were downward cast;
And when she at her table gave me food 715
She did not look at me. Her voice was low,
[D, 380] Her body was subdu'd. In every act
Pertaining to her house affairs appear'd
The careless stillness of a thinking mind,
Self-occupied, to which all outward things 720
Are like an idle matter. Still she sigh'd,
But yet no motion of the breast was seen,
[D, 385] No heaving of the heart. While by the fire

---

693 *continuing her error, DW wrote* My tears have flow'd as if my body were not such *and the line was then erased but not corrected*
695 mind, &
696 hope,'] hope" "that
698 home." "It
701 tedious,] tedious
706 me;] me
708 away,] away
709 {B / being
711 life,] life
714 cast;] cast
720 Self-occupied,] Self occupied,
721 sigh'd,] sigh'd

739	*~~My tears~~ {H / have flow'd as if my body were not such*	
740	*As others are, and I could never die.*	
741	*But I am now, in mind, and in my heart*	[E, 695]
742	*More easy, and I hope," said she "that Heaven*	
743	*Will give me patience to endure the things*	
744	*Which I behold at home." It would have griev'd*	

[20r]

745	*Your very soul to see her. Sir,* [ ]	
746	*The story linger in my heart; I fear*	[E, 700]
747	*'Tis long and tedious, but my spirit clings*	
748	*To that poor Woman: so familiarly*	
749	*Do I perceive her manner and her look*	
750	*And presence, and so deeply do I feel*	
751	*Her goodness, that, not seldom, in my walks*	[E, 705]
752	*A momentary trance comes over me*	
753	*And to myself I seem to muse on one*	
754	*By sorrow laid asleep, or borne away*	
755	*A human being destin'd to awake*	
756	*To human life, or something very near*	[E, 710]
757	*To human life when he shall come again*	
758	*For whom she suffer'd. Sir, it would have griev'd*	
759	*Your very soul to see her: evermore*	
760	*Her eyelids droop'd, her eyes were downward cast;*	
761	*And when she at her table gave me food*	[E, 715]
762	*She did not look at me. Her voice was low,*	
763	*Her body was subdu'd. In every act*	
764	*Pertaining to her house affairs appear'd*	
765	*The careless stillness of a thinking mind,*	
766	*Self-occupied, to which all outward things*	[E, 720]
767	*Are like an idle matter. Still she sigh'd,*	
768	*But yet no motion of the {breast / heart was seen,*	
769	*No heaving of the heart. While by the fire*	

745 The upper part of the last two words, "I feel," is trimmed away; the bottoms of the "I" and the "f" are visible.

768 The middle three letters of "heart" are erased; the first and last letters were used as parts of the overwriting.

We sate together, sighs came on my ear;
I knew not how, and hardly whence they came. 725
I gave her for her Son, the Parish Boy,
A kerchief and a book wherewith she seem'd
Pleas'd; and I counsell'd her to have her trust
In God's good love, and seek his help by prayer.
I took my Staff, and, when I kiss'd her Babe, 730
The tears stood in her eyes. I left her then
[D, 390] With the best hope and comfort I could give;
She thank'd me for my will; but for my hope
It seem'd she did not thank me.
I return'd
And took my rounds along this Road again 735
Ere on its sunny bank the primrose flower
[D, 395] Had chronicled the earliest day of spring.
I found her sad and drooping; she had learn'd
No tidings of her Husband: if he liv'd
She knew not that he liv'd; if he were dead 740
She knew not he was dead. She seem'd the same
[D, 400] In person and appearance; but her house
Bespake a sleepy hand of negligence;
The floor was neither dry nor neat, [the hearth
Was comfortless, and her small lot of books,] 745
[D, 405] Which, one upon the other, heretofore,
Had been pil'd up against the corner panes
In seemly order, now with straggling leaves
Lay scatter'd here and there, open or shut,
As they had chanc'd to fall. Her Infant Babe 750
[D, 410] Had from its Mother caught the trick of grief
And sigh'd among its playthings. Once again
I turn'd towards the garden-gate, and saw

---

725 and] &
732 *last three words over erasure, probably the mistaken beginning of the next line* give;] give
736 the *alt* a *(WW, pencil)*
737 *alt* Was seen to give an earnest of the spring *(WW, pencil)*
744 neat,] neat the hearth *inserted (WW, pencil)*
745 *WW penciled the line over an illegible erasure (perhaps the MS. D reading:* The windows too were dim and her few books*)* comfortless & books,] books

---

751 See the note to l. 449 of the MS. B Reading Text, above.

770 *We sate together sighs came on my ear,*
771 *I knew not how, and hardly whence they came.* [E, 725]
772 *I gave her for her Son, the Parish Boy,*
773 *A kerchief and a book wherewith she seem'd*
774 *Pleas'd; and I counsell'd her to have her trust*
775 *In God's good love, and seek his help by prayer.*

[20v]

776 [ ]*ook my Staff and when I kiss*[ ]*d her Babe,* [E, 730]
777 *The tears stood in her eyes, I left her then*
778 *With the best hope and comfort I could give*
779 *She thank'd me for my will, but for my hope*
780 *It seem'd she did not thank me.*
I return'd
781 *And took my rounds along this road again* [E, 735]
782 *Ere on its sunny bank the primrose flower*
~~with grateful promise~~
783 *Peep'd forth to give an earnest of the spring.*
784 *I found her sad and drooping; she had learn'd*
785 *No tidings of her Husband: if he liv'd*
786 *She knew not that he liv'd; if he were dead* [E, 740]
787 *She knew not he was dead. She seem'd the same*
788 *In person and appearance; but her house*
789 *Bespake a sleepy hand of negligence;*
790 *The floor was neither dry nor neat, the hearth*
791 *Was comfortless, and her small lot of books,* [E, 745]
792 *Which, one upon the other, heretofore*
793 *Had been pil'd up against the corner panes*
794 *In seemly order, now, with straggling leaves*
795 *Lay scatter'd here and there, open or shut*
796 *As they had chanc'd to fall. Her Infant Babe* [E, 750]
797 *Had from its Mother caught the trick of grief*
798 *And sigh'd among its playthings. Once again*
799 *I turn'd towards the garden gate, and saw*

---

776 Owing to trimming, only the bottom part of this line survives; the two opening words should be "I took."

783 Traces of WW's pencil writing above the line probably read "Peep'd forth"—which may have been a copying instruction for DW's erasure and correction of the MS. E alternate reading: "Was seen."

More plainly still that poverty and grief
Were now come nearer to her: the earth was hard, 755
[D, 415] With weeds defac'd and knots of wither'd grass;
No ridges there appear'd of clear black mold,
No winter greenness; of her herbs and flowers
It seem'd the better part were gnaw'd away
Or trampl'd on the earth; a chain of straw, 760
[D, 420] Which had been twisted round the slender stem
Of a young apple-tree, lay at its root;
The bark was nibbled round by truant sheep;
Margaret stood near, her Infant in her arms,
And, seeing that my eye was on the tree, 765
[D, 425] She said, 'I fear it will be dead and gone
Ere Robert come again.' Towards the House
Together we return'd, and she inquir'd
If I had any hope. But for her Babe
And for her little friendless Boy, she said, 770
[D, 430] She had no wish to live, that she must die
Of sorrow. Yet I saw the idle loom
Still in its place. His Sunday garments hung
Upon the self-same nail, his very Staff
Stood undisturb'd behind the door. And when 775
[D, 435] I pass'd this way beaten by autumn winds,
She told me that her little Babe was dead
And she was left alone. She now, I learn'd,
After her Infant's death had taken up
The employment common hereabouts, and gain'd, 780
By spinning hemp, a pittance for herself;
And, for that end, had hir'd a Neighbour's Boy
To help her in her work. That very time
Most willingly she put her work aside
And walk'd with me a mile, and, in such sort 785
[D, 441] That any heart had ach'd to hear her, begg'd

---

755 her:] her
766 "I
767 again."
770 said,] said
775 door. And] door, and
779–784 *A faint pencil mark runs vertically through these lines, but it may be accidental since the passage was not deleted in later texts.*
780 and] &
782 {N / neighbour's}
785 and,] &,

800 *More plainly still that poverty and grief*

801 *Were now come nearer to her,* {;} *the earth was ha*[ ] [E, 755]
802 *With weeds defac'd and knots of wither'd grass;*
803 *No ridges there appear'd of clear black mold,*
804 *No winter greenness; of her herbs and flowers*

[21[r]]

805 *It seem'd the better part were gnaw'd away*
806 *Or trampled on the earth; a chain of straw* [E, 760]
807 *Which had been twisted round the slender stem*
808 *Of a young apple-tree, lay at its root;*
809 *The bark was nibbled round by truant sheep.*
810 *Margaret stood near, her Infant in her arms,*
811 *And, seeing that my eye was on the tree,* [E, 765]
812 *She said "I fear it will be dead and gone*
813 *Ere Robert come again." Towards the House*
814 *Together we return'd, and she inquir'd*
815 *If I had any hope. But for her Babe,*
816 *And for her little friendless Boy, she said* [E, 770]
817 *She had no wish to live, that she must die*
818 *Of sorrow. Yet I saw the idle loom*
819 *Still in its place. His Sunday garments hung*
820 *Upon the self-same nail; his very Staff*

821 *Stood undisturb'd behind the door,* {.} {*A* / ~~*and*~~} *when* [E, 775]

ensuing

822 *This way the ~~following~~ winter I return'd*
823 *She told me that her little Babe was dead*
824 *And she was left alone. She now, I learn'd,*
825 *After her Infant's death had taken up*

thr{ough / [?os] these [?parts]}

826 *The employment common*^ ~~*hereabouts,*~~ *& gain'd* [E, 780]
827 *By spinning hemp, a pittance for herself*
828 *And, for that end, had hir'd a neighbour's boy*
829 *To help her in her work. That very time*
830 *Most willingly she put her work aside,*
831 *And walk'd with me a mile, &, in such sort* [E, 785]
832 *That any heart had ach'd to hear her, begg'd*

---

801 The final two letters of "hard" are worn away.
821 Deletion by erasure.
822 The erased line may be the MS. E reading: "**I** **p**ass'd this way **b**eaten **b**y autumn wind**s**." Traces of WW's pencil writing survive above the line.
825 WW's interlining (825/826) obliterates the punctuation, if any, after "death."

That, wheresoe'er I went, I still would ask
For him whom she had lost. We parted then,
Our final parting; for, from that time forth,
[D, 445] Did many seasons pass ere I return'd 790
Into this tract again.
Nine tedious years,
From their first separation nine long years,
She linger'd in unquiet widowhood,
A Wife and Widow. Needs must it have been
A sore heart-wasting. I have heard, my Friend, 795
[D, 450] That in yon broken arbour she would sit
The idle length of half a sabbath day
And, when a dog pass'd by, she still would quit
The shade, and look abroad. On this old Bench
[D, 455] For hours she sate; and evermore her eye 800
Was busy in the distance, shaping things
That made her heart beat quick. You see that Path?
Now faint; the grass has crept o'er its grey line;
There to and fro she pac'd through many a day
[D, 460] Of the warm summer, from a belt of hemp 805
That girt her waist spinning the long-drawn thread,
With backward steps. Yet, ever as there pass'd
A man whose Garments shew'd the Soldier's red,
Or crippled Mendicant in Sailor's Garb,
[D, 465] The little Child who sate to turn the wheel 810
Ceas'd from his toil, and she with faltering voice,
Expecting still to hear her Husband's fate,
Made many a fond inquiry; and when they
Whose presence gave no comfort were gone by,
[D, 470] Her heart was still more sad. And by yon gate 815

---

794 {W / wife}
795/796 From some who half believed that she was craz'd *(WW, pencil)*
797 The idle *del to* Idly the *(WW)*
798 when *del to* if *(WW)*
800 sate &
805 summer; [?flax] *erased, overwritten* hemp *(?WW)*
808 {G / garment's *with apostrophe erased*}
811 toil, *alt* work task *(WW, pencil)* and] &
813 inquiry,
814 by,] by

799–800 See the note to ll. 490–491 of the MS. B Reading Text, above.
804–811 See the note to ll. 495–511 of the MS. B Reading Text, above.
808 See the note to l. 499 of the MS. B Reading Text, above.
810–818 See the note to ll. 501–509 of the MS. B Reading Text, above.

833 *That, wheresoe'er I went, I still would ask*
834 *For him whom she had lost. We parted then,*
835 *Our final parting; for, from that time forth,*

[21v]

836 *Did many seasons pass ere I return'd* [E, 790]
837 *Into this tract again.*
Nine tedious years,
838 *From their first separation, nine long years,*
839 *She linger'd in unquiet widowhood,*
840 *A Wife and Widow. Needs must it have been*
841 *A sore heart-wasting. I have heard, my Friend* [E, 795]
842 *That in yon broken arbour she would sit*
843 *The idle length of half a sabbath day*
844 X *And, when a dog pass'd by she still would* {*quit* / [?*sit*]}
845 *The shade, and look abroad. On this old Bench*
846 *For hours she sate; and evermore her eye* [E, 800]
847 *Was busy in the distance, shaping things*
848 *That made her heart beat quick. You see*
that Path {, / ?}
849 *Now faint* {, / ?} {*T* / *the grass has crept o'er its grey line;*}
850 *There to and fro she pac'd through many a day*
851 *Of the warm summer; from a belt of hemp* [E, 805]
852 *That girt her waist spinning the long-drawn*
thread
853 *With backward steps. Yet, ever as there pass'd*
854 *A Man whose garments shew'd the Soldier's red,*
855 *Or crippled Mendicant in Sailor's garb*
856 *The little Child who sate to turn the wheel* [E, 810]
857 *Ceas'd from his task, and she with faltering voice,*
858 *Expecting still to hear her Husband's fate,*
859 *Made many a fond inquiry; and when they*
860 *Whose presence gave no comfort were gone by*
861 *Her heart was still more sad. And by yon Gate* [E, 815]

844 The X probably marks the copying error.
848–849 Deletion by erasure.

Which bars the Traveller's road she often stood
And, when a Stranger Horseman came, the latch
Would lift, and in his face look wistfully,
Most happy if, from aught discover'd there
[D, 475] Of tender feeling, she might dare repeat 820
The same sad question. Meanwhile, her poor Hut
Sank to decay: for he was gone, whose hand,
At the first nippings of October frost,
Clos'd up each chink, and with fresh bands of straw
[D, 480] Chequer'd the green-grown thatch. And so she liv'd 825
Through the long winter, reckless and alone,
Until her House by frost, and thaw, and rain
Was sapp'd, and, when she slept, the nightly-damps
Did chill her breast; and, in the stormy day,
[D, 485] Her tatter'd clothes were ruffl'd by the wind, 830
Even at the side of her own fire. Yet still
She lov'd this wretched spot nor would for worlds
Have parted hence; and still that length of road
And this rude Bench one torturing hope endear'd,
[D, 490] Fast rooted at her heart, and here, my Friend, 835
In sickness she remain'd; and here she died:
Last human tenant of these ruin'd Walls."
The Old Man ceas'd: he saw that I was mov'd;
From that low Bench, rising instinctively,
[D, 495] I turn'd aside in weakness, nor had power 840
To thank him for the tale which he had told.
I stood, and, leaning o'er the garden gate,
Review'd that Woman's sufferings, and it seem'd
To comfort me while with a Brother's love
[D, 500] I bless'd her, in the impotence of grief. 845
At length towards the Cottage I return'd

---

824 and] &
830 tatter'd] tatterd
834 endear'd,] endear'd
841 which] that *del to* which *(WW, pencil); a probable copying error corrected, since* which *is in MSS. D and M, and in* Excursion, *1814*
842 gate, *del to* wall *(WW, pencil)*
843 and] &

---

826 See the note to l. 517 of the MS. B Reading Text, above.
831–835 See the note to ll. 522–526 of the MS. B Reading Text, above.
837 See the note to l. 528 of the MS. B Reading Text, above.

862 *That bars the Traveller's road she often stood,*
863 *And, when a Stranger Horseman came, the latch*

[22ʳ]

864 *Would lift, and in his face look wistfully,*
865 *Most happy if from aught discover'd there*
866 *Of tender feeling she might dare repeat* [E, 820]
867 *The same sad question. Meanwhile her poor Hut*
868 *Sank to decay: for he was gone whose hand,*
869 *At the first nippings of October frost,*
870 *Clos'd up each chink, and with fresh bands of straw*
871 *Chequer'd the green-grown thatch. And so she liv'd* [E, 825]
872 *Through the long winter reckless and alone,*
873 *Until her House by frost, and thaw and rain*
874 *Was sapp'd; and when she slept, the nightly damps*
875 *Did chill her breast; and, in the stormy day,*
876 *Her tatter'd clothes were ruffled by the wind* [E, 830]
877 *Even at the side of her own fire. Yet still*
878 *She lov'd this wretched spot nor would for worlds*
879 *Have parted hence; and still that length of road,*
880 *And this rude Bench one torturing hope endear'd*
881 *Fast rooted at her heart,* ; } *and here, my Friend,* [E, 835]
882 *In sickness she remain'd, and here she died,*
883 *Last human tenant of these ruin'd Walls.*
884 *The Old Man ceas'd: he saw that I was mov'd;*
885 *From that low Bench rising instinctively,*
886 *I turn'd aside in weakness, nor had power* [E, 840]
887 *To thank him for the Tale which he had told.*
888 *I stood, and leaning o'er the Garden wall*
889 *Review'd that Woman's sufferings, & it seem'd*
890 *To comfort me while with a Brother's love*
891 *I bless'd her in the impotence of grief.* [E, 845]
892 *At length towards the Cottage I return'd*

Fondly, and trac'd with milder interest
That secret spirit of humanity,
Which, 'mid the calm oblivious tendencies
[D, 505] Of Nature, 'mid her plants, and weeds, and flowers, 850
And silent overgrowings, still survived.
The Old Man, seeing this, resum'd and said,
"My Friend, enough to sorrow have you given,
The purposes of wisdom ask no more;
[D, 510] Be wise and chearful, and no longer read 855
The forms of things with an unworthy eye.
She sleeps in the calm earth, and peace is here.
I well remember that those very plumes,
Those weeds, and the high spear-grass on that wall,
[D, 515] By mist and silent rain-drops silver'd o'er, 860
As once I pass'd, did to my heart convey
So still an image of tranquillity,
So calm and still, and look'd so beautiful
Amid the uneasy thoughts which fill'd my mind,
[D, 520] That what we feel of sorrow and despair 865
From ruin and from change, and all the grief
The passing shews of being leave behind,
Appear'd an idle dream that could not live
Where meditation was: I turn'd away
[D, 525] And walk'd along my road in happiness." 870
He ceas'd. Ere long, the sun, declining, shot
A slant and mellow radiance which began
To fall upon us where beneath the trees
We sate on that low Bench; and now we felt,
[D, 530] Admonish'd thus, the sweet hour coming on. 875
A linnet warbled from those lofty Elms,
A thrush sang loud; and other melodies,

---

850 & flowers,
852 and said,] & said
857 here.] here
859 and] &
863 & look'd
864 mind,] mind
866 & all
867 behind,] behind
871 declining,] descending, *del to* declining *(WW); a probable copying error corrected, since* declining *is in MSS. D and M (corrected), and in* Excursion, *1814*
873 the] thee *a miswriting*

871–883 See the note to ll. 526–538 of the MS. D Reading Text, above.

893 *Fondly, and trac'd with ~~milder~~ interest* {more mild
894 *That secret spirit of humanity,*

[22v]

895 *Which, 'mid the calm oblivious tendencies*
896 *Of Nature, 'mid her plants, and weeds, and flowers* [E, 850]
897 *And silent overgrowings still surviv'd.*
noting
898 *The Old Man, ~~seeing~~ this, resum'd, and said,*
899 *"My Friend, enough to sorrow have you given,*
900 *The purposes of wisdom ask no more;*
901 *Be wise and chearful, and no longer read* [E, 855]
902 *The forms of things with an unworthy eye.*
903 *She sleeps in the calm earth, and peace is here,*
904 *I well remember that those very plumes,*
905 *Those weeds, and the high spear grass on that wall,*
906 *By mist and silent rain-drops silver'd o'er,* [E, 860]
907 *As once I pass'd did to my heart convey*
908 *So still an image of tranquillity,*
a
909 *So c{a}lm and still, and look'd so beautiful*
910 *Amid the uneasy thoughts which fill'd my mind*
911 *That what we feel of sorrow and despair* [E, 865]
912 *From ruin and from change, & all the grief*
913 *The passing shows of being leave behind*
914 *Appear'd an idle dream that could not live*
915 *Where meditation was: I turn'd away*
916 *And walk'd along my road in happiness."* [E, 870]
917 *He ceased. Ere long, the sun, declining, shot*
918 *A slant and mellow radiance which began*
919 *To fall upon us where beneath the trees*
920 *We sate on that low Bench: & now we felt,*
921 *Admonish'd thus, the sweet hour coming on.* [E, 875]
922 *A linnet warbled from those lofty Elms,*
923 *A thrush sang loud, & other melodies,*

---

909 Deletion by erasure.
917 The erasure is probably of the last eight letters of the MS. E reading: "de**s**cending."

At distance heard, peopled the milder air.
The Old Man rose, and hoisted up his load;
[D, 535] Together, casting then a farewell look 880
Upon those silent walls, we left the shade
And, ere the stars were visible, we reach'd
A Village Inn, our evening resting-place.

The End.

---

879 and] & hois{lif}ted *(WW)*
882 we *del to* had *(WW, pencil)*

924 *At distance heard, peopled the milder air.*
lifted
925 *The Old Man rose, & ~~hoisted~~ up his load;*
926 *Together, casting then a farewell look* [E, 880]
927 *Upon those silent Walls we left the shade*
had
928 *And, ere the stars were visible, ~~we~~ reach'd*
929 *A Village Inn—our Evening resting-place.*

The Pedlar

Transcriptions of Additions to MSS. E and M

~~At distance I beheld a grove~~, of trees
Upon open
on that a grove
That ~~midway~~ open level stood ~~alone~~,
[?in] {[?] I hope [?]
The wish for port {[?to] which my steps were bound
~~Thither I came at length and there I found~~
hard
And ~~where at length~~ I from the beating sun [?ob]
~~Obtained a shealter~~
Not only shelter from the beating sun
Found shelter, and obtained a livelier joy
amid the the
Thither I came at length beneath ~~a~~ shade
{by
Spread {a a brotherhood of lofty elm
Appeard a ~~roofless~~ House,^four naked
walls
That stared upon each other I look round
espied
And there beheld a venerable [?man]
{ to
A friend whom in that place I hoped {[?to] meet
~~and then with lively joy~~
~~espy~~
Did I ~~behold~~ him on the cottage bench
Recumbent in the shade as if
And there espied upon the cottage Bench
Recumbent in the shade, as if asleep
I look round
{[?t]
And to my wish & {& to my hope espied
[?Man]
One whom I loved ~~a~~ venerable ~~Man~~
~~Upon a~~ the the ~~cottage he lay bench~~ he lay
[?the]
I found him lying on the Cottage
re was he seen upon the cottage
The ~~[?] did I see him on the cottage~~ bench
Recumbent in the shade as if asleep

The additions to MS. E are presented out of manuscript order to accommodate facing photographs and transcriptions of the most interesting and complicated passages.
A revision of MS. E, ll. 12–22, these lines on 1ᵛ contribute to *Excursion*, I, 26–36 (*PW*, V, 8). Pencil drafting in WW's hand underlies lines near the bottom:
[? ?were ?bound ? ?wished ?for] port
The port
[? ? ? ? ?venerable ?]

[E, outside back cover]

from con } at last
Till ~~throught~~ [?the]} straint of poverty the loom
Was parted with & little left
But naked
The loom was parted with & little left
B }
[?A]} ut the bare wall where reckless and
alone
She liv'd till throught neglect & unconcern

in her needs & loves
In what she needed & in what she loved
[?by]
Made poorer every day till at the last
The loom was parted with & nothing left
But the bare walls where reckless & alone
linger'd in
She ~~liv'd till through~~ neglect & unconcern
Till the house [?by]
Untill the house by frost & thaw & rain
Was sappd

The drafts on the outside back cover are attempts to recast MS. E, ll. 825–828. The leaves of MS. E have been stitched into stiff cardboard covers, with a woodcut of a bird on the back cover and one of a squirrel on the front.

[E, 1^{r}]

In his heart
Where ~~fear~~ solemn apprehension dread & awe
Sate daily, no uncherished visitatant
The milder spirit yet was wanting, yet
Love was

[E, 20^{r}]

And so She liv'd
~~Through the long winters long & desolate~~
In objects of her need & of her love
day after day made poorer & till at
Made poorer every day ~~till at the~~ last
The loom was parted with & nothing left
But naked walls where joyless & alone
Through the long winters long & desolate
She lingerd in neglect & unconcern
Untill her house by frost & thaw & rain
Was sapp'd

[M, 1^{v}]

Transcendent holiness that did not need
i}
The imperfect officeces of prayer & pray}se

[M, 2^{r}]

visitation from the
Of ~~pure communion~~ with the living God
Thought was not in enjoyment it expired
No thanks he breathed he proffered no request
~~And in that adoration~~ that transcends
Rapt into still communion that transcends
The imperfect offices of prayer & praise
~~In adoration blessedness & love~~
g}
His mind was a thanksk}iving to the power

E, 1^{r} This draft—written over DW's "Part First" erased—is a revision of ll. 175b–176a in MS. E (see also *Excursion*, I, 185b–187, and *apparatus criticus*; *PW*, V, 14).

E, 20^{r} Like the drafts on the outside back cover of MS. E, this passage is a revision of MS. E, ll. 825–828.

M, 1^{v} This and other additions to MS. M are written on paper inserted into the notebook after it went to STC. Therefore WW's additional drafts date from after STC's return from Malta in August, 1806 (see the headnote to *The Pedlar*, above). This passage on 1^{v} is a revision of MS. M, l. 233, and contributes to *Excursion*, I, 215–216 (*PW*, V, 15). Below WW's lines is "Pacchiaretti" in STC's hand; this is the name of a sherry that also appears in other notebooks owned by STC (*The Notebooks of Samuel Taylor Coleridge*, ed. Kathleen Coburn (3 vols.; London, 1957–1973), entries 371, 870, 1955, 2761, 3040, 4107.

M, 2^{r} A revision of MS. M, ll. 231–235, these drafts contribute to *Excursion*, I, 212–218 (*PW*, V, 15).

Thought was not in enjoyment it expired
No thanks he breathed he proffered no request
Rapt into still communion that transcends
The imperfect offices of prayer & praise
His mind was a thanksgiving to the power
That made him it was blessedness & love.

[M, 23r]

its pride of neatness. From the border lines
Composed of da[?] {isy} and resplendent thrift
~~The~~ [?ha] {~~F~~ f} ~~lowers~~
Flowers straggling forth ~~[?] encroached upon the paths~~ had on those paths encroached
Which they were used to deck: Carnations, once
Prizd for supassing beauty, and no less
For the peculiar pains they had required
Hung down their languished heads without support.
The cumbrous Bindweed &

had lost her elder Child
Twas well, for he was eating chearful bread
And useful work's might learn a serving boy

[M, 23v]

With a kind Master on a distant farm
Now happily apprenticed.

M, 23r The first draft is a revision of MS. M, ll. 698–701, and contributes to *Excursion*, I, 722–728 (*PW*, V, 32–33). The second draft, continuing onto 23v, is a revision of MS. M, ll. 728–730, and contributes to *Excursion*, I, 760–762 (*PW*, V, 34)

Appendixes

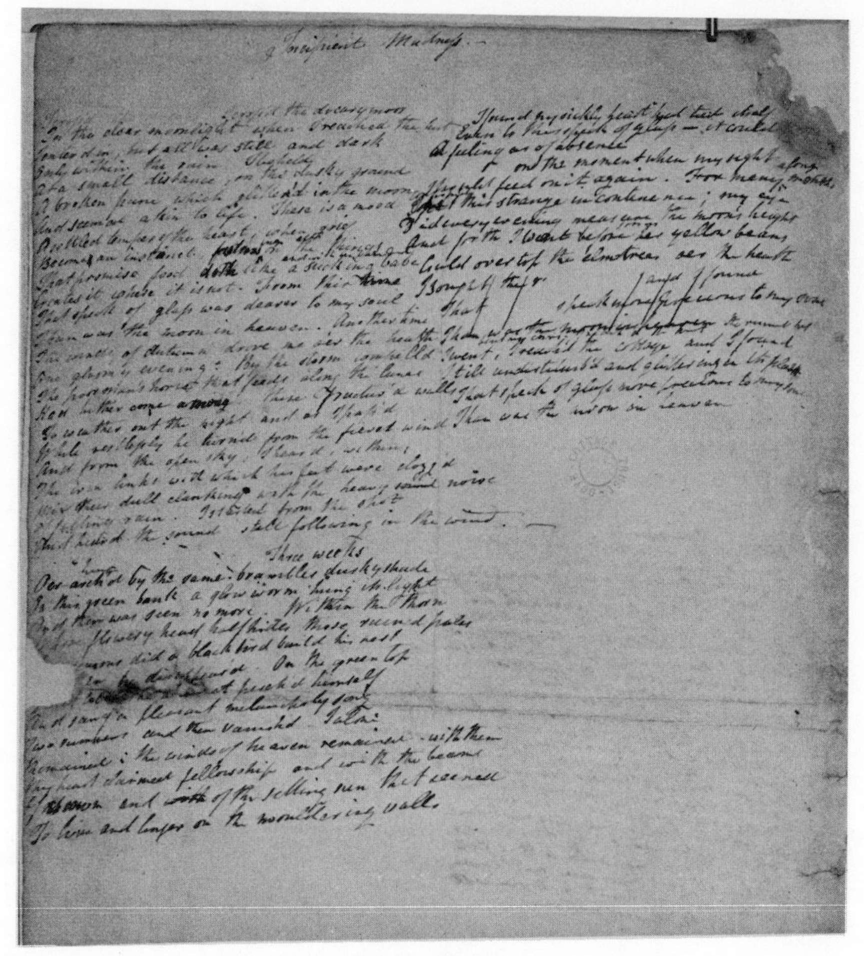
Incipient Madness.

Incipient Madness

Appendix I

The Baker's Cart and *Incipient Madness* Fragments

On the leaf preceding *Ruined Cottage* MS. A in DC MS. 13 are two fragments related to the poem's origins: what Mark Reed has called *The Baker's Cart* appears on 4^r, and *Incipient Madness* is on 4^v. In *The Baker's Cart*, elements that would later become part of *The Ruined Cottage* emerge. The woman is nameless and has five children instead of Margaret's two, but her poverty, her pitcher, her "low and fearful voice," and her mind "Sick and extravagant" all suggest the later poem. Work on *Ruined Cottage* MS. A probably followed quickly after *The Baker's Cart*, hence spring 1797 is the probable date for the fragment's composition.

Incipient Madness, so titled by Wordsworth, faces *Ruined Cottage* MS. A. In MS. A, the poet tried several drafts about a passerby who hears within a ruined cottage a poor man's horse—the melancholy clanking of its foot chains mixing with the sound of a beating rainstorm—and sees there a broken pane of glass glittering to the moon. Such gothicism no doubt helped inspire *The Ruined Cottage* but does not fit with the more simple story the poem later became. Wordsworth's work on *The Ruined Cottage* increasingly focused on the unbalanced minds of Robert and Margaret; the teller of the tale, confronted with the ruin that reminds him of their tragedy, remains sane and calm. Wordsworth transferred these drafts about the poor man's horse and the pane of glass from *Ruined Cottage* MS. A to the opposite verso—probably in spring 1797—and used them as the basis for *Incipient Madness*.

The reading texts of *The Baker's Cart* and *Incipient Madness* represent the fragments in their most advanced states. In *The Baker's Cart*, however, it is uncertain how Wordsworth intended to use incomplete passages of revision, and they are excluded from the reading text.

Transcription of these fragments follows the conventions set out in Editorial Procedure, above. As in *Ruined Cottage* MS. A on leaf 5, Wordsworth wrote in two vertical columns on leaf 4. For ease of presentation, the left-hand and right-hand columns are here labeled 1 and 2, respectively; 1a and 1b designate the top and bottom halves of the left-hand column on 4^v. *The Baker's Cart* is shown in two photographs and *Incipient Madness* in four, the first of them a photograph of the entire sheet. In both fragments the main text is in the left-hand column, with Wordsworth's revisions in the right-hand column. Line numbers correspond to those of the reading texts. At the bottom of leaf 4, a strip of paper 4.4 centimeters high has been removed (the text is not affected), leaving the sheet 24.5 centimeters wide by 34.6 centimeters high. *The Baker's Cart* fragment begins 14.7 centimeters below the top of the page; *Incipient Madness* begins at the top.

[The Baker's Cart]

I have seen the Baker's horse
As he had been accustomed at your door
Stop with the loaded wain, when o'er his head
Smack went the whip, and you were left, as if
You were not born to live, or there had been 5
No bread in all the land. Five little ones,
They at the rumbling of the distant wheels
Had all come forth, and, ere the grove of birch
Concealed the wain, into their wretched hut
They all return'd. While in the road I stood 10
Pursuing with involuntary look
The wain now seen no longer, to my side
[ ] came, a pitcher in her hand
Filled from the spring; she saw what way my eyes
Were turn'd, and in a low and fearful voice 15
She said, "That waggon does not care for us."
The words were simple, but her look and voice
Made up their meaning, and bespoke a mind
Which being long neglected and denied
The common food of hope was now become 20
Sick and extravagant—by strong access
Of momentary pangs driv'n to that state
In which all past experience melts away
And the rebellious heart to its own will
Fashions the laws of nature. 25

1–4 Cf. *The Borderers*, ll. 1333–1336 (PW, I, 180):
I have heard
The boisterous carman, in the miry road,
Crack his loud whip and hail us with mild voice,
And speak with milder voice to his poor beasts.

I have seen the Baker's horse
As he had been accustomed at your door
Stop with the loaded wain, when o'er his head
Smack went the whip and you were left as if
You were not born to live, or there had been
No bread in all the land. Five little ones
They at the rumbling of the distant wheels
Had all come forth And ere the grove of birch
Concealed the wain, into their wretched hut
They all return'd. While in the road I stood
Pursuing with involuntary look
The wain now seen no longer, to my side
came, a pitcher in her hand
Filled from the spring, she saw what way my eyes
Were turn'd and in a low and fearful voice
She said — that waggon does not care for us
The words were simple but her look and voice
Made up their meaning, and bespoke a mind
Which being long neglected and denied
The common food of hope was now become
Sick and extravagant, — by strong access
Of momentary feelings driv'n to that state
In which all past experience melts away
And the rebellious heart to its own will
Fashions the laws of nature.

1 I have seen the Baker's horse
2 As he had been accustomed at your door
3 Stop with the loaded wain, when oer his head
4 Smack went the whip and you were left, as if
5 You were not born to live, or there had been
6 No bread in all the land. Five little ones
7 They at the rumbling of the distant wheels
8 Had all come forth and ere the grove of birch
9 Concealed the wain, into their wretched hut
10 They all return'd. While in the road I stood
11 Pursuing with involuntary look
12 The wain now seen no longer, to my side
13 — came, a pitcher in her hand
14 Filled from the spring she saw what way my eyes
15 Were turn'd and in a low and fearful voice
16 She said—that waggon does not care for us
17 The word were simple but her look and voice
18 Made up their meaning, and bespoke a mind
19 Which~~e~~ being long neglected and denied
20 The common food of hope was now become
21 Sick and extravan{ga/g}nt,—by strong access
22 Of momentary pa{ngs/in} driv'n to that state
23 In which all past experience melts away
24 And the rebellious heart to its own will
25 Fashions the laws of nature.

A faint red margin line, observed by WW, runs 2.0 centimeters from the left edge.
19 Deletion by erasure.
23 In "melts," WW crossed the "l" as well as the "t," with separate strokes.

my eyes were turned nor can forget

and fearful voice

by misery and rumination deep
Tied to dead things and seeking sympathy
In stocks and stones

forget
my eyes were turned nor can I well
With what a low and fearful voice [?she] [?s]aid
The low with which she said
by misery and rumination deep
Tied to dead things and seeking sympathy
In stocks and stones

This draft, related to ll. 14–16 of *The Baker's Cart*, begins opposite l. 12 of col. 1. WW elevated the last word of the first line ("forget") in order to observe a faint red margin line 3.9 centimeters from the right edge.

Incipient Madness. —

I cross'd the dreary moor
In the clear moonlight; when I reached the hut
I enter'd in, but all was still and dark—
Only within the ruin I beheld
At a small distance, on the dusky ground, 5
A broken pane which glitter'd in the moon
And seemed akin to life. There is a mood,
A settled temper of the heart, when grief,
Become an instinct, fastening on all things
That promise food, doth like a sucking babe 10
Create it where it is not. From this time
I found my sickly heart had tied itself
Even to this speck of glass. It could produce
A feeling as of absence [ ]
[ ] on the moment when my sight 15
Should feed on it again. Many a long month
Confirm'd this strange incontinence; my eye
Did every evening measure the moon's height
And forth I went soon as her yellow beams
Could overtop the elm-trees. O'er the heath 20
I went, I reach'd the cottage, and I found
Still undisturb'd and glittering in its place
That speck of glass more precious to my soul
Than was the moon in heaven. Another time
The winds of Autumn drove me o'er the heath 25
One gloomy evening. By the storm compell'd,
The poor man's horse that feeds along the lanes
Had hither come among these fractur'd walls
To weather out the night, and as I pass'd
While restlessly he turn'd from the fierce wind 30
And from the open sky, I heard, within,
The iron links with which his feet were clogg'd
Mix their dull clanking with the heavy noise
Of falling rain. I started from the spot
And heard the sound still following in the wind.— 35
Three weeks
O'er-hung by the same bramble's dusky shade

On this green bank a glow worm hung its light
And then was seen no more. Within the thorn
Whose flowery head half hides those ruined pales, 40
[Three] seasons did a blackbird build his nest
[And] then he disappear'd. On the green top
[Of th]at tall ash a linnet perch'd himself
And sang a pleasant melancholy song
Two summers and then vanish'd. I alone 45
Remained: the winds of heaven remained—with them
My heart claimed fellowship and with the beams
Of dawn and of the setting sun that seemed
To live and linger on the mouldering walls.

Incipient Madness

I cross'd the dreary moor
In the clear moonlight when I reached the hut
I enter'd in, but all was still and dark
Only within the ruin I beheld
At a small distance, on the dusky ground
A broken pane which glitter'd in the moon
And seemed akin to life. There is a mood
A settled temper of the heart, when grief
Become an instinct, fastening on all things
That promise food doth like a sucking babe
Create it where it is not. From this time
That speck of glass was dearer to my soul
Than was the moon in heaven. Another time
The winds of Autumn drove me o'er the heath
One gloomy evening: By the storm compell'd
The poor man's horse that feeds along the lanes
Had hither come among these fractur'd walls
To weather out the night and as I pass'd
While restlessly he turn'd from the fierce wind
And from the open sky, I heard, within,
The iron links with which his feet were clogg'd
Mix their dull clanking with the heavy noise
Of falling rain. I started from the spot
And heard the sound still following in the wind.

I found
Even to
A feeling or
on
Thought feel
Upon this stra
I did every even
And forth I
Could over to
I bought they
That
Than was
I went, I
Still under
That speck
Than was

Incipient Madness.—

1 ~~I cross'd the dreary~~ I cross'd the dreary moor
2 In the clear moonlight when I reached the hut
3 I enter'd in, but all was still and dark
4 Only within the ruin I beheld
5 At a small distance, on the dusky ground
 r } {in
6 A broken pane which glitte[?]} 'd {~~to~~ the moon
7 And seemed akin to life. There is a mood
8 A settled temper of the heart, when grief
 i } {fastens ing all
9 Become~~s~~ an inst[?a]}nct, {[?]^on the things
 {doth and with [?unbounded]
10 That promise food {and like a sucking babe
 {time
11 Creates it where it is not. From this {hour
 That speck of glass was dearer to my soul
24 Than was the moon in heaven. Another time
 {A
25 The winds of {autumn drove me o'er the heath
26 One gloomy evening: By the storm compell'd
27 The poor man's horse that feeds along the lanes
 {among
28 Had hither come {~~within~~ these fractur'd walls
29 To weather out the night and as I pass'd
30 While restlessly he turn'd from the fierce wind
31 And from the open sky, I heard, within,
32 The iron links with which his feet were clogg'd
 {noise
33 Mix their dull clanking with the heavy ~~sound~~ {
34 Of falling rain. I started from the spot
35 And heard the sound still following in the wind.—

---

1 Deletion by erasure.
6 Deletion by erasure.
11/24 WW's added lines are on 4^{v}, col. 2.
26 The colon may have been converted to a period.
28 Deletion by erasure.

Three weeks

long
O'er-arch'd by the same brambles dusky shade
On this green bank a glow worm hung its light
And then was seen no more. Within the thorn
Whose flowery head half hides those ruined pales
Three seasons did a black bird build his nest
Then he disappeared. On the green top
Of [illegible] wall [illegible] perch'd herself
And sang a pleasant melancholy song
Two summers and then vanish'd. I alone
Remained: the winds of heaven remained—with them
My heart claimed fellowship and with the beams
Of ~~morn~~ and ~~with~~ of the setting sun that seemed
To love and linger on the mouldering wall.

36 Three weeks

-hung
37 Oer-arch'd by the same bramble's dusky shade
38 On this green bank a glow worm hung its light
39 And then was seen no more. Within the thorn
40 Whose flowery head half hides those ruined pales
41 [ ] seasons did a blackbird build his nest
42 [ ] then he disappear'd. On the green top
43 [ ]at tall ash a linnet perch'd himself
44 And sang a pleasant melancholy song
45 Two summers and then vanish'd. I alone
46 Remained: the winds of heaven remained—with them
47 My heart claimed fellowship and with the beams
{ dawn
48 Of {[?morn] and ~~with~~ of the setting sun that seemed
49 To live and linger on the mouldering walls

36–49 These lines, less neatly written than those on 4^v, col. 1a, may be a later addition.
41–43 The opening letters are torn away. A transcript by Gordon Graham Wordsworth (the poet's grandson, who died in 1935) found by John Finch in DCP has the following readings: 41, "Three"; 42, "And"; 43, "Of that." Fragments of ascenders in ll. 41 and 43 support these readings.

I found my sickly heart had tied itself
Even to this speck of glass — it could produce
A feeling as of absence on the moment when my sight
Should feed on it again. For many months
Upheld this strange incontinence; my eye
Did every evening measure the moon's height
And forth I went before her yellow beams
Could overtop the elmtrees o'er the heath
I sought it then &
That speck unseen precious to my soul
Than was the moon in heaven
I went, I reach'd the cottage and I found
Still undisturb'd and glittering in its place
That speck of glass more precious to my soul
Than was the moon in heaven

12 I found my sickly heart had tied itself
13 Even to this speck of glass—it could produce
{A
14 {a feeling as of absence
15 on the moment when my sight
a long
16 Should feed on it again. ~~For~~ many^months
Confirm'd
{~~Con~~
17 {I felt this strange incontinence; my eye
18 Did every evening measure the moon's height
soon as
19 And forth I went before her yellow beams
20 Could overtop the elm-trees oer the heath
I sought the [?r] and I found
That speck more precious to my soul
Than was the moon in heaven
the ruined hut
bent my course I reach'd the hut
21 I went, I reach'd the cottage and I found
ce
22 Still undistuturb'd and glittering in its pla[?]
23 That speck of glass more precious to my soul
24 Than was the moon in heaven

Here WW adds lines to fit after l. 11 on 4v, col. 1a.

Appendix II

Wordsworth's Notes

The Fenwick Note

That part of the Fenwick note to *The Excursion* concerning *The Ruined Cottage* and *The Pedlar* is given here. The only surviving manuscript is a copy of Isabella Fenwick's lost original made by Wordsworth's daughter and son-in-law, Dora and Edward Quillinan, which concludes: "To dearest Miss Fenwick are we obliged for these notes, every word of which was taken down by her kind pen from my Father's dictation. The former portion was transcribed at Rydal by Mr Quillinan, the latter by me & finished at the Vicarage Brigham this *Twenty fifth day of Augst 1843, D. Q.*" (DCP). The section of the manuscript presented here is in Dora's hand; internal evidence related to the date of Southey's death suggests late April 1843 for Wordsworth's comments.

The Excursion.

Something must now be said of this Poem but chiefly, as has been done through the whole of these notes, with reference to my personal friends, & especially to Her who has perseveringly taken them down from my dictation.[1] Towards the close of the first book, stand the lines that were first written beginning "Nine Tedious years" & ending Last human tenant of these ruined walls."[2] These were composed in 95.[3] at Race Down & for several passages describing the employment & demeanour of Margaret during her affliction I was indebted to observations made in Dorsetshire & afterwards at Alfoxden in Somersetshire where I resided in 97. & 98. The lines towards the conclusion of the 4th book, "Despondency corrected," beginning, "For the Man who in this Spirit" to the words "intellectual soul"[4] were in order of time composed the next either at Race Down or Allfoxden, I do not remember which. The rest of the Poem was written in the Vale of Grasmere chiefly during our residence at Allan Bank. The long Poem on my own education was, together with many minor Poems, composed while we lived at the Cottage at Town End. Perhaps my

---

[1] A penciled note on the opposite page reads "Miss Fenwick—."

[2] MS. B reading text, ll. 482–528.

[3] An ink stroke before the "95." probably represents Dora's initial thought of writing "1795." As indicated on pp. 3–4, above, WW's memory is in error about this date.

[4] *The Excursion*, IV, 1207–1275 (*PW*, V, 148–150). These lines, originally part of the addendum in MS. B, were composed at Alfoxden in the spring of 1798.

purpose of giving an additional interest to these my Poems in the eyes of my nearest & dearest Friends may be promoted by saying a few words upon the character of the Wanderer, the Solitary, & the Pastor, & some other of the persons introduced—and first of the principal one the Wanderer. — My lamented friend Southey (for this is written a month after his decease)[5] used to say that had he been born a Papist, ~~that~~ the course of life which would in all probability have been his, was the one for which he was most fitted & most to his mind, that of a Benedictine Monk in a Convent furnished, as many once were & some still are, with an inexhaustible Library. Books, ~~were in fact~~, as appears from many passages in his writings & was evident to those who had opportunities of observing his daily life,—were in fact[6] his passion; & wandering,[7] I can with truth affirm, was mine, but this propensity in me was happily counteracted by inability from want of fortune to fulfill my wishes. But had I been born in a class which would have deprived me of what is called a liberal education, it is not unlikely that being strong in body, I should have taken to a way of[8] life such as that in which my Pedlar passed the greater part of his days. At all events I am here called upon freely to acknowledge that the character I have represented in his person is chiefly an idea of what I fancied my own character might have become in[9] his circumstances. Nevertheless much of what he says & does had an external existence that fell under my own youthful & subsequent observation.[10] An Individual named Patrick, by birth & education a Scotchman, followed this humble occupation for many years & afterwards settled in the Town of Kendal.— He married a kinswoman of my wife's, & her Sister Sarah was brought up from early Childhood under this good man's eye.[11] My own imaginations I was happy to find clothed in reality &

---

[5] Southey died on 21 March 1843.

[6] The phrase "in fact" was inserted.

[7] This comma, and the following one, are later additions in pencil. The preceding semicolon (after "passion") was altered from a comma by the addition of a pencil dot.

[8] The word "in" was overwritten "of."

[9] The "in" was inserted above the line.

[10] On 27 March 1843—about a month before the Fenwick note—WW wrote Henry Reed about *Matthew*: "The character of the School Master about whom you inquire, had like the Wanderer in the Excursion a solid foundation in fact & reality, but like him it was also in some degree a Composition; I will not & need not call it an invention—it was no such thing. But were I to enter into details I fear it w[o]uld impair the effect of the whole upon your mind, nor could I do it at all to my own satisfaction" (*Wordsworth and Reed*, ed. Leslie N. Broughton [Ithaca, 1933], p. 96). The poet repeated this sentiment in the Fenwick note to *Matthew*: "This and the other poems connected with Matthew would not gain by a literal detail of facts. Like the Wanderer in the Excursion, this Schoolmaster was made up of several both of his class & men of other occupations. I do not ask pardon for what there is of untruth in such verses, considered strictly as matters of fact. It is enough, if, being true & consistent in spirit, they move & teach in a manner not unworthy of a poet's calling" (DCP).

[11] "Childhood" is underlined in pencil, and Mary Wordsworth adds "her ninth year"; she also corrects "eye" to "roof." An ink X next to "Childhood" refers to a pencil draft by Mary on the opposite page, now partially erased: "[?Aunt ?Sarah] went to Kendal when she was 10 years old [?&] Mr. Patrick died within 2 years after —M. W." Written over that partially erased sentence is the following one, also in Mary's hand: "Sarah went to Kendal on our Mother's death but Mr P. died in the course of a year or two." Below this, the poet's grandson, Gordon Graham Wordsworth, wrote, "Mrs Hutchinson d. March 31, 1783. James Patrick March 2 1787 GGW." Notes about family history that Mary wrote for her son William in November 1851 provide more information in her account of the three daughters of Alex and Elizabeth Robison: "Margaret the oldest, was, in conjunction with our grandmother, a Godmother to my Sister who was named after the two, Margaret. Margaret Robison became the Wife of James

fresh ones suggested by what she reported of this man's tenderness of heart, his strong & pure imagination, & his solid attainments in literature chiefly religious whether in prose or verse. At Hawkshead also, while I was a school boy, there occasionally resided a Packman (the name then generally given to this calling) with whom I had frequent conversations upon what had befallen him & what he had observed during his wandering life, &, as was natural, we took much to each other; & upon the subject of Pedlarism in general, as then followed, & its favorableness to an intimate knowledge of human concerns, not merely among the humbler classes of society, I need say nothing here in addition to what is to be found in the Excursion & a note attached to it.[12]

[*Wordsworth's comments on the Solitary and the Pastor are here omitted.*]

And now for a few words upon the scene where these interviews & conversations are supposed to occur. The scene of the first book of the Poem is, I must own, laid in a tract of country not sufficiently near to that which soon comes into view in the second book to agree with the fact. All that relates to Margaret & the ruined cottage &c was taken from observations made in the South West of England & certainly it would require more than seven leagued boots to stretch in one morning from a common in Somersetshire or Dorsetshire, to the heights of Furness Fells & the deep vallies they embosom. For thus dealing with space I need make, I trust, no apology; but my friends may be amused by the truth. In the Poem I suppose that the Pedlar & I ascended from a plain country up the vale of Langdale. . . .

[*The description of the scene in later books of* The Excursion *is here omitted.*]

Now for a few particulars of, fact respecting the persons whose stories are told or characters described by the different speakers. To Margaret I have already alluded. I will add here that the lines beginning, "She was a woman of a steady mind" "& live on earth a life of happiness"[13] faithfully delineate as far as they go, the character possessed in common by many women whom it has been my happiness to know in humble life, & that several of the most touching things which she is represented as saying & doing are taken from actual observation of the distresses & trials under which different persons were suffering, some of them Strangers to me, & others daily under my notice. I was born too late to have a distinct remembrance of the origin of the American war, but

---

Patrick of Kendal the intellectual Pedlar—whose Character, suggested to your Father that of the Wanderer in the 1st Book of the Excursion—The details of which he gathered from Conversations with your Aunt Sarah,—who was taken by her Sister's godmother from her home upon the death of our Mother, when she was 8 ["9" was overwritten "8" and "eight" was added] years old — She went to School at Kendal—but the most important part of her education was gathered from the stores of that good Man's mind. — She remained one of his Household some time after his death—until, I know not how many years afterwards, she (Your Aunt S.) joined my Brother Tho[s.] & myself at Sockburne" (DCP). Thompson, pp. 234–238, shows that Sara was in fact eight years old when she went to Patrick's home, spending nearly four years with him before his death on 2 March 1787. The little else that is known about James Patrick is summarized in Thompson; see also Francis Nicholson and Ernest Axon, *The Older Nonconformity in Kendal* [Kendal, 1915], pp. 346, 461, 477, 481, 496, and a photograph of Patrick's memorial tablet facing p. 496.

[12] See Note to *The Excursion*, below. Thompson demonstrates (pp. 239–246) that WW could have known six pedlars in Hawkshead, and that the "Packman" referred to here is probably David Moore.

[13] MS. E reading text, ll. 445–451. A draft for these lines is in *Peter Bell* MS. 2 and probably dates from 1799; they were not incorporated into the poem until MS. E.

the state in wh I represent Robert's mind to be ~~in~~ I had frequent opportunities of observing at the commencement of our rupture with France in 93. opportunities of which I availed myself in the Story of the Female Vagrant as told in the Poem on Guilt & Sorrow. . . .

Note to *The Excursion*

When *The Excursion* was published in 1814, Wordsworth provided the following note to "Much did he see of men" in the line corresponding to MS. E, line 300:

In Heron's Tour in Scotland is given an intelligent account of the qualities by which this class of men used to be, and still are, in some degree, distinguished, and of the benefits which Society derives from their labours. Among their characteristics, he does not omit to mention that, from being obliged to pass so much of their time in solitary wandering among rural objects, they frequently acquire meditative habits of mind, and are strongly disposed to enthusiasm poetical and religious. I regret that I have not the book at hand to quote the passage, as it is interesting on many accounts.

In the 1827 edition of *The Excursion*, the note was altered:

At the risk of giving a shock to the prejudices of artificial society, I have ever been ready to pay homage to the Aristocracy of Nature; under a conviction that vigorous human-heartedness is the constituent principle of true taste. It may still, however, be satisfactory to have prose-testimony how far a Character, employed for purposes of imagination, is founded upon general fact. I therefore subjoin an extract from an author who had opportunities of being well acquainted with a class of men, from whom my own personal knowledge emboldened me to draw this Portrait.

"We learn from Caesar and other Roman Writers, that the travelling merchants who frequented Gaul and other barbarous countries, either newly conquered by the Roman arms, or bordering on the Roman conquests, were ever the first to make the inhabitants of those countries familiarly acquainted with the Roman modes of life, and to inspire them with an inclination to follow the Roman fashions, and to enjoy Roman conveniences. In North America, travelling merchants from the Settlements have done and continue to do much more towards civilizing the Indian natives, than all the Missionaries, Papist or Protestant, who have ever been sent among them.

"It is farther to be observed, for the credit of this most useful class of men, that they commonly contribute, by their personal manners, no less than by the sale of their wares, to the refinement of the people among whom they travel. Their dealings form them to great quickness of wit and acuteness of judgment. Having constant occasion to recommend themselves and their goods, they acquire habits of the most obliging attention, and the most insinuating address. As in their peregrinations they have opportunity of contemplating the manners of various Men and various Cities, they become eminently skilled in the knowledge of the world. *As they wander, each alone, through thinly-inhabited districts, they form habits of reflection and of sublime contemplation.* With all these qualifications, no wonder, that they should often be, in remote parts of the country, the best mirrors of fashion, and censors of manners; and should contribute much to polish the roughness, and soften the rusticity of our peasantry. It is not more than twenty or thirty years, since a young man going from any part of Scotland to England, of purpose *to carry the pack*, was considered, as going to lead the life, and acquire the Fortune, of a Gentleman. When, after twenty years' absence, in that honourable line of employment, he returned with his acquisitions to his native country, he was regarded as a Gentleman to all intents and purposes."

Heron's Journey in Scotland, Vol. i. p. 89.[14]

[14] Robert Heron, *Observations Made in a Journey through the Western Counties of Scotland; in the Autumn of MDCCXCII*... (2 vols; Perth, 1793), I, 89–92. WW omits a paragraph between the first and second ones; the first italics in the second paragraph are WW's addition, but *to carry the pack* is in the original.